The Roots
of
Whitman's Grass

The Roots
of
Whitman's Grass

T. R. RAJASEKHARAIAH

RUTHERFORD • MADISON • TEANECK
Fairleigh Dickinson University Press

Associated University Presses, Inc.
Cranbury, New Jersey 08512

SBN: 8386 7493 3

Printed in the United States of America

To

Professor Gay Wilson Allen
Whose love of Whitman is great
and love of truth greater

CONTENTS

7

INTRODUCTORY NOTE

THAT WALT WHITMAN MIGHT BE INDEBTED IN SOME WAY TO THE ancient poets of India was suspected as early as 1856 by Thoreau, who said he found *Leaves of Grass* "wonderfully like the Orientals," meaning especially the Sanscrit poems, and he asked Whitman if he had read them. Whitman replied "No," and asked to be told about them, but many years later he named "the ancient Hindoo poems" as "embryonic facts of 'Leaves of Grass.'" Other readers of Whitman also continued to see puzzling similarities, such as Edward Carpenter, a British minor poet who visited Whitman in 1877 and later compiled a list of parallels in *Leaves of Grass* and the *Upanishads, Mahâparinibbâna, Suttanta,* and the *Bhagavad Gita*—but also of the Chinese *Sayings of Lao-tzu.* However, he saw in these parallels only "the same loving universal spirit . . . making its voice heard from time to time, harmonizing the diverse eras, enclosing continents, castes, and theologies."

In 1866 Lord Strangford, a distinguished British Orientalist, thought Whitman's verse "pure Persian," imbued "with not only the spirit, but with the veriest mannerism, the most absolute trick and accent of Persian poetry. . . ." Since Whitman could not read Persian (very few in England or the United States could), and not much Persian poetry had been translated into English, this is a remarkable statement, as Lord Strangford himself very well knew.

In the twentieth century several scholars have made comparative studies of Whitman and Indian literature. One was Dorothy Mercer, who completed a doctoral dissertation at the University of California in 1933 on *"Leaves of Grass* and the *Bhagavad Gita:* A Comparative Study."* Recently V. K. Chari published a study of *Whitman in the Light of Vedantic Mysticism,* and O. K. Nambiar in *Walt Whitman and Yoga* proposed *Leaves of Grass* as a modernized guide to Yoga (perhaps better called an American version of Yoga).

Meanwhile Malcolm Cowley decided independently that "Most of Whitman's doctrines, though by no means all of them, belong to the mainstream of Indian philosophy." Seeing Whitman in this "mainstream" gave Cowley a new attitude toward him, and he recommended this approach as the best means of understanding Whitman rather than American sources and influences, such as New England Transcendentalism. But Cowley doubted that Whitman had directly drawn upon Indian philosophy, and presumed that a "mystical experience" might have given him intuitive insight resembling Indian mysticism.

Yet not until Mr. Rajasekharaiah began his researches had anyone rigorously explored the ways by which Whitman might have actually gained some knowledge of Indian philosophy and literature. In 1965 while at the University of Minnesota on a Fulbright fellowship this Indian scholar wrote to me to ask if I could give him any clews to books and articles on India in English that Whitman actually read or might have read. I replied that aside from a few articles which Whitman had torn from magazines and annotated (now in the Duke University Library) and Alger's *Oriental Poetry,* there was little evidence of his readings in this field. (In the 1870s he did own a copy of the *Gita,* but how soon he read it no one really knows.) But I pointed out that in the early 1850s Whitman, according to his brother George, spent many hours in the New York libraries, one of which almost certainly was the Astor, which published a catalogue of its holdings in 1853. This catalogue would show what Whitman could have read.

Mr. Rajasekharaiah came to New York in the spring of 1966 and compiled a list of 500 items (books and articles) that were accessible to Whitman between 1850 and '55. In reading this large batch of material he found many passages which, he thought, so closely paralleled Whitman's ideas, imagery, or stylistic characteristics that he became convinced Whitman had actually used them.

So many sources have been claimed for Whitman from so many different authors and countries that the claims tend to cancel each other. Yet we know now that Whitman did read widely and erratically and that he drew ideas and suggestions from far more books than he ever admitted, or perhaps was even aware of. And of all his plausible sources, India—by whatever inadequate or distorted interpretations by journalists and amateur Orientalists— must be reckoned with. In my judgment Mr. Rajasekharaiah's findings are more convincing as parallels or similarities than actual sources. I would have preferred a comparative study from him rather than so definite a source study. However, the form in which he has presented his material is more challenging than the comparative studies of Mercer, Chari, and Nambiar, and may well get more attention. Every reader will be forced to decide for himself which example is actual or possible source or only a striking parallel, and in the process of deciding he will come to understand Whitman better than he ever did before encountering this lively and provocative examination of the "roots" of *Leaves of Grass*. I seriously doubt that the Indian cult of the Cusa grass gave Whitman his major symbol, and yet what an interesting parallel! This book is crowded with many other interesting similarities, coincidences, mysteries, and perhaps even some direct sources.

                                                Gay Wilson Allen

PREFACE

"SOME FUTURE TILTER AT WINDMILLS WILL ATTEMPT TO PROVE
that the man whom we knew as Walt Whitman was an uncul-
tured imposter,"[1] said John Townsend Trowbridge sixty-six years
ago, as if suspicious that something of the imposter was to be proved
in a man of whom an admirer said, "I want no other God than
Walt Whitman; I want no other Bible than 'Leaves of Grass.' "[2]

In spite of what might be regarded as a Quixotic feat in these
pages at the critical windmills of over a century of Whitman
scholarship, the aim of this book is not to expose Walt Whitman
as an imposter. The problem of originality in art is too subtle to be
so easily trifled with, and the question of whether Whitman was
a great poet has already been so answered with the authority
both of wisdom, which finds the answer, and of time, which tests
the answer, that neither the discovery of his "pose," nor of his
"alias," nor even of his "roots," can possibly alter the verdict. Nor
is such an alteration the whole import of this book. For, after
all is said and done, *Leaves of Grass* is one of the world's masterpieces even if it is not the work of one of the world's masters.
That is the only mystery about Whitman, and it will have to survive this book. It will survive, if these pages are taken, as I trust
they will be, in the spirit in which they are written—that the
ugliest history is more meaningful than the most beautiful myth.

I sincerely hope that the disclosure of these pages will initiate
a truer, and therefore a more profitable and less dazed, understanding of Whitman's poetry. His literary reputation, though a

---

[1] *My Own Story: With Recollections of Noted Persons* (Boston: Houghton, Mifflin & Co., 1903).

[2] Thomas Harned: quoted from the Foreword to *Rivulets of Prose,*
ed. Carolyn Wells and Alfred F. Goldsmith, New York, (Greenberg,
1928, p. xvii.)

hasty comprehension of its significance may point in that direction, need not suffer by taking away the god-mask he wore to cover his human face. We all wear masks, and if Whitman stumbled upon a divine one in the antechambers of the literary hall, he at least played the role that accident so thrust upon him with a talent that compels moral scruples to yield to aesthetic considerations. That, I am sure, is marvel enough in an act that—if we still believe in one of the world's earliest masters, Aristotle—is imitation. The only aim of this book is to show that marvel: the bible of a man who was not a Christ.

I am grateful to the United States Educational Foundation in India and the Committee on International Exchange of Persons in Washington, D.C., for making it possible for me to go to the United States in the first place, without which the research that went into the making of this book would have been impossible; to the Conference Board of Associated Research Councils in the U.S.A. for readily extending its grant for a year more to help me conduct the investigation; to Professor Allen Tate, who enthusiastically approved of my plans for a book, read the manuscript, and thought much of it; to Professor Gay Wilson Allen without whose sustained interest and generous encouragement I would have despaired of publishing a work that threatened to say so much that is disagreeable about a poet the world has already accepted as great; and to Dr. Charles Angoff for boldly lending the book the imprint of Fairleigh Dickinson University Press.

ACKNOWLEDGMENTS

I WISH TO THANK CHARLES E. FEINBERG, DETROIT, MICHIGAN, for permission to print the following unpublished material in the Feinberg Collection: Whitman's note pinned to the copy of J. C. Thomson's *Bhagavadgita,* and Whitman's entry on the flyleaf of H. D. Thoreau's *A Week on the Concord and Merrimack Rivers.*

I also wish to thank Columbia University Press and Harvard University Press for permission to quote copyrighted material, as follows:

C. J. Furness, ed., *Leaves of Grass by Walt Whitman, Reproduced from the Facsimile First Edition,* Facsimile Text Society, Columbia University Press, New York, N.Y., 1939, pp. ix-xi.

C. J. Furness, ed., *Walt Whitman's Workshop, A Collection of Unpublished Manuscripts,* Harvard University Press, Cambridge, Mass., 1928, pp. 190–191 and 201.

And I can never sufficiently thank Mrs. Mathilde E. Finch for her inestimable help in getting the manuscript fit for the press.

T. R. R.

The Roots
of
Whitman's Grass

PART ONE:

The Grass

1

THE RIDDLE

THE FIRST MAN TO SUSPECT THE INFLUENCE OF INDIAN THOUGHT
on Whitman's poetry was Emerson. He described *Leaves of Grass*
(with what Cebría Montoliu calls "charming irony"[1]) as "a remarkable mixture of the Bhagvat Ghita and the *New York
Herald*."[2] Thoreau too, an ardent votary of Indian philosophy
himself, had no difficulty in noticing the Oriental element in
Leaves of Grass, which to him was "Wonderfully like the
Orientals." But when he asked Whitman if he had read them, he
answered, "No; tell me about them."[3] The answer, Allen observes
diffidently, "may have been disingenuous or it could have been
modesty before a man who obviously knew a great deal about
Oriental scriptures."[4] Later on, however, when the garrulity of
advancing age was possessing him, Whitman admitted that he had
"read the ancient Hindoo poems" in preparation for *Leaves of
Grass*.[5] Therefore, it would seem that, like most of his statements
about himself and his works,[6] the earlier denial should be taken
with suspicion[7] and explained as disingenuousness rather than
modesty, and as an attempt to "hide his source."[8]

But the denial was accepted in good faith by Thoreau, and, if he
still had any lingering doubts, they might well have been satisfied
by Whitman's subsequent request to him for a reading list on
Oriental literature that would answer "questions concerning man's
origin, purpose, and destiny."[9] Like Emerson and Thoreau, every
reader and critic of Whitman has perceived the exotic element in
his poetry, which—unless explained away in the ingenious manner
of Margaret Lacey that "the more evolved a man becomes, the more

21

certain he is to reach a stratum of thought we sometimes call Oriental"[10]—must at least be traced to the East, if not specifically to India. But Whitman's categorical disavowal of any Oriental knowledge, acceptance of which was made easy by the absence of any established evidence of his actual reading of Indian works and by his undeniably original manner of expression, naturally forced those critics to conclude that Indian thought had no impact whatever on his poetry, or at most if there was any, that it was indirect and diffuse, coming through an intermediary source like English Romanticism, or German Transcendentalism, or Neoplatonism, or —closer to home—American Transcendentalism, which might be called "the offspring of a German father and a Hindu mother."[11] This last supposition was amply supported by the circumstance that "Orientalism was very much in the American intellectual atmosphere of the 1840's and 50's."[12]

This minimized and attenuated theory of Oriental, or, to be precise, Indian, influence on Whitman appears to have satisfied critical inquiry for a long while, until, in recent times, research and analysis of his poetry exposed its inadequacy by clearly showing that Whitman differed in very important respects both from German thought (apart from coming into a knowledge of it not only superficially but late in his poetic career[13]) and from New England Transcendentalism.[14] And this in spite of the powerful initial effect Emerson had on him! Besides, even while both biography and criticism unquestioningly acquiesced in the first denial and ignored the later confession, there has been on the part of those of Whitman's readers and critics who had any knowledge of Indian philosophy a continued and insistent awareness that there is a good deal in *Leaves of Grass* that resembles—not always vaguely—and parallels—often very closely—the philosophical thought of India. Moving even farther from the Neoplatonists and the English Romanticists, twentieth-century criticism, though like the earlier readers still unable to point to actual literary sources, has tended more and more toward Indian philosophy to explain not only the content but even the quality of Whitman's thought. A recent work by an Indian scholar has demonstrated the un-Hegelianism of Whitman's thought and its affinity—almost identity—with the Hindu Vedantic mysticism.[15] But the fog that

Whitman so skillfully built around the vision of his poetry, both from inside and out, is thick enough to force even the most enlightened and rational of the critics to fall back upon the uncritical doctrine of a mystical revelation that R. M. Bucke in his extreme personal enthusiasm assiduously propagated years ago.

2

CRITICAL EXPLANATIONS

FROM THE POINT OF VIEW OF LITERARY CRITICISM, THERE ARE (if we must call them so) two mysteries in Whitman: one is the "remarkable accession of power"[16] that suddenly transformed a writer whose "tales, essays, sketches, and even poems [were] in no way distinguishable from that 'mighty tide of ditch-water' which Carlyle tells us flows day by day from the power-presses of civilization" into "the greatest [poet] of a great country."[17] The second, the significance of which appears to have been underestimated in the overemphasis accorded to the first or implicitly regarded as a mere detail, is the equally remarkable acquisition of knowledge. For two things happened on that miraculous day in July 1855 when *Leaves of Grass* was so dramatically thrust upon an unsuspecting world. Not only was a great poet born, but a poetry —a poetry absolutely different from what was so far known to the American reader, a book that contained "incomparable things said incomparably well."[18] It was a magnificent lyric utterance, but at the same time profound philosophical poetry, and it was this philosophic content that roused Emerson enthusiastically to prophesy a great career for its author.[19] But in the sense of wonder with which early biography and criticism examined the extraordinary event, the astonishingly original power of saying things incomparably well appears to have driven to the shadows the equally astonishing circumstance of having those incomparable things to say. The general reaction seems to have been that, if the change from the conventional and sentimental manner of the pre-1855 days of the poet could be explained and understood, the change from the equally conventional and sentimental stuff that occurred in the transformation would be automatically explained too. The formal lyricism of Whitman's poetry also contributed to the confusion of the issue, which consequently came to be regarded as of an essentially biographical nature. Almost every critic, finding himself called upon to answer the riddle of Whitman's transformation from a "worse than mediocre"[20] writer into the titanic genius of *Leaves of Grass* has, as the first principle on which to understand his poetry, attempted to discover an event in his life that brought about the "miracle."

Stated in simple terms, as Bucke put it, the Sphinxian riddle was: "Where did he get the stuff to put into it? How did he get it all in a minute, as it were? Or if it was in him before, why did it not show itself?"[21] The most popular as well as the most persistent of the answers given to this riddle is the "mystic revelation theory" of Bucke himself, according to whom Whitman had an illumination "in June, probably in 1853, when he had just entered upon his thirty-fifth year."[22] Convenient as it is, and even fashionable in certain areas of modern criticism, one can easily notice the weakness of this mystic hypothesis. For one thing, there is nothing in *Leaves of Grass* that a purely poetic imagination cannot discover on its own flight without the borrowed wings of superhuman grace. And, even if this—one might call it a literary sacrilege—can be overlooked, the fact that prior to June 1853 a good many of the thoughts of the 1855 poems are already present in rudimentary shape in the 1847–48 notebooks speaks against the theory. Moreover, as Roger Asselineau contends, it does not explain the sudden appearance, answer the question why it happened in 1853 and not some other year, nor account for the "transmutation of the vision into poetry."[23] Besides, it underestimates, even ignores the enormous amount of industry that Whitman put into the making of his poetry in those long years of preparation. What little evidence has been offered to prove that revelatory event in Whitman's life falls to the ground upon closer examination. The so-called references in Whitman's own writing to the new experience are only poetic lines, part of the stuff of his poems, and not even, like some of the entries in his notebooks, his record of personal experience. The most important allusion, according to Bucke's claim, is the following passage of two lines:

I cannot be awake for nothing looks to me as it did before,
Or else I am awake for the first time and all before has been
   a mean sleep.

The passage is among the "First Drafts and Rejected Lines," No.
131 on page 287 (Vol. 3) of *The Complete Writings*.[24] It bears
Bucke's editorial footnote: "Referring to his recent illumination;
probably written 1853." Regarded as a personal confession, which
it is not, or even as a poetic passage independently found by
itself, the lines can be said to have reference to some profound
illuminating or awakening experience. That is how one would
speak of such an experience. But the entry is not from a diary or
a confession in a letter, and it is curious that Bucke has failed to
notice that the same two lines occur as part of a four-line fragment describing, very obviously, the ecstasy of feeling accompanying or following a sexual experience:[25]

Can ? make me feel so exuberant yet so faintish?
The rage of an unconquerable fierceness is conquered by the
   touch (of the) tenderest hand.
I cannot be awake for nothing looks to me as it did before,
Or else I am awake for the first time and all before has been
   a mean sleep.

There are many such passages scattered all through Whitman's
experimental fragments and tentative drafts. They are capable
of misleading a hasty or predisposed observation into "mystical"
explanations, but turn out, upon scrutiny, to be mere poetic ejaculations of sexual emotion. The following illustrations will suffice:
Item No. 135 on page 40 of *Notes and Fragments* has these words:

I am a look—mystic—in a trance—exaltation
Something wild and untamed—half savage.
Common things—the trickling sap that flows from the end
   of the manly maple.

And No. 134 on the same page:

To be at all in any callous shell;
I think if there were nothing more developed, the clam in its

callous shell in the sand were august enough.
I am not in any callous shell;
I am cased with supple conductors all over
They take every object by the hand and lead it within me.
There are thousands, each one with his entry to himself.
They are always watching with their little eyes, from my
head to my feet.

The latter, with some verbal change, was inserted in section 27
of "Song of Myself."[26] One can easily read a profound meaning—
philosophical, scientific, or even mystic—into these lines. This has
been done with them in their final position in the poem, in
ignorance that when the passage was originally composed it ended
with two more lines, which have an unmistakable sexual connotation:

One no more than a point lets in and out of me such bliss
and magnitude.
I think I could lift the girder of the house away if it lay
between me and whatever I wanted.[27]

Strangely enough, eagerness to find mystic meanings in a poetic
line could force a philosophic suggestion out of these last two
lines too. In fact, the phrase "one no more than a point" could be
regarded as the Whitmanesque way of describing the Soul, of
which the Upanishads said:

A person (purusha) no bigger than the thumb abides in the
midst of self.[28]

The omnipresent spirit, extending over the space of the heart,
which is the size of a finger, resides within the body.[29]

The other entries in Whitman's early notebooks, which Malcolm
Cowley calls "sidelong references to such an experience,"[30] are
merely stray thoughts of a poetic imagination stirred by philosophical questions, mostly suggested, as will be seen in the course of
this study, by readings in philosophical works. If Whitman did
actually have a revelation, one can hardly imagine it possible for
him, with his egotism and his self-adoration amidst his admiring

band of "hot little prophets,"[31] to have kept from telling them. He even denied having any religious experience in his life, which the mystic theory would imply. Bucke himself reports of how "one day talking about religious experiences, Whitman said, 'I never had any particular religious experiences—never felt I needed to be saved—never felt the need of spiritual regeneration.' "[32] Mysticism is indeed the very heart and soul of Whitman's poetry, but it does not necessarily involve an actual mystical experience.

If the mystic theory of Bucke was raised upon the foundation of the element of mysticism in Whitman's poetry, the second striking element in Whitman, sex, appears to have supplied the ground for the "romantic hypothesis" first advanced by Binns,[33] and supported and even developed by Bazalgette,[34] Sélincourt,[35] and Emory Holloway.[36] But again, the evidence on which this attractive theory of a love affair that inspired the transfiguration of Whitman depends, crumbles at the slightest touch. The new poetic thought and line ushering in the transformed poet are already seen emerging in the notebook of 1847 before he "left Brooklyn for New Orleans on Feb. 11, 1848";[37] and the poem "Once I Passed through a Populous City," generally used to establish the amorous episode, has been found to be the later revision of another poem "inspired by a 'Calamus' friendship with a man."[38] Further, the homosexual nature of Whitman that research has established now beyond doubt, effectively discredits the romantic view. Besides, that nothing of any significance happened to Whitman during his southern sojourn is attested by his own brother:

> I was in Brooklyn in the early fifties, when Walt came back from New Orleans. We all lived together. No change seemed to come over him: he was the same man he had been, grown older and wiser.[39]

Apart from showing clearly that the visit to New Orleans had nothing whatever to do with Whitman's emergence as poet of *Leaves of Grass,* George's testimony further points out that the *Leaves* came out of the "barrels" of Whitman's writing at that period, and not from the sudden mystic enlightenment of a Buddha, as Bucke tried to prove in his *Cosmic Consciousness.*[40] Said George, "He wrote what mother called 'barrels' of lectures. We did not know what he was writing. He did not seem more abstracted than usual. . . . We were all at work—all except Walt. But we know he was printing the book."[41] He further added, "Altogether, Walt's life was uneventful, containing no startling events, so far as I know."[42]

Equally unconvincing is the "phrenological theory" maintained by Hungerford,[43] which found the origins of Whitman's poetry in the elevated image that Fowler's "chart of bumps" had given him of himself as a "type of perfect humanity."[44] For the confusions and disturbances of Whitman's personal nature, the uncomfortable awareness of the anomaly of his sexual character, and perhaps even for the blind gropings of unrealized ambition, the pseudo-scientific assurances of the phrenological verdict may have acted as a favorable medical opinion, but it is too much of an exaggeration to transfer "the springs of courage"[45] to the achievements of Whitman's poetry. An astrologer's encouragement does not account for an Alexander's victory, even if it sets him on the battlefield. Unsatisfactory too, for the same reason, is the "compensation theory" of Jean Catel,[46] to whom Whitman's poetry results from a self-idealization on the part of a socially maladjusted, disappointed, ambitious youth, rushing for recompense into an imaginary world created by his unconscious. For, all art being some kind of compensation, it exaggerates the principle merely in order to explain the excessive "I" in Whitman's poetry, and, while so doing, notices only the psychological implications of it, ignoring the broader and more significant philosophical foundations on which the "I" is raised.

Each of these explanations, like the men in the story of the elephant, concentrates upon one aspect or element of the poetry of Whitman, and attempts to discover the entire truth in terms of it. Also noticeable in them is the fallacy of identifying the world of his poems with the world of his private personal life—considerably persuaded by Whitman's insistence upon the autobiographical character of his poetry—and the fallacy of using the poetry to explain the person in order to explain the poetry better.

While these, though in different ways, seem to answer Bucke's first question "Where did he get the stuff to put into it?" with the implied suggestion of his next two questions—namely, that it was in him before, (their concern being only to discover what

might describe how he "got it all [out] in a minute, as it were"),
there are others who proceed on the assumption that Whitman got
it all from somewhere outside himself—in other words, from a
literary source. The most important of these intellectual influences
that are held to explain the genesis as well as the "stuff" of his
poems is Emerson, the High Priest of Oriental thought in nineteenth-century America. Although in the early days of Whitman
criticism, partly under the misdirection of Whitman himself and
partly from an impulse to assert the poet's prophetic originality,
the influence of Emerson was almost completely denied, later research and comparative analysis have incontrovertibly established
the fact that it was both early and deep. But the role played by
Emerson in Whitman's poetic emergence can be exaggerated.
As W. S. Kennedy proudly observed, "the latter sweeps an orbit
vaster than [Emerson's] own, and has in every respect a broader
and more massive nature."[47] In fact, while Emerson definitely
roused Whitman's ambition, inspired the poetic programme—
and no doubt by his example suggested the philosophical direction, thereby kindling his enthusiasm toward Oriental thought—
and even supplied him with many words and ideas, *Leaves of Grass*
has more in it, even of the Orient, than could be traced to him, or
for that matter to the *Dial,* with its other Oriental enthusiasts. For
instance, Emerson, to quote Malcolm Cowley, "had nothing to
do with notions like metempsychosis or Karma, or the universe
pictured as a road for traveling souls.[48] Yet these philosophical and
religious doctrines were of the very essence of the 1855 *Leaves of
Grass* as they are of Whitman's total poetic philosophy. And
Leon Howard has pointed out the fundamental difference between
Whitman's notion of "identity" and that of New England Transcendentalism.[49]

Like Emerson, Margaret Fuller can only be said to have in-
flamed Whitman's ambition to become the great American poet of
her prophecy, but, as Esther Shephard has observed, "in so much as
the *Leaves of Grass* is an 'evangel-poem,' and that to a considerable extent, Whitman did not get his inspiration from [her]."[50]
Whitman had read and reviewed the works of Carlyle in his
journalistic days, and there are striking analogies between their
writings, as F. M. Smith has noticed and listed.[51] Carlyle was
probably the source of a few ideas, such as the Poet-Prophet,

preference of Nature over Art, belief in the truth of all religions, and so on. But the manifest differences of Whitman as man and poet from Carlyle prove that his influence was merely casual and fragmentary and that he was one of many minor sources. The influence of Frances Wright and Volney has been overestimated too; as Cowley says, "there is hardly a hint of them in Whitman's fundamental thinking."[52] All of Frances Wright's gift to Whitman can be indicated, as Goodale has done,[53] in his "Pictures,"[54] having her *A Few Days in Athens* for a source, and in the fact that his notions of the ideal woman and the joys of oratory, his prose in his political thinking, and his essay on the Eighteenth Presidency show her influence. Volney's *Ruins* has acted as "a store-house of information," providing the entire section of Whitman's notes on "Religion—gods" in *Notes and Fragments,* besides some words and phrases in "Salut au Monde!"[55] But they can hardly have inspired his poetry, or have carried it into the philosophy of "Song of Myself." And George Sand, for whom Esther Shephard makes a spectacular claim,[56] again is barely more than one of many sources from which Whitman drew his manifold inspirations. Perhaps a detail for the plan of his poetic career, even for the pose he assumed as a poet-prophet, and some ideas and phrases besides were owing to George Sand. But if in what he proposed to do he used Sand's hero as a model and imitated him, in what he actually did there is very much more than what the model gave him. The plagiarism Miss Shephard accuses him of is mostly of pattern and not of substance.

By many tributaries is the mighty river of Whitman's work fed, but not one of these has brought it the main stream of thought.

3

A HINDU SMILE

EITHER UNABLE TO FIND ACTUAL SOURCES OR EVIDENCE OF WHIT-
man's use of them, or persuaded by their personal enthusiasm and
his misdirection, critics have generally found it irresistible to attribute all the novel thought as well as the novel expression of
Leaves of Grass to an absolute originality of genius. But many have
recognized the remarkable resemblance its thought bears to Indian
philosophy. The earliest to put such an observation in print (to
overlook Lord Strangford, who, in an article written in 1866,
noticed Whitman's Oriental style and said, "Whitman managed
to acquire or imbue himself with not only the spirit, but with the
veriest mannerism, the most absolute trick and accent of Persian
poetry"[57]) was M. D. Conway, who admired "the singular genius,
whose writings, although he had no acquaintance with Oriental
literature, have given the most interesting illustration of it."[58]
Though Conway regarded Asia as "the key to both Whitman and
the Transcendentalists,"[59] he seems to have been influenced by
Whitman's denial, for farther on in the same article he says: "I
could not help suspecting he must have had masters; but he declared that he had learned all that he knew from omnibus-drivers,
ferryboat pilots, fishermen, boatmen, and the men and women of
the markets and wharves. These were all inarticulate poets, and
he interpreted them."[60] If Conway, apparently in implicit trust in
Whitman's word, declared Whitman's "singular" originality,
Edward Carpenter, in spite of being an equally enthusiastic personal admirer of the poet, is not so easily taken in, probably because

he himself had a first-hand knowledge of Oriental literature and philosophy. Louis Cazamian speaks of the influence of "Hindu mysticism" on Edward Carpenter.[61] "How much exactly," says Carpenter,[62] "Walt Whitman may have known of the Vedic or other early writings is doubtful, but that he had read here and there among them, quite enough to gain an insight into the heart of them . . . is quite certain. 'These are really the thoughts of all men in all ages and lands, they are not original with me.' In the Vedic scriptures, and in lineal succession from these, in the Buddhist and Platonist and Christian writings [and so on], the root is to be found. . . . It would be hard to imagine anything more subtle and profound than passages in the Upanishads. . . . He seems to *liberate* the good tidings and give it democratic scope and worldwide application unknown in the older prophets, even in the sayings of Buddha." This certainty on the part of Carpenter appears to be the result not merely of resemblances noticed between Indian works and *Leaves of Grass* (a list of which "parallels" he gives in an appendix[63]) but of an actual knowledge of Indian literature that Whitman betrayed in one of his conversations with him, reported as follows:

> Going to Oriental literature, Whitman spoke of 'Sakuntala,' the Indian drama, its 'modernness'—the comic scenes especially being as of the times of Shakespeare; and of the great Hindu epic, the 'Ramayana'; and told the story of Yudisthura, which occurs as an episode in the latter.[64]

If Carpenter noticed parallels mostly with the *Upanishads* of India, William Norman Guthrie[65] regarded the *Bhagavad-Gita* as the key to understanding Whitman: "Yet, in spite of every effort to be clear, he [Whitman] is steadily misunderstood by most readers for years, unless they have chanced to study the Idealist philosophers of Germany, the Mystics of Christian centuries, the Neoplatonists, or better yet, for interpreting Emerson and Whitman, the Bhagavad Gita." Unable to suggest that Whitman read the *Gita* or any other Indian works, Guthrie yet observes how "Vedantic views are at times expressed [by Whitman] with such originality and energy as to have brought a smile of delight to the serene immobile countenance of a Hindu friend, to whom [he] read them."[66] Kennedy considered Whitman's religious philosophy Hegelian,[67] but did not fail to notice "the resemblances between Oriental poetry and portions of *Leaves of Grass*."[68] He found particularly striking

> the similarity of the verses of the old Vedic hymns to those of Walt Whitman. Max Mueller (*History of Ancient Sanscrit Literature,* London, 1860, p. 149) speaks of single lines in the Vedas of sixty-eight syllables each. These hymns are familiar to most readers, but I add one verse (or line) for the sake of complete illustration:
>
> > O Agni, thou from whom, as a newborn male, undying flames proceed, the brilliant smoke goes toward the sky, for as messenger thou art sent to the gods.[69]

Repudiating the similarity often claimed between Carlyle and Whitman, Gabriel Sarrazin asserted that "wholly unlike Carlyle . . . Walt Whitman, in his confident and lofty piety, is the direct inheritor of the great Oriental mystics, Brahma, Proclus, Abou Said."[70] To Karl Knortz "Whitman is the poet of identity. . . . The Brahmanical motto 'Tat Tvam Asi' is his."[71] Wayland Hyatt Smith noticed the "blending of the Orient and the Occident in Walt Whitman."[72] Elsa Baker wrote an article on "what Whitman learned from the East."[73] With quotations taken at random from Whitman's poetry "to show, or rather suggest, that the philosophy that underlies Christian Science and finds lyrical expression in Walt Whitman's 'Leaves of Grass' is identical with that of Hindu Vedanta," Charles G. Garrison[74] declared that, though "beyond mere citation little can be said," in his fundamental ideas, namely, There is but One Self; Man is that self; The Unreality of the Rest; and The Universe is Consciousness; and in his scheme of salvation, "Whitman is substantially identical with Hindu Vedanta." Romain Rolland[75] was struck by the affinities Whitman has with Vedantic thought, though he was not persuaded of a direct Indian origin for them, and, like most others, was forced to regard them as product of the poet's imaginative intuition, partly influenced by the background and spirit of the times. An extensive comparative analysis of the *Bhagavad-Gita* and *Leaves of Grass* compelled D. F. Mercer[76] to the inference that, notwithstanding

that the *Gita* could not on evidence be claimed as Whitman's
source, the Brahmin thought—diffuse and indefinite as it may be—
exerted a direct influence on Whitman, probably through his readings of the commentaries and expositions of Indian philosophy available in his time. Malcolm Cowley, probably the stoutest supporter
in recent times of the Eastern element in Whitman's poetry, says,
"Even though Whitman had probably read none of them [Indian
works] in 1855 . . . the system of doctrine suggested by the poem
["Song of Myself"] is more Eastern than Western, it includes notions like metempsychosis and Karma, and it might be one of those
Philosophies of India that Dr. Zimmer expounds at length."[77]
Even an early newspaper sensed the Oriental quality of Whitman's
poems. In a clipping from the *Literary World* of 19 November
1881, preserved by Whitman, is this interesting comment:

> Yet the prevalent tone of his verses is curiously Asiatic as
> though he were an incarnation of Brahma and a Pantheist.[78]

Richard Chase, comparing "Song of Myself" and "The Wasteland" as philosophic poems, made the observation that "it is probable, one may add, that both 'Song of Myself' and 'The Wasteland'
were influenced by the Bhagavad-Gita, which may be loosely described as thematically similar to these two poems."[79] And, according to Bliss Perry, Whitman "was Oriental rather than Western"
in his "capacity for brooding imaginative ecstasy." He added that
"his fondness for naming himself in his verse, his dervish-like passion for the endless Open Road, and even his catalogue method
have been noted as having singularly close parallels in the poetry of
the East."[80]
   If Western readers of *Leaves of Grass* have been left with a
feeling of uncertainty and vagueness about the nature of the influence of Indian thought on Whitman, the reaction of Indian
readers, like that of Guthrie's Hindu friend, has been one of instantaneous recognition of the definiteness of Whitman's intimate
knowledge of Indian philosophy. As Emory Holloway reports,[81]
"When long after Whitman's death, Tagore visited America, he
declared that no American had caught the Oriental spirit of
mysticism so well as he." Mercer quotes the President of the
Vedantic Society of Calcutta as writing to her that "Walt Whit-

man must have studied the Bhagavadgita, for in his *Leaves of Grass* one finds the teachings of Vedanta; the 'Song of Myself' is but an echo of the sayings of Krishna."[82] Swami Vivekananda called Whitman "the Sanyasin of America."[83]

To the Western reader the effect of Whitman's poetry may have been what John Burroughs described as follows: "Had Whitman descended upon us from some other world he would hardly have been a greater puzzle to the average reader and critic."[84] To the Indian it is all native notes, though sung in a slightly wild, foreign voice.

In noticing Lord Strangford's article referred to earlier, Allen remarked that his observation "might have started interesting and fruitful discoveries in comparative literature, but no one at that time, not even Lord Strangford, pursued the comparison any further."[85] The remark can generally be applied to most critics who have noticed the parallels of Whitman's with Eastern thought, but obviously the secrecy with which the gestation years of his poetic career are shrouded (in large part by his own design) made impossible any further inquiry that might have led to a greater knowledge of his sources even if it reduced the "surprising" element of originality.

4

WHITMAN'S CLAIMS

WHITMAN'S INITIAL DENIAL OF HAVING READ ANY ORIENTAL works is not hard to explain in the light that research has shed on his career and methods as a poet. It was in keeping with the myth he deliberately created and which his band of "hot little prophets" ardently perpetuated—that of a "rude, natural poet" whose "knowledge was not to any large extent derived from that source [books], but from real life . . . and, above all, as Rawley says of Bacon, 'from some ground and notions from within himself.' "[86] One can easily see—after his imagination was strongly touched by the impassioned call for a Poet by Emerson and Fuller, and once his groping, uncertain ambition had stirred and fixed its direction—how Whitman must have felt and pondered hard the need for a new kind of poetry uttered with a new voice, to be able to fulfill their prophecy. Realizing that "America needs her own poems, in her own body and spirit. Different from all hitherto—freer, more muscular, comprehending more and unspeakably grander. Not importations or anything in the spirit of importance,"[87] he would "take no illustrations whatever from the ancients or the classics, nor from mythology, nor Egypt, Greece or Rome—nor from the royal and aristocratic institutions and forms of Europe,"[88] and "make no quotations and no references to any other writer."[89] Then of himself he could say, "Self-reliant, with haughty eyes, assuming to himself all the attributes of his country, steps Walt Whitman into literature, talking like a man unaware that there was ever hitherto such a production as a book; or such a being

37

as a writer." And he could further claim that "Nature may have given the hint to the author of the 'Leaves of Grass', but there exists no book or fragment of a book which can have given the hint to them."[90]

The deliberate desire to be "different" on the one hand, and on the other the subsequent violent championing of the "self-made" nature of his poetry—part of the "ways he chose for pushing his gospel and advertising his philosophy"[91]—seem to indicate that Whitman set great store on being accepted as a poet absolutely original, uninfluenced, and new, the maker of a book that belonged to no known type of poetry in form or feeling. This is a desire most poets have, but it was obviously exaggerated in his case, ending up in his claiming an originality in which "he makes no allusions to books or writers; their spirits do not seem to have touched him."[92] The vehement assertion of originality involves, as can be noticed, a pointed denial of indebtedness to anybody, as if he were conscious of not being easily accepted as an original poet or were at least doubtful of being so taken. For after all he had written lyric poetry, or—what he was so fond of reminding himself—"subjective" poems, a kind of verse in which borrowings and influences, unlike those in drama or story or epic, will not easily show themselves up, and there was no need for so much calculated effort at pointing out the unborrowed splendor of it. There is no doubt, besides, that he had, even as a lyric poet, produced a new variety of verse, different both in content and shape from those so far known. And like a proud magician he commends and announces his trick. The efficacy of the trick lies in its novelty; so he must carefully produce the impression of unqualified originality and must do so by the creation of the myth of a writer into whose equipment "reading did not go for so very much."[93] Later he might dismiss the virtue of originality as not very valuable, and say, "Walt Whitman's philosophy . . . is not the least of his peculiarities—one must not say originalities, for Whitman himself disclaims originality."[94] Here he was obviously pointing to his own line in "Song of Myself."[95] Or he might even comment light-heartedly on the plagiarism of all great writers: "Do you ever think, Horace, what infernal plagiarists the big fellows are— big lawyers, big preachers, big writers,—even Shakespeare, Longfellow; how much they borrow and never pay back?"[96] But that was when he was quite satisfied that he had built himself a literary position the strength of which no attempt at brick-pulling could challenge. When we realize that Walt Whitman would even assiduously maintain that he "never cared so very much for E [merson]'s writings, prose or poems,"[97] and that the "touch . . . of Emerson-on-the-brain . . . came late and was only on the surface"[98] (forgetting that the entire Preface of the first edition of *Leaves of Grass* bore Emerson's influence deep down) in the mere assurance that no proof of having read him could be advanced against his assertion; and when we realize that he would claim, after his position as a Messianic teacher of mankind had been secured, that one of those "big fellows," Hegel (falsely again) is the one "who advances me to light on these [profound metaphysical questions],"[99] and that he himself was "the greatest *poetical* representative of German philosophy,"[100] it is not difficult to suspect a deliberate intention on the part of Whitman to create certain impressions, and to agree with Furness, who says:

> The impasse is created by the sophomoric pose of complete independence from all precedent works which Whitman struck and maintained through the early stages of his career. . . .

> Whitman made a consistent effort to cache deftly his sources of inspiration as well as of information until his own literary reputation became sufficiently well-grounded to permit him to indulge in a more magnanimous attitude.[101]

The "sophomoric pose" helped the myth of the poet who created a poetic masterpiece all out of himself, as it were, like a magician producing a rabbit out of the hat, and that in a trice. It was in him before, though it did not show itself, or, to use Whitman's own words, *"Leaves of Grass* was there unformed, all the time, in whatever answers as the laboratory of the mind."[102] As Bucke puts it, "The 'Democratic Review' essays and tales came from the surface of the mind and had no connection with what lay below— a great deal of which, indeed, was below consciousness. At last the time came when the concealed growth had to come to light."[103] As regards the equipment, or the material that goes into the composition of poetry, "Reading did not go for so very much in Walt Whitman's education—he found he could get more from things themselves than from pictures or descriptions of them drawn by others," said the official portrait.[104] For, "urged forward by an invincible impulse of growth and expansion within, he attained a mental level unprecedented . . . in the history of humanity,"[105] and thus "Whitman's wonderful book, *Leaves of Grass* is the reflection of an inner illumination."[106] Therefore, all his philosophical ideas and doctrines had to be attributed to his own "intellect [which,] had it stood alone, was great enough to have entitled him to rank among the foremost thinkers of the race, as witness, among a hundred other proofs, his comprehensive vision and acceptance of evolution in both the inorganic and organic worlds before Darwin published the 'Origin of Species,' or Spencer began his encyclopaedic treatise."[107] And if Bucke made this attribution in ignorance of the fact that Whitman had read at least the reviews in the periodicals of the 1840's of the "Vestiges of Creation," which, as Conway noted, "had the good effect of popularizing the idea of evolution,"[108] a modern biographer-editor has speculated on the likelihood that a note of Whitman on the idea of justice ("The quality of Justice is in the soul—It is immutable," etc.) occurred to him "through mystical illumination," just because he is not certain "whether he [Whitman] had by this time read Emerson's 'Compensation.' "[109]

But the accumulated evidence that research and comparative study have brought up in recent years despite the confusion created by Whitman's mispersuasions, has exploded a large part of this myth. Most of the ideas and thoughts that Whitman expresses in an original manner have been paid back to their sources. It has been shown that *Leaves of Grass* was not all "in him before," and that the essays and tales that "came from the surface of his mind" were not absolutely innocent of any connection with it, and that only the growth of the book was concealed. We know that "in no sense . . . was the 'Leaves of Grass' an impromptu. It was the result of a purpose which had been slowly forming for years,"[110] and that "it was out of this deep scrutiny, and after this long period of meditation upon the nature and method of the poet's task that *Leaves of Grass* came into being."[111] We also know the immense amount of preparation and experimental labor that went into it. Kennedy himself admitted that "the transmutation from conventional poetry and prose took Whitman several years of experiment.

Eight years passed in the gestation of the 'Leaves of Grass.' The leap was not a sudden one."[112] And in two articles the same writer traced the sources of many of Whitman's ideas to Pindar, Plutarch, Plato, Montaigne, Rousseau, Dickens, George Sand, Michelet, Carlyle, and Emerson.[113]

All this establishes the important role that reading played in Whitman's poetic activity. Here again it is largely in terms of comparative analysis or indirect evidence that research has been able to arrive at its discovery. In the vast Whitman material preserved there is a significant lacuna for those gestation years. The notebooks collected by Holloway[114] and Furness[115] are more records of the poet's developing thought and experimental line than journal of his personal life. Whitman has said that "during those eight years they [the poems of the 1855 edition] took many shapes; that in the course of those years he wrote and destroyed a great deal."[116] What else was destroyed at the same time the world will never know. But then, if we had it, it might have been like the notebooks we now have, indicating the thoughts that were being shaped into his new poetry rather than showing evidence of his reading or gathering material from the reading of those years. It is within the limits of reasonable speculation to think that in his extreme eagerness to assert the originality of his poems he destroyed the notes of his reading, lest it be proved later that in giving hints to his poems, Nature was not quite as unassisted as he would have the world believe. He must still have had the same feeling when, as Shephard observes, he "spent much time during those last years in Camden sorting out and burning papers that were too surely his own, as he said, to be left."[117] Whether, however, he deliberately destroyed them or they were lost, the fact is, we do not have his notes of the reading of those years as we have of the years subsequent to 1855.[118]

Nevertheless, there is sufficient testimony to Whitman's reading in those preparatory years. In the authorized version of his biography by Bucke, the assertion that "reading did not go for so very much in Whitman's education," is accompanied by the qualifying admission that "still his aim was to absorb humanity and modern life, and he neglected no means, books included, by which this aim be furthered." Bucke further admits that though his "special education" was "in absorbing into himself the whole city and country about him," he "went occasionally to the libraries and museums of all sorts."[119] George Whitman, the poet's brother, reported: "Walt had very few books. He was not a book collector. But he spent a good many hours in the libraries of New York."[120] In another authentic account of those years, Thomas A. Gere, a friend of Whitman, exclaimed: "What enjoyable nights they were when Walt would come to us after a long study at home or in some prominent New York library!"[121] That apart from the use of libraries for absorbing humanity Whitman used some other intellectual or literary means is avouched by the following state- ment of the official portrait (to which, incidentally, the large number of magazine articles clipped and preserved among his papers[122] bear additional testimony): "Those years he used to watch the English quarterlies and Blackwood's, and when he found an article that suited him he would buy the number, perhaps second-hand, for a few cents, tear it out and take it with him on his next sea-beach excursion to digest."[123] All this humanizes our poet a little and presents something very much better than the superman of the myth—"a man earthly . . . and alive";[124] a poet who produced a human miracle in the hard but human way of genius, and knew the labor that went into it, and undertook it.

Contrary to the implication of the concessional admission the authorized biography made, namely, that literary means played a secondary role in Whitman's education, Newton Arwin's analy- sis[125] shows the enormous impact of books on Whitman's poetry. Arwin traces the influence of science and the scientific thought of the day on Whitman and discovers how he absorbed the ideas and thoughts of nineteenth-century America through reading. "At the end of [his] long chapter," as Cowley says, "one is left with a feeling of respect for Whitman's mass of information, but also with a diminished sense of his individuality."[126] We thus travel a long way from the "cosmic vision" and the "mystical revelation" that suddenly brought the poet "the mental expansion,"[127] and find that a considerable amount of his "stuff" was not there in him at all, but was gathered diligently through years of reading. The mystical illumination gives way to "literary derivation." As Arwin observed, "it was in the mental soil that had been harrowed and seeded by the poets and novelists, by the preachers and lecturers and essayists that 'Leaves of Grass' took root and sprouted."[128]

As regards his reading habits, the official biography offers this description: "He seldom read any book deliberately through, and there was no more apparent system about his reading than in anything else that he did, that is to say, there was no system about it at all. If he sat in the library an hour, he would have half a dozen to a dozen volumes about him, on the table, on the chairs, and on the floor. He seemed to read a few pages here and there, and pass from place to place, from volume to volume, doubtless pursuing some clue or thread of his own. Sometimes (though very seldom) he would get sufficiently interested in a volume to read it all."[129] Although Whitman's well-known habit of heavily underlining and annotating the pages of his reading[130] induces us to take this apparently authorized account with suspicion, the unsystematic nature of his reading and his habit of gathering quick surface impressions, can be established by an analysis of his treatment of sources. Bliss Perry observed that "his methods of reading were mainly casual and impressionistic."[131] The relatively fewer books and the large mass of newspaper and magazine articles in his personal possession indicate that his reading inclined toward periodicals, whose brief and immediate nature probably suited his temperament and the habits of a long journalistic career. The kind of notes he has made of his reading, as we have them in *Notes and Fragments,* also supports the statement that "he gave the newspapers and magazines the greater portion of his attention. He read widely in the periodical field."[132] But there were books in his preparatory days, books like *The Age of Reason, The Rights of Man,* Carlyle's *Past and Present, A Few Days in Athens,* and a host of others, from whence ideas and thoughts, and often words, phrases, and whole sentences, seeped into his avid imagination and enlarged the stuff of his poetry. For during the early journalistic years of his life, as Holloway says, "Whitman reviewed more books and knew more about books than any contemporary editor in Brooklyn, if not in New York, exclusive of the editors of the literary periodicals. It was he who introduced the literary miscellany into the *Eagle* and who gave prominence to book reviewing through its columns. In the course of two years he quoted from nearly a hundred more or less well-known authors and reviewed more than a hundred books."[133]

Thus, whatever gave Whitman "the remarkable accession of

power," the acquisition of knowledge that his poetry carried was the result of human labor. He wanted to be a great poet; to be a great poet, of the kind he envisaged under the inspiration of Emerson and Fuller, he had to have great things to say—a message to give if he must play the role of a Vates, a Prophet-Poet. To give a message, he had to have it; and, simply, to have it meant to go and acquire it.

And Whitman, as the vast area over which his interests took him in his known reading itself indicates, acquired it from many sources. No one source can account for the entire literary event of *Leaves of Grass*—the initial personal aspiration of becoming a great poet, the direction the aspiration took, the plan on which his great poetry was composed, the new content put into it, the different form in which it was presented, and much else that made his work the puzzle that it is. One may notice, for instance, the apparent disparity between the announcements of the Preface and the actual contents of the poems of the first edition with which he gave to America its "first distinctive poem," as he called it.[134] The Preface declares the coming of a national bard, whose song is "the great psalm of the republic," but in the poems themselves, as John Kinnaird has observed, "we are really never in a consciously American world, but always within the purely magical universe of Whitman's 'self' and its strange visitations."[135] The source or inspiration of the poems, and the source or inspiration of the nationalistic scheme of the poet, are evidently two different—albeit in him related—things.

Whitman's is truly the art of Emerson's description: "In poetry, we require the miracle. The bee flies among flowers, and gets its mint and marjorum, and generates a new product, which is not mint and marjorum, but honey."[136] Like a bee, the assiduous mind of Whitman has gathered its mint and marjorum, and, though, as every reader of his has found, it has not always produced the honey, it *has* generated a new product. And the industry with which it has collected its raw material from innumerable sources, far and wide, is undeniable.

5

SLIPS AND ENVELOPES

THE SECRECY WITH WHICH THE YEARS OF WHITMAN'S PROBA-
tionary period in regard to his intellectual activities are surrounded;
the many ways in which he has mystified the world into accepting
the originality of his genius; the fact that *Leaves of Grass* is "not
based on one or a dozen sources; but it was Whitman's achievement to fuse 'hints' from hundreds of books with an authentic
product of his own fantasy"[137] are difficulties enough in discovering tracks of his ideas. "Whitman was so successful in hiding his
tracks," said Brinton, "that he seemed to end where most writers
begin."[138] Not inconsiderable is the challenge posed by his method
of composition, which achieved a poem in the installment pattern,
by agglomeration of bits and fragments, composed at different
times, under different immediate stimuli, and by ordering them
together into a whole subsequently, often breaking that order and
re-forming them, in another poem and in another shape. Commenting upon the various corrections, revisions, and later layers
of revision found in "The Manuscript of Whitman's *Passage to
India,*" Fredson Bowers remarked: "On the evidence there is little
doubt that Whitman was working into his long poem pieces from
separate and shorter works which at some time had been set up in
proof but are not otherwise preserved so far as I know."[139] The
remark applies to all his long poems. Aside from working into a
later poem pieces from others, frequently from his own prose,
which might be regarded a mere peculiarity, his basic principle of
poetic composition itself was, as evidence shows, fragmentary.

In 1887 he imparted to a young friend (Harrison S. Morris) some idea of his method of collecting material for a poem. The following is a transcript of Mr. Morris's notes:

"He said an idea would strike him, which, after mature thought, he would consider fit to be the special 'theme' of a piece. This he would revolve in his mind in all its phases, and finally adopt, setting it down crudely on a bit of paper—the back of an envelope or any scrap,—which he would place in an envelope. Then he would lie in wait for any other material which might bear upon or lean toward that idea, and, as it came to his mind, he would put it on paper and place it in the same envelope. After he had quite exhausted the supply of suggestion, or had a sufficient number to interpret the idea withal, he would interweave them in a 'piece' as he called it. I asked him about the arrangement or succession of the slips, and he said, 'They always fall properly into place.' "[140]

This envelope method of ordering fragments properly into place, or, to use Furness's description, "slowly and painstakingly gathering together the stuff of fantasy, vagrant flashes and half gleams" and "draw[ing] out . . . with arduous labour . . . the full essence of his thought, eventually building into vivid inescapable prison-patterns of sound the captured sense,"[141] makes the task of tracking the source of the captured sense often well-nigh impossible. And then, Whitman possessed the extraordinary power of transforming the sense he captured into "inescapable prison-patterns of sound" all his own. The following examples will illustrate both aspects of his composition.

In his 1865 poem "A Broadway Pageant" is a passage obviously describing India:

The Originatress comes,
The nest of languages, the bequeather of poems, the race of eld,
Florid with blood, pensive, rapt with musings, hot with passion,
Sultry with perfume, with ample and flowing garments,
With sunburnt visage, with intense soul and glittering eyes,
The race of Brahma comes.[142] (Italics added)

With one word missing, "with" in the middle of the last line, the italicized part of the above passage occurs again as a quotation in his eulogy on "The East—What a subject for a poem!" in *Specimen Days*.[143] An analysis of these lines will throw an interesting light on the art of this shaper of words.

The word "florid," of which he is very fond when describing the Orient, is from his own note, collected in *Notes and Fragments*,[144] beginning: "The florid, rich, first (?) phases of poetry, as in the Oriental poems." The rest of the passage is almost entirely from the lines he read in Alger's *The Poetry of the East*,[145] of which he had a copy. On page 23 of his Introduction, Alger describes Indian poetry as follows:

> The poetry we should expect, and have found [in India] is as the clime,—vast in mystery, warm with passion, far-vistaed with reverie, rich in jewels, redolent with perfumes, brilliant in colours, inexhaustible in profusion.

A little later, on page 27, Alger observes that "The Hindu Muse is pre-eminently characterized by *pensiveness, love* of meditation. Her children see everything in reverie. The world is suspended in Maya or illusion, and they mildly think on it."

On the flyleaf of his copy of Alger's book, Whitman has written: "Given me by WRA the author in Boston it must have been in 1861 or '2. Have often read (dabbled) in the 'Introduction to Oriental Poetry' pp 3 to 92 and over and over again . . . two or three of my jaunts thro' the war, I carried this volume in my trunk—read in it—sometimes to hospital groups, to while away the time."[146]

One of Malcolm Cowley's grounds for assuming Whitman's ignorance of Oriental literature at the time of the first edition of *Leaves of Grass* is the absence in the 1855 poems of any "words from the Sanskrit (notably 'Maya' and 'Sudra')" which "are used correctly in some of the poems written after 1858."[147] This might lead to the impression that Whitman "had read seriously about the East only at a fairly later date . . . perhaps under the influence of Alger's anthology."[148] But then in the poem, "Are You the New Person Drawn Toward Me?" written in 1860, Whitman, like Alger, uses the words maya and illusion together. If Alger's book did come to him in 1861 or 62, we have another and earlier source for his knowledge of the words. And abstention from use of such words in 1855 may be part of the intention to "make no quotations or allusions to any other writer," in accordance with which he had dropped the name of "Ahimoth, brother of Death," when he reprinted the 1850 "Resurgemus"[149] as "Europe" in 1855.

Another example of Whitman's transformation of phrases gathered from his sources is equally illuminating. In Alger's anthology a fragment from a Hindu poem is offered as an example of Hindu imagination:

> I will cite but one brief fragment more which like a quick, broad flash lights up to our ignorance the dark stage and canvas of the Hindu fancy. . . .

> "With the noise of the musical instruments, and the eager noise of the spectators,
> The din of the assembly rose up like the roaring of the sea,
> When, lo! wearing his white raiment, and the white sacrificial cord,
> With his snow-white hair and his silvery beard, and the white garland round his head,
> Into the midst of the arena slowly walked the Brahmin with his son,
> Like the sun with the planet Mars in a cloudless sky."[150]

With "New Themes Entered Upon" in "1876, '77," Whitman wrote in *Specimen Days* for the "Night of Oct. 28," the following passage:

> The heavens unusually transparent—the stars out by the myriads—the great path of the Milky Way, with its branch, only seen of very clear nights—Jupiter, setting in the west, looks like a huge hap-hazard splash, and has a little star for companion.

> Clothed in his white garments,
> Into the round and clear arena slowly entered the brahmin,
> Holding a little child by the hand,
> Like the moon with the planet Jupiter in a cloudless night-sky.
>
>   Old Hindu Poem.[151]

Kennedy noticed the parallelism between Whitman's "Old Hindu Poem" and Alger's "fragment," but maintained that Whitman was "quoting from memory very imperfectly."[152] But that it is not the imperfection of quoting from memory but a conscious adoption is evident from the fact that the lines are adapted to the night, the moon, the clear heavens, and the Jupiter that Whitman saw in the west. Furthermore, Alger's fragment, along with his other illustrations, was reproduced from "a valuable article on 'Indian Poetry' in the October number of the Westminster Review for 1848,"[153] and Whitman had that article in his possession, "much scored and annotated."[154]

In one of his "Notes on the Text of 'Leaves of Grass,'" Bucke painstakingly compares the "Lines taken verbatim from pages forty one and two of the 1855 edition (describing the battle)" with the accounts of a battle given in the "Life and Character of the Chevalier Paul Jones, a captain in the Navy of the United States during the Revolutionary War," and finds many words "borrowed by Whitman in his brief and animated account," and, in many instances, even the same arrangement of words and phrases. Almost the entire account of the old-time sea-fight in "Song of Myself" is a verbal transcription, except for the rearrangement of details and occasional words and phrases of his own linking the borrowed phrases together. Yet to the inordinate personal enthusiasm of Bucke it was an illustration of Whitman's insistence on—a habit that was a law for him—"actual observation of the facts at first hand by himself or else obtained from some entirely trustworthy person."[155] To a dispassionate reader it seems to be an illustration of poetic methods not quite in consonance with the law of art.

These and innumerable other examples of Whitman's borrowings (research has shown that he borrowed not only hints and suggestions, or ideas and phrases, but even entire slices of the thought and experience of others) to put into his poetry—however transformed into authenticity they might be by the power of the poetic tongue—indicate that his genius lay more in the act of imaginative rendering of thought than in the creation of the thought itself.

Another interesting aspect of his method of composition is illustrated by the following. In an early notebook Whitman wrote:

Amelioration is the blood that runs through the body of the universe.—I do not lag—I do not hasten—(it appears to say) I bide my hour over billions of billions of years—I exist in the

?

void that takes uncounted time and coheres to a nebula, and in further time cohering to an orb, marches gladly round, a beautiful creature, in his place in the processions of God, where new comers have been falling in the ranks for ever, and will be so always—I could he balked no how, not if all the worlds and living beings were this minute reduced back into the impalpable film of chaos—I should surely bring up again where we now stand and go on as much further and thence on and on—My right hand is time, and left hand is space—both are ample—a few quintillions of cycles, a few sextillions of cubic leagues, are not of importance to me—what I shall attain to I can never tell, for there is something that underlies me, of whom I am a part and instrument.[156]

This beautiful passage, on which critical attention has rightly showered its praise, is an exquisitely imaginative description of the universe, and what it appears to say. But when *Leaves of Grass* came to be written, a large part of the utterances of the universe was attributed to the poet's "I," and the prose passage was disintegrated and distributed among the verse. Some of it was given, duly, to the earth, which may be regarded as synonymous with universe, in the poem, "A Song of the Rolling Earth."

> Amelioration is one of the earth's words,
> The earth neither lags nor hastens. . . .[157]

But the rest of it all goes into "Song of Myself":

> Before I was born out of my mother [. . .]
> My embryo has never been torpid [. . .]
>
> For it the nebula cohered to an orb [. . .]
> . . . .
> There is no stoppage, and never can be stoppage,
> If I and you and the worlds,[. . . . .

.................] were this moment reduced back to a
pallid float [. . .]
We should surely bring up again, where we stand,
And as surely go as much farther, and then farther and
    farther.
. . . .
A few quadrillions of eras, a few octillions of cubic leagues do
    not hazard the span, or make it impatient,
They are but parts. . . . anything is but a part.

See ever so far. . . . there is limitless space outside of that.
Count ever so much. . . . there is limitless time around that.[158]

Even this apparent incongruity of the poet's self's saying what the
universe should appear to say has been accepted as the result of
the imaginative identification of the Poet's self with the universe,
which may well be, considering that there is in the poem a much
more varied identification than that—with God, with the Cosmic
Soul, the Universal Man, son of Manhattan, and so on. We
might ignore for a while that all this complicated mass of identification was supposed "to articulate and faithfully express in
literary or poetic form, and uncompromisingly my [Whitman's]
own physical, emotional, moral, intellectual, and aesthetic personality, in the midst of, and tallying, the momentous spirit and
facts of its immediate days, and of current America."[159] But unless
we raise the phrase "out of my mother" to the subtlety of a metaphysical conceit, and completely overlook the implications of the
words "If I and you and the worlds" in the lines quoted above,
it is difficult to accept the identification with the earth. And then
it is the earth, not the entire universe, with which he is trying his
imaginative exercise, for it is as the earth that he can say:

My sun has his sun and round him obediently wheels,
He joins with his partners a group of superior circuit,
And greater sets follow, making specks of the greatest inside
    them.[160]

This brief peep into his methods of poetic composition creates
an irresistible impression that Whitman's art is basically one of
verbal assemblage, that it is the work of patient craft more than

of urgent vision, and that—skillfully transformed into a shape often verbally different, broken up into bits and worked up and placed in carefully chosen contexts and positions, or fused with new combinations and significances—his material has an undeniable look of original conception, defying any attempt to trace it to its true source.

6

FAINT CLUES AND INDIRECTIONS

BECAUSE NEW ENGLAND TRANSCENDENTALISM IS INADEQUATE
as a source for all the recognizably Indian ideas[161] of Whitman,
and because the subjective illumination theory is hard to accept
against the knowledge of the literary derivation of his other ideas,
his later admission of having read "the ancient Hindoo poems"
deserves more serious notice than critics have so far given it. However, except for its definite indication that he had read them before
the writing of the first edition of *Leaves of Grass,* Whitman's
admission is too vague to be very helpful, inasmuch as it does not
specify which poems he read. The description—and one suspects
that its indefiniteness, particularly when compared to the precision with which he mentions other books in the same list, is, like
the earlier denial, rather deliberate—might apply to almost the
entire range of Hindu philosophical writings. It might merely
mean the epic poems, the *Ramayana* and the *Mahabharata,* of his
knowledge of which we have plenty of other evidence. But that
does not take us very far in our inquiry, because, although like
most literature of Ancient India, the epics have their philosophical
content, by themselves they can hardly be supposed to have given
him the ideas that we notice in his poems. It might mean the
Vedas, to which he often refers in his prose works; or the
Bhagavad-Gita, to which, considering that he did possess a copy of
it "with marginal notes throughout" added by himself, he strangely
makes no reference at all; or, it might mean the *Upanishads* of
India. For all these are "ancient Hindoo poems." Furthermore, to
be on the safe side, we should probably guard ourselves against

53

overenthusiastic acceptance of the admission itself in our eagerness
to stress the contradiction between the earlier and the later declarations. For it may well be like his other claim of being "the greatest
poetical representative of German philosophy," or a detail in the
cosmic posture of his

> Having studied the new and antique, the Greek and Germanic
>   systems,
> Kant having studied and stated, Fichte and Schelling and
>   Hegel,
> Stated the lore of Plato, and Socrates greater than Plato,
> And greater than Socrates sought and stated, Christ divine
>   having studied long.[162]

Therefore, we are to be wary in accepting his statements, both
avowals and denials, and seek some kind of involuntary evidence,
what might be called a statement he never made, a sort of cir-
cumstantial evidence, or, to use Whitman's own phrase, "faint
clews and indirections."[163]

The chief ground upon which intelligent literary criticism, as
contrasted with personal admiration found elsewhere, is forced to
assume Whitman's ignorance of Indian philosophy is the absence
of definite evidence of his reading Indian works. There is a good
deal of exaggeration in this position, because in most cases the evidence in his notebooks of his knowledge or ignorance of books,
whether by direct statements or references or by the absence of
such statements or references, is misleading and untrustworthy.
Such claims to an actual study as are made within the poems
themselves, like the one quoted above, research has shown to be
just poetic pose, and, when carried over to the plain truths of
prose, as was frequently done by Whitman, to be downright
boast or misguided exaggeration. The innumerable references to
authors and books in his prose writings as well as in scrapbooks
and notebooks are not always reliable evidence of the nature and
extent of his reading and knowledge of the books in question. In
many cases, as in the notes on Goethe, or the four German metaphysicians, or Cervantes,[164] he has collected his points from books
about books, or critical accounts, or journalistic surveys, and
gathered a superficial or second-hand information about the authors
and the works. Besides, most of his entries in the section "Pre-

paratory Reading" about the authors, such, for example, as the ones on Spencer, Swedenborg, Cervantes, Schiller, the English poets, Plutarch, Richter, and Tasso, are of a biographical nature,[165] of the sort found in periodical magazines or literary reviews. A disproportionately large part of those notes on authors consists merely of dates and events in their lives. Only in a few instances do the notes testify to an unmistakable reading of the original work.

Moreover, with the exception of a few fragments, all the material printed in *Notes and Fragments* under the misleading title "Preparatory Reading and Thought"[166] belongs to the years subsequent to the first edition of 1855. There is not a single reference in it to any reading prior to 1855 beyond the following: Fragment no. 154 (p. 127) on Alexander Smith's poems; no. 155 (p. 127) on Bayard Taylor's poems; no. 157 (p. 127) on Gerald Massey's (of 1855, but no date mentioned); his notes on the magazine article "Imagination and Fact" (no. 6, p. 77); a reference to De Vere's "Comparative Philology" (no. 48, p. 96); and the comment on Emerson's writings (no. 163, pp. 128–129). Even the "Notes on English History," as Bucke's footnote explains, were made about 1855–56, "because they are written on the back of the unused copies of the flytitle of the 1855 'Leaves of Grass.' "[167]

And in his early notebooks, of the years before 1855, collected by Holloway and Furness, there is no record of any reading whatsoever. There is no reference to Emerson or an admission of having read him in those notebooks recording the formative years of the 1855 poems. He even calculatedly and energetically denied having read the Philosopher of Concord. But all the mystification it succeeded in creating in the early stages of critical investigation could not conceal for long how much the 1855 *Leaves of Grass* owed to Emerson. Even Kennedy, in a long study, traced forty-three passages in Whitman that had close parallels of thought and language with Emerson, though, inspired by his unswerving faith in the originality of his master, he maintained that "the great genius appropriates material on every hand and makes it his own by the weight of his mind," and explained the "Identities of Thought and Phrase in Emerson and Whitman" thus: "It simply shows that two philosophers talking about life and its conduct must use somewhat the same language and cover the same ground, especially when they are contemporaries and living amid similar thought."[168]

Absence of explicit reference to his reading of a book or an author seems to be of no reliable value in determining Whitman's ignorance of the book or the author. Merely because "Whitman does not refer to it [the *Bhagavad-Gita,* in this case,] in his note-books of the early 1850's where he mentions most of the books he was poring over," Malcolm Cowley, who came nearest to discovering the secret of Whitman, is forced to the conclusion that "in spite of the recognizably Indian ideas expressed in the poem ["Song of Myself," which he rightly regards as very important] I would hazard the guess that the ideas are not of literary derivation." The inability to find proofs of the literary derivation of those ideas further drives him to the sad legacy of nineteenth-century Whitman criticism, the mystical hypothesis that Whitman "reinvented them for himself, after an experience similar to the one for which the Sanskrit word is Samadhi, or absorption," and to the statement that "it was a truly extraordinary achievement for him to rediscover the outlines of a whole philosophical system chiefly on the basis of his own mystical experience and with little help from his reading."[169]

We are forced, then, by indirections to find directions out. Let us first consider the considerable number of references that Whitman makes to India in his prose works and notebooks. They are not superficial, as is generally supposed. Upon closer examination, they testify to a knowledge deeper and more serious than an American newspaper reader's understanding of a distant, ancient land with its strange, wise ways. They indicate a special interest, a profound personal enthusiasm that frequently expresses itself in eulogy. To this interest the mass of material clipped from newspapers and magazines, read and preserved among his scrapbooks, also bears testimony. It has been observed that "Asia was of special interest to Whitman and many clippings relate to that continent."[170] His vast notes on the geography, history, and general culture of the countries of the East, collected in *Notes and Fragments,* are not the product of casual inquiry.

Scattered all through his prose writings are allusions to India. They are all, of course, of the years subsequent to the first edition of *Leaves of Grass,* and do not throw any direct light on our problem of tracing Whitman's knowledge of Indian ideas prior to 1855. Yet they deserve some notice, because they indicate that he knew something, and they may help us to a knowledge of its extent and source as well as method of acquisition. They are therefore presented here in the order in which they appear in his *Complete Writings*.[171]

The first of these is the passage for the "Night of Oct. 28," with the "Old Hindu Poem" shaped from Alger's illustration of Hindu fancy, already noticed in these pages. The following is an entry for "the Dawn" of "July 23, 1878," and is a paean on the East:

> The EAST—what a subject for a poem! Indeed, where else a more pregnant, more splendid one? Where one more idealistic-real, more subtle, more sensuous-delicate? The East, answering all lands, all ages, peoples; touching all senses, here, immediate, now—and yet so indescribably far off—such retrospect! The East—long-stretching—so losing itself—the Orient, the gardens of Asia, the womb of history and song—forth-issuing all those strange, dim cavalcades—
> Florid with blood, pensive, rapt with musings, hot with passion,
> Sultry with perfume, with ample and flowing garments,
> With sunburnt visage, intense soul and glittering eyes.
>
> Always the East—old, how incalculably old! And yet here the same—ours yet, fresh as a rose, to every morning, every life, to-day—and always will be.[172]

Of the significance of the three lines of verse in the passage something has been said already. The whole rhapsodical passage follows the description of the early dawn when

> . . . the moon well up in the heavens, and past her half, is shining brightly—the air and sky of that cynical-clear, Minerva-like quality, virgin cool—not the weight of sentiment or mystery, or passion's ecstasy indefinable—not the religious sense, the varied all, distill'd and sublimated into one, of the night just described [in the previous entry for "July 22d 1878," "Hours for the Soul," in these words: "I am convinced there are hours of Nature, especially of the atmosphere, mornings and evenings, address'd to the soul. Night transcends, for that pur-

pose, what the proudest day can do"]. Now, indeed, if never before, the heavens declared the glory of God. It was to the full sky of the Bible, of Arabia, of the prophets, and of the oldest poems. There, in abstraction and stillness . . . the copiousness, the removedness, vitality, loose-clear-crowdedness, of that stellar concave spreading overhead, softly absorbed into me, rising so free, interminably high, stretching east, west, north, south, and I, though but a point in the centre below, embodying all. . . .

As if for the first time, indeed, creation noiselessly sank into and through me its placid and untellable lesson. . . . The spirit's hour—religion's hour—the visible suggestion of God in space and time—now once definitely indicated, if never again.[173]

The long, involved quotation shows that the intense enthusiasm for the East following the profound meditation on "the visible suggestion of God in space and time" marks Whitman's philosophic thoughts as having an Eastern association; otherwise the eulogy on the East would be inconsequential and difficult of explanation. The connection between the passages is too obvious to be overlooked.

In his essay on "Carlyle from the American Points of View"[174] Whitman said: "The most profound theme that can occupy the mind of man . . . is doubtless involved in the query: What is the fusing explanation and tie—what the relation between the (radical, democratic) Me, the human identity of understanding, emotions, spirit &c. on the one side, of and with the (conservative) Not Me, the whole of the material objective universe and laws, with what is behind them in space and time, on the other side?" And, regarding Kant's answer to that query as partial, and Schelling's as a mere suggestion of an answer, he examines (though his summary is "indebted to J. Gostwick's abstract") G. F. Hegel's "fuller statement of the matter" thus:[175]

According to Hegel the whole earth, (an old nucleus-thought as in the Vedas . . .) with its infinite variety, the past, the surroundings of today, or what may happen in the future, the contrarieties of material with spiritual, and of natural with artificial, are all, to the eye of the *ensemblist,* but necessary sides and unfoldings, different steps or links, in the endless process of creative thought, which, amid numberless apparent failures and contradictions, is held together by central and never-broken unity—not contradictions or failures at all, but radiations of one consistent and eternal purpose; the whole mass of everything steadily, unnervingly tending and flowing toward the permanent *utile* and *morale,* as rivers to oceans. . . .

Extent of Whitman's knowledge of Indian philosophy apart, the passage clearly demonstrates an awareness of the nature of Hindu thought acute enough to point out that Hegel's answer to "the most profound theme that can occupy the mind of man" is "an old nucleus-thought as in the Vedas." Both the feeling of the "visible suggestion of God in space and time" and the thought of "the central and never-broken unity" of things remind him of India. (The reference in the former passage is to the East in general, of course, but the fact that the verse lines used in "A Broadway Pageant" allude to "the Originatress," the "race of Brahma," gives to it a more specific implication.) It is also curious that in the same line of thought it occurs to him to use a simile most frequently used in Hindu writings, as these examples will show:

The man whose passions enter his heart as waters run into the unswelling ocean, obtaineth happiness. (The *Bhagvat-Geeta*)

As the rapid streams of full-flowing rivers roll on to meet the ocean's bed . . . (*Ibid.*)

As all rivers flowing into the ocean disappear and lose their respective appellations and forms, so the person who has acquired a knowledge of and faith in God . . . is absorbed into the Supreme. (*Moonduk-Oopunishud*)[176]

A little later in the same essay, Whitman declares the superiority of the answers given to his query by the philosophical poets of ancient times over the system of the four German masters: "While the contributions which German Kant and Fichte and Schelling and Hegel have bequeathed to humanity—and which English Darwin has also in his field—are indispensable to the erudition of America's future, I should say that in all of them, and of the best of them, when compared with the lightning flashes and flights of the old prophets and *exaltés,* the spiritual poets and poetry of all lands (as in the Hebrew Bible), there seems to be, nay certainly is, something lacking—something cold, a failure to satisfy the deepest emotions of the soul—a want of living glow, fondness, warmth, which the old *exaltés* supply, and which the keenest modern philosophers so far do not."[177]

It would not be far wrong to infer from such an explicit assertion that Whitman's own soul found its answers rather in the "lightning flashes and flights" of the old prophets than in the modern philosophers whom he and many of his critics claimed as his teachers.

Among the maxims and excerpts collected by him from his reading is a Buddhistic saying: "If you hate a man, don't kill him, but let him live." Presenting this as a sample of his "common-place book down at the creek," he makes a comment on the samples that may throw an interesting light on his poetic processes. He says:

> I ought not to offer a record of these days, interests, recuperations, without including a certain old, well-thumb'd commonplace book, filled with favorite excerpts, I carried in my pocket for three summers, and absorb'd over and over again, when the mood invited. I find so much in having a poem or fine suggestion sink into me (a little then goes a great ways) prepar'd by these vacant-sane and natural influences.[178]

Speaking of the function of literature in modern society, where the "problem of humanity . . . is to be finally met and treated by literature," because "the priest departs and the divine literatus comes," Whitman mentions, as an example of the literature in which the entire genius of a nation resides, "the far-back cumbrous old Hindu epics, as indicating the Asian eggs out of which European chivalry was hatch'd."[179] In another elaborate footnote, again as an illustration of "the literature, songs, esthetics, &c. of a country" whose importance is "principally because they furnish the materials and suggestions of personality for the women and men of that country," he speaks of Indian literature with a detail that signifies a special knowledge of it:

> After the rest is satiated, all interest culminates in the field of persons, and never flags there. Accordingly in this field have the great poets and literatuses signally toil'd. They too, in all

ages, all lands, have been creators, fashioning, making types of
men and women, as Adam and Eve are made in the divine fable.
Behold, shaped, bred by Orientalism, feudalism, through their
long growth and culmination, and breeding back in return—
(when shall we have an equal series, typical democracy?)—
behold, commencing in primal Asia, (apparently formulated, in
what beginning we know, in the gods of the mythologies, and
coming down thence,) a few samples of the countless product,
bequeath'd to the moderns, bequeath'd to America as studies.
For the men, Yudisthura, Rama, Arjuna . . .

Among women, the goddesses of the Egyptian, Indian and
Greek mythologies . . .[180]

The passage above is obviously the product of actual reading
of the two epics of India, the *Ramayana* and the *Mahabharata,*
and of the *Purana* or *Puranas* that narrate mythological stories of
gods, as the phrase "types . . . formulated . . . in the gods of the
mythologies" suggests.

Whitman's next reference to Indian literature:[181] "Hindus,
with hymn and apothegm and endless epic" which are among the
monuments that "stand . . . along the great highways of time . . .
those forms of majesty and beauty . . . beacons" that for us "burn
through all the nights," is not the vague description that comes
from general knowledge, because it makes a definite allusion to the
varieties of Hindu works—one may presume, the Vedic "hymn,"
the "apothegm" of Vishnu Sharma's *Hitopadesha,* or the *Laws of
Menu,* and the "endless epic" of the *Ramayana* and the *Mahabharata,* all of which were available in English translation, "bequeath'd
to America as studies" in Oriental art.

To illustrate another point he is making, that "the altitude of
literature and poetry has always been religion—and always will
be," Whitman again mentions, first in the list, the Indian Vedas
as one "of such poems only in which, (while singing well of persons and events, of the passions of man, and the shows of the
material universe,) the religious tone, the consciousness of mystery,
the recognition of the future, of the unknown, of Deity over and
under all, and of the divine purpose, are never absent, but indirectly
give tone to all."[182]

Among his "first class poets" who are "to hold up high to eyes
of land and race the eternal antiseptic models," for whom the

"rule and demesne" is "not the exterior, but interior; not the macrocosm, but microcosm, not Nature, but Man," are regarded "the old singers of India," though they were "to their days and occasions."[183]

In his note on "British Literature" he says: "While there is much in [Shakespeare] ever offensive to democracy," Shakespeare being "incarnated, uncompromising feudalism in literature . . . of the great poems of Asian antiquity, the Indian epics . . . I should say they substantially adjust themselves to us . . . with our notions, both of seriousness and fun, and our standards of heroism, manliness, and even the democratic requirements. . . . I rejoice at the feeling for Oriental researches and poetry, and hope it will go on."[184]

The note on "Darwinism—(Then Further More)" mentions India among "the antique races and lands" in which, "giving cast and complexion to their art, poems, and their politics as well as ecclesiasticism, all of which we [the Americans] more or less inherit . . . appear those venerable claims to origin from God himself, or from gods and goddesses—ancestry from divine beings of vaster beauty, size, and power than ours."[185]

Pointing out America's "Lacks and Wants Yet," as compared to "most foreign countries, small or large . . . each [of which] has contributed after its kind, directly or indirectly, at least one great undying song, to help vitalize and increase the valor, wisdom, and elegance of humanity," he mentions, again first in the list, "the stupendous epics of India."[186] And among "those precious legacies—accumulations . . . from the far-off—from all eras—and all lands" that America "is to receive . . . cheerfully," India has its bequest too.[187]

In "Our Eminent Visitors—Past, Present and Future," Whitman again speaks of the old masterpieces, "the interminable Hindu epics,"[188] and his essay on "The Bible as Poetry" begins with a reference to "those autochtonic bequests of Asia—the Hebrew Bible, the mighty Hindu Epics," and observes that "all the poems of Orientalism, with the Old and New Testaments at the centre, tend to deep and wide (I don't know but the deepest and widest,) psychological development—with little, or nothing at all, of the esthetic, the principal verse-requirement of our day." After the reading of such works, Whitman exclaims, the western writers appear "the most shallow, impudent, supercilious brood on earth.' "[189]

Probably the nicest compliment Whitman paid to Indian literature, as well as the strongest direct evidence to his actual reading of it, occurs in the same essay a little farther on:

> The finest blending of individuality with universality (in my opinion nothing out of the galaxies of the Iliad, or Shakespeare's heroes, or from the Tennysonian 'Idylls,' so lofty, devoted and starlike,) typified in the songs of those old Asiatic lands. Men and women as great columnar trees. Nowhere else the abnegation of self towering in such quaint sublimity; nowhere else the simplest human emotions conquering the gods of heaven, and fate itself. (The episode, for instance, toward the close of the "Mahabharata"—the journey of the wife Savitri with the god of death, Yama,
>> "One terrible to see—blood-red his garb,
>> His body huge and dark, bloodshot his eyes,
>> Which flamed like suns beneath his turban cloth,
>> Arm'd was he with a noose,"
> who carries off the soul of the dead husband, the wife tenaciously following, and—by the resistless charm of perfect poetic recitation!—eventually redeeming her captive mate.)[190]

The verse lines Whitman quotes above are not from Alger's *The Poetry of the East,* or the article on "Indian Epic Poetry" of the *Westminster Review* of October 1848, the known material of his Indian readings, both of which, with other extracts, illustrate that epic story. It is apparent, therefore, that he got the passage from another source. It is a negligible detail in which translation he read the episode, but it certainly is a curious circumstance that his lines are so like and yet at the same time so different from the lines of Sir Edwin Arnold in his translation of "Savitri; or Love and Death,"[191] reproduced here for comparison:

> ... when, lo! before her rose
> A shade majestic. Red his garments were,
> His body vast and dark; like fiery suns
> The eyes burned beneath his forehead-cloth;
> Armed was he with a noose, awful of mien.
> This Form tremendous stood by. . . .

Oriental poetry is mentioned once more, though in a general sort of way, in Whitman's note on "Five Thousand Poems" in which he regards the poetry of the whole earth as combining "in one aggregate and electric globe or universe, with all its numberless parts and radiations held together by a common centre or verteber."[192]

The earliest reference to India that can be found in all his writings is in the "Sundown Papers; From the Desk of a School master," written in 1840. Paper No. 8 describes a reverie, in which the author "wandering over the earth in search of Truth . . . after having lived too with the rude Tartar in his tent, and installed [himself] in all the mysteries which are known to the Lamas of Tibet," came down "to a more southern clime, and disputed with the Brahmins, who profess to believe in a religion that has existed for more centuries than any other one for years."[193]

The pieces collected in *Notes and Fragments* have a considerable number of direct references to India. Some of them are notes made from reading material that touched on India, such as books, journals, and newspapers, from all of which he augmented his "storehouses of information"[194] on the geography, history, population, religion, etc., of "Hindostan." But a great many of these are expressions of personal enthusiasm and deep-seated understanding.

In the way Bucke presents these notes and fragments in his edition, they are regarded as capable of throwing light upon the genesis, intention, and meaning—in a word, the entire background—of *Leaves of Grass*. But it is for the later editions of the book, rather than for the first edition of 1855, that they have any significance. They belong very largely to the fifties, as Bucke notes in his preface; and, it seems from the recorded dates of many of them, to the later fifties, at least later than the first edition of Whitman's poems. Even the fragments discussing "the Meaning and Intention of Leaves of Grass" (part I of *Notes and Fragments*) concern later editions, as the famous note on "The Great Construction of the New Bible," written in 1857,[195] indicates. Therefore, to the question whether Whitman had studied or read Indian literature, or any other, for that matter, and was influenced by such study or reading in the poems of 1855, the notes have no valuable answer to give, except part III and the list of "Magazine and Newspaper articles" in part V. Reserving our examination of the list of articles for a later occasion, we shall briefly glance at the notes for their references to India without connecting them to Whitman's poems.

The first of these is in the section headed: "Memoranda from Books and from his own Reflections—indicating the Poet's Reading and Thought Preparatory to writing 'Leaves of Grass'." In that brief note, he speaks of the common ancestry of the European and Asian races:

> Then the inhabitants of India and the descendents of the Keltic and Teutonic nations are all of one family and must all have migrated from one country. Whether that country was Persia or Cashmir or a country further east is not easily determined—but it seems that, accordingly, the white man of Europe and the tawny man of India have a common ancestry.[196]

Note 10, containing a direction to himself for a self-teaching exercise,[197] is undoubtedly of considerable significance to us, because it refers to the famous Yoga discipline of India, but inasmuch as it does not explicitly mention India, it will have to be overlooked for the present. In number 54, using that adjective of which he is so fond in describing Oriental poetry, he mentions "the *florid,* rich, first(?) phases of poetry, as in the Oriental poems," and observes how the "very ancient poetry of the Hebrew poets, of Ossian, of the Hindu singer and ecstatics, of the Greeks, of the American aborigines, the old Persians and Chinese, and the Scandinavian Sagas, all resemble each other."[198] There is a brief reference in note 57: "Menu preceded both [Zoroaster and Moses] 1700 B.C."[199] Note 60, a brief commentary on ancient civilizations, mentions India.[200] Note 62, containing Whitman's "notes on the phases of development of man,"[201] has a critical comment on India:

> India represents meditation, oriental rhapsody, passiveness, a curious school-master teaching of wise precepts and is the beginning of feudality, or the institution of the lord and the serf—much of the late-age lord or fine gentleman so nice and delicate dates back to Hindustan.[202]

The passage ends with a note on the antiquity of Hindustan. In the one that follows, the literature of "Hindustan" is mentioned as one of "the first" in the history of universal literature.[203] In his projected plan for "A volume—(dramatic machinery for localities, characters, etc.) running in idea and description through the whole range of recorded time" the "Hindoostanee" is not forgotten.[204]

In the notes Whitman made for his "Sunday Evening Lectures," there is a summary of the doctrines of the four German metaphysicians, Kant, Fichte, Schelling, and Hegel. Once more, in his discussion of Hegel's philosophical ideas, he is reminded of India and the *Vedas:*

> Strictly speaking the transcendental metaphysics present no new contribution to morals, to the formation or guidance of character, the practice of virtue or for the better regulation either of private life or public affairs. With respect to such morals, virtue, or to heroism and the religious incumbency the old principles remain, without notable increase or diminution, the same today as we trace them in farthest India, Egypt, Greece, the Vedas, the Talmud, the Old Testament, Epictetus, Zerdusht, the divine teachings of Christ.[205]

The Hegelian concept of the One all-pervading Spirit again puts him in mind of India:

> Penetrating beneath the shows and materials of the objective world we find, according to Hegel, (though the thought by itself is not new but very antique and both Indian and Grecian) that in respect to human cognition of them, all and several are pervaded by *the only absolute substance* which is SPIRIT, endued with the eternal impetus of development, and producing from itself the opposing powers and forces of the universe.[206]

And in his enthusiastic applause for the achievement of the past, as recorded in note No. 176, the Hindu is the second of "those stages all over the world . . . leaving their memories and inheritances."[207]

Part III of "Notes and Fragments," the section of "Shorter

Notes, Isolated Words, Brief Sentences, Memoranda, Suggestive
Expressions, Names and Dates" has also some interesting references to India:

Item 1 mentions "Ramayana."[208] No. 4, about "Religion-Gods,"
contains a mass of tidbits, chiefly about the Hindu pantheon:

> . . . Chiven (god of desolation and destruction) . . . Brahm,
> Buddha. . . . Vishnu, preserver of the world, image of the
> Lingam the male sign. . . . Manu preceded Moses 2100 B.C. . . .
> Brahma to create. Vishnu, to preserve. Chiven (Siva) to destroy.
> In India—the Vedas—all the three deities from "the eternal"
> Siva. . . . Pouranas treat of mythology and history. Vedas—
> the fourth—concerning ceremonies, is lost. Boudha, Bhudda
> (Fot, Phtah, Mercury) the Boudha doctrine is found in book of
> 3000 B.C. Hermes, author of Egyptian Vedas. All seems to go
> back to Manu who preceded Zoroaster, Moses and the rest,
> and must have been 2100 B.C. and more definitely embodied on
> the banks of the Ganges, the Indian theology with Brahma,
> Vishnu and Chiven. Manu son or grandson of Brahma. . . .
> Krishna (? thence Christ).[209]

This is one of the few memoranda in *Notes and Fragments* indicating the poet's reading truly preparatory to the writing of
Leaves of Grass, for, as Goodale has traced,[210] this entire section,
with the possible exception of one phrase, was made up from
Volney's *Ruins,* a book that Whitman has been proved to have
possessed in his early years. The phrase excepted is, "Manu son
or grandson of Brahma," which is repeated in note 30 with the
additional words, "and first of created beings".[211] Of this phrase
the source appears to be another, as will shortly be seen.

Item 6 carries a short note that "Buddhism was the state religion
of India from the 3rd century before to the 6th century after
Christ,"[212] apparently put down from some article in a newspaper or a periodical just as with note 9: "Tamerlane, 1400 A.D.
in time his (Zinghis Khan) successor. He extended his rule to
Hindostan, founding the Mogul rule there which terminated
1803."[213] A statistical note, 10 mentions: "Hindoos 142,000,-
000."[214]

The first explicit evidence in the pages of *Notes and Fragments*
of Whitman's pre-1855 acquaintance with Indian works is pre-

sented in the following "Notes" made "on a magazine article (1848) on Indian Epic Poetry."[215]

> The Ramayana is the most ancient having one separate distinct thread. Vedas, there are four. One was written 1400 B.C., other anterior.
>
> Two most ancient Indian poems—the Ramayana of almost unknown antiquity, one continued thread of action—the Mahabharata full of mixed episodes and legends.
>
> Ramayana by the poet Valmiki. Probably Valmiki and Homer were contemporaries—perhaps V. was the earlier of the two.
>
> The Athenian historical pet was Theseus; the Dorian, Hercules; the Hindostanee—Brahmanic, Rama. . . .
>
> The style of a great poem must flow on "unhasting & unresting."
>
> Vyasa, poet of the Mahabharata.[216]

Passing mention may be made of the fact that the comment on the style of a great poem, like the other observations in the notes, is taken from the article itself, which says that "Valmiki's style . . . greatly resembles that of Homer; each flows on in that 'unhasting and unresting' continuity which only belongs to the heroic age of a literature."[217]

Note 30 carries that developed line about Menu, mentioned earlier: "Menu son or grandson of Brahma and first of created beings." The line is an exact copy of Sir William Jones's description in his preface to the translation of the *Laws of Menu,* from which Thoreau quotes the same words in *A Week on the Concord and Merrimack Rivers.* A copy of *A Week* was given to Whitman by Thoreau in 1856. The phrase could have come to Whitman from either Jones or Thoreau. For the Westminster article said only, "Menu son or the grandson of Brahma." Whitman's fragment also carries a reference to "Indian epic poetry—[and asks] who was Veias?" The significance of this name "Veias" will be discussed later. For the present the point to be noticed is that the entire fragment appears to have been written earlier than the others in the neighborhood, because in all of them, as in the previous one we have noted, he carries the correct spelling of the name "Vyasa," and knows who he was. Therefore, if it is an earlier note, then the phrase, "the first of created beings," came not from

Thoreau's book, unless he had read another copy of *A Week* before Thoreau's gift in 1856, but from Sir William Jones himself.[218] Note 33 again refers to Menu by mere name,[219] and note 51 to the Indian Epics and their authors: "Valmiki—author of Ramayana. Vyasa—Mahabharata."[220]

In the Harned Collection of Whitman's manuscripts, preserved in the Library of Congress, Washington, D.C., is a sheet in Whitman's hand, which speaks of the superiority of Asiatic achievement over that of the West in religion and poetry:

> How different the more cultivated, more mathematical; cold and continent, & in important respects far more valuable, European intellect & aestheticism, - - - yet in religion & poetry the old Asiatic land dominates to this day, and will until above the world shall rise peaks still higher than the Hebrew Bible Roman Iliad, & the chants & psalms & great epics of India.[221]

In "Walt Whitman's letter to Moncure D. Conway in answer to his letter of Oct. 12 (1860?). Written throughout in Whitman's hand, but intended to be signed by O'Connor," are two more references to India:

> . . . and offering to the world, in himself, an American personality, & real Democratic Presence, that not only the best old Hindu, Greek, and Roman worthies would at once have responded to. . . .
> The idea, however, which is this man's highest contribution, and which, compared even with the vastness of Biblical & Homeric poetry, still looms & towers—as, athwart his fellow-giants of the Himalayas, the dim head of Kunchainjunga rises over the rest—is the idea of Totality of the All-successful, final certainties of each individual man, as well as the world he inhabits.[222]

Unless dismissed as the result of an exaggerated self-praise, usual with Walt Whitman, as his adulatory reviews earlier referred to indicate, the phrases suggest that he might genuinely have felt that his poetry, whether deliberately fashioned after the great models or not, had in it the quality of thought to which "the best old Hindu . . . worthies would at once have responded."

At any rate, they testify to his awareness of what the old Hindu worthies were like.

Pinned to the copy of J. C. Thomson's *Bhagavadgita* presented to him by Thomas Dixon, are his notes on the Indian Epics, made from Thomson's exhaustive introduction, and supplemented by other sources:

> The Ramayana
> Valmiki's beautiful epic—the war for the recovery of the woman [the word is struck off] princess Sita wife of Rama, abducted by Ravana.
> The Mahabharata
> immense old Hindu poem—war carried on between two branches of a family the Kurus (the elder) & the Pandavas the (Younger) for old Hastinapura (? modern Delhi)—this war fills 20000 slokas of the M—about one quarter as the work at present exists—the other three quarters are didactic & legendary episodes interpolated since—woven in by various redactors, successive editions, different times—The Bhagavadgita is one of these episodes of the M.[223]

That he was aware of the doctrine of metempsychosis and its Indian origin is vouched for by these lines from his "Notes on English History."

> Pythagoras is supposed to have introduced into Greek metaphysics the idea of metempsychosis.
> Probably both the Druids and Pythagoras drew their philosophy, numbers etc., etc. from the same source (from the Indus or the Nile?). An oriental origin to all.[224]

He knew that the word "Buddha" means "intelligence,"[225] and that "Mercury is probably the same as Bhuda, also Woden,"[226] having gathered the latter information from an 1845 periodical.

The long list presented of direct references to India found among Whitman's prose writings—in many cases merely names and dates —is at least sufficient to indicate that India was of considerable special interest to him, and, as seen from quite a few apparently superficial allusions, there is the suggestion of not only deep enthusiasm but a fairly sizable knowledge of India's history as well as literature, philosophy, and religion. Also evident in many instances is the fact that, though the time and source of his acquiring the knowledge cannot be fixed with any certainty, the kind of knowledge he possessed and the zeal he felt for India are not such as come from light reading.

Most significant of all the testimonies we have to Whitman's interest in and knowledge of India, is the supreme declaration of his poetic and personal love for India, the "Passage to India" itself. But since it is a poem, we shall have to ignore it as evidence. However, just a look at the initial thought that later grew into the poem is enough to convince that his understanding of India was not of a vague, general, or fanciful kind, but of a deeper, intelligent, and informed one. Found in a notebook that he maintained for the composition of "Passage to India," is the "Spinal Idea," as he called it, of the poem, reproduced here from extracts with a specific allusion to India:

> Passage to India. . . . The Spinal Idea: That the divine efforts of heroes & their ideas, faithfully lived up to will finally prevail, and be accomplished however long deferred. Every great problem is *The Passage to India* (put this in literally). . . . What other passage to India? A religious sentiment is in all these heroic ideas & underneath them. What Thou too O my Soul, (what is thy) takest thou passage to India? To The mystic wisdom—the lore of all old philosophy TO All the linked transcendental streams, their sources, To vast and mighty poems the Ramayana, the Mahabharata, The Vedas with all their hymns & sacred odes. And you O my Soul? Have not you & I long sought the passage to India. Sought the Source, sought some fond and ? strait Some Suez or some Darien Panama? (what are the straits) O Love! passage to India—Pride of man! passage to India. Other after the rest: Passage to India, O, my soul.[227]

Whether the almost religious adoration with which in this rhapsodic utterance India is regarded by him as the symbol of man's spiritual quests represents the fiction of a mere poetic imagination or the genuine reality of his own spiritual experience is a question that need not hold us here. But it is unmistakable that in "The mystic wisdom—the lore of all old philosophy . . . all the linked transcendental streams, their sources . . . vast and

mighty poems the Ramayana, the Mahabharata, the Vedas, with
all their hymns & sacred odes," there is a knowledge and understanding of the nature and quality of India's philosophy and literature far beyond the casual information that nineteenth-century
American newspapers and periodicals could supply.

7

DIRECTIONS

BUT, WITH THE EXCEPTION OF THE PASSAGE IN "SUNDOWN Papers" and a couple of other fragments, all the references and allusions to India gathered from Whitman's prose are of the years after 1855, and hence are of no significance to the question of how much his *Leaves of Grass* was influenced by Indian philosophy. For the later editions are merely the superstructure raised on the foundation of the first *Leaves of Grass,* and the best part of the philosophical ideas his later poems adumbrate are in essence present in "Song of Myself." Therefore, if his knowledge of Indian philosophy influenced him significantly, it should be in the making of the first *Leaves of Grass,* and the question before us is whether or not Whitman had read any philosophical works of India then available in translation in America. The fact of his later readings and even possession of copies of Indian works or scholarly books about India has already been established by evidence. Also evident in the later poems is the effect of such readings in a direct and explicit manner, as in his use of Sanskrit words, like "sudra" in "Chanting the Square Deific" (1865–66), "maya" in "Are You the New Person Drawn Toward Me?" (1860), "avatars" in "Salut au Monde!" (1866), and "nirvana" in "Twilight" (1887). We know that he had come into the possession of a copy of Alger's *Poetry of the East,* given to him by the author "in 1881 or '2," and, apart from his own testimony to his having "read (dabbled) over and over again" the introductory pages and recited the poems to the soldiers, Kennedy's investigation has shown how much he borrowed of phrases and hints from the pieces of the anthology.[228]

And, according to Asselineau, "Later he even bought scholarly books on the East, such as William Dwight Whitney, *Oriental and Linguistic Studies: The Veda; The Avesta; The Science of Language* (New York, 1873), and J. Muir, *Religious and Moral Sentiments rendered from Sanskrit* (London and Edinburgh, 1875), both now in the Library of Bryn Mawr College."[229] He also came to possess a copy of J. Cockburn Thomson's 1855 translation of the *Bhagavadgita,* presented to him, according to an entry on the flyleaf, by Thomas Dixon of Sunderland in "Dec. 1875." Among direct evidences of his later reading may also be mentioned his request to Thoreau for a list of reading material about India, to which Thoreau replied on 12 December, 1856 from Concord, as follows:

> Our acquaintance with the ancient Hindoos is not at all personal. The full names that can be relied upon are very shadowy. It is, however, tangible works that we know. The best I think of are Bhagvat Geeta (an episode in an ancient heroic poem called the Mahabarat), the Vedas, the Vishnu Purana, the Institutes of Menu, etc.[230]

Whether or not the reading list recommended was of any use to Whitman, it appears from the next letter of Thoreau, written on April 26, 1857 from Concord, that Whitman discussed the books with Thoreau:

> I see [wrote Thoreau] that you are turning a broad furrow among the books, but I trust that some private journal all the while holds its own through their midst.[231]

But the fact that, among all Whitman's readings as recorded in the notes of his "Reading and Thought," there is not one word of reference, explicit or implicit, to any one of the books recommended by Thoreau, in spite of the obvious impression he created on him of "turning a broad furrow" among them, seems to suggest that either Whitman did *not* read them (probably not having to), or that the journal that held "its own through their midst" was destroyed with the papers he burned in his last years in Camden. If he did not read them, he would not have been able to create such an impression on Thoreau, which leads to the only other alternative—barring, of course, the unpleasant likelihood of a vague reference to them in his report to Thoreau—that he had already read them or known of them.

The 1840 article of the *Long Island Democrat*, 20 October, describing the reverie of his search for truth, evidences an early interest of Whitman in India and its philosophical or religious speculations; a passion for the mysterious Orient that has enticed the imagination of all poets. But in none other has that passion taken such an ardor, such profound implications, as in Whitman, a fact to which "Passage to India" bears witness.

We cannot resist the implication that for some strange reason Whitman suppressed all evidence of his reading of Indian works. Even the copy of the *Bhagavadgita* that he is known to have possessed was never seen by any one of his friends and admirers who have described his library. His own description of his room in Camden in 1891, mentions many books: "the Bible . . . Homer, Shakespeare, Walter Scott, Emerson, Tickner's Spanish Literature, John Carlyle's Dante, Felton's Greece, George Sand's Consuelo, a very choice little Epictetus, some novels, the latest foreign and American monthlies, quarterlies, and so on," but no *Gita*.[232] Perhaps by that time he had given away the "presentation copy" to Mrs. Anne Montgomerie Traubel.[233] For a man so profoundly interested in India, as his prose writings and private notes suggest, for a philosopher-poet whose imagination assumed the cosmic proportions of the Absolute, the giving away of the one book which—among all the books he read or preserved to the end of his life—bore the closest parallel to his own poetry, appears strange. If, for this reason and the other mentioned elsewhere,[234] one has to assume the existence of another copy, there is no evidence of what happened to it.

Yet, of Whitman's early reading about India there is some direct evidence. Among the magazine and newspaper articles studied and preserved by Whitman are (to ignore others of a historical or political or general nature): "a magazine article 'Indian Epic Poetry' dated October 1848, much scored and annotated," "Leaves torn from a book on the 'Heetopades of Veeshnoo Sarma,'" a "magazine article 'Laws of Menu,' May 1845," and "'The Hindu Drama,' magazine article dated April 1857, much scored and annotated."[235]

While it would be idle to pretend that a few magazine articles such as these could have been a sufficient source for the kind of knowledge of Indian philosophy that roused the response of Emerson and Thoreau, we cannot be insensible to the implications of the evidence. For one thing, these few articles could not possibly be all the material that Whitman, with his well-known voracity for knowledge and special interest in the East, can be imagined to have read. Secondly, an examination of even this apparently meagre material shows that there is more in them than appears at first sight; for, as will be seen later, they are not merely brief historical surveys of the subjects they touch upon, but contain critical interpretation, illustration, and suggestion for further reading, and have considerable discussion of the philosophy of India. Furthermore, the fact that they have been "much scored and annotated" clearly indicates that Whitman did not read them casually but rather studied them. Even if we ignore the last of these articles, the others are all of the years before 1855. Whitman's declaration of absolute ignorance of the Orientals to Thoreau in 1856, therefore, wears the look of a lie, and the later pretense of taking advantage of Thoreau's reading list, of a deliberate trick, because, if nothing else, these articles themselves give the entire reading list.

Before we examine the significance of this bit of evidence to Whitman's pre-1855 knowledge of Indian philosophy, a few more pieces of evidence, though not of the direct kind, must be mentioned, just because they are of the years prior to the first edition of *Leaves of Grass,* and take very little time to scan.

In "Pictures," an unpublished poem of Whitman preserved by him in a notebook, on the title page of which he had instructed himself to "break all this [the whole poem] into pictures," occur these lines:

> Here is one singing canticles in an unknown
>   tongue, before the Sanskrit was,
> And here a Hindu sage, with his recitative in
>   Sanskrit. . . . [236]

"Pictures," as Holloway editorially observes, "was an attempt at a poem like 'Faces' or 'Salut au Monde!' and the manuscript "certainly dates before 1855, and probably about 1850."[237] By

1850, therefore, Whitman was aware that Hindu philosophical literature was the product of sages who sang in Sanskrit.

Among the "First Drafts and Rejected Lines and Passages from the Leaves of Grass, largely Antecedent to the 1855 edition," collected by Bucke in the 1899 *Notes and Fragments,* but absent in the 1902 *Complete Writings,* is the following passage:

> Asia, steppes, the grass, the winter appearances,
> ....
> The ancient Hindoostanee with his deitees.
> The great old Empire of India; that of Persia and its expe-
>   ditions and conquests;
> The Sanskrit—the ancient poems and laws;
> The ideas of Gods incarnated by their avatars in man and
>   woman;
> The falling of the waters of the Ganges over the high rim
>   of Saukara;
> The poems descended safely to this day from poets of three
>   thousand years ago.[238]

The passage is not entirely rejected, however, which is the reason for its disappearance from this section in the later edition. It is broken up into bits, and, in keeping with Whitman's already observed method of fragment-assemblage, appears in different poems. We have no evidence that this piece was one of those "antecedent to the 1855 edition," but there is reason to suppose it was, because the lines appear in 1856 poems. For instance, section 6 of "Salut au Monde!" has:

> I see the site of the old empire of Assyria, and that of Persia,
>   and that of India,
> I see the falling of the Ganges over the high rim of Saukara.
> I see the place of the idea of the Deity incarnated by avatars
>   in human forms.

And section 3 of the same poem has:

> I hear the Hindoo teaching his favorite pupil the loves, wars,
>   adages, transmitted safely to this day from
> poets who wrote three thousand years ago.

Section 7 of "Song of the Broad-Axe," also of 1856, is given one
relevant phrase, "the most ancient Hindustanee."

Many of the items of description in the passages quoted above
are derived from the "magazine article 'Indian Epic Poetry' dated
Oct. 1848, much scored and annotated." The line, "I see the falling of the Ganges over the high rim of Saukara," is a typical
Whitmanesque adaptation of the following description of the fall
of Ganges in Millman's translation, given as one of the illustrations
of Indian poetry in the article:

> Falling from heaven upon the peaks of Sankara and thence
>   falling upon the earth,
> The waters flowed in winding currents, sending forth a heavy
>   sound.[239]

One may notice the resemblance of the line-structure between
this specimen of Indian poetry and Whitman's, though in the
hurry of transcribing the words into his own page, Whitman
misspells Sankara into Saukara. David Goodale, obviously carried
away by the other identities of line between "Salut au Monde!"
and Volney's *Ruins,* mistakenly regards Whitman's line as a
transformation of Volney's "You see the winding course of the
Ganges."[240]

And the line, "The ideas of Gods incarnated by their avatars in
man and/woman," or the changed, "I see the place of the idea of
the Deity incarnated by avatars in/ human forms," is only a
Whitmanization of a sentence in the same article: "The subject of
the Ramayana is the descent or avatar of Vishnu, in human form,
to save the world from Ravana. . . . "[241]

The other lines of the passage, or passages, like "The Sanskrit—
ancient poems and laws," "The ancient Hindoostanee with his
deities," and "The poems descended safely to this day from/
poets of three thousand years ago," are not indicative of any special
knowledge, and can be taken, like his Sundown Paper's journey,
to have come from a newspaper, magazine, or hearsay. Or they
can be suggestions from the articles on India listed in his possession. But the developed line he put in section 3 of "Salut au
Monde!": "I hear the Hindoo teaching his favorite pupil the
loves, wars,/adages, transmitted safely to this day from poets/who

wrote three thousand years ago," has more than the information of newspapers, the articles in question, and Volney's *Ruins,* as a slight analysis will show.

The description of "the Hindoo teaching his favorite pupil the loves, wars, adages," deserves attention. The articles nowhere describe the Hindu tradition out of which the philosophical speculations of India came into being, of private personal communication to a pupil seeking knowledge in devotion. Whitman's words, "the loves," "wars," "adages," and the word "laws" from the earlier line, are a succinct reference to the principal varieties of Indian literature available, at any rate in translation, for the nineteenth-century American reader. The "ancient poems," of course, are the *Vedas,* or, the epics that were the subject of the article "Indian Epic Poetry," and Whitman knew about them, because the article has many extracts from both the *Ramayana* and the *Mahabharata.* The word "wars" naturally refers to the epics, the stories of both of which center on a battle. The word "adages," like the word "apothegms" noted elsewhere, is a reference to the *Heetopades of Veeshnoo Sarma,* a collection of wise aphorisms, of which, again, he at least possessed "pages torn out of a book." The word "laws" of the rejected line obviously refers to the *Laws of Menu,* an article on which he also possessed. That leaves us with a word and a phrase to account for: "loves" and "the Hindoo teaching his favorite pupil." That they are not sheerly a way of describing things in general fancy is evident from the definiteness and meaning with which he is using the other words. Similarly, then, must the word "loves" allude to something precise, naturally a piece of romantic literature, and be traceable to memory rather than fancy. But, ignoring the article on "The Hindu Drama" as being of 1857, there is no reference to the romantic literature of India in any of the articles in question, unless in the allusions "Indian Epic Poetry" makes to Sir William Jones's translation of Calidasa's *Sakuntala.* From Carpenter's testimony we know that Whitman had read *Sakuntala,* and either he had read it before he wrote the line we are examining, or the word refers to a "poem" itself, the "Gita Govinda," a long poem dealing with the "loves" of Krishna and Radha. H. T. Colebrooke translated this poem as the "Song of Jayadeva" in Volume Three of the *Asiatic Researches,* available in the libraries of New York in the days when Whitman was reading these and other periodicals and used "to loaf in the libraries" there.[242]

But the phrase is more significant. To be fair, it can be the outcome of a knowledge of the Hindu tradition, or as well be the result of a mere verbal borrowing, like many of his, from some page he read. In both cases, it leads to a source other than these articles, even all the other articles about India in the periodicals from which these were clipped, because none of them has such a thought or phrase. There must, therefore, be some other source. In the 1785 translation of the *Bhagvat-Geeta* by Charles Wilkins, the book of which Emerson was put in mind at sight of *Leaves of Grass,* is the following description in the prefatory letter of Warren Hastings: "Arjoon is represented as the favorite and pupil of Kreeshna, here taken for God himself, in his last Oōtar, or descent to earth in a mortal frame."[243]

Among the "Literary Notes and Reviews" of Whitman collected from the *Brooklyn Daily Times* is his review of Emerson's "Brahma" on 16 November, 1857. In defending the poem against unintelligent criticism, his acuteness of understanding of Indian philosophy is apparent when he sums up in one single sentence the entire Vedanta system:

> Some of the papers are poking fun at Emerson on account of the unintelligibility of his little Mystic Song entitled 'Brahma' in the new Atlantic Monthly. The name of the poem is a facile key to it; Brahma, the Indian Deity, is the absolute and omnipresent god, besides whom all is illusion and fancy, and to whom everything apparent reverts in the end. This pantheistic thought Emerson expresses, not only clearly, but with remarkable grace and melody.[244]

But this was in 1857, over two years after he published his own mystic songs, at whose unintelligibility many more papers poked fun. Yet the deep knowledge of those words, unless of course the words were borrowed, could not have come to him during those two years. He had much in those two years to keep him busy. The failure of his first edition led him to attempt to sing its glories himself in three long anonymous reviews, which, as Esther Shephard says,[245] he set up himself and printed; he had other journalistic activities; and he had begun work on the second edition of

Leaves of Grass. It is hardly imaginable that he had time to acquaint himself with Indian philosophy then.

In another note, date unknown, now in the Trent Collection, he makes some "comments on Emerson," and shows a similar knowl-edge of the Oriental concept of God:

His idea of God (as in the Oversoul) is not the modern Scientific idea, now rapidly advancing, far more sublime & re-splendent, and reflect'g a dazzl'g light upon Democracy, its twin, but the old old Oriental idea of God. . . . [246]

8

MORE DIRECTIONS

WE SHALL NOW RETURN TO THOSE ARTICLES ABOUT INDIA THAT
were found in Whitman's possession. These are the only documentary evidence there is for his pre-1855 knowledge of India.
We may recall Bliss Perry's statement that "the periodical literature of the forties was Whitman's only university, so far as intellectual stimulus was concerned."[247] That Whitman was an ardent
reader of the periodicals is evident from the enormous mass of
articles and clippings from newspapers and magazines found in his
possession after his death. It even looks as if he had more patience
and enthusiasm for the brief articles than for books. We discover
that of all the periodicals from which he gathered his articles, his
favorites appear to be *The Westminster Review, The Whig
Review,* and *The Edinburgh Review.* The largest portion of the
clippings listed in *Notes and Fragments* comes from the *Whig
Review;* next from the *Edinburgh,* the *Westminster,* the *Black-
woods* in that order; then a few from *Graham's, Sartain's, Harper's* and *The Eclectic.*

Once again ignoring the newspaper clippings as of but transitory
interest, we find that—with the exception of no. 438, magazine
article (May 1839) "American and the Early English Poets,"
no. 516, "The Dying Gladiator" from the *Penny Magazine* of
12 January 1833, no. 554, "Philosophy, Psychology and Metaphysics" from the *Eclectic,* April 1871, and one or two more of
later years—the period covered by these periodical articles is from
1845 to 1859, the heaviest concentration being in the late forties,

1845–49, with a few belonging to the 1850s. Whitman seems to have done a great deal of reading in these years, 1845 to 1849. That his reading in these periodicals was not casual—that is, he did not, as the official account might lead us to think, just happen to pick up a periodical in the second-hand bookstalls of the road-side and cut out any article he took a liking to—but that he was a regular reader of these periodicals is proved by two facts. One is that he himself is reported to have said to Thayer, a friend of his: "I used to read all the quarterlies and the magazines I could lay hands on. I read 'em through; and so I stored up in my memory all sorts of odds and ends, which I pulled out and used whenever they came in handy."[248] The second is that, from almost every number of the same periodical during those years, Whitman has cut out his articles. There is, for instance, the *Whig Review,* which has contributed to his collection from its issues of January 1845 (article no. 417), February '45 (no. 444), May '45 (nos. 357, 439, and 518), July '45 (no. 469), October '45 (nos. 14 and 425), January '46 (no. 424), September '46 (nos. 494 and 535), October '46 (no. 404), November '46 (no. 13, though Bucke by mistake puts it as December '46), May '47 (nos. 274 and 299), September '47 (no. 285), and so on. It is reasonable to suppose that he read the other numbers, and, not finding anything of great preservable interest in them, threw them away, or what was preserved from them was possibly lost in transit from Washington, D. C. to Camden along with other papers he said were lost. We also find that the area of interest covered among these periodicals is almost the entire gamut of human knowledge, from theology to travel, that it is covered with considerable profundity, and that the variety and the scholarship with which the subjects are treated in them could fairly form the equipment of a student, not just the information of the curious.

Of the material about India mentioned above, I have been able to identify with some hesitation the "Leaves torn from a book on 'The Heetopades of Veeshnoo Sarma.'" There were in those days, at least in the city of New York, three English translations of Vishnu Sharma's *Hitopadesha,* one by Sir Charles Wilkins in 1787, another by Francis Johnson in 1847, the third, with the original Sanskrit text and also a Bengali translation, edited by Lakshami Narayan Nyalankar in 1830. Of the three, the trans-

lation of Wilkins alone spells the names of the title in the manner
of the "Leaves" in Whitman's possession, and obviously, therefore, they are from Wilkins. But Bucke's description has a helpless vagueness about it; it might mean that the book from which
the "Leaves" were torn either contained the "Heetopades," or, as
in the case of the pages about the *Laws of Menu* torn from
Thoreau's *A Week,* merely discussed them. While the other
"Indian" articles are still extant among collections of Whitman
material, the "Leaves" appear to have been lost in the confusion
that attended Whitman manuscripts after they passed from Bucke's
hands. However, the *Dial* magazine published selections from
"The Heetopades" in its July 1842 number, and on the top of its
pages the name of the magazine is not printed, only the date, year,
page number, and the name, "Veeshnoo Sarma." A brief prefatory
note announces that the sentences are taken from Charles Wilkins's
translation, and the aphorisms are printed under the title, "Extracts from the Heetopades of Veeshnoo Sarma," in pages beginning 82 top and ending 85 bottom. I should think, therefore, that
Whitman's "Leaves" were torn from that journal, for, as far as I
have been able to discover, there was no other "book" in those
days which either contained or discussed the "Heetopades." Besides, the little piece " 'Editor's Table,' annotated," in the list of
the articles in Whitman's possession,[249] appears also from the
Dial of December 1842, and the undated "Chaucer" may possibly
be from the *Dial* of October 1843.[250] I have labored the point in
order to suggest the evidence it offers of Whitman's reading of
the *Dial* in those early years. This evidence supports Asselineau's
statement: "He [Whitman] must also have read articles about the
East in the Dial from 1840 to 1844."[251]

Otherwise this little item is not of very great significance for
Whitman's knowledge of Indian thought, inasmuch as the "hitopadesha" of Vishnu Sharma are fundamentally of an ethical
nature, precepts for practical conduct in society and worldly wisdom, although many of them, in a condensed utterance, echo the
characteristic ideas of Hindu philosophy, as in the following:[252]

> Whatsoever cometh to pass, either good or evil, is the conse-
> quence of a man's own actions, and descendeth from the power
> of the Supreme Ruler.

It is said, Fate is nothing but the deeds committed in a former state of existence; wherefore it behoveth a man vigilantly to exert the powers he is possessed of.

The difference between the body and the qualities is infinite; the body is a thing to be destroyed in a moment, whilst the qualities endure to the end of creation.

That, in a nutshell, is the Hindu doctrine of Karma and Whitman's concept of "Prudence," which he so elaborately sets forth in his 1855 Preface as well as in "Song of Prudence." Both the early thoughts of his notebooks and the developed ones of his later poetry, such as "Says" and "Thoughts," bear an impress of the "Heetopades," and it even appears probable that he was personally influenced by these apothegms and tried to live in their light.

It is possible that his early thought, "I know that my body will (decay),"[253] is a reflection of Vishnu Sharma's line, but he surely echoes the last of the extracts in section 4 of "A Song of the Broad-Axe" when he says "And nothing endures but personal qualities."

Though his contempt for riches and disgust for people with a "morbid appetite for money" are already there in the young (journalist) days of his life[254] when the purer, unworldlier imagination of youth has a natural dislike of earthly possession, the thought as he sets it down in his 1847 notebook may have borrowed some strength from the following:

Where have they, who are running here and there in search of riches, such happiness as those placid spirits enjoy who are gratified at the immortal fountain of happiness?

Whitman's entry on the folly of rich men is as follows:

The dismal and measureless fool called a rich man, or a thriving, who leaves untouched those countless and ever (?) spread tables thick in immortal dishes, heaped with the meats and drinks of God, and fancies himself smart because he tugs and sweats among cinders, and parings, and slush[.][255]

* * * * * * * * *

The following might have given a hint to Whitman's well-known habit of addressing a part of himself:

Why dost thou hesitate over this perishable body composed of flesh, bones and excrements? O my friend, (*my body,*) support my reputation!

Perhaps the goodness of the poet that "appoint[s]" a "common prostitute" with "an appointment," saying, "Not till the sun excludes you do I exclude you,"[256] was in some dim way, in the alchemy of Whitman's imagination, affected by his reading the "Heetopades" which said:

Good men extend their pity even unto the most despicable animals. The moon doth not withhold the light, even from the cottage of a Chandala.[257]

Hospitality is to be exercised even towards an enemy when he cometh to thine house. The tree does not withdraw its shade even from the woodcutter.

Besides these, in all probability, suggestions were gathered consciously or unconsciously from other wise sayings such as these:

What is religion? Compassion for all things which have life. What is happiness? To animals in this world, health.[258]

He, whose inclination turneth away from an object, may be said to have obtained it.[259]

A wise man should relinquish both his wealth and his life for another. . . .

Every book of knowledge, which is known to Oosana or to Vreehaspatee, is by nature planted in the understanding of women.

Oosana and Vreehaspatee were the wisest of the Hindu sages. I wonder if this apothegm of Vishnu Sharma had, in some strange way, anything to do with Whitman's pointed assertion to Traubel that "two sorts of people ought to understand Leaves of Grass offhand—women and doctors,"[260] and to Carpenter that "what lies behind *Leaves of Grass* is something that few, very few, (only one here and there, perhaps oftenest women,) are at all in a position to seize."[261]

If the "Leaves torn from a book on the 'Heetopades of Veeshnoo Sarma,' " are from the *Dial* of July 1842, the next, in point of time, of the early Indian material is "a magazine article, 'Laws of Menu' May 1845." The article is a review by J. D. Whelpley, whom Whitman seems to have regarded with some esteem as a writer, for he had preserved some of his articles. Item no. 424 of the list, "Phrenology, a Socratic dialogue," from the *Whig Review* of Jan. 1846, is by Whelpley, and so is no. 425, "On Style," from the October 1845 number of the same magazine. Besides the article on the "Laws of Menu," J. D. Whelpley wrote a few more about India in the other *Whig Review* issues of the same year. The March number carried an article on "The Hindoos, their Laws, Customs, and Religion," and it looks as if Whitman did read it, because there are echoes of the article in his notebooks.

J. D. Whelpley opens his sketch with an observation of how "the author of the Zendavesta . . . brings the first family of men out of Cashmere, or Little Thibet, it is uncertain which. . . . The first seat of man may, therefore, be sought rather in the Caucasus of India." (pp. 290–91)

Whitman transcribed this into fragment 7 of part II of *Notes and Fragments* in this manner: "Then the inhabitants of India and the descendents of the Keltic and Teutonic nations are all of one family and must have migrated from one country. Whether that country was Persia or Cashmir or a country further east is not easily determined."[262]

In the course of his historical survey of India's ancient past, Whelpley speaks of "Buddha, whom the Chinese pagans worship under the name of Fo, and who is identified with the Woden or Odin." (p. 291). Whitman in his notes on English History recorded: "Deities: . . . Mercury is probably the same as Bhuda, also Woden."[263]

Whelpley's article is a general account of Hindu history, and, despite its title, has very little of their ways of life and social and religious practices. It does not involve itself in any philosophical discussion, but it mentions sources of further knowledge. Sir William Jones is mentioned once, and a reference is made to his *Works* and the *Asiatic Researches* from which its ideas are obviously taken. Another footnote mentions Jones's translation of *Sakuntala,* and reference is made to the Reverend W. Ward's two-volume *View of the History, Literature and Mythologies of the Hindoos,* Vol. I. Allusions of a passing nature are made to Menu, the *Vedas,* and the *Puranas.*

To the April number Whelpley contributed another article on India, called "Castes and Occupations of India." This is merely an account of the social institutions of the Indian people, but to any one interested in a knowledge of the country it contained some useful suggestions. It mentions Alexander's conquest of India, which Whitman might have mentally noted to put into "Passage to India:" "The tale of Alexander on his warlike marches suddenly dying"; gives a name, "Menes," King of Egypt, that slips into Whitman's enormous mass of notes; refers in a footnote to Sir William Jones's translation of the *Laws of Menu,* and later to the Reverend W. Ward on "the Hindoos"; and has lines that might have struck Whitman's eagerness to know about the East and its strange ways, such as the following:

> For twelve days the neophyte must sleep upon a bed of cusa grass, (which is singularly sacred). (p. 401)

> Thrice they bathe . . . worshipping the *Lingam,* a little idol. . . . The manner of bathing and worship is minutely prescribed in the Shastras. . . . Reading in the Vedas is highly meritorious. (p. 402)

> Siva's worshippers, a murderous and bloody sect delight in blood and self-torture. (p. 402)

The account given of the religious practices of the Hindu sects is neither flattering nor encouraging to a foreigner's interest in the mysterious land of Vedic wisdom; at any rate, not such as could rouse Whitman's enthusiasm for it, but it is possible—judging from his deep interest in words, which he gathered from all sorts of sources and often coined in his own way, and from his habit of collecting "odds and ends" from his reading to throw them into a new fusion—that the word "Shastras" of Whelpley, misspelt, like "Saukara" for "Sankara," became the "Shastas" of line 1100 of "Song of Myself," first edition (Section 43), joined with the correctly reproduced "Vedas." And the sanguinary phrase, "bloody sect delight in blood," probably suggested the "blood" he put into the company of his favorite epithet for the East, "florid," to become the "florid with blood" of "A Broadway Pageant."

The "Laws of Menu" article appeared in the *Whig Review's* May 1845 number, to which Whitman himself had contributed a story entitled "The Boy-Lover," and from which he cut out two more articles, No. 357 of the list, "Petrarch," and No. 439, "Thoughts on Reading." The "Laws of Menu" ends on page 521 of the *Whig Review,* and on page 525 commences a long nineteen-page review, by Tayler Lewis, of the book *Vestiges of the Natural History of Creation.* This work, as Conway has already been quoted to have said, "had the good effect of popularising the idea of evolution," but, as both the review by Lewis and the one in the *Edinburgh Review* of July 1845 indicate, it seems to have met with considerable adverse criticism for its unorthodox mechanical theory of the Universe. However, though unfavorable, Lewis's review elaborately discusses the ideas of the book, the concept of natural evolution, the principle of "Law (order) and development" governing all phenomena, the "awkward phrase, *law-creation,*" which denies "the direct act of God," and so on. Apparently Bucke had not heard of this book or read its reviews when he claimed for the author of *Leaves of Grass* the vision that anticipated Darwin, for many of the astonishing "mystic" ideas of Whitman are here in the pages of this 1845 review. The new book acknowledges as

The First Cause . . . a vital power which developed itself into a law; this law being the expression of all the phenomena. . . . Matter . . . possess[es] *necessary, inherent* properties of motion, attraction &c. . . . All has been carried on by a machinery. . . . [There is] *reason, intelligence, science* . . . in the heavens. . . . Two words . . . constitute the very soul of this work . . . *law* and *development*. . . . Law and development . . . may be compared to an immense machine which . . . developed out of the First Cause. This machine contains in itself all subsequent developments. Nothing is external to it; nothing *has* happened, nothing *is* happening, and nothing *can* happen, which is not *now* provided for in it, and which has not made a part of its complicated structure *from the beginning*. . . . The bursting of a planet, the eruption of a volcano, the rustle of a leaf, and the motion of the almost invisible particle of dust as it floats in the air, have each had, from all eternity, some part assigned for their future production. Some little spring or cog, which for ages has revolved in some great wheel, invisible and without effect, has been so adjusted as to strike in its appointed place and time, thus producing a new development. (pp. 529–31)

For example, a certain species of vegetation . . . is by virtue of a hidden law contained in its organization . . . suddenly developed into a new species in the first stages of animal life; "a process by which," says our author, *"the whole train of animated beings, from the simplest and oldest up to the highest and most recent, are to be regarded as a series of advances of this principle of development."* In this way the plant becomes an animal, the reptile a fish, the fish an inhabitant of the dry ground, and terrestrial animals rise in the ascending scale, until the *developement* reaches the Simia tribe . . . [and] . . . the monkey loses its tail, and man comes out. . . . Man our author regards as but the *initial* of a grand growing type. . . . (pp. 537–38)

Whitman's echoes of these lines are too many and too well-known to need specific mention. Even the theory of evil presented in the *Vestiges,* of which the orthodox Lewis naturally speaks in derision, enters into Whitman's "mystic vision":

. . . In his great perplexity [with regard to the question of evil and pain] he [the author] turns . . . to the consoling position, that the Deity must proceed by fixed laws, and that their operation is *generally* useful. Gravitation was not intended to injure legs, but to keep things stable on earth,—still those who will break it . . . must suffer the consequences. "If the rash boy lose his hold of the branch, it will unrelentingly pull him down; and yet it was not a primary object of this great law of gravitation to hurt boys—the evil is, therefore, only a casual exception from something in the main good." (p. 541)

With the last two sentences the following lines of Whitman may be compared:

The Law of gravity is the law under which you make your house plumb but that is not what the law is specifically made for.[264]

The power by which the carpenter plumbs his house is the same power that dashes his brains out if he falls from the roof.[265]

Whelpley's article is a review of Sir William Jones's translation: *The Institutes of Menu*. Whitman appears to have cultivated a particular esteem for Menu and his "Laws." His notes mention him many times, particularly stressing his antiquity. And in addition to this article, he had cut pages from Thoreau's *A Week* about the *Laws of Menu*, where Thoreau, with a quotation from Jones (transcribed by Whitman into his notes), discusses in wholehearted praise "one of the most attractive of those ancient works."[266]

The *Laws of Menu* is not, as the English title suggests, merely a book of legal jurisprudence, setting down a code for social or political conduct, legislation, government, and so on, but a whole encyclopedia of knowledge and principles for total human behavior. It is, as the Sanskrit title signifies, *Manava Dharma Shastra,* or the Science of Human Conduct, a complete "system of duties, religious and civil, and of law in all its branches; which the Hindus firmly believe to have been promulgated in the beginning of time by Menu, son or grandson of BRAHMA, or, in plain language, the first of created beings."[267] Though a large part of its 2685 verses deals with the Hindu social institutions, the duties of the different orders of society, the obligations of the different stages of life, the observation of ceremonies, and the like, the book gives expression to the theological and cosmogonical ideas of the Hindu system, and contains a good deal of philosophical thought. Among the subjects discussed in it are: the Creation, the Various Orders in Creation, Education, Marriage, Economics and Private Morals, Diet, Purification, Women, Devotion, Government and Public Law, Judicature, Private and Criminal Law, Conduct in Times of Distress, Penance and Expiation, and, in the last chapter, Transmigration and Final Beautitude.

Whelpley presents a chapter-by-chapter summary of the *Institutes of Menu,* with occasional quotations, and I reproduce (Appendix I,a) a few excerpts that either gave Whitman a knowledge of Hindu ideas or offered suggestions for his own thought.

In the abstract of the article, one can easily see that there is an adequate, if not a very elaborately developed, representation of some of the basic thoughts of Hindu philosophy, such as the Concept of the Universal Soul, the Law of Karma, or, one's actions bearing rewards or punishments according to their virtuousness or wickedness, the Doctrine of Transmigration, and that of the Final Absorption, thoughts which are the very essence of the philosophy of the 1855 "Song of Myself." However, since the 1855 *Leaves of Grass* displays an understanding of these ideas far deeper than could be gained from the reading of even an intelligent summary like Whelpley's, we may simply observe that before 1855 Whitman was not so ignorant of Oriental thought as he and his biographers have given us to believe. Yet, in the knowledge we have of the poet's remarkable power of taking hints from his reading and developing them with the magic of his imagination, we might notice some areas of the article on which that skill operated. A few of Whitman's startlingly original thoughts can be traced here. Take for instance the following paragraphs from his notes on "Lectures on Religion":

> There are in things two elements fused though antagonistic. One is that bodily element, which has in itself the quality of corruption and disease; the other is the element, the Soul, which goes on, I think, in unknown ways, enduring forever and ever.
> The analogy holds in this way—that the Soul of the Universe is the Male and genital master and impregnating and animating spirit—Physical matter is Female and Mother and waits barren and bloomless, the jets of life from the masculine vigor, the undermost first cause of all that is not what Death is.[268]

One can easily see their origin in Menu's passage on creation. And his strange conception of a triad in him that the Inscription poem celebrates, in which he set his name to his verses, "Signing for Soul and Body"—or the line in "Pioneers! O Pioneers!": "I too with my soul and body,/We, a curious trio, picking, wandering on our way"—may have, in spite of its "increase or diminution" to Kennedy's or Furness's meaning,[269] been born here in the "three souls" that "inspire every human being." Quite as possibly, the famous prayer in "Passage to India" in which the poet's soul addressed the Supreme Soul as

O Thou Transcendent,
Nameless, the fibre and the breath,
Light of the Light, shedding forth the universes, thou centre of
    them
Thou mightier centre of the true, the good, the loving,
Thou moral, spiritual fountain . . .

has its dim roots in the extracts about "the key of all heathen mystery" with which Whelpley ended his review.

A hundred other lines in Whitman can be read back to the article, but they are not significant. However, one cannot help remarking the possibility that the Menu passages instructing the Brahmin in the contemplation of the Universal Soul in the various parts of his body, caused the idea of the sanctity of the body and regard for it as not inferior to the soul at least to germinate in Whitman's mind. For, if in the exalted understanding of the Brahmin, a man "may contemplate the subtle ether in . . . his body; the air in muscular motion and sensitive nerves; the supreme solar and igneous light in his digestive heat and his visual organs; in his corporeal fluids, water; in his flesh, earth; in his heart, the moon; in his auditory nerves, . . . guardians of eight regions of the world; in his progressive motion, Vishnu; in his muscular force, Hara; in his organs of speech, Agni; in excretion, Mitra; [and] in procreation, Brahma," it would not be impossible for Whitman to be "the poet of the Body" at the same time that he is "the poet of the Soul," and to assert, as though he were contemplating Brahma in procreation, that "Copulation is no more rank to me than death is."[270]

The beautiful poem "Sleepers" ("that fantasia of the unconscious," as Cowley calls it[271]) may have found its initial inspiration in the line of Menu that speaks of the "spirit which can only be conceived by a mind slumbering." Elsewhere in Whitman's other Indian readings we will find elaborate analyses of the state of "deep sleep" in which "matter and spirit, the object enjoyed and the enjoyer, are as one, notwithstanding the necessary distinction between them."[272]

And if the unorthodox, even "irreligious," scientific doctrine of evolution was wholeheartedly accepted by Whitman and reconciled with his profound religious faith without any conflict (a point on which criticism has lovingly dwelt), there is enough suggestion in Whelpley's account of Menu that the Hindu philosophy also had accepted it, as in the brief summary of "the other efforts of thought [by which] Brahma originated the forms of things, in succession, ending with Man."

How much more of the *Laws of Menu* went into Whitman's philosophy or poetic equipment can be seen in the following further example. The *Dial* printed these extracts from Jones, in which the Hindu concept of Justice is discussed, under the heading "Reward and Punishment":

Justice, being destroyed, will destroy; being preserved, will preserve; it must therefore, never be violated. Beware, O judge, lest Justice, being overturned, overturn both us and thyself.

The only firm friend, who follows men even after death, is Justice; all others are extinct with the body.

The soul is its own witness; the soul itself is its refuge; offend not thy conscious soul, the supreme internal witness of men.

O friend to virtue, that supreme spirit, which thou believest one and the same with thyself, resides in thy bosom perpetually, and is an all-knowing inspector of thy goodness or of thy wickedness.

Compare with these the following entry in Whitman's early notebook, about which Holloway in an editorial footnote remarked: "It would be interesting to know whether this truth came to Whitman through mystical illumination or whether he had by this time read Emerson's 'Compensation' (1841)."[273]

Justice is not varied or tempered in passage of laws by legislatures—Legislatures cannot alter it any more than they can love
or pride or the attraction of gravity. The quality of justice is
in the soul.—It is immutable . . . it remains through all times
and nations and administrations . . . it does not depend on
majorities and minorities. . . . Whoever violates it pays the
penalty just as certainly as he who violates the attraction of
gravity. . . . Whether a nation violates it or an individual, it
makes no difference.

The consciousness of individuals is the test of Justice.—What
is mean or cruel for an individual is so for a nation.

It is also possible that the paternal tone of Whitman's Messianic
voice, which imparts profound teachings of truth to the world,
calling, "Come my children,/Come my boys and girls,"[274] had its
precedent and justification in the following laws of Menu that the
Dial also carried under another section entitled "Teaching":

> A Brahmin, who is the giver of spiritual birth, the teacher of
> prescribed duty, is by right the father of an old man, though
> himself be a child.
> Cari, child of Angiras, taught his paternal uncles and cousins
> to read the Veda, and, excelling them in divine knowledge, said
> to them "Little sons."
> They, moved with resentment, asked the gods the meaning
> of that *expression;* and the gods, being assembled, answered
> them, "The child has addressed you properly;"
> For an unlearned man is in truth a child; and he who teaches
> him the Veda is his father: holy sages have always said child to
> an ignorant man, and father to a teacher of scripture.

The *Dial's* extracts of the *Laws* appeared in its January 1843
number. Whitman's "leaves" on "Heetopades" were cut from
the July 1842 issue. His reading of the *Dial* cannot be limited
to that number only. His interest in Oriental knowledge was
strong enough to make him realize that of all the journals of
the day, the *Dial* was the major source of Eastern thought.
Further, even a casual glance at the pages will bear evidence to
his reading of its other numbers. A few of the passages from them

that have powerful indications of having entered into Whitman's poetry are examined here.

In the July 1841 *Dial,* under the title "Wheat Seed and Bolted Flour," in this passage: "There is no Past; there is no Future. *Now* alone is. The Past is the circulating sap; the Future is the folded petal. Now is the Life; and God is now; and now is God. . . ." (No. x)

Here are the lines from Whitman, wonderfully transformed:

> There was never any more inception than there is now,
> Nor any more youth or age than there is now;
> And will never be any more perfection than there is now,
> Nor any more heaven or hell than there is now.[275]

Examine the following "Orphic Saying" from the *Dial* of July 1840: "Every soul sees at times her own possibility of becoming a God; she cannot rest in the human, she aspires after the God-like. . . . Men shall become gods. . . ." and Whitman's claim: "Who knows but I too shall in time be a God so pure and prodigious as any of them?" or "I think the soul will never stop, or attain to any growth beyond which it shall not go."[276]

How far the following other "Orphic Sayings" have entered into Whitman's pages, poetry or prose, may be seen without illustration:

> Engage in nothing that cripples or degrades you. Your first duty is self-culture, self-exaltation: you may not violate this self-trust. Your Self is sacred, profane it not. . . . (No. v)

> . . . Every synthetic fact is supernatural and miraculous. . . . Divinely seen, natural facts are symbols of spiritual laws. . . . God, man and nature are miracles." (No. VII)

> A man's period is according to the directness and intensity of his light. Not erudition, not taste, not intellect, but character, describes his orbit and determines the worlds he shall en-lighten. . . . (No. LXIX)[277]

> Individuals are sacred: creeds, usages, institutions as they cherish and reverence the individual. The world, the state, the

church, the school are all felons whensoever they violate the sanctity of the private heart. . . . A man is divine; mightier, holier than rules or powers ordained of time. (No. xcii)

Whitman's poem "Faces," celebrating the "testimony" that human faces bear, "slumbering or awake," to "their descent from the Master himself,"[278] appears to have its origin in this July 1840 Orphic Saying from the *Dial* called "Transfiguration":

> Never have we beheld a purely human face; as yet, the beast, demon, rather than the man or God, predominate in its expression. The face of the soul is not extant in flesh. Yet she has a face, and virtue and genius shall one day reveal her celestial lineaments. . . . (No. xlix)

Of the magic of the poetic power by which, as Whitman himself described it, "the great poet absorbs the identity of others and experience of others . . . presses them all though the powerful press of himself [and] loads his own masterly identity,"[279] another illustration is given here.

The April 1842 *Dial* has a poem called "Like by Like," an extract from Henry More's "Psyche-Zoa or Life of the Soul," in an article entitled "Days from a Diary":

> "Well sang the wise Empedocles of old,
> That earth by earth, and sea by sea,
> And heaven by heaven, and fire more bright than gold,
> By flaming fire, so gentle love descry
> By love, and hate by hate. And all agree
> That like is known by like."

This "mint and marjorum" becomes the "honey" of our poetic bee, first a prose note in his "Preparatory Reading and Thought," then later a whole short poem. Here they are:

> The secret is here: Perfections are only understood and responded to by perfections.
> This rule runs through all and applies to mediocrity, crime and all the rest; each is understood only by the like of itself. . . .[280]

In 1860 he wrote a poem of two lines called "Perfections":

Only themselves understand themselves and the like of them-
    selves,
As souls only understand souls.

And those magnificent lines describing the profound symbolic
significance of "What is the grass?" in section 6 of "Song of
Myself" bear too close a resemblance to the following poem
entitled "Correspondences" (in an article called "Glimmerings")
in the January 1841 *Dial* to be accidental, or a mere coincidence:

"All things in Nature are beautiful types to the soul that will
    read them;
Nothing exists upon earth, but for unspeakable ends.
Every object that speaks to the senses was meant for the spirit:
    Nature is but a scroll,—God's handwriting thereon.
Ages ago, when man was pure.........................
....
Everything stood as a letter or word of language familiar,
    Telling of truths which *now* only the angels can read.
Lost to man was the key of those sacred hieroglyphics,—
....
....
Thus does the word of God distil like the rain and the dew-
    drops,
Thus does the warm wind breathe like to the Spirit of God,
And the green grass and the flowers are signs of the regener-
    ation.
....
    O thou Spirit of Truth! visit our minds once more!
Give us to read, in letters of light, the language celestial,
    Written all over the earth—written all over the sky.

For the lyric poet that Whitman is—and he made much of the
subjective character of his poems[281]—and for a poet supposed to
have been visited with an "illuminating experience," far too much
seems to have come in from outside, from some one else's experience. This is not to underestimate his poetry, but only to recognize
the enormous part reading has played in it and the strange method
by which he has organized his reading into his own shape. Who

can tell but that his profound self-discovery of the early notebook: "I cannot understand the mystery, but I am always conscious of myself as two—as my soul and I; and I reckon it is the same with all men and women,"[282] is a mere thought suggested by the reading of these lines from the *Dial's* Jan. 1842 number:

A man, and the object upon which he acts, are two separate and distinct things.

A man, and the instrument by which he acts, are also two separate and distinct things.

My hand is an instrument by which I act; My hand therefore is not me.

My whole body is a combination of instruments by which I act; my body, therefore, is not me.[283]

Examples of this kind can be multiplied, but my purpose is merely to show the evidence on which Whitman can be taken to have read the other extracts from Menu quoted from the *Dial*. One last passing reference to one more detail from the pages of the *Dial* will be made. In its October 1841 issue it carried a review, with excerpts from the text, of that strange but fascinating book by Bailey, *Festus*. Whitman had among his magazine articles one on *Festus,* dated "Dec. 45."[284] I have not been able to trace a "Dec. 45" review of *Festus* at all. The *Whig Review* notices the book in its January and February 1847 numbers, and the *Westminster's* December 45 number (or *Eclectic's* or *Edinburgh's*) does not have it. Unless Bucke's date is a mistake, Whitman's article must be from some other accidentally read periodical. In his *Notes and Fragments,* Whitman also refers to *Festus:* "Theories of Evil—Festus, Faust, Manfred, Paradise Lost, Book of Job."[285] That *Festus* had a hand in the third of the four gods of "The Square Deific" has been noticed by George Sixbey,[286] but, as far as I know, not much attention otherwise seems to have been given to Bailey's book, or the article on it, which, as the following random selections will show, has supplied much more to Whitman that just a suggestion for his Lucifer. They are, first, from the *Dial,* "Festus," which presents its review in the form of a dialogue, with extracts from the book:

LAURIE. . . . Do not consider it as a book, as a work of art at all;
but as a leaf from the book of life. His postscript gives a faith-
ful account of what he has done.

> "Read this, World? He who writes is dead to thee,
> But still lives in these leaves. He spake inspired."
> (pp. 234–35)

> First of all,
> Care not about the name, but bind thyself,
> Body and Soul, to nature hiddenly;
> . . . .
> The bard must have a kind, courageous heart,
> . . . .
> He must believe the best of everything;
> Love all below, and worship all above.
> All animals are living hieroglyphics,
> . . . . .mean something more
> To the true eye than their shapes show; for all
> Were made in love, and made to be beloved. (p. 238)

> . . . .
> And though these scenes may seem to careless eyes
> Irregular and rough and unconnected,
> . . . .
> A meaning, a purpose may be marked
> Among them of a temple reared to God,
> It has a plan, but no plot. . . . (p. 244)

> Evil is
> Good in another way we are not skilled in. (p. 244)

Though Whitman's optimism, love, and sense of the divinity of
all things did not take roots here, assuredly he learned here his
own "postscripts":

> Indeed this is no book, but more a man. . . .
> No printed leaves, but human lips. . . .[287]

> Camerado, this is no book,
> Who touches this touches a man. . . .[288]

No one will get at my verses who insists upon viewing them as a literary performance, or attempt at such a performance, or as aimed toward art or aestheticism.[289]

If he scandalized orthodox readers of *Leaves of Grass* by calling Christ a "comrade" or "brother,"[290] or by claiming to "know that the spirit of God is the brother of [his] own,"[291] or by writing that "The soul addresses God as his equal—as one who knows his greatness—as a younger brother,"[292] it looks as if he did not need a mystical experience for it, because in *Festus* Lucifer says to the hero,

> Knowest thou not
> God's Son to be the brother and the friend
> Of spirit everywhere? (p. 255)

If Whitman has given a poetry, "leaving [out] all outside heroes and events, the stock of previous bards," of something "more close and deep," namely "ONE'S-SELF,"[293] for *Festus,* the same achievement was claimed:

> One bard shows God as He deals with states and kings;
> Another as he dealt with the first man;
> Another as with heaven, and earth, and hell;
> Ours writes God as He orders a chance soul,
> Picked out of earth at hazard, like oneself,
> It is a statued mind and naked heart
> Which he strikes out. Other bards draw men dressed
> In manners, customs, forms, appearances,
> Laws, places, times, and countless accidents
> Of peace or polity; to him there are not;
> He makes no mention, no account of them. . . .

The "spiritual arrogance" with which Whitman writes in his early notebooks: "If I walk with Jah in Heaven and he assume to be intrinsically greater than I it offends me, and I shall certainly withdraw from Heaven,"[294] and, "If the presence of God were made visible immediately before me, I could not abase myself,"[295] appears to lose a good deal of its mystical quality when we see this description of *Festus* in the January 1847 number of the

Whig Review, of which, as has been shown, he was a fairly regular reader:

> Accordingly the book is, without exception, the most irreverent thing we have seen. Instead of putting his shoes from off his feet when he comes to holy ground, he [Festus, or, his author] rather puts on an additional pair. He wears his loftiest looks in the awfulest Presence; and gives us the gratifying information, that
>
>> "Men have a claim on God; and none who hath
>> A heart of kindness, reverence and love,
>> But dare look God in the face and ask His smile."
>
> . . . He evidently belongs to that class of worshippers whose motto is, "let us go boldly to the throne of grace"; and who *do* go boldly, as if their Master were their equal. (p. 47)

Not only for Lucifer, but for his "Santa Spirita" too, *Festus* appears to have given a hint, in the Angel of Earth who protests:

> Think not I lived and died for earth alone.
> My life is ever suffering for love.
> In judging and redeeming worlds is spent
> Mine everlasting being. (p. 48)

The poem "Festus" and the poetry of Whitman are worlds apart; however, the poet Whitman comes very close to Festus. For the personality he assumed as a poet, and some of his doings—or sayings about his doings—as a poet, Festus appears to have been as much a model as the vagabond hero of George Sand.[296]

The most revealing part of this parallel study is the one that follows, which is the reason for my dwelling so long on *Festus.*

Section 5 of "Song of Myself" has been regarded as undoubtedly the most important passage of the whole poem and of crucial significance in the understanding of it. Allen describes it as "one of the most magnificent passages in the literature of mysticism, conveying a sense of union with God, brotherhood with men and women, and sympathy with all living things, however small, lowly or common," although Whitman "was a mystic in the sense that intellectually and spiritually he believed *love* to be the creating, unifying, and life-giving principle of the universe." By many others, like Canby and Schyberg "the whole passage has often been assumed to be an esoteric description of some physical experience."[297] The passionate advocate of the true mystic vision, Bucke looked upon it as irrefutable evidence of Whitman's illumination: "the first direct mention . . . on the third page of his first writing after the new faculty had come to him."[298] The striking sexual imagery in which the passage symbolically represents the "consummated marriage of body and soul," Miller observes, "constitutes the basic paradox in the poem. Whereas normally the mystical state is achieved only through a mortification of, or escape from, the senses, the poet of 'Song of Myself' asserts that it is through the transfigured senses that he reaches mystical consciousness."[299] Whichever way we look at it, it is a piece of beautiful verse, not in spite of the sexual connotation, but probably because of it. The power with which the fusion, or equivalence of the sexual and the spiritual is suggested is astonishing. But a good part of the astonishment is lost, as well as of the profounder implications, when we notice that the sexual foundation of the spiritual enlightenment may possibly owe something to the following passage in *Festus,* described by our reviewer:

Next follows [after Lucifer's assurance of immortality to Festus] a pretty fine love-scrape, wherein our hero revels in the most voluptuous images and anticipations, protesting to the fair object, that in vain he

"Strives to love aught of earth or heaven but her:
She is his first, last, only love; nor shall
Another ever tempt his heart."

In this state of mind he is visited with a most supernatural insight, with "the ken of Angels," so that neither sky, nor night, nor earth hinders him from seeing quite "through the forms of things into their essence," and even through the mysteries of life, death, and immortality, all of which, by the way, is the work of love and Lucifer. (Italics added)

"This wild and whirlwind touch of passion,
Which, though it hardly lit upon the lip,
With breathless swiftness sucked his soul out of sight,
So that he lost it, and all thought of it." [p. 53]

It is hard not to notice how the last four lines of the verse might also have suggested the passage on "touch" in Whitman's early notebook,[300] later worked into "Song of Myself," section 28. From such instances it is clear that the world of Whitman's poetry is the world of poetic fantasy, the creation of imagination without positive correspondences in his own actual personal life. And such a large portion of the world he creates is, at least in the early stages, structures raised upon bits and scraps of material taken from elsewhere that—our wonder at the spectacle notwithstanding —one has to be careful about using his poetry to explain his life, or his life to explain his poetry, as we normally do with lyric poets. The evidence so far seen describes a poetry born out of poetic skill rather than of genuine personal or poetic experience, the power of transforming suggestions and hints rather than of creating an original suggestion, the power of Coleridge's Secondary Imagination, not of ordering an experience, but of reordering it. Even his "Answerer" appears to have been raised on the hints of these lines from *Festus:*

> "He is an universal favourite;
> Old men admire him deeply for his beauty;
> Young women for his genius and strict virtue,
> And young men for his modesty and wisdom;
> All turn to him, whene'er he speaks, full-faced,
> Like plants to the sun, or owls to a rush light"

[because by this time Festus has had his "supernatural insight" into the essence of things, and] "not a promise has Lucifer made to him, but is fulfilled," [as a result of which,] after solving all the mysteries, pocketing all the secrets, and sipping all the delights of creation; . . . after various short excursions, one through space, one to Everywhere, one to Hell, one to Nowhere, one to a lady's drawing-room, besides sundry other places too numerous to mention, extracting and concentrating the essence of them all, . . . our hero mounts the throne of the world, and gives his law to the nations. . . . (p. 54)

Whitman's claims to the deep meanings of his poetry are well-known. "What lies behind *Leaves of Grass* is something that few, very few . . . are at all in a position to seize. It lies behind almost every line; but concealed, studiedly concealed; some passages left purposely obscure. . . ."[301] The deep meaning of his poems is, of course, undeniable, but the claim resembles that of *Festus,* of which the reviewer says:

> Doubtless the meaning [of the book] is occult—so very occult, we fear, that no one, not even the author himself, can find out what it is; for the author takes care to inform us that the book is very deep, "the meaning always dwelling in the word in secret-sanctity." (p. 54)

Sufficient evidence has been seen of Whitman's enthusiasm for the *Whig Review* and his quite regular reading of it during the early years. He had collected and preserved eight articles from its 1845 issues. From the July number he cut the article on "Society and Civilization" by John Quincy Adams, and from the October issue, the article on "Scotch School of Philosophy" and Whelpley's "On Style." Bucke's list mentions an article on "Plato" (No. 349), undated, and the August 1845 number of *Whig Review* carried Tayler Lewis's "The Study of Plato." There is, thus, a reasonable ground for supposing that Whitman read the September number of that year too, which contained an article by E. B. Green, entitled "The Bhagvat Geeta—And The Doctrine of Immortality."

Green's article is not specifically a review of Charles Wilkins' 1785 translation of the Indian classic, but a critical discussion of the Hindu concept of Immortality, with particular reference to the "Gita," principally, and to the *Vedas,* and the *Laws of Menu,* from all of which he quotes extensively in the course of his analysis. It begins with an extract from the *Vedas,* and a brief summary of the Hindu ideas of metempsychosis and Karma, with which, we might mention, the author has no patience.

> It is written in the Vedas, "The Soul should be known, that is, it should be distinguished from nature; for then it will not return, it will not return." In this passage, under a form peculiar to the East, we find the enunciation, of one of the fundamental problems of philosophy (that of the immortality of the soul). . . . It is the general belief of the Orientals, that the soul of a dying man, after leaving this present body, will be born again into the world under some new form . . . and this rebirth . . . is the

return of the soul. The expiation of certain crimes consists, according to the description in laws of Menu, in the soul's living a thousand successive lives, in the bodies of a thousand different spiders. . . . (p. 267)

With this as the starting point, E. B. Greene begins to "examine this doctrine of the transmigration of souls." But since it is not our purpose to review the writer's opinions so much as to find how much of the actual philosophical doctrines of India Whitman came to gather directly from reading this article, we shall concern ourselves with the passages quoted from the original Indian works themselves and ignore the author's treatment, except for a couple of paragraphs that seem to have offered interesting hints to Whitman.

At the outset of his examination, Green refers to the two schools of thought that hold opposing views about the relative importance of body and soul.

In all ages of the world there have been philosophers who held that *the soul built the body,* that is, that the character and form of the body was dependent on the character of the soul. . . . At this time, . . . many of our phrenologists and other materialists, believe that it is *the body which builds the soul,* that is, that the soul is a function of . . . some portion of the organism. (p. 267)

At a later point in the discussion, after presenting the Hindu concept of death and immortality, the writer makes the following observations:

What is death, or the transition from this life to that which is to come? . . . Death is the passage of a vital agent from one state of existence to another. . . . For the soul . . . does not cease to live. To die, therefore, is not to cease from all life, but to cease from this present *form* of life which we enjoy in the body. (p. 274)

When the body is destroyed the particles are not destroyed; they go into new relations; what was once wheat or grain is now a man, and what was once a man is now some animal—"all flesh is grass." (p. 275)

The soul lives now in the body, is dependent upon the body for its communion with outward nature, it cannot learn or know anything of the visible world except through the medium of the senses, and without the cunning organization of the ear, human speech and the communion of man with man, and therefore, human sympathies, and, in short, human life, would be impossible.

The last of the paragraphs reproduced above is Green's impatient answer to the Hindu emphasis, as suggested in the first two, on the importance of the soul and the relative insignificance of the body which is its fugitive abode, and so are the following lines with which the discussion ends:

It seems to us . . . that the theory of future existence of the soul, independent of any body, spiritual or material, is unphilosophical. . . . Now the soul, in order to [have] communion with other souls, must have some mode of activity, and some means of recognizing the activities of other souls; that is, it must exist in actual relations . . . in a body. . . . We would not be misunderstood; we do not believe the soul to be the substance of the body. We hold that the soul and body are distinct, though not separate. . . . (p. 278)

We shall now pass on to the original Indian texts presented in the article. From the *Vedas* two more verses dealing with creation are quoted, one of which is reproduced here, the other being a development of it.

As the spider spins, and gathers back its thread (say the Vedas) ; as plants sprout out of the earth; as hairs grow on a living person; so is this universe produced from imperishable nature. *By contemplation the Vast One germinates.* (p. 274)

The Hindu theory of the genesis of the universe is presented with eleven quotations from the *Laws of Menu* (Appendix I, c).
The impact of these extracts on Whitman will be traced later. Green quotes four more laws of Menu on one aspect of the twin doctrines of Karma and Transmigration, which achieve their supreme Whitmanesque expression in "Song of Prudence," while

reverberating in other pages, as the "law" that "cannot be eluded" [302] "for all that a person does or thinks is of consequence."[303] One of them is reproduced here:

> Action, either verbal, mental, or corporeal, bears good or evil fruit, as itself is good or evil; and from the actions of men proceed their various transmigrations in the highest, the mean, and the lowest degree. . . . (p. 277)

The rest of the article's extracts from Hindu texts are all from the *Bhagvat-Geeta* of Wilkins' translation, and bear upon the Indian doctrines of Immortality, the nature of the Supreme Being, the nature of the Soul, the Divinity of Creation, and the final absorption of the Individual soul into the Universal Soul. Although our concern is to discover Whitman's pre-1855 knowledge of Indian philosophical ideas, not to assess its effect on his poetry, and although his reading of the article under notice is a matter of conjecture, however reasonable, a word about the *Gita* is, I think, in order. For, of all the books in the literature of the world, the one work that bears the closest resemblance to "Song of Myself," both in literary technique and philosophical content, and which offers a model to the lyricism as well as the metaphysics of the poem in which the poetic "I" identified itself with the Absolute Self—at the same time supplying the "recognizably Indian ideas" of *Leaves of Grass*—is the *Bhagvat-Geeta,* as even the extracts from it in Green's article will show.

With his obvious enthusiasm for J. D. Whelpley's writings and the *Whig Review,* it would again not be unreasonable to assume that Whitman may have seen the January 1849 *Whig* issue, which carried another article by Whelpley, entitled "Middle-Asiatic Theology." In spite of its slightly misleading title, the article is on Indian theology and its philosophical doctrines. Not so much a critical analysis as a general survey, very often superficial, and the result of the author's readings in the *Asiatic Researches* and the works of the Reverend W. Ward, by the latter of which it is deeply influenced in its attitude to the subject, it yet presents an informative summary of the basic Hindu philosophical thought and the different systems that have sprung from it, like Yoga, Nyaya, Mimamsa, Vedanta, Vysesika, and Sankhya, as well as

Buddhism. A few excerpts from the survey that look as if they might have caught either Whitman's intellectual curiosity or poetic fancy are rendered here (Appendix I, d).

In the course of his article Whelpley refers to the *Asiatic Researches* three times, to Ward on the "Hindoos" five times, to Sir William Jones's *Works* once, and once to the *Laws of Menu,* thus offering a reading list for any one interested in a further knowledge of Indian thought.

From these explorations into "faint clews and indirections," we shall now return to the direct evidence of the two remaining articles of Bucke's list on India. "The Hindu Drama" may be dismissed with casual notice, first because it is of April 1857, and secondly because it has no bearing on Indian philosophical ideas. It is a review in the *Westminster* magazine of four translations of Indian dramas: Kalidasa's *Sakoontala* by Monier Williams and *Vikramorvasi* by E. B. Cowell into English, *Malavika and Agnimitra* by Albrecht Weber into German, and Shoodraka's *La Chariot d'Enfant* by Méry and Gerard de Nerval into French. But Whitman's penchant for collecting interesting words to use in his writings appears to have operated in the reading of this article. He seems to have picked up his title for the poem "Halcyon Days" from this quotation from *Sakoontala:* "Unceasing are the charms of halcyon days. . . ."

But there was another article on Hindu Drama in the *Westminster Review* seven years earlier, in its October 1850 number, this time reviewing two books, *Vikramorvasi,* edited by Monier Williams, and *Maha-vira-charita,* edited by F. H. Trithen. If Whitman had read it, which is not unlikely, he would have noticed its references to Jones's *Works* and his *Sakuntala,* and Max Mueller's *Rig Veda* edition, probably scoring the following sentence:

Its [India's] epics will still prove that poetry once dwelt there; the "Bhagavad Geeta" will reveal to us its philosophy. (p. 19)

The "magazine article, 'Indian Epic Poetry,' dated Oct. 1848, much scored and annotated," was cut from the *Westminster Review.* Though the apparent occasion is a critical notice of a Greek translation of the *Mahabharata* by Demetrius Galanus, and an Italian translation of the *Ramayana* by Gaspare Górresio, the article's scholarly analysis of the Indian epics, with many extracts from their English translations (one of which is Millman's) includes a survey of the history and nature of Indian poetry. The evident part of the much scored and annotated reading of the article by Whitman is seen both in his notes of the "Preparatory Reading and Thought" and his poems, as well as his prose writings. Some of the thoughts and words that entered his own pages are noted here:

> We little think [thus begins the article], while we read of the glories of Grecian and Roman history, that during those very centuries which they seem to have monopolised, the sun still witnessed other empires in other parts of the earth, whose histories were full of interest in those days, and not without importance even in our own time. Contemporaneous with these romance-lands of European antiquity, flourished the great empires of Persia and India. . . . Each had its own heroes and its chivalrous deeds; each had its own laws and institutions, and its generations of minds to be trained and influenced thereby. . . . While all this [development of language in Greece and Rome] was passing, India was witnessing the rise and decline of as noble a speech as these, with a literature entirely her own, exemplifying in itself all those changes which scholars love to trace in the classical languages of Europe.

Whitman reproduces all this in his own characteristic phrasing in notes nos. 60 and 63 of "Preparatory Reading," and the line in the article: "In *these* early *times* the bards *are* the historians," becomes his "In *those* early *days* the bards *were* the *only* historians."[304] (Italics added) His notes on the *Ramayana* and the *Mahabharata*,[305] together with the observation about "the style of a poem," are taken from the article itself. Two of the lines of a rejected fragment, as noted earlier, entering into "Salut au Monde!" owe themselves to the article. Another of those exotic words of Whitman, the "gymnosophist" of line 1099, "Song of Myself," 1855, along with its preceding phrase, "rapt and austere in the woods," is obviously from this passage in the article:

We get [in the story of the *Ramayana*] many a pleasant glimpse of quiet hermitages, . . . such as doubtless abounded from the earliest ages in Hindostan, to offer their shelter to those contemplative minds which fled from the tumults of their times. It was in one of these hermitages that Alexander found the Gymnosophists, when, in reply to his inquiries, they only stamped on the ground, as a silent admonition to the conquerer of his mortality.

That in spite of the three long quotations from the *Ramayana* and one long and eight small ones from the *Mahabharata* given in the article—with the entire story of both the Epics briefly narrated —Whitman's knowledge of the Hindu epics (with which he could discuss their characters in a conversation with Edward Carpenter[306] as well as mention them as fine examples of human personality in his *Democratic Vistas*) was not from this limited account, is evidenced by one circumstance. In his essay, "Bible as Poetry," which again praises the principle of characterization in ancient Indian poetry, Whitman mentions an episode from the *Mahabharata* and quotes a passage from it. The article on "Indian Epic Poetry" also has extracts from the same episode of the Epic but they touch on other phases of it, without that passage quoted by Whitman describing Yama or the god of Death. He must therefore have read the Epic itself, at least in part, because, again, the passage did not come from Alger, whose own extracts are reproduced from this article. And if Whitman read the *Mahabharata* in full, he could hardly have missed the *Bhagavadgita,* which is an episode in its sixteenth chapter.

An interesting little detail strikes our attention as we peruse this article in relation to the question of Whitman's pre-1855 knowledge of Indian thought. It has been remarked that only in his later poems do Sanskrit words like "maya," "sudra," and "nirvana" appear, which has encouraged critics like Malcolm Cowley to assume that Whitman's Indian knowledge was of late origin. In other words, with his well-known affection for strange and foreign words, he would have used them in the early poems had he known them. But strangely enough, this 1848 article, from which he uses so many other words and phrases, has the very phrase, "maya or illusion," which he does not use until 1860.

But the whole scene [of Yudhisthara's descent to Hell] was only a *máyá*, or illusion to prove his virtue; the sorrows suddenly vanish, the surrounding hell changes into heaven.

One implication of this would be that the use of the term in this article does not carry the full force of its significance, whereas Whitman's use of it has all the Vedantic depth in it, and so, the knowledge of the philosophical thought was not of these years. But, in terms of direct evidence alone, as we have observed in his 1857 comment on Emerson's "Brahma," he has betrayed a remarkably precise knowledge of it. Therefore, it appears that his not using those Indian words in the early poems is not because he did not know them. The word "sudra" occurs in Whelpley's articles on "The Hindoos" and "Castes and Occupations of India."

Considering Whitman's power of absorbing suggestions and ideas and of transforming them into effective use in his own poetry, it would not be surprising if these two following passages from the article he read so avidly had something to do with much of the "American scene" he puts into the philosophical "Song of Myself," following his own assertion that the American bard "incarnates its geography and natural life and rivers and lakes,"[307] and with his insistence that "America does not repel the past or what it has produced under its forms."[308]

The same freeness of expression characterizes each [Valmiki and Homer]; the words flow carelessly from the poet's lips, as the natural voice of his emotions; and the open fullness of his heart faithfully mirrors itself in his song. In each, too, we find the same repetition of favourite phrases and images; . . . and both poets abound with that vivid fellow-feeling with nature, which so strongly characterizes the half-civilized age of an heroic people. The gigantic peaks of the Himalayas are ever present to Valmiki's mind, as Ida and Olympus to Homer's; and his poem reflects a thousand influences from his country's vast scales of geography and scenery. . . .

Thus closes the Mahabharata, the new mythic world, which a modern Columbus has opened! Greatly as our times are distinguished by discovery and progress, we are yet continually reminded, amidst its changes, of the world of the Past, out of which the Present is born . . . The heroic times and youth of the race thus rise up in earth's later days, in startling contrast with our science and commerce, as if Nature would expressly teach us that there lies a romance in the past which can never grow obsolete to man.

A good deal of Valmiki and Homer described in the first of the above passages is in Whitman. And when we put together the poet's "Singing my days,/Singing the great achievements of the present, . . ./Yet first to sound, and ever sound, the cry with thee O Soul,/The Past! The Past! The Past!"[309] and his soul's seeking the "passage to India," to "The Mystic wisdom," and "the Source,"[310] with his subsequently uttering the prayer of "a battered, wreck'd old man" "reporting myself once more to Thee,"[311] it is not difficult to conceive that Whitman genuinely regarded himself as "a modern Columbus," and, what is more, *was* one. In some strange, mystic way, the two poems, "Passage to India" and "Prayer of Columbus" are an affidavit not only of Whitman's poetic enthusiasm, but also of his poetic career. He had discovered India for America.

In the January 1849 *Westminster Review,* under the section "Foreign Literature," there is a review of "Lectures upon Ancient History by Frederick von Raumer," presenting long textual extracts on ancient Indian religious thought. In them is a critical summary of the early Vedic religion, its theories of creation, transmigration, and the fixed order of the universe, later theological ideas, the Hindu Trinity, the "doctrine of the emanation of the universe from the divinity," Shaivism, and a long account of the Buddha and his teachings. The survey of Indian religion is followed by that of Egyptian religious beliefs and practices, and the long extract on Egypt appears to have supplied some of Whitman's own notes on Egypt.[312] One of his favorite words, en masse, seems to come from this review, which ends thus:

But while we avoid the old error of condemning all ancient religions but one, *en masse,* as frantic follies, we need not fall into the more recent mistake of supposing either the Indian or the Egyptian systems models of profound wisdom.

In the extract on Hindu religion, there is a passage describing the concept of the Trinity that developed in India:

> Thus, according to the Indian mode of expression, Bram (the Almighty) brought forth Bhavani, the all-generative nature; who again produced three sons—Brahma, Vishnu and Shiva. Bram now soon retired into the background, and the three symbols of one God became gradually regarded as three independent beings, exercising peculiar and separate functions. Some felt that the question here was of distinction, but not of a contrariety, and that the Trinity merely comprehended the whole idea of Godhead.

From what initial suggestion and through what complicated progression Whitman's "Square Deific" emerged it is hard to say, but the "Bhavani" of this passage bears some resemblance to the fourth of the Square.

PART TWO:

The Roots

1

THE POETIC PROGRAMME

IN A "VERY EARLY NOTE, THE PAPER TORN AND ALMOST FALLING
to pieces from age," Whitman has recorded one of his well-known
directions to himself:

> For example, whisper privately in your ear . . . the studies
> . . . be a rich investment. . . . Enter into the thoughts of the
> different theological faiths—effuse all that the believing Egyp-
> tian would—all that the Greek—all that the Hindoo, worship-
> ping Brahma—the Kooboo adoring his fetish stone or log—the
> Presbyterian—the Catholic with his crucifix and saints—the
> Turk with the Koran.[1]

Though fragments of the latter part of this passage, slightly
altered and developed, enter into section 43 of "Song of Myself,"
which describes the faith "enclosing all worships ancient and
modern," it does not appear to have been originally intended for a
poem. Considering the self-instructions in it, it looks like a personal resolution made early in life for the programme of his poetic
enterprise. For, as he wrote in another note, the leading characteristics of his works were to be "to unite all sects, parties, states,
lawyers, disputants, young men, women (universology)—[in
order that he could] be one whom all look toward with attention,
respect, love."[2] Another fragment in which he briefly sums up the
central ideas of past religions—Egyptian, Greek, and Hebrew—
alludes to the "new religion" which it was his intention to found.

117

?Spinal idea of a "lesson." Founding a new American religion (? No religion). That which is comprehensive enough
to include all the doctrines and sects and give them all places
and chances, each after its kind.[3]

This then was the plan on which Whitman was to "make *the
Works*,"[4] and achieve "The Great Construction of the New
Bible."[5] And although the final resolution to "make *the Works*"
and the definite idea of the "New Bible" were recorded in the
years 1856 and 1857 respectively, from the nature of his early
readings and notes he appears to have had the objective clearly in
mind before he started writing the first edition. To his early interest in the various religions of the world, many of his notes and
fragments bear ample testimony. He even had a "look at [a]
theological dictionary [in] 1855."[6]

Though most of his "Notes for 'Lectures on Religion'"[7] were
evidently made after 1855, a large part of their thoughts echo
"Song of Myself," indicating that they sprang from the interest
in comparative religion of his preparatory days. A considerable
portion of his "Shorter Notes, Isolated Words," belongs to the
history of philosophy and religion. An entire section on "Religion-
gods,"[8] of notes taken, as Goodale has shown, from Volney's
Ruins, is of the early years, because some of them enter into his
experimental compositions. The basic character of the thoughts of
his early 1847–'48 notebooks[9] is of a philosophical or religious
kind. The notes he has made on "two fragments of paper both
torn and, indeed, destroyed" about "those stages, Egyptian, Hindu,
Hebraic, Greek, Christian," not only declare his deep enthusiasm
for "their memories and inheritances in all continents" (about
which he has no "complaint" because he "stand[s] silent and ad-
mirable before the monuments of the great soul of man in all
lands and in every age"[10]), they also contain suggestions of his
early zeal in the studies of the past. For they are of the same
tenor as the thoughts on religion elsewhere recorded as material
for his proposed lectures on the subject, on "a series of slips of
paper . . . quite old" and, according to Bucke, "probably
belong[ing] to early fifties," the period of Whitman's preparation:

Premonitory . . . That the Past and the Present [are] to be
treated with perfect respect. . . . That I stand with (not their

slave) admiration and boundless awe before all the growths of
the Past, of men in all ages, all lands, the present, civilizations,
religions, politics. . . . I do not condemn the Past or the
Present. Shall I denounce my own ancestry—the very ground
under my feet? . . . Do you suppose religion consists in one
particular form or creed—the Christian or any other? No, it is
the whole universal heart of man . . . processions of races,
swiftly marching and countermarching over the fields of the
Earth—the sublime creeds of different eras . . .—religions,
the new ones arriving out of the old ones. . . . When I stand
off, silent, and view how in the Present, as perhaps in the
Past . . . the divine ideas of spirituality, of the universal soul
of the woman and the man, of another sphere of existence, of
conscience and perfect justice and goodness have been serenely
preserved . . . I receive the great inheritance with welcome joy.[11]

Whether out of this evident desire to make "new combinations,
more copious, more turbulent than earth's preceding times, in-
augurating a new world mental or spiritual as any,"[12] and the
consequent wide reading among whatever sources were available
to him in the "sublime creeds of different eras," Whitman acquired a coherent system of thought, or even a profound one, is
another question. Perhaps Whitman himself was sensible of it
when he admitted with his characteristic subtlety that "a certain
vagueness almost passing into chaos (it remains to be acknowledged) is in a few pieces and passages; but this is apparently by
the deliberate intention of the author,"[13] and declared:

> Do I contradict myself?
> Very well then I contradict myself,
> (I am large, I contain multitudes.)[14]

And despite his contradictions and chaos perhaps he did achieve
his ambition of "the Great Construction of the New Bible" at
least for some—like his friend Thomas Harned who in genuine
reverence said: "I want no other God than Walt Whitman; I
want no other Bible than 'Leaves of Grass.' "[15] But most critics
would agree with Symmonds that "it is useless to extract a coherent system of thought from his voluminous writings . . . he is
full of contradictions."[16]

However that may be, it is beyond doubt that Whitman's poetic plans as well as his personal enthusiasm inclined toward religion and philosophy at an early stage in his life. But his writings of the journalistic days do not suggest a particularly philosophical or religious temperament; it is only in the notebooks of those gestation years that metaphysical interest and speculation find their expression. And the first of his profound questions about the mystery of being is heard at about the same time as the new poetic line emerges.[17] The growth of his personal philosophical meditations on the "greatness, immortality and purity" of the soul, its "dilation," the equal divinity of body and soul or mind and matter, is simultaneous with the assumption of the messianic role to "take each man and woman of you to the window" and "point you to the endless and beginningless road along whose sides are crowded the rich cities of all living philosophy." Both rub shoulders with the new poetic experiment on the theme of *"Myself"* in which the lyric "I" begins to open its wings to soar into the cosmic proportions of the metaphysical "Me," remembering its own "crucifixion and bloody coronation" and the "nails driven through" its hands. The vital connection among these three, namely, the private philosophical cogitation, the consciousness of the prophet's role he would play, and the experiment on the new verse in which to impart his message, seems to suggest that the new poetry he wrote was not an accident but the outcome of his new philosophical speculations and acquisitions, and that all three were products of the early resolution he "whisper[ed] in [his] ear" to undertake those studies that would "be a rich investment."

The absence of Whitman's own records of these studies makes impossible any accurate story of the years of preparation that went into the realization of his ambition. Yet, from the notebooks preserved, mixed up and unreliable as most of them are with regard to dates, and from the reading material, a large part of which can be dated, one can fairly reconstruct the picture of those mysterious eight or nine years of Whitman's intellectual life. A good deal of the mystery vanishes when we realize the importance of the fact that the 1847 notebooks already indicate the emergence of the new Whitman, both as poet and as man. Not only by this time has his ambition been roused and the direction of his aspirations settled, but the first fumbling steps toward his new literary life are visibly taken. From these initial steps that grope and stumble a little uncertainly, not with the uncertainty of the path but with that of strength, to the athletic achievement in both the poetry and the philosophy of *Leaves of Grass,* is a long period of eight years. He had his dream "to be an American prophet-poet, to make the American people a book which should be like the Bible in spiritual appeal and moral fervour, but a book of the New World and the New Spirit";[18] he labored hard and deep to gather his "most comprehensive equipment ever attained by a human being,"[19] as the evidence of research into his reading proves; he had his "period of meditation upon the nature and method of the poet's work";[20] and during this period, "he wrote and destroyed a great deal."[21]

But eight years of dedicated industry are a trifle too long for the production of twelve poems, however brilliant in craftsmanship and profound in substance they may be. In other words, the miraculous suddenness of it all disappears and we see the story of *Leaves of Grass* in its true light of slow, deliberate, and industrious evolution. Even if, according to the official account, "early in the fifties the 'Leaves of Grass' began to take a sort of unconscious shape in his mind," and "in 1854 he commenced definitely writing out the poems that were printed in the first edition,"[22] from the first experiments of 1847 or 1848 to the time of the book's "unconscious shape" in the fifties there is sufficient length of time for the "accession of power" on the part of an aspiring poet who knew what he wanted to do. Thus if there is any miracle in Whitman's career, it is the miracle of all genius. The transformation in him did not occur in 1855, or "June, probably 1853," but in 1847. The beginnings of the change are already there, and the change was consummated over a period of years, involving all the stages, phases, and processes in which poets grow. We do not see them, in the sense that we do not see them in print, as we do those of other poets and thereby perceive the gradual stages by which they have developed. For Whitman did not publish any poems during those years, as ordinarily poets do, thus helping us to trace their career and, as it were, keep abreast of them; he did not do so because he was not writing poems in those days at all. He was writing one great "Poem" with which to answer Emerson's prophetic call, and was busy cherishing a Miltonic purpose and "gathering forces" in shy hiding.

The careful planning, the almost superhuman patience with

which, as we know, he constructed his poem, the meditation on its content and technique, the acquisition of material to go into it, were matters enough to keep him occupied. He knew the need for all that devoted attention. His was not the ordinary ambition that labors for the quick proceeds of success or money to keep the pot boiling. He had done enough of that kind of writing already in both prose and verse. He was now writing for a more noble, a more sacred, a more serious objective. That "special desire and conviction"[23] had to be nurtured with all the ardor and steadfastness he was capable of, and reared upon all the patience and labor he could give it. Not seeking the ordinary rewards of literature, he had to give to the world a work totally extraordinary.

And when he gave it, it was so. It was not even a book of so many poems, each with a title of its own, dealing with a theme of its own. It was a book of Poetry, like the Bible or some other holy scripture; not of independent pieces, but of one connected, related, integrated writing.[24] Thus for eight long years he had worked upon one long poem, in this sense, and the apparent grace and mastery of expression were acquired after many assays, from what we now know of his methods of composition, at each word, phrase, and passage, over each thought and its manner of expression, and over the general order as well as the arrangement of individual portions of the piece. It was not the magical palace of Aladdin, but the pyramid of long, hard, lonely, and unseen labor of years, growing inch by inch, brick by brick, with which he finally announced himself. The "long foreground"[25] that Emerson suspected for the power of his poetry is very much there. But we do not see it. When at last the "concealed growth" came to light, it looked like an "explosion."[26]

Whether Emerson and Fuller supplied the initial inspiration to Whitman's ambition, or by suggesting definite nationalistic designs, merely aided in the articulation of the unconscious and vague aspirations already there but dormant is of very little significance, but the importance of Emerson in the awakened life of Whitman appears to be much more than that. Many of his entries in the notebook of 1847 are thoughts of a personal nature, different from the experimental poetic lines in them, although, as his practice often is, they subsequently become the stuff of his poems. In these personal thoughts the new man of philosophical mind is clearly seen, as is the new poet of Cosmic Self in the experimental verse that follows.

The literary event in his career that ushered in the new kind of writing, and the biographical event of some influence that powerfully shaped his attitude to life into a serious philosophic frame thus appear coincident. This philosophical bent of mind he came to acquire might have invisible roots in the psychology of a highly sensitive man who, in addition to the imaginative sorrows of youth, was further prey to the agonizing "perturbations" of an anomaly in his own nature, but Emerson was doubtless the occasion for the enthusiasm. As Allen remarks, commenting on Catel's hypothesis noted earlier in our pages: "the subjective philosophy of the post-Kantians in America, and of Emerson especially, provided both a framework and rationalization for the psychological adjustments, which his inner nature compelled him to make. Perhaps he was only dimly aware of his great debt to Emerson, but Transcendentalism, like a religion, opened up a new life for Walt Whitman."[27] And the light in which Whitman regarded the writings of the man whom he had once with genuine feeling called "Master," aware of his "great debt" to him (though he later found it advantageous or gratifying to deny it) is unmistakably shown in these observations "written as note to a magazine article, date May 1847":

> The superiority of Emerson's writings is in their character—they mean something. He may be obscure, but he is certain. . . . He has what none else has; he does what none else does. He pierces the crusts that envelope the secrets of life. He joins on equal terms the few great sages and original seers. . . . No teacher or poet of old times or modern times has made a better report of manly and womanly qualities, heroism, chastity, temperance, friendship, fortitude. . . . His words shed light to the best souls; they do not admit of argument. . . . A few among men (soon perhaps to become many) will enter into Emerson's meanings: by these he will be well-beloved. The flippant writer, the orthodox critic, the numbers of good or indifferent imitators, will not comprehend him; to them he will indeed be a transcendentalist, a writer of sunbeams and moonbeams, a strange and unapproachable person.[28]

Bucke editorially notes that the passage "to judge by paper and writing goes back to early fifties," and that "W[hitman] (it would seem) knew Emerson pretty well in those days."[29] The words

"strange and unapproachable person" appear to have led Bucke
into assuming a personal acquaintance between Emerson and Whitman in the early fifties. There is no evidence of a meeting between
the two before 1855, when Emerson had "his first personal visit
and two hours with"[30] Whitman in Brooklyn, or of any correspondence prior to Whitman's sending a copy of his first edition
to Emerson. And Emerson's famous congratulatory reply has all
the look of a letter to a perfect stranger. However, from the nature
of those observations, one can see that Whitman knew Emerson's
writings more than "pretty well" in those early days,[31] and was
not one of those to whom Emerson was "a writer of sunbeams and
moonbeams." There is in them more than a reviewer's assessment;
there is a note of personal ardor, of one who has entered "into
Emerson's meanings" and recognized the "great sage" who "pierces
the crusts that envelope the secrets of life."

A good deal of the light Emerson "shed . . . to the best souls,"
of whom Whitman was definitely one, was gathered in the Orient,
especially India, though on the solitary strength of one assumption—that Emerson had not read the *Bhagavadgita* till 1845—
Carpenter[32] concludes that Emerson's fundamental ideas, such as,
for instance, the Over-soul, were all his own, or the product of
Neoplatonic thought. But Emerson, as Carpenter's own list in an
appendix shows, had read the *Mahabharata* in 1830, the *Vedas* in
1839, the *Laws of Menu* in 1834 and 1838, and Sir William Jones
in 1822, 1838, and 1840, to mention only a few of his Indian
studies before the publication of the *Essays* or the *Dial*.

Catching in Emerson, as he did beyond doubt, a direction both
for his perturbed mind and his unborn poetry, Whitman could
hardly have escaped the Oriental enthusiasm of Emerson. His
readings in the *Dial*, which illustrated in its pages the new and
fascinating vein of thought and feeling the Transcendentalists of
New England had created with their deep passion for Oriental
writings, must certainly have strengthened and extended it.

It is not hard to conceive how in those formative years of his
career when the great poetic dream had shaped itself in his mind,
Whitman turned not only to philosophy as the key to his ambition, but to Oriental philosophy. All great poets are teachers,
men who join "on equal terms the few great sages and original
seers." If he aspired to be the great poet of America, he had to be

an American Vates, one who created a poetry that would bring philosophy home to American readers. Emerson had said: "But genius was religious."[33] And from his example and that of the other Transcendentalists, Whitman must have realized in which direction his own quest lay.

2

THE QUEST

IF THUS WITH A CLEARLY FORMULATED LITERARY PROGRAMME TO "enter into the thoughts of the different theological faiths," Whitman started the studies that would be "a rich investment" for his "religious canticles,"[34] and under the stimulation of his readings in the Transcendental *Dial* developed an Oriental direction for them, the source of his information was not necessarily confined to the *Dial* and the few literary periodicals from which, as we have seen, he collected some of his early knowledge of Eastern philosophical thought. That his readings on India captured his imagination is sufficiently indicated by the underscoring and annotating done to the passages of the articles he possessed. In many of the critical notices he read there were suggestions for further reading to satisfy a stronger interest in the philosophical works of India. They all mentioned the principal works available in translation in America during those years. With his appetite whetted by these scattered readings, Whitman could not have resisted the obvious opportunities to intensify his Oriental knowledge. And the libraries of the city of New York, where (according to his own brother's and others' testimony already mentioned) he spent "a good many hours," possessed not only the books recommended by the periodicals, but a great deal of other material on India.

Though we know from many witnesses that Whitman used to "loaf in libraries," we do not have a precise knowledge of which libraries he was usually in the habit of visiting during his frequent trips to New York. "Mannahatta" had quite a few libraries in

126

those days, but if we ignore the private and specialized ones, the most important and popular were the Astor, the Mercantile Library Association, and the New York Society Libraries, all three of which had abundant Indian material during the 1840s and 1850s. Of these, the New York Society Library, the oldest, was founded in 1700 (then called Public Library), and passing through a number of changes in name and location, was finally in 1836 moved to the corner of Broadway and Leonard Street.[35] Broadway being one of Whitman's favorite haunts in New York, it is possible that he visited this library more often than the others. According to its 1850 catalogue, which follows the 1838 one, the Society Library had the following books and journals on India.[36]

The *Bhagvat-Geeta,* translated by Charles Wilkins, 1785. (Catalogue p. 477)

The *Heetopades of Veeshnoo Sarma,* translated by Charles Wilkins, 1787. (p. 477)

Calidasa's *Cloud Messenger* from Sanskrit, translated by H. H. Wilson, 1814.

Asiatic Researches: or Transactions of the Society Instituted in Bengal for Enquiring into the History, Antiquity, the Arts and Sciences and Literature of Asia; of the years 1798–1818. (p. 611)

Sir William Jones's *Works,* 6 vols., 1799. (p. 234)

Thomas Maurice's *Indian Antiquities,* 7 vols., 1800. (p. 287)

Thomas Maurice's *History of Hindoostan,* 2 vols., 1795. (p. 287)

H. T. Colebrooke's *Digest of Hindoo Laws.*

The Asiatic Journal, 1824–1836.

The Asiatic Annual Register, 1799–1805; and several other books on the history of India.

The Mercantile Association Library was incorporated in 1820, and as early as 1830 it possessed 40,000 volumes housed in Clinton Hall on Nassau and Beekman Streets. Its 1837 catalogue, among a large number of historical sketches, travel accounts, and the like, lists the following scholarly works on India:

Rev. W. Ward's *A View of the History, Literature, Religion and Manners of the Hindoos,* 2 vols., (Hartford, 1826). (p. 29 of catalogue)

Issac P. Cory's *Ancient Fragments of the Phoenician, Chaldean, Egyptian, Tyrian, Charthagian, Indian, and Other writings,*

and an Inquiry into the Philosophy and Trinity of the Ancients,
London, 1832. (p. 45)
Sir William Jones's *Works,* 13 vols., London, 1807. (p. 264)
Maurice's *Indian Antiquities.* (p. 70)
Asiatic Researches ... 7 vols., London, 1811. (p. 113)
Oriental Collections of Ouseley. (p. 70)
   An 1840 supplementary catalogue records the addition, among
other volumes, of:
Hindoos: an Account of the Origin and Antiquity of the Hindoos,
   their Religion, Character, Manners, Customs, Literature, etc.
   2 vols., (Library of Entertaining knowledge), London, 1835.
   (p. 18)
   The Astor Library, established in 1849, developed a regular
Oriental section by 1851. The first set of Oriental books was pur-
chased in Europe, and brought home toward the end of December
1851. Although the Library came to be in regular public service
in its own building after 1 February 1854, the volumes were kept
open for "limited" public use till then in 32 Bond Street. Its 1854
catalogue of books "relating to the Languages and Literature of
Asia, Africa, and the Oceanic Islands," lists over two hundred
items on India, covering a comprehensive area of subjects like
history, travel, philology, and grammar, and including original
works and translations, and a considerable number of scholarly
books in English as well as German and French. Reducing the immense inventory to only such items as are in English and deal
with the philosophy, religion, and literature of India, and as could
constitute a sufficient source for a satisfying knowledge of Indian
thought, we have the following:
Ramayana of Valmeeki, translated from the original Sanskrit,
   with explanatory notes, by William Carey and Joshua Marshman, Vol. I, containing the First Book, London, 1808. (p. 293)
Bhagvat Geeta ... translated by Charles Wilkins, 1785. (p. 295)
Vishnu Purana, a system of Hindu Mythology, translated from the
   Sanskrit by H. H. Wilson, London, 1840. (p. 297)
Megha Doota—or Cloud Messenger: a poem in the Sanskrit
   language. By Kalidasa—translated into English verse with notes
   and illustrations, by H. H. Wilson, 2nd edition, London, 1843.

Selected Specimens of the Theatre of the Hindus, translated from the original Sanskrit by Horace Hayman Wilson, 2nd edition, 1–2, London, 1835. (p. 297)

Sacontala: or the Fatal Ring, an Indian drama by Calidas—translated from the original Sanskrit and Pracrit [Sir William Jones], London, 1792.

Heetopades of Veeshnoo-Sarma, in a series of connected fables, interspersed with moral, prudential and political maxims; translated from an ancient manuscript in the Sanskrit language—with explanatory notes, by Charles Wilkins, Bath, 1787. (p. 299)

Hitopadesá ... By Francis Johnson, London, 1847. (p. 299)

Hitopadesha ... with the Bengali and the English translations revised—Edited by Lakshami Narayan Nyalankar, Calcutta, 1830. (p. 299)

Sankhya Karika or Memorial Verses on the Sankhya philosophy by Iswara Krishna; translated from the Sanskrit by Colebrooke— Also the Bhashya or Commentary of Gaurapada, translated and illustrated by an original comment by H. H. Wilson, (Orient Trans. Fund) Oxford, 1837. (p. 300)

Manava-Dherma-Sastra; or the Institutes of Menu. Edited by Graves Chamney Haughton, Vol. I Sanskrit Text; Vol. II English Translation, 1–2, London, 1825.

Rig-Veda-Samhita, the Sacred Hymns of the Brahmins, together with the Commentary of Sayanacharya. Edited by Dr. Max Mueller, London, 1849, 2 vols. [with Introduction and prefaces in English]. (p. 291)

Translations of the Samhita of Sama Veda by J. Stevenson, (Orient Trans. Fund) London, 1841. (p. 292)

Translations of Several Principal Books, Passages, and Texts of the Veds, and of some controversial works on Brahmanical theology—by Raja Rammohun Roy, London, 1842. (p. 292)

Among scholarly accounts or critical dissertations:

Historical Sketch of Sanskrit Literature, with copious Bibliographical Notices of Sanskrit Works and translations from the German of Adelung, with numerous additions and corrections, Oxford, 1832.

Thomas Maurice: *Indian Antiquities.*

John Crawfurd: *Sketches* chiefly relating to the History, Religion,

Learning and Manners of the Hindoos, 2 vols., London, 1792.

Rev. W. Ward: *A View of . . . the Hindoos,* 3rd edition, 1–4, London, 1817–1820.

I. P. Cory: *Ancient Fragments.*

Sir William Jones: *Works,* London, 1799, 6 vols.; Supplemental volumes, London, 1801, 2 vols.

Astor had the publications of almost every society conducting Oriental researches, including those in Germany and France. Among the English, the chief ones are:[37]

Journal of the American Oriental Society, Boston and New York, Vols. 1–4, 1842–1854.

Asiatic Researches . . . 1799–1811.

Transactions of the Royal Asiatic Society of Great Britain and Ireland, London, 1827–1835, 3 vols.

Journal of the R.A.S., 1834–1852.

Journal of the Asiatic Society of Bengal from its commencement to 1843, Calcutta, 13 vols., 1832–43.

New Asiatic Miscellany—consisting of original essays, transactions, and fugitive pieces, Calcutta, 1789, 2 vols.

Oriental Collections . . . by Ouseley, London, 1797–98, 2 vols.

Oriental Translations Fund: Collection of the Publications of, London, 1829–1850.

Even the abridged list given above shows that for any one inquiring after a deep understanding of the faith of "a Hindoo, worshipping Brahma," the libraries of New York in the 1840s and 1850s offered adequate facilities. Whitman's visits to any of these libraries cannot be established on any kind of documentary evidence, because neither the Mercantile nor the Society Library has maintained records of its users, and the only records of the Astor Library are of the years after 1859.[38] It is equally difficult to be precise in the matter of dates. But the testimony of his brother and his friend and his own "official" declaration help us to fix the period of his visits to the libraries generally in the years of his preparation for *Leaves of Grass.* As for his reading any of the books or journals in those libraries, we are again thrown back upon indirect evidence, the "faint clews," that a comparative analysis throws up in the nature of parallels and echoes, often too many and too precise to be accidental. But the fact that almost every one of his fundamental ideas, as well as the scattered thoughts of his notes, can be traced to one or the other of these works listed above, supports the probability of his having read them.

One of the difficulties in discovering the tracks of his thoughts is the vastness and variety of the material available to him among these libraries in the 1840s. There were the original Indian works themselves in translation; a considerable number of scholarly accounts of the philosophy, religion, and literature of the Hindus, many containing extracts from the original works; and then the immense number of journals and transactions publishing the researches conducted by learned societies. From any one of these three different sources an intelligent American reader could gather a powerful understanding of Indian philosophy. Furthermore, the same text or the same idea or set of thoughts, often the same phrase, could be found in more than one of these sources. Therefore it is generally impossible to pin down a particular idea or thought of Whitman to any one of these books and exclude the possibility of his having come upon it in the pages of another. The only certainty is that Whitman found the knowledge of India he was seeking among these books, and that these books in various different ways presented the entire content of Indian philosophical thought.

A large part of the difficulty in establishing an accurate picture of his reading in these books is caused by two circumstances: first, the notebooks of those years, which would certainly have, however dimly, reflected his reading, are not extant, whether by accident or by design. The second is his power of imaginative expansion of a thought, in which lyric increase it often loses its original significance and grows into a meaning all his own, sometimes in strange combinations and relationships. However, with the help that our knowledge of his methods of composition gives us, it is possible to maintain with considerable certainty that a particular book or page was read by Whitman, though part of the thought he gathered from it may have been subsequently affected by, or fused with, thoughts he absorbed from another.

Among the books mentioned above, the most significant for Whitman's knowledge of Indian philosophy are, the *Bhagvat-Geeta, The Vishnu Purana, Sankhya Karika, Manava-Dherma-Sastra* or the *Institutes of Menu, Sama Veda Sanhita,* and Roy's *Translations* in the first section of original works; Sir William

Jones' *Works,* Rev. W. Ward's *View,* and Maurice's *Indian
Antiquities* in the section of scholarly expositions; and the *Asiatic
Researches,* and the *Transactions of the R.A.S.* in the section of
Oriental research publications. Any one of these was sufficient to
educate Whitman in Hindu thought; even the critical accounts
such as Ward's or Jones's, or the *Researches* and the *Transactions,*
contain both original extracts and erudite discussions of Indian
philosophy. And if the volumes of the Astor Library were available only after their arrival in New York on December 24, 1851,
and then only for "limited" use till 1854, the *Bhagvat-Geeta* was
available in the New York Society Library as early as 1838; the
Mercantile had the Reverend W. Ward in 1837; both of them
had Jones's *Works, Asiatic Researches,* and Maurice's *Antiquities*
in the 1840's; and the Mercantile Association acquired the *Transactions* along with Roy's *Translations* sometime after its 1844
catalogue.

3

WHAT IS THE GRASS?

WE MAY BEGIN OUR EXAMINATION OF WHITMAN'S READING among these books with the *Asiatic Researches,* not only because they were available in all three libraries and he could have had access to them very early, but also because the articles he had cut from his favorite periodicals made repeated references to these publications as the source of information on India, and so probably interested Whitman in them. The *Asiatic Researches,* or Trans- actions of the Society instituted in Bengal for inquiring into the history and antiquities, the arts and sciences and literature of Asia, were the principal means by which knowledge of the Orient was first brought to the West. They form the foundation of all the later interest and enthusiasm that Western scholars developed for the East, as well as of a good part of their own scholarship. Representing the dedicated work of brilliant Oriental scholars like Sir William Jones, H. T. Colebrooke, J. D. Paterson, and a host of others, the *Researches* cover a vast range—from the geography and history of the countries of the East to their religious and metaphysical speculations. Through scholarly accounts and discussions, and translations of the hitherto unknown works of those nations, they present an almost exhaustive discovery of Asian achievement in the fields of arts and sciences.

Of the many articles on India that the volumes of *Asiatic Re- searches* carried, particularly noticeable are the following, which, in discussion, extract, and comparative study, deal with the religious and philosophical ideas of the Hindus:

Volume I has a fifty-six page article by Sir William Jones, entitled "On the Gods of Greece, Italy and India," in which he examines, in a comparative survey, the pantheons of the three major civilizations of the early times, the mythologies that formed the background of their theological notions and religious worship, and the parallelism noticeable among their myths and gods. There is also an account of "The Literature of the Hindus" by an Indian scholar, supplemented with a commentary by the President of the Society, Sir W. Jones himself. And there are two "Discourses" "on the Hindus," one by Jones, another by H. T. Colebrooke, the former discussing the nature and quality of Hindu philosophy, the latter, the Hindus and their ways of life.

The third volume has two articles, one "On the Mystical Poetry of the East," by Sir W. Jones, and the other by Lt. Francis Wilford, "On Egypt and the Nile from the Ancient Books of Sanskrit." The first of these presents specimens of Eastern mystic poetry, in the author's own translation, after a penetrating discussion of the nature of mysticism itself, and of its Eastern variety as illustrated in the mystical poetry of the Persians and the Hindus. The famous mystic poem, *Gita-Govinda* of Jayadeva, celebrating the love of Krishna and Radha, accompanies the article. Wilfred's article is a scholarly study of the ancient books, the "Puranas" of India. It runs to an impressive two hundred pages nearly, and, in its elaborate analysis of their contents, examines the myths and fables of the Hindus as well as their religious and philosophical concepts.

Volume 5, in an "advertisement" presents a comparative study of the *Laws* of Menu and of Moses with extracts from both arranged in juxtaposition. It also has a number of very informative articles on Hindu life: H. T. Colebrooke's "Enumeration of Indian Classes"; Wilford's "On the chronology of the Hindus," which is a study of the "Puranas" of India, its only "historical records"; John Bentley's "Remarks on the Principal Aeras and Dates of the Ancient Hindus"; the first of H. T. Colebrooke's three articles "On the Religious Ceremonies of the Hindus, Bra'mens especially"; and the translation of a chapter from one of the Puranas.

The second and the third installments of Colebrooke's exhaustive account of the Hindu ceremonies, with frequent extracts from their scriptures, appear in the seventh volume of the *Researches,* which also has an erudite article "On the Sanskrit and Pracrit Languages" by the same writer.

Volume No. 8 contains J. D. Paterson's researches "On the Origin of Hindu Religion," in which he traces the history of Hindu religious ideas, and studies the gods of Hindu faith and their philosophical background, while attempting a comparison with the gods and myths of Rome and Greece. In the same volume is H. T. Colebrooke's pioneer study of Indian scriptures, "On the Vedas, or the Sacred Writings of the Hindus," which, with extracts from the pieces, analyzes the contents of the *Vedas,* the *Brahmanas,* the *Aranyakas,* and the *Upanishads.*

Whitman's reading in the *Asiatic Researches* is not purely a matter of conjecture, or a sort of theoretical conclusion, based, on the one hand, upon our knowledge of his reading in the libraries of New York and his proven interest in the Orient, and, on the other, upon the availability of the volumes in those libraries, though of course the validity of such a logical assumption cannot be totally disregarded. He had noticed how the periodical writers had used the *Researches* as their own chief source. (Years later, he even declared, "I rejoice at the feeling for Oriental researches and poetry, and hope it will go on."[39]) It would therefore, not be far wide of the mark to suppose that these were the pages to which he first applied himself in his quest for knowledge of "the sublime creeds of different eras."[40] How much of his poring over them entered into his memory or notes, and through what involved transformation, combination, and development and in what relationship with his other readings of the same nature it finally found its place in the pages of his poetry or prose, cannot with precision be stated. But there is no doubt whatever that he read them, and gathered from them considerable material to mold into his own shape later in his writings.

One of Whitman's fundamental ideas—almost the very base of his metaphysics—is the doctrine of "Identity," which to him is a "knit" achieved by "opposite equals"—namely, of sex.[41] The entire creation, for him, is the product of two principles, "two elements fused though antagonistic," and "the Soul of the Universe is the Male and genital master and the impregnating and animating spirit—Physical matter is Female and Mother and waits barren and bloomless, the jets of life from the masculine vigour."[42]

The concept, the sexual symbolism, and the words of this passage have their roots in the pages of the *Asiatic Researches,* as the following extracts will show:

> Yavana is a regular participle form of the root *yu,* to mix; But since *yóni,* or the *female nature,* is also derived from the same root, many *Pandits* insist that Yavanas were so named from their obstinate assertion of a superior influence in the *female* over the *linga,* or male nature, in producing an offspring. . . . They [the Hindus] represent Narayana *moving* (as his name implies) on the waters, in the character of the *first male,* and the *principle* of all nature. . . . The *chaos* is also called PRACRITI, or crude Nature; and the male deity has the name PURUSHA, from whom proceeded *Sacti* or power, which, when it is ascribed to the earth, in contradistinction to the waters, is denominated Áhára Sacti, or, the *power of containing* or conceiving; but that *power,* in its first state, was rather a *tendency* or *aptitude,* and lay dormant or inert until it was excited by the *bija,* or vivifying principle, of the plastick ISWARA. This power, or aptitude, of nature is represented under the symbol of *yóni,* or *bhaga,* while the *animating principle* is expressed by the linga. Both are united by the creative power, BRAHMA; and the yóni has been called the *navel* of Vishnu; not identically, but nearly; for though it is held, in the Védánta, that the Divine Spirit penetrates or pervades all nature, and though the *Sacti* be considered as an emanation from that Spirit, yet the emanation is never wholly detached from its source, and the penetration is never so perfect as to become a total union or identity.[43]

> For my part, I have no doubt that *Iswara* and *Isi* of the Hindus . . . mean, I conceive, the *Powers of Nature* considered as Male and Female.[44]

> . . . This power and matter, are two distinct and co-existent principles in nature; the one agent, the other patient; the one *male,* the other *female;* and . . . creation was the effect of the mystical union of these principles.[45]

In *The Vishnu Purana* and Ward's *View,* which we shall notice later on, the same concept is presented in the discussion of the Hindu theory of creation:

The "mother," or literally, "the womb of the world" (Jagad-yóni) means "the passive agent in creation," operated on or influenced by the active will of the creator.[46]

In conformity with these ideas, God is spoken of by the Hindoo sages as the active power, and matter as passive in the work of creation, and hence the terms male (purusha) and female (prakriti) are frequently found in their writings: "God, when the active and passive powers are united, possesses form" (Agastya, p. 246). "The supreme cause exists in two parts like the seed of the cicer arietinum, which represents the active and passive powers of nature" (Vishnu, p. 249). "In creation the active power directed the passive" (Agastya, p. 247).[47]

And, as we have noticed in the periodical article, there are passages in the *Laws of Menu* expounding the same idea.

Wilford's long article has all the appearance of having supplied many more suggestions. It is likely that Whitman's insistence upon the importance of the physical principle, or body, as equal to that of the spiritual, or soul, and his mystical recognition of his own consanguinity with the phenomena of nature, as well as certain expressions of his, like "the Universal Mother," had their first dim sprouts in the following passages in which Wilford discusses some Hindu notions.

They [the Hindus] make frequent hómas, or oblations, to fire and perform acts of worship to the sun, the stars, and the powers of Nature, which they consider as *múrtis* or images,[48] the same in kind with ourselves, but transcendently higher in degree. The Moon is also a great object of their adoration; for, though they consider the Sun and Earth as the two grand objects in the system of the universe, yet they know their reciprocal action to be greatly affected by the influence of the lunar orb . . . and seem even to have an idea of *attraction* through the whole extent of nature. . . . Elemental fire was the great and powerful deity whose influence contributed chiefly toward the generation and perfection of natural bodies: while the ocean . . . afforded the nutriment that was necessary; and the *Earth* was the vase, or capacious receptacle, in which the grand operation was performed; hence ORPHEUS described the Earth as the Universal Mother: and that is the true meaning of the *Sanskrit* word *Ambá*. Such is the system of the *Hindus* who admit an equal concurrence of the two principles [male and female].[49]

There is a legend in the *Servarasa* of which the figurative meaning is more obvious. . . . This divine pair [Sati, and Mahádéva, who "at the beginning of the fourth Veda . . . is described as *Mahapurusha* or the Great Male,"] had once a dispute on the compartive influence of the sexes in producing animated beings and each resolved, by mutual agreement to create apart a new race of men. The race produced by Mahádéva . . . devoted themselves exclusively to the worship of the male deity. . . . PARVATI . . . created a multitude . . . who adored the female power only. [The latter defeated the former, and Mahádéva in anger drove them away; they were the Yavanas.] . . . The tale . . . was invented to establish that the good shape, strength and courage of animals depend upon the superior influence of the female parent. . . . There is a sect of Hindus . . . who, attempting to reconcile the systems, tell us . . . that PARVATI and MAHADEVA found their concurrence essential to the perfection of their offspring.[50]

I wonder if the legend inspired the following thoughts that Whitman records in his 1847 notebook:

When I see where the east is greater than the west,—where the sound man's part of the child is greater than the sound woman's part—or where a father is more needful than a mother to produce me—then I guess I shall see how Spirit is greater than matter.[51]

In the course of his analysis of Hindu beliefs and concepts, Wilford presents a brief exposition of the Vedanta notion of God, and of the Universe as Divine Emanation.

It f[ol]lows from the principal tenet of the Vedantís, that the only being, which has absolute and real existence, is the Divine Spirit, infinitely wise, infinitely benign, and infinitely powerful, expanded through the universe: not merely as the *soul of the world,* but as the *provident ruler of it;* sending forth rays or emanations from his essence, which are the pure vital souls of all animated creatures, whether *moveable* or *immovable;* that is, (as we should express ourselves) both *animals* and *vegetables,* and which he calls back to himself, according to certain laws established by this unlimited wisdom. . . .[52]

There is one very strong proof of Whitman's reading the *Asiatic Researches*. One of his most beautiful poems is "Eidólons," which, dealing in a full treatment with a theme that is the very essence of the philosophy suffused through the length and breadth of his poetry—namely, the "resistless gravitation of spiritual law" in all beings—asserts "the spiritual reality of each individual self."[53] This lovely poem was first published in 1876, but the idea is not of the later years; it is there in essence in the 1855 poems. As Miller observes, "In 'Eidólons' one finds re-enacted on a minor scale the drama of the whole of *Leaves of Grass*."[54]

Kennedy, in his "elucidations and analyses of difficult poems in 'Leaves of Grass,'" examines the source for the "germ-idea" of this poem, and makes the following remarks:

> If we inquire where Walt Whitman got the germ-idea of his wonderful Eidólon poem, we shall soon discover that he did *not* get it from the ancients or from Bacon. Epicurus, Empedocles, Democritus, Lucretius, held that all objects are continually giving off emanations, effluxes (called eidóla, or απορροίαι), from their surfaces, by means of which we are enabled to apprehend their colors and other properties. Then from the old idea of ghosts wrapped up in the word *eidóla* came the meaning of *delusions* which is what Bacon means by his "idols." Shakespeare and other Elizabethans use the word *idea* as meaning image, idea and *eidólon* having a common root, and with Plato ideai were the archetypal models, or images, of which created things are the imperfect archetypes. Still we are no nearer to Whitman's model. The fact is that he is original in his application of the term *eidólon* to the class of ideas he connects with it. But he is certainly not original in the main thought of the poem. In reading it I at once recalled the work by Balfour Stewart and P. G. Tait, The Unseen Universe. This book was published in 1875. I remember the sensation. I read it, while in college, with eager interest. Whitman's Eidólons was written just about this time, and published in 1876. There can be little doubt that he got his idea for the poem from that remarkable and curious book, the central idea of which is this: *"Thought conceived to affect the matter of another universe simultaneously with this may explain a future state."* . . . But Whitman takes the idea and expands it, applying it in detail, item by item, in a most startling and powerful manner. . . .

Kennedy also "elucidates" the central idea of the poem thus:

> But Whitman (following out German thought) gives it a
> wider application: he conceives of the great globes of space and
> all objects on them as being but emanations, or phantoms, pro-
> jected by the Soul, the great eidólon. Eidólons are the real
> substratum underneath all objects. The whole living, working
> universe is forging but eternal eidólons, or souls, the real en-
> tities. The visible world is only appearance. . . .[55]

Whether the word "eidólon" also came from the book *The
Unseen Universe,* Kennedy does not inquire. But the fact is that
the term "eidólon" never occurs in the book, even in the Greek
quotations, of which there are quite a few. Also although the
central idea of the book is that "the things which are seen are
temporal, but the things which are not seen are eternal," and that
there is a *"close* and vital union" between the two universes of
the Seen and the Unseen, nowhere is mentioned the idea of souls
being eidólons, or emanations of God.[56] From the point of view
of time, however, Kennedy's contention that Whitman got the
idea from *The Unseen Universe* looks plausible. But then, as he
himself notices, "the basic thought of Eidólons may also be found
in Song of Prudence, Unnamed Lands and Assurances," and
"Song of Prudence" was published in 1856, "Unnamed Lands" in
1860, and "Assurances" in 1856, though the word "eidólon" is not
used in any one of them. The actual source of both the word and
the thought in fact is a page in the *Asiatic Researches.*

In his account of the Hindu practice of worshiping "the sun, the
stars, and the powers of nature" as emanations of the Supreme
Spirit, Wilford offers an explanation of it in terms of the underlying Vedanta concept, with these words:

> "PRITHVI, or *Earth,* and RAVI, the *Sun* are severally
> *trimúrtis,* or forms of the three great powers acting jointly
> and separately, but with different natures and energies; and by
> their mutual action, excite and expand the rudiments of material
> substances. The word *múrti* or form, is exactly synonymous with
> εἴδωλον; and, in a secondary sense, means an image: but in its
> primary acceptance it denotes any *shape* or *appearance* assumed
> by a celestial being. Our *vital souls* are, according to the Védanta,

no more than images, or εἴδωλα, of the *Supreme Spirit;* and Homer places the *idol* of HERCULES in Elysium with other deceased heroes, though the God himself was at the same time enjoying bliss in the heavenly mansions. Such a *múrti,* say the Hindus, can by no means affect with any sensation, either pleasing or painful, the being from which it emanated, though it may give pleasure or pain to collateral emanations from the same source; hence they offer no sacrifices to the Supreme Essence, of which our own souls are *images,* but adore him with silent meditation.[57]

If the Vedanta regards the Earth, the Sun, the stars, and "our vital souls" as *"múrtis,"* or "images," or "eidólons," so did Whitman in these stanzas from "Eidólons":

    Exalté, rapt, ecstatic,
The visible but their womb of birth,
Of orbic tendencies to shape and shape and shape,
    The mighty earth-eidólon.

    All space, all time,
(The stars, the terrible perturbations of the suns,
Swelling, collapsing, ending, serving their longer, shorter use,)
    Filled with eidolons only.
. . . .
    And thee my soul,
Joys, ceaseless exercises, exaltations,
Thy yearning amply fed at last, prepared to meet,
    Thy mates, eidolons.

    Thy body permanent,
The body lurking there within thy body,
The only purport of the form thou art, the real I myself,
    An image, an eidólon.

The precise correspondence noticeable between Whitman's lines and the Vedanta concept of the pages of *Researches* leaves no doubt about his gathering both the term and the idea from here, though, in keeping with his practice of not using suggestive foreign words, he refrained from the use of the term in the earlier poems. He must assuredly have made notes of his reading in the *Researches,* considering the time element, and later destroyed them, or written the poem, in a tentative form at least, much earlier than he actually published it.

Among the many wonders that *Leaves of Grass* has been to its readers and critics, its title has come in for its share of puzzlement as well as admiration, not entirely without reason. "The leaves growing out of Whitman's title," said Esther Shephard, "are strange and fanciful, and they are indeed 'leaves of anything but grass,' but the title *Leaves of Grass,* is nevertheless one of the happiest inspirations of Whitman's genius and we are glad that he was stubborn enough to retain it."[58] The "official portrait" of Whitman also took care to draw the reader's attention to it. "In examining this book," wrote Bucke, "the first thing that presents itself for remark is its name, by no means the least significant part. It would indeed be impossible to select for the volume a more perfect title. Properly understood, the words express what the book contains and is. Like the grass, while old as creation, it is modern, fresh, universal, spontaneous, not following forms, taking its own form, perfectly free and unconstrained, common as the commonest things, yet its meaning inexhaustible by the greatest intellect, full of life itself and capable of entering into and nourishing other lives, growing in the sunshine (i.e. in the full broad light of science) perfectly open and simple; yet having meanings underneath. . . ."[59] If we subtract a few words that spring from a slightly excessive personal warmth, the observation is substantially correct, though one cannot help mischievously wondering how, apart from our having to explain the prominent grass imagery in the poems in a less comprehensive way, any other title, like "Drops of Rain," or "Waves of the Sea," or "Notes of the Air," or even "Leaves of the Sky," or "Leaves of the Earth," would have been a less "perfect" one. Probably with no less zeal would the volume have been accepted and with no less meaningfulness explained in terms of the title. However, there is no denying that the grass is the heart of the matter of the book, and the use of it in the naming of it is not only appropriate but almost an aesthetic necessity. And the grass is so central to the meaning of the poems, being so much present in them both symbolically and materially, that it is possible that the notion of such a title preceded the composition of the poems. Perhaps in the ultimate analysis, it is not the title of the book but the use of the grass in the book that is "one of the happiest inspirations of Whitman's genius."

Whitman's own satisfaction with the title is reported by Traubel to whom he said:

> I am well satisfied with my success with titles—with Leaves of Grass for instance, though some of my friends themselves rather kicked against it at the start—particularly the literary hair-splitters, who rejected it as a species of folly. 'Leaves of Grass,' they said: 'there are no *leaves* of grass; there are *spears* of grass: that's your word, Walt Whitman: spears, spears: But *Spears* of Grass would not have been the same to me. Etymologically, *leaves* is correct—scientific men use it so. I stuck to leaves, leaves, leaves, until it was able to take care of itself.[60]

Unlike the literary hair-splitters among Whitman's friends, the critics have been as much satisfied as he was with the fitness and significance of the title, which has been "able to take care of itself" in their midst. Yet, many have been intrigued by it—by the words "grass" and "leaves," by the strange combination of the two words; by the use of it in the book, and by the possible source for it.

According to Roger Asselineau,[61] the grass of the title is "grass, the anonymous mass of herbacious plant," and Whitman has chosen it "because it symbolizes for him the universal presence of life, not only in space, but also in time, even beyond death"; and he has "purposely used the word 'leaf' in its botanical sense." He adds: "thus, *Leaves of Grass* represents the universal brotherhood of all living things permeated in all places and times by the same immortal burning force. The title admirably characterizes this book and fairly sums up one of its essential themes, the eternal cycle of life." And, so far as the title is concerned, the word "Leaves" may have been borrowed from Mrs. Parson's *Fern Leaves from Fanny's Portfolio* from which Whitman probably borrowed the idea of the binding of his first edition, too.[62]

This is fairly the reaction of most critics that have remarked upon the name of Whitman's book, except for Furness, who has no such reverence for the profound philosophical involvements of the title. In what is so far the most elaborate analysis of the question, he says:

> Both in its title and style of binding, *Leaves of Grass* seems to me to show the result of contemporary influences. One of these was the example furnished by "Fanny Fern." . . . May not *Fern Leaves* have suggested *Leaves of Grass*? . . .
>
> The title of Whitman's poems probably grew out of a general trend of the times, which may have influenced Fanny Fern herself. "Leaves" in literary titles of the 40's and 50's were rampant. . . .
>
> So much for the "Leaves;" now, why leaves "of grass"? Perhaps, Walt, the handy-man about Brooklyn printshops, was simply using the normal lingo of printer's devils, familiar to him since early boyhood. "Grass," in printer's slang, means a person who does casual work around the shop, and applies as well to the work such a person does. . . . May not Whitman, with his customary interest in the language of the "divine average" man, have adopted this ironical phrase? This might account for the use of the word *grass* in so unusual a connection as *Leaves of Grass*.
>
> There has also been much conjecture about the uncommon combination of "leaves," rather than "blades," with the word "grass." Leaves, in this case, might have been used literally, for printers are accustomed to handling their paper in the form of "leaves," rather than pages; and Whitman's poems, rolling off the press . . . were actually "leaves" of "grass," printed sheets of poetic composition probably regarded by the shop as effusions of dubious merit.[63]

The reasoning is very ingenious, but for two reasons one has to agree with Allen, who regards the explanation as unconvincing.[64] One objection to it has been advanced by Charles M. Adams, who, questioning the validity of such an assumption of the meaning of the word "grass," asks if anywhere in his poetry Whitman has used the word in the connotation of Furness.[65] The second is the extraordinary esteem in which Whitman held himself and his work.

Even since what might be called thought, or the budding of

thought, fairly began in my youthful mind, I had a desire to attempt some worthy record of that entire faith and acceptance ("to justify the ways of God to man" is Milton's well-known and ambitious phrase) which is the foundation of moral America.

No one will get at my verses who insists upon seeing them as a literary performance. . . . I hope to go on record for something different—something better, if I may dare say so.[66]

I claim everything for religion. . . . Yet I have been called irreligious, an infidel . . . as if I could have written a word of the Leaves without its religious root-ground.[67]

The basis on which the work stands will probably finally be discovered and agreed to be the Religious basis—the reference of every possible event to a divine purpose, and unfolding.[68]

What name? Religious Canticles. These perhaps ought to be the *brain*[,] the *living spirit* (elusive, indescribable, indefinite) of all the "Leaves of Grass."

Hymns of ecstasy and religious fervor.[69]

It is true that these statements asserting the religious nature of his poems were made in retrospect, years after the publication of the first edition, and are appreciably exaggerated. Yet some of his early notes, like the one quoted elsewhere, referring to his preliminary plans, suggest that he was aware at the time of publishing the 1855 poems that in them "one deep purpose underlay others— and that [was] the religious purpose."[70] And the Preface, which unfolds the exalted notion he held of a poet, rules out the faintest possibility of his "ironically" looking upon himself as "a person who does casual work around the shop," or upon his poems "as effusions of dubious merit."

It is not, as has been suggested, the word "leaves" or the word "grass," but the use of grass, consciously and purposefully in its symbolic significance in the poems, that offers the true clue to the title. Whitman's imaginative interest in the grass, though not in all its subsequent full-blooded philosophical significance, is already seen in the early notebook of 1847:

Different objects which decay, and by the chemistry of nature,
their bodies are [blank] into spears of grass.
Bring all the art and science of the world, and baffle and
humble it with one spear of grass.[71]

But it is only a "spear" of grass, though a little later, in an experimental verse passage, it becomes a "leaf."

And saw the journey-work of suns and systems of suns,
And that a leaf of grass is not less than they. . . .[72]

In another note, apparently of the pre-verse-experimentation
days, his wonder at the grass is again expressed:

. . . superb wonder of a blade of grass growing up green and
crispy from the ground . . .[73]

This deep interest in the grass, Asselineau suggests,[74] may
probably have been the result of his early reading of Carlyle's
Heroes and Hero-Worship, where this line occurs:

To us also, through every star, through every blade of grass,
is not a God made visible, if we will open our minds and eyes?

And his use of the word "leaves" with reference to a human
being, as in his regarding his poems as "leaves" of himself, is in
evidence again in another of his early notebooks:

There is a quality in some persons which ignores and fades
away the [blank] around the hearts of all the people they meet—
To them they respond perhaps for the first time in their lives—
now they have ease. . . . They can be themselves—they can expose their secret failings and crimes—Most people that come
to them are formal or good or eminent—are repugnant to them—
They close up their leaves to them.[75]

All this shows that Whitman's interest in "grass" and his conception of a man as a book of "leaves" are already formed before
the poems of the first edition were shaped for the press. Even the
unusual combination "leaf of grass" is already made, whether, as

he claimed, from a knowledge of the scientists' etymologically correct use of it, or not. Therefore it seems as if the use of the title had nothing to borrow from the "general trend of times," but that it grew from within, from the impulses that operated and shaped the inner world of his own thoughts and poems. And the basic suggestion that started the initial train of thought that later ended in the title as well as the phrase "leaves of grass" appears to have come to Whitman from the pages of *Asiatic Researches*.

In H. T. Colebrooke's essays "On the Religious Ceremonies of the Hindus and of the Bra'mens especially," a study based upon the *Laws of Menu*, the dictates of the *Vedas*, and other holy writings, occur the following descriptions:

> The priest then takes up two leaves of *cusa* grass, and with another blade of the same grass, cuts off the length of a span, saying "Pure leaves! be sacred to VISHNÚ;" and throws them into a vessel of copper or other metal. Again he takes two leaves of grass. . . . He sprinkles both the leaves with water, and throws them away . . . and then concludes the ceremony of hallowing butter; during the course of which, while he holds the leaves of grass in both hands, he recites this prayer, "May the divine generator (VISHNU) purify thee by means of (this) faultless pure leaf; and may the sun do so by means of (his) rays of light! be this oblation efficacious!"

> With blades of *cusa* grass held in his right hand, he must strew leaves of the same grass on three sides of the fire. . . .[76]

> The bride's father presents to him a cushion made of twenty leaves of *cusa* grass, holding it up with both hands. . . . The bridegroom . . . taking it . . . recites the following prayer: "May those plants over which Soma presides, and which are variously dispersed in the earth, incessantly grant me happiness."

> The bride offers the oblations of rice mixed with leaves of Sami [grass] . . . letting fall the offerings on the fire.[77]

It seems more than probable that Whitman got not only his "uncommon combination" of leaves of grass here, but even his

profound fascination with grass. His poetic sense of the "sacredness" of "the anonymous mass of herbacious plant" might easily
have been the result of the religious sacredness of it in the Hindu
world, of which again other articles in the *Researches,* as well as
all the other books on India, like Jones's, Ward's and Maurice's,
speak in their accounts of Hindu practices. In his discourse "On
the Origin and Family of Nations," for instance, Sir William
Jones explains the holiness that grass has for the Hindus:

> . . . We know that the name (Cush) is venerated in the high-
> est degree; and given to a sacred grass, described as *Poa* by
> KOENIG, which is used with a thousand ceremonies in the
> oblations to fire, ordained by MENU to form the sacrificial
> zone of the Bráhmans, and solemnly declared in the Véda to
> have sprung soon after the *deluge,* whence the *Pauránicks* con-
> sider it as the *bristly hair of the boar* which supported the globe
> [in one of Vishnu's avatars].[78]

In another essay, called "Botanical Observations on Select Indian Plants," Jones says again:

> Every lawbook, and almost every poem in Sanskrit contains
> frequent allusions to the holiness of this plant [cusa]. . . . Some
> of the leaves taper to a most acute evanescent point; whence the
> *Pandits* often say of a very sharp-minded man, that his intellects
> are *acute as the point of* a Cusa-leaf.[79]

Whelpley's article, noticed earlier, also referred to the sacredness of the Cusa grass, and another note in the *Asiatic Researches*
explained:

> CUS'HA; pronounced more correctly cusá with a palatal *s;*
> a grass held sacred by the Bráhmens from time immemorial. . . .[80]

There is, as we shall observe later on, a good deal of the Hindu
"Yogi" in the prophetic personality Whitman assumed for his
poetic activity. But at the moment one may notice how he resembles the Brahmin priest oblating the "pure leaves . . . sacred to
Vishnu" when he offers "the bouquets of the incomparable feuillage of these States," saying,

Whoever you are! how can I but offer you divine leaves, that
you also be eligible as I am?[81]

Though the words, "rapt and austere in the woods, a gymnosophist," of section 43 of "Song of Myself" came from "Indian
Epic Poetry," two earlier phrases of the same section, "honouring
the gods . . . saluting the sun," apparently echo the description of
those ceremonies in Colebrooke's account:

> Having concluded this ceremony, and walked in a round
> beginning the south, and saluted the sun . . . he [the priest]
> should sit down and spread the *cusa* grass before him . . . he
> should invoke the gods. . . .[82]

Whitman's habit of calling his verses his "leaves" may have taken
another hint from the article "On the Literature of the Hindus,"
where these lines occur:[83]

> [Hence] the verses of them (Vedas) are said in the Gita to
> be the *leaves* of that holy tree to which the Almighty is com-
> pared.
> The wise have called the Incorruptible One an Aswattha,
> with its roots above and its branches below; the leaves of which
> are the sacred measures. He who knows the tree knows the
> Vedas.

What Whitman did with the other pages of *Asiatic Researches*
is hard to fix with any definiteness. That in the wide ground they
covered and the scholarship with which they treated it they were
capable of giving both a comprehensive picture of India and a
specific knowledge of its philosophical ideas is clear from the list of
articles supplied above. So far, our extracts from the *Researches*
have been of such passages as were, at least among the books on
India in the libraries of New York, found only in them and not
in others, and therefore with some assurance it could be suggested
that Whitman must have got those ideas from them. The rest of
the pages of *Researches* have information to be found equally in the
other books, and so we enter here into a zone of relative uncertainty. However, one or two very striking passages from some of
the other articles that might have affected Whitman's thinking may
be given brief attention.

H. T. Colebrooke's exhaustive survey of "the Vedas or the Sacred Writings of the Hindus," in the course of its exposition of the Vedic and the Upanishadic thought, frequently presents extracts from all the "sacred writings." One such extract is: "the Song of 'Vach,' daughter of Ambhrina, in praise of herself as the supreme and universal soul. Vach, it should be remembered, signifies speech; and she is the active power of Brahmá, proceeding from him." Here is the song, abridged:

> I uphold both the sun and the ocean. . . . the firmament . . . and fire. . . . I support the moon. . . . I grant wealth to the honest votary. . . . Me, who am the queen . . . first of such as merit worship, the gods render, universally, present everywhere, and pervader of all beings. . . . Hear then the faith, which I pronounce. Even I declare this self, who is worshipped by gods and men: I make strong whom I choose; I make him *Brahmá,* holy, and wise. . . . I pervade heaven and earth . . . my origin is in the midst of the ocean; and, therefore, do I pervade all beings, and touch this heaven with my form. Originating all beings, I pass like the breeze; I am above this heaven, beyond this earth; and what is the great one, that am I.[84]

While we do not hold that the philosophic arrogance of the lyric "I" in Whitman had its origins here, the formal resemblances, at any rate, between his "Song of Myself" as the cosmic "Me," and Vach's "song" "of herself as the supreme and universal soul," are remarkable, and it is a fair speculation that the uprising aspirations for a "different" kind of poetry he was seeking to create may have found an interesting model in Vach. And the sacred hymn of the Hindus, called *Gayatri,* in one of Colebrooke's essays on the Hindu ceremonies, may also have had some suggestions:

> On the effulgent power, which is BRAHME himself, and is called the light of the radiant sun, do I meditate; governed by the mysterious light which resides within me for the purpose of thought; that very light is the earth, the subtile ether, and all which exists within the created sphere; it is the threefold world, containing all which is fixed or moveable; it exists internally in my heart, externally in the orb of the sun; being one and the

same with that effulgent power. I myself am an irradiated manifestation of the Supreme BRAHME.[85]

In section 44 of "Song of Myself," adapting, as we have seen,
thoughts originally meant for the earth, Whitman describes the
immortality of his soul with these words:

Rise after rise bow the phantoms behind me.
Afar down I see the huge first Nothing, the vapour from
    nostrils of death,
I know I was even there. . . . I waited unseen and always,
And slept while God carried me through the lethargic mist,
And took my time . . . . and took no hurt from the fetid
    carbon.[86]

In the whole of that passage which describes, as Miller says,
that "there was never a period when the self did not exist," Whitman uses "the imagery of physics and evolution."[87] But the phrase,
"the vapour from nostrils of death," in which death does not
seem to have been used figuratively, and its combination with "the
huge first Nothing," strongly suggest that the source of the basic
elements of the imagery is the picture of creation presented in the
following extracts from the "Sacred Writings of the Hindus": a
hymn from *Rig-Veda,* a passage from *Vrihadaranyaca,* the third
from *Aitareya Aranya.*[88]

Then was there no entity, nor nonentity; no world, nor sky
nor aught above it: nothing, anywhere. . . . But THAT
(Supreme Being) breathed without afflation. . . . Other than
him, nothing existed. . . . Darkness there was; (for) this universe was enveloped with darkness, and was undistinguishable
(like fluids mixed in) waters: but that mass, which was covered
by the husk, was (at length) produced by the power of contemplation. First desire was formed in his mind: and that became the original productive seed. . . .
    Nothing existed in this world before (the production of
mind): this universe was encircled by death eager to devour;
for death is the devourer.
    Originally this (universe) was indeed SOUL only; nothing
else whatsoever existed, active (or inactive). HE thought,

"I will create worlds:" thus HE created these (various) worlds. . . .

HE thought, "there are indeed worlds; I will create guardians of worlds." Thus HE drew from the waters and framed, an embodied being (*Purusha,* a human form).

Whitman's religious zeal for procreation which is "just as divine as spirituality,"[89] may have been reared on the foundations of such thought of the *Aitareya Aranya* of the *Vedas* as the following:

This (living principle) is first, in man, a fetus, or productive seed [that "flowed" from the "generative organ" of "Purusha" framed by the Supreme being], which is the essence drawn from all the members (of the body) : thus the man nourishes himself within himself. But when he emits it into woman, he procreates that (fetus) : and such is its first birth.

It becomes identified with woman; and being such, as is her own body, it does not destroy her. She cherishes his own self, thus received within her; and, as nurturing him, she ought to be cherished (by him). . . . Since he supports the child before and after birth, he cherishes himself: and that, for the perpetual succession of persons; for thus are these persons perpetuated. Such is his second birth.

This (second) self becomes his representative for holy acts (of religion) : and that other (self), having fulfilled its obligations and completed its period of life, deceases. Departing hence, he is born again (in some other shape) : such is his third birth.

This was declared by the holy sage. "Within the womb, I have recognized all the successive births of these deities. A hundred bodies, like iron chains, hold me down: yet, like a falcon, I swiftly rise." Thus spoke VAMADEVA, reposing in the womb: and possessing this (intuitive) knowledge, he rose, after bursting that corporeal confinement; and ascending to the blissful region of heaven . . . became immortal.[90]

Whitman's acceptance of, nay, more, insistence on sex is not merely the result of its physical joy—he is not the poet of sex in that sense—but of the recognition that it is the "living principle" of things. There is in it, besides, an awareness that sex is "for the perpetual succession of persons":

I draw you close to me, you women,
I cannot let you go, I would do you good,
I am for you, and you are for me, not only for our own sake,
    but for others' sake,
Envelop'd in you sleep greater heroes and bards,
They refuse to awake at the touch of any man but me.[91]

And that is why he swore "the oath of procreation" to "produce boys to fill" his place when he is "through."[92]

The same extract from *Aitareya* cited above declares the following on the nature of the soul:

What is this soul? that we may worship him. Which is the soul? Is it that by which (a man sees)? . . . hears? . . . smells . . . ? . . . utters . . . ? . . . discriminates . . . ? . . . the heart (or understanding)? . . . mind (or will)? Is it sensation? or power? or discrimination? or comprehension? or perception? or retention? or attention? or application? . . .

All those are only various names of apprehension. But, this (soul, consisting in the faculty of apprehension) is BRAHMÁ; . . . these gods . . . the primary elements, earth, air, the ethereal fluid, water and light: these, and the same joined with minute objects and other seeds (of existence), and (again) other (beings) produced from eggs, or borne in wombs, or originating in hot moisture, or springing from plants; whether horses, or kine, or men, or elephants, whatever lives, and walks or flies, or whatever is immovable (as herbs and trees): all that is the eye of intelligence. . . .

Whitman's lines in "Starting from Paumanok" bear a startling resemblance to the above passage.

Was somebody asking to see the soul?
See, your own shape and countenance, persons, substances,
    beasts, the trees, the running rivers, the rocks and sands.[93]

All that is, is the soul, said the *Veda;* and Whitman, "having look'd at the objects of the universe," finds "there is no one nor any particle of one but/has a reference to the soul."[94]

As regards God, Whitman announces:

I hear and behold God in every object, yet I understand God
not in the least. . . .[95]

One of the prayers from *Yajurveda* in Colebrooke's essay said:

FIRE IS THAT (original cause) ; the sun is that; so is air;
so is the moon; such too is that pure BRAHME, and those
waters, and that lord of creatures. Moments (and other meas-
ures of time) proceeded from the effulgent person, whom none
can apprehend (as an object of perception). . . . Of him, whose
glory is so great, there is no image. . . . He . . . pervades all
regions . . . he, severally and universally remains with (all)
persons. . . .
    . . . Recognizing heaven, earth, and sky (to be him), knowing
the worlds, discovering space and (*swar*) the solar orb (to be
the same), he ["the votary"] views that being: he becomes that
being; and is identified with him . . .

Whitman declares in almost the same phrases,

I see something of God each hour of the twenty four, and
    each moment then,
In the faces of men and women I see God, and in my own face
    in the glass. . . .[96]

In "Song of the Answerer," Whitman presents what apparently
is a list of the virtues of his ideal man, who, incidentally, was himself by implication:

Divine instinct, breadth of vision, the law of reason, health,
    rudeness of body, withdrawness,
Gayety, sun-tan, air-sweetness, such are some of the words of
    poems.[97]

An earlier line, probably a tentative step toward this, greatly
modified later, is as follows:

Spirituality, the unknown, the great aspirations of the soul,
    the idea of justice, divinity, immortality.[98]

Against the philosophical background of Whitman's readings at least, one might wonder if the "withdrawness" was not the spiritual "abstraction" which, in the conversation with Maitreyi, his wife, Yagnawalcya declares is necessary for "immortality," because "affections are relative to the soul, which should therefore be contemplated and considered in all objects, since everything is soul.[99]

There are innumerable passages in all these accounts dealing with the idea that life, or *Brahme,* is felicity or *anandamaya.* One that most eminently brings out this Vedantic notion is in the *Taittiriyaca Upanishad* quoted by Colebrooke. It is the story of Bhrigu, who sought from his father, Varuna, directions for the knowledge of *Brahme,* and was told: "That whence all beings are produced, that by which they live when born, that towards which they tend, and that into which they pass, do thou seek, [for] that is *Brahme."* Many times does Bhrigu go and meditate in "devout contemplation" only to find answers that were unsatisfactory, like food, or body, breath, or life, and intellect, to be *Brahme,* but finally "he knew *Ananda* (or felicity) to be *Brahme:* for all beings are indeed produced from pleasure; when born, they live by joy; they tend towards happiness; they pass into felicity."[100] Whitman's own message is primarily the message of joy.

I have elsewhere suggested that Whitman's meaningful use of the word "loves" in his account of "the Hindoo, teaching his favourite pupil," must refer either to *Sakuntala* or to the *Gita-Govinda.* The latter, a long mystic poem celebrating the loves of Krishna and Radha, is the specimen of "the mystical poetry" of the Hindus presented by Sir W. Jones in his article. The poem itself may be ignored as of no special significance, but the introductory article deserves some attention for its account of mysticism and of the Vedantic thought, which is essentially mystical. Following some long quotations from Barrow and Necker on the nature of mysticism, Jones examines the Vedantic concept and sums it up as follows:

They (Vedantís and Súfis) concur in believing that the souls of men differ infinitely in *degree,* but not at all in *kind,* from the divine spirit, of which they are particles, and in which they will

ultimately be absorbed; that the spirit of GOD pervades the
universe, always immediately present to his work, and consequently in substance . . . that from eternity without beginning,
to eternity without end, the supreme benevolence is occupied in
bestowing happiness, or the means of attaining it . . . that nothing has a pure absolute existence but *mind* or spirit; that *material substances,* as the ignorant call them, are no more than gay
pictures presented continually to our *minds* by the sempiternal
spirit.[101]

Considering how Whitman played "the sempiternal spirit" in
his poems, one may lightheartedly wonder if his "pictures" were
so presented too, but cannot fail to notice how close his thoughts
come to the mystic doctrine.

4

TRANSCENDING THE MOON

OF GREATER SIGNIFICANCE THAN THE *Asiatic Researches,* PER-
haps of even fundamental importance to Whitman's knowledge of
Indian philosophy, are the *Transactions* of the Royal Society of
Great Britain and Ireland, among the three volumes of which is a
most elaborate and systematic account, with original texts, of the
entire body of Hindu philosophical thought. Astor library had the
set in its Oriental section, and the Mercantile acquired it sometime between its 1837 and 1866 catalogues. Some of the most important contributions to its pages by the earliest of the Oriental
scholars of the west are as follows:

Volume I: Article 2: On the Philosophy of the Hindus, Part I,
H. T. Colebrooke, pp. 19–43. [With a general
introduction on Hindu philosophical speculations
and their basic tenets, the author, whose researches
formed the foundation of subsequent Western scholarship, presents two systems of Hindu thought,
namely *Sankhya* and *Yoga.*]

Article 7: On the Philosophy of the Hindus, Part
II, H. T. Colebrooke, pp. 92–118. [Two more
systems, *Nyaya* and *Vysheshika,* are studied.]

Article 10: Analytical Account of Panchatantra, illustrated with occasional translations, H. H. Wilson, pp. 155–200. [A study of the full text of Vishnu
Sharma of which *Hitopadesha* is only a part.]

Article 23: On the Srávacs or Jains, Major J. Delamaine, pp. 413–438. [An account of the tenets and practices of Jains in India.]

Article 24: On the Philosophy of the Hindus, Part III, H. T. Colebrooke, pp. 439–460. [The *Mimamsa* System.]

Article 29: On the Sráwacs or Jains, F. B. Hamilton, pp. 531–536.

Article 33: On the Philosophy of the Hindus, Part IV, H. T. Colebrooke, pp. 549–579. [An account of the non-orthodox schools like Buddhism, Jainism, Charvaka, etc.]

Volume II: Article 1: On the Philosophy of the Hindus, Part V, H. T. Colebrooke, pp. 1–39. [The *Vedanta*.]

Article 13: Sketch of Buddhism, B. H. Hodgson, pp. 222–257.

Volume III: Article 26: Colonel Vans Kennedy on the Vendanta system, pp. 412–436. [Part of a controversy with regard to Colebrooke's interpretation of some Vedantic doctrines.]

The five articles of H. T. Colebrooke present, with texts from the *Vedas,* the *Upanishads,* the *Sutras,* and commentators like Sankara, an exhaustive analysis of all the schools of Indian philosophy. If Whitman had read nothing else he would have gathered from these a profound understanding not only of the fundamental doctrines of Indian philosophy but of the whole body of thought raised on their foundation. And Whitman, as will be evident from the following examination, did read these essays in the *Transactions.*[102]

One of the fine lyric passages of "Song of Myself" is lines 1290—1298 of the first edition:

I hear you whispering there O stars of heaven,
O suns . . . . O grass of graves . . . . O perpetual transfers and promotions . . . . if you do not say anything how can I say anything?

Of the turbid pool that lies in the autumn forest,
Of the moon that descends the steeps of the sloughing twi-
light,
Toss, sparkles of day and dusk . . . . toss on the black stems
that decay in the muck,
Toss to the moaning gibberish of the dry limbs.

I ascend from the moon . . . . I ascend from the night,
And perceive of the ghastly glitter the sunbeams reflected
And debouch to the steady and central from the offspring
great or small.[103]

The utter Whitmanesque lyricism of these lines clothes a profound philosophic thought, namely, of "perpetual promotions and
transfers," the insight of which the poet has acquired, thereby
realizing that life is "the leavings of many deaths" and no doubt
he has died himself "ten thousand times before."[104] In fact, the
theme of the entire section, finally numbered 49, is death and immortality. Death, the "bitter hug of mortality," does not alarm
him, because he "recline[s] by the sills of the exquisite flexible
doors," and "mark[s] the outlet, and mark[s] the relief and
escape." To use Miller's words, "Death is not an end of the self,
but an outlet for it into the Transcendent, a relief from life, an
escape into the permanent union with the Absolute."[105] This "promotion" to the Transcendent is described with a powerful imagery
in the last three lines of the passage quoted. To quote Miller
again:

Paradoxical, but surely intentional, is the use of the scientific
to symbolize the spiritual truth. The "ghastly glimmer" of the
moon is but "sunbeams reflected." The moon and night, suggestive of death, are but the "off-spring" of the "steady and
central" sun. The figure is apt: death is an "off-spring" of God,
a birth into the "steady and central" Transcendental Reality.
The poet sees in death the ultimate permanent union he has
fleetingly achieved in his mystical experience.[106]

But that this union is not achieved in any "mystical experience,"
even of the kind imagined by Miller, that the "apt" figure is not
intentionally selected from the scientific world, that, though

"moon" and "night" symbolize death they are suggestive more of what is not "steady and central" light, being mere reflections, and that the whole passage is the product of Whitman's characteristic treatment of a thought he had read in Colebrooke's essays, however brilliantly lyricized, can be seen looking at the following paragraphs dealing with the Vedanta notion of "death and immortality":

They concur even in the limit assigned to mutation and change; deeming all which is sublunary, mutable, and that which is above the moon subject to no change in itself. Accordingly, the manes doomed to a succession of births, rise, as the *Védas* teach, no further than the moon: while those only pass that bourne who are never to return. But I am here anticipating on the *Vedanta*.[107]

The passages anticipated discuss death, transmigration, and the future state, and are as follows:

"The soul is subject to transmigration. It passes from one state to another, invested with a subtile frame consisting of elementary particles, the seed or rudiment of a grosser body. Departing from that which it occupied, it ascends to the moon; where, clothed with an aqueous form, it experiences the recompense of its works; and whence it returns to occupy a new body with resulting influence of its former deeds. But evil-doers suffer for their misdeeds in the seven appointed regions of retribution.

"The returning soul quits its watery frame in the lunar orb, and passes successively and rapidly through ether, air, vapour, mist, and cloud into rain; and thus finds its way into a vegetating plant, and thence, through the medium of nourishment, into an animal embryo. . . .

"But he who has attained the true knowledge of GOD does not pass through the same stages of retreat, proceeding directly to reunion with the supreme being, with which he is identified, as a river, at its confluence with the sea, merges altogether. . . .

"The soul, together with the vital faculties absorbed in it having retired within its proper abode, the heart, the summit of that viscus flashes, and lightens the passage by which the soul is to depart. . . . A hundred and one arteries issue from the heart, one of which passes to the crown of the head: it is named *sushumna*.

By that passage, in virtue of acquired knowledge, and of recollection of the meditated way, the soul of the wise, graced by the favour of BRAHME, whose dwelling is in the heart, issues and meets a solar ray; and by that route proceeds, whether it be night or day, winter or summer. The contact of a sunbeam with the vein is constant, as long as the body endures: rays of light reach from the sun to the vein, and conversely extend from this to the sun. . . ."

The soul of him who has arrived at the perfection of divine knowledge, and is consequently liberated, "quitting its corporeal frame, ascends to the supreme light which is BRAHME."[108]

These are all extracts from the *Brahmasutras* enunciating Vedanta notions. In his final summary of the system Colebrooke reverts to the concept that

In death it [the soul] has absolutely quitted its gross corporeal frame.

Subject to future transmigration it visits other worlds, to receive the recompense of works or suffer the penalty of misdeeds. Sinners fall to various regions of punishment. . . . The virtuous rise to the moon, where they enjoy the fruits of their good actions; and whence they return to this world to animate new bodies, and act in them, under providence, conformably with their propensities and predispositions, the trace of which remains.

The wise, liberated from worldly trammels, ascend yet higher, to the abode and court of BRAHME; or, if their attainment of wisdom be complete, they at once pass into a reunion with the divine essence.[109]

In another part of the same essay the idea is dwelt upon again:

The mystic syllable *óm* . . . is the subject of devout meditation. . . . If the devotion be restricted to the sense indicated by one element, the effect passes not beyond this world; if to that indicated by two of the elements, it extends to the lunar orb, whence however the soul return to a new birth; if it be more comprehensive, embracing the import of the three elements of the word, the ascent is to the solar orb, whence, stripped of sin, and liberated as a snake which has cast its slough, the soul proceeds to the abode of *Brahme,* and to the contemplation of (*purusha*) him who resides in a corporeal frame: that is, soul reposing in body (*puri-saya*).[110]

Whatever be the scientific absurdity of the thought, it has its obvious attraction for the poetic imagination, and Whitman turned it into account in his lines. Like the liberated soul of Vedanta, his self not only does not stop at the moon, but "recline[s] by the sills of the exquisite flexible doors," "the hundred and one arteries [which] issue from the heart," marking "the outlet," "the passage" by which the soul "issues and meets a solar ray" to ascend "to the supreme light" that is "steady and central."

The following makes an interesting study in Whitman's art of poetic composition, at the same time offering further proof of his reading of Colebrooke's essays.

In 1872 he published a poem called "As a Strong Bird on Pinions Free," in an independent pamphlet containing a few other pieces. It entered, with considerable alterations and additions, into *Leaves of Grass* subsequently, but under a new title, "Thou Mother with Thy Equal Brood." A "reworking of old themes and ideas,"[111] the poem is "what may be called a sequel to 'By Blue Ontario,' a vision and a prophecy (like the discarded Apostroph) of the grandeurs of the New World Civilization."[112] The "strong bird" personifies America, which he "regarded as a culmination of past civilizations," and he sings a "special song" for its future to prophesy "that the nation would surpass them all, and eventually achieve the 'destinies of the soul,' whatever these were."[113]

The imagery and the symbolism of the poem are suggested in these lines:

As a strong bird on pinions free,
Joyous, the amplest spaces heavenward cleaving,
Such be the thought I'd think of thee America,
Such be the recitative I'd bring for thee. (Sec. 2)

The vision and the prophecy are seen in these extracts:

Thou! mounting higher, diving deeper than we knew, thou
    transcendental Union!
. . . .

. . . .

Thought of man justified, blended with God,
Through thy idea, Lo, the immortal reality!
Through thy reality, Lo, the immortal idea! (Sec. 2)

. . . .

Ascending from such gestation, taking and giving continual
    strength and life,
World of the real—world of the twain in one,
World of the soul, born by the world of the real alone, led to
    identity, body, by it alone,

. . . .

I watch thee advancing, absorbing the present, transcending
    the past,

. . . .

I but thee name, thee prophesy, . . .

. . . .

Thee in thy only permanent life, career, thy own unloosen'd
    mind, thy soaring spirit,

. . . .

(Thy soaring course thee formulating, ...) (Sec. 5)

. . . .

(Lo, where arise three peerless stars,
To be thy natal stars my country, Ensemble, Evolution, Free-
    dom,
Set in the sky of Law.)

Land of unprecedented faith, God's faith,
Thy soil, they very subsoil, all upheav'd,
The general inner earth so long so sedulously draped over,
    now hence for what it is boldly laid bare,
Open'd by thee to heaven's light for benefit or bale.

. . . .

In many a smiling mask death shall approach beguiling thee,
    thou in disease shalt swelter,

. . . .

But thou shalt face thy fortunes, thy diseases, and surmount
    them all,

. . . .

They each and all shall lift and pass away and cease from
    thee,
While thou, Time's spirals rounding, out of thyself, thyself
    still extricating, fusing,

Equable, natural, mystical Union thou, (the mortal with
  immortal blent,)
Shalt soar toward the fulfilment of the future, the spirit of the
  body and the mind,
The soul, its destinies.

The soul, its destinies, the real real,
(Purport of all these apparitions of the real;)
In thee America, the soul, its destinies,
. . . .
Thou mental, moral orb—thou New, indeed new, Spiritual
  World!
The Present holds thee not—for such vast growth as thine,
For such unparallel'd flight as thine, such brood as thine,
The Future only holds thee and can hold thee. (Sec. 6)

Aside from its magnificent national theme, which is manifestly
Whitman's own, the entire poem, with its imagery, symbolism, and
thought, is raised upon the foundations of the following passage in
the *Transactions* explaining the Jaina concepts of "mócsha" and
"baddha":

VI. *Baddha* is that which binds (*badhnáti*) the embodied spirit.
It is confinement and connexion, or association, of the soul with
deeds. It consists in a succession of births and deaths as the
result of works (*carman*).
VII. *Mócsha* is liberation; or deliverance of the soul from the
fetters of works. It is the state of a soul in which knowledge
and other requisites are developed.
  Relieved from the bondage of deeds through means taught by
holy ordinances, it takes effect on the soul by the grace of the
ever-perfect ARHAT or JINA.
  Or liberation is continual ascent. The soul has a buoyancy or
natural tendency upwards, but it is kept down by corporeal
trammels. When freed from them it rises to the region of the
liberated.
  Long immersed in corporeal restraint, but released from it; as
a bird let loose from a cage, plunging into water to wash off the
dirt with which it was stained, and drying its pinions in the
sunshine, soars aloft; so does the soul, released from long confinement, soar high, never to return.

Liberation then is the condition of a soul clear of all impediments.

It is attained by right knowledge, doctrine and observances: and is a result of the unrestrained operation of the soul's natural tendency, when passions and every other obstacle are removed.[114]

Let us forget the date of the poem's publication, which is not always the date of its composition in Whitman's case, and substitute the term "soul" for America, and make the slight modifications necessary; it is then not hard to see in the prophecy Whitman is uttering that he is only the "ever-perfect ARHAT or JINA," the Supreme Soul of the Jains, granting the "grace" by which his nation, her "fetters of works" all surmounted, "extricating herself," shall "soar toward the fulfilment of the future," like a bird that "soars aloft."

The simile of the soaring bird on its pinions free does not occur anywhere else among the books we are examining, and the idea of the emancipated soul ascending beyond the moon to the supreme light, though found in one or two other places such as the *Bhagvat-Geeta,* is not stated with the repetitive and elaborate detail of Colebrooke. The Reverend W. Ward's *View* also has accounts of the different systems of Hindu philosophy, presented through translation of texts that enunciate the doctrines, but, as Colebrooke has noticed in his essay, Ward's rendering of *Vedanta sara,* or, the Essence of Vedanta, "is no version of the original text and seems to have been made from an oral exposition through the medium of a different language, probably the Bengalese,"[115] and so does not give a correct or complete account of the Vedanta school. The part played by Ward's book in Whitman's poetry will be set forth in the coming pages, but its role seems to have been confined to its Sankhya and Yoga chapters, and Colebrooke's elaborate textual exposition of Vedanta appears to have been Whitman's major means of the knowledge of "the Hindoo, worshipping Brahma." But again, the indications are that Whitman did not study these various schools of thought systematically or approach them intellectually as a student of philosophy does. Rather, he went over them like an interested reader, reacting more emotionally than scientifically, not collecting thoughts in an organized method, but gathering impressions and hints in a rambling sort of way, later to weave a conscious or unconscious pattern, regardless of harmony, from elements often dissimilar, discordant, or even contradictory, that he picked from different areas of his reading. Some of the bits from the pages of Colebrooke that have gone into his lyrical amalgam are easily noticeable:

> The Sánc'hya philosophy . . . affirms two eternal principles, soul and matter; (for *pracriti* or nature, abstracted from modifications, is no other than matter:) and reckoning, with these two permanent principles, such as are transient, they enumerate twenty five.[116]

> It is for contemplation of Nature, and for abstraction from it, that union of soul with nature takes place, as the halt and the blind join for conveyance and for guidance: (one bearing and directed; the other borne and directing). By that union of soul and nature, creation, consisting in the development of intellect and the rest of the principles, is effected.[117]

To Whitman's own affirmation of the two principles that go to make "identity," and to his notion, "All tends to the soul,"[118] considerable support must have come from these paragraphs.

Elsewhere I have suggested that "The Sleepers," once called "Night-Poem" (1856) and later "Sleep-chasings" (1860), has unmistakable indications of Indian inspiration because of its obvious Vedantic quality. The central idea of the vision in which the poet "wander[s] all night . . . travelling around the globe with the ease of his cosmic flights in 'Song of Myself,' "[119] is the identity of the poet's soul with "the journeymen divine . . . the actor and the actress, the voter, the politician, the emigrant and the exile," in a word, with every other being, through which identification the realization dawns that "the soul is always beautiful," This identity with all is achieved in the night, which "symbolizes the world of spirituality," and in sleep, which "represents death's release of the soul."[120]

Some of the Vedantic passages that suggest this release of the soul in a state of sleep, when, liberated from the trammels of individuality, it achieves union with the Supreme Soul, are found in Colebrooke's essays too:

The *Vedanta* considers the individual soul to be temporarily, during the period of profound sleep, in the like ["ecstatic"] condition of reunion with the Supreme, which it permanently arrives at on its final emancipation from body.[121]

Three states of soul in respect of the body are recognized. . . . In profound sleep the soul is absent, having retired by the channel of the arteries, and being as it were enfolded in the supreme diety. It is not, however, blended with the divine essence, as a drop of water fallen into a lake, where it becomes indistinguishable; but, on the contrary, the soul continues discriminate, and returns unchanged to the body which it animates while awake.[122]

Almost immediately following this passage on the state of sleep is the one on "the liberated soul" ascending higher than the moon to the "supreme light" quoted earlier, and this is followed by an account of "three degrees of liberation or deliverance" that, according to Vedanta, can be achieved by man, the third of which is "effectual in life-time (*jivan mukti*), and enables the possessor of it to perform supernatural actions; [such] as evocation of shades of progenitors, translation of himself into other bodies called into existence by the mere force of his will, instantaneous removal to any place at his pleasure, and other wondrous performances."[123]

Whitman's identification with the sleepers is not the incorporation of a "jivan-mukta" into "bodies called into existence by the mere force of his will," but a far more spiritual union with all living beings; he becomes them. But the identification with the Supreme Soul of the philosophic passage and the identification with the Universal Soul of Whitman's lyric passage are not very different. Incidentally, of the other kind, the "wondrous performance" of the jivan-mukta, one may hear a faint echo in these lines of "Song of Myself":

I find I incorporate gneiss and cool and long-threaded moss
    and fruits and grains and esculent roots,
And am stucco'd with quadrupeds and birds all over,
And have distanced what is behind me for good reasons,
And call anything close again when I desire it.[124]

To return to "The Sleepers": Like the Vedantic soul's identity in sleep with the Supreme Soul, Whitman's identity with that of the several or all beings and things in the world is also temporary. He will "stop only a time with the night," and "rise betimes," and even as the Vedantic soul again in sleep returns to the Supreme, so does Whitman's return to the night and "love" it:

> I love the rich running day, but I do not desert her in whom
> I lay so long:
> I know not how I came of you, and I know not where I go
> with you. . . . but I know I came well and shall go well.

Night to him is not death, but the time of sleep, i.e., of identity. A line, quoted in Colebrooke, says, "While a man sleeps without dreaming, the soul is with *Brahmé*."[125] But Whitman dreams poetically.

One of the basic concepts of Hindu philosophy concerns the nature of the soul, which, according to it, is eternal, unalterable, and immaterial, and therefore for its fruition it is invested initially with a "subtile" body, composed of "elementary rudiments," which in turn is invested with a "gross" body, composed of matter. At death the latter perishes or returns to the elements out of which it was made, while the former, subtle and imperishable, endures. The Sankhya school presents this idea in the pages of Colebrooke thus:

> Soul, termed *Purusha, Pumas,* or *Atman;* which is neither produced nor productive. It is multitudinous, individual, sensitive, eternal, unalterable, immaterial.
> The theistical Sánc'hya [Yoga] recognizes the same principles [the twenty-five principles in which Sankhya sums up the totality of knowledge]; understanding, however, by *Purusha,* not individual soul alone, but likewise GOD (Iswara), the ruler of the world.
> . . . .

The soul's wish is fruition or liberation. For either purpose, it is in the first place invested with a subtile person, towards the formation of which the evolution of principles proceeds no further than the elementary rudiments (carika 40). This is composed then of intellect, consciousness [or egotism], and mind, as well as the rest of the organs and instruments of life, conjoined with particles, or elementary rudiments, of five sorts: thus seventeen principles enter into its composition.

This person, or subtile frame, termed *linga, linga-sarira,* or *sucshma-sarira,* is primeval, produced from original nature at the earliest or initial development of principles. It is unconfined; too subtile for restraint or hindrance (and thence termed *ativáhica,* surpassing the wind in swiftness) : incapable of enjoyment until it be invested with a grosser body, affected nevertheless by sentiments. . . .

The grosser body, with which a soul clad in its subtile person is invested for the purpose of fruition, is composed of the five elements; or of four, excluding the ethereal, according to some authorities; or of one, earth alone, according to others. That grosser body, propagated by generation, is perishable. The subtile person is more durable, transmigrating through successive bodies, which it assumes, as a mimic shifts his disguises, to represent various characters.[126]

The "carika 40" and 39, which are presented in Colebrooke's exposition are as follows:

Subtile (bodies), and such as spring from father and mother, together with the great elements, are three sorts of specific objects. Among these, the subtile bodies are lasting; such as issue from father and mother are perishable. (carika 39)

(Subtile body), primeval, unconfined, material, composed of intellect, with other subtile principles, migrates, else unenjoying; invested with dispositions, mergent. (carika 40)[127]

Whitman is referring to this gross body composed of "the five elements; or of four, excluding the ethereal," when he says in "A Song of the Rolling Earth," section 1:

> Air, soil, water, fire—these are words,
> I myself am a word with them—my qualities interpenetrate
>   with theirs—my name is nothing to them. . . .

and to the invisible, imperishable "subtile" body when he asks,

> How can the real body ever die?
> . . . .
> Why, what do you suppose is the body?
> Do you suppose this that has always existed—this meat, bread,
>   fruit, that is eaten, is the body?
> No, those are visible parts of the body, materials that have
>   existed in some way for billions of years now entered into
>   the form of the body.
> But there is the real body too, not visible.[128]

To this awareness of the distinction of the perishable and the durable bodies that envelope the soul, Whitman gives a veiled expression in these words of his prose elegy on Carlyle:

> And now that he has gone hence, can it be that Thomas Carlyle,
> soon to chemically dissolve in ashes and by winds, remains an
> identity still? In ways perhaps eluding all the statements, lore
> and speculation of ten thousand years—eluding all possible
> statements to mortal sense—does he yet exist, a definite vital
> being, a spirit, an individual—perhaps now wafted in space
> among those stellar systems, which suggestive and limitless as
> they are, merely edge more limitless, far more suggestive sys-
> tems? I have no doubt of it.[129]

But the clearest echo is heard in these lines:

> For not life's joys alone I sing, repeating—the joy of death!
> The beautiful touch of death, soothing and benumbing a few
>   moments, for reasons,
> Myself discharging my excrementitious body to be burn'd, or
>   render'd to powder, or buried,
> My real body doubtless left to me for other spheres,
> My voided body nothing more to me, returning to the purifi-
>   cations, further offices, eternal uses of the earth.[130]

> Thy body permanent,
> The body lurking there within thy body. . . .[131]

Among the first drafts and rejected fragments of Whitman are these two experimental lines:

> O I see now that I have the make of materialism and things,
> And that intellect is to me as hands or eyesight, or as a vessel.[132]

In these two lines a whole set of Sankhya stanzas can be detected. The first of the twenty-five principles of the school is "Nature, *Pracriti,* or *Múla-pracriti,* . . . the universal material cause . . . eternal matter." Intellect is the second, "called *Buddhi* or *Mahat* . . . the first production of nature, increate, prolific, being itself productive of other principles." Egotism, the product of intellect, produces "five subtile particles, rudiments, or atoms, denominated *Tanmátra,* . . . themselves productive of the five grosser elements," earth, water, fire, air and space, and "eleven organs of sense and action": the eye, the ear, the nose, the tongue, and the skin being "instruments of sensation," and voice, hands, feet, excretory organs, and the organ of generation being instruments of action; all these external, and the mind, internal, the eleventh organ. "These eleven organs, with the two principles of intelligence [or intellect] and consciousness are thirteen instruments of knowledge" for the soul.[133]

> The five senses and the understanding [intellect] form that clothing or receptacle of spirit which is made up of knowledge. . . . The five organs and thought form that receptacle of spirit which is wholly made up of intellect. The five organs are the mouth, the hands, [etc.][134]
> Mind is the instrument (of the soul).[135]

It can readily be seen how this account of the nature of the soul and its relation to the faculties it possesses has entered into Whitman's thinking. In one of his own notes on his poetry, commenting on the "Philosophy of Leaves of Grass," he wrote:

> He (Whitman) evidently thinks that behind all the faculties of the human being, as the sight, the other senses and even the emotions and the intellect stands the real power, the mystical identity, the real I or ME or YOU.[136]

Whitman's use of the word "egotism" has a definite philosophical connotation: it is more than personal pride, or egoism; it is the principle of being. It is in that same sense that Sankhya uses it as equivalent to consciousness, which is the third of its principles.

> 3. Consciousness, termed *Ahancára,* or more properly egotism, which is the literal sense of the term: the peculiar and appropriate function of it is (*abhimána*) selfish conviction, a belief that, in perception and meditation, "I" am concerned; that the objects of sense concern ME; in short, that I AM. It proceeds from the intellectual principle.[137]

And from the Sankhya nation of Nature, or *Pracriti,* as "universal material cause . . . eternal matter," may have also arisen Whitman's notion "that Materials are just as eternal as growth."[138]

Another doctrine most peculiar to Hindu thought is that of the three qualities of matter as constituting the fundamental principle of nature and being responsible for variety in creation. It is common to all schools of Indian philosophy and is found in all accounts of it in the books and journals we are examining. We shall notice it briefly here, though Whitman found it elsewhere too—probably even earlier than his reading Colebrooke—in the *Laws of Menu* and the periodicals. The notion, we must remember, is bound up with the doctrines of Karma and Transmigration.

> The *Sanc'hya,* as other Indian systems of philosophy, is much engaged with the consideration of what is termed the three qualities (*guna*): if indeed quality be here the proper import of the term; for the scholiast of CAPILA understands it as meaning, not quality or accident, but substance, a modification of nature, fettering the soul. . . .
> The first, and highest, is goodness (*sattwa*). It is alleviating, enlightening, attended with pleasure and happiness: and virtue predominates in it. In fire it is prevalent; wherefore flame ascends, and sparks fly upwards. In man, when it abounds, as it does in beings of a superior order, it is the cause of virtue.
> The second and middlemost is foulness or passion (*rajas* or *téjas*). It is active, urgent, and variable; attended with evil and misery. In air it predominates: wherefore wind moves transversely. In living beings it is the cause of vice.

The third and lowest is darkness (*tamas*). It is heavy, and obstructive: attended with sorrow, dulness, and illusion. In earth and water it predominates, wherefore they fall or tend downwards. In living beings it is the cause of stolidity.

These three qualities are not mere accidents of nature, but are of its essence and enter into its composition. . . .

They co-operate for a purpose, by union of opposites: as a lamp, which is composed of oil, a wick, and flame, substances inimical and contrary.[139]

This doctrine of the soul fettered by the "qualities" of matter has its echoes in Whitman. In the long description of his Concept of Prudence, which is merely the Hindu notion of Karma, he speaks of how "the indirect is always as great and real as the direct. The spirit receives from the body just as much as it gives to the body."[140] And the way in which he uses the words "matter" and "qualities" together in the following first draft lines, as well as the central idea in them, seems to indicate that the term "qualities" is employed in the deep philosophical connotation of the Hindu thought. These were, as Bucke notes, "written 1855 or 1856."

(? Superfluous?)

Thought

Of that to come—of experiences—of vast unknown matter
    and qualities lying inert—much doubtless more than known
    matter and qualities;

Of many a covered embryo—owner and faetus—Of the long
    patience through millions of years—of the slow formation,

Of countless germs waiting the due conjunction, the arousing
    touch,

Of all these tending fluidly and duly to myself, and duly and
    fluidly to reappear again out of myself.[141]

Since our interest is not in the philosophical systems of the Hindus themselves so much as in the passages of the *Transactions* that seem on the basis of expression to have been Whitman's source of their ideas, we shall ignore the rest of Colebrooke's account of Sankhya and Yoga. For, although many more elements of these systems entered into Whitman's metaphysics, they appear to have come from Ward's *View* rather than Colebrooke's essay, probably because the latter is mostly textual, succinct in its comments, and except in the case of Mimamsa and Vedanta, combines two schools in one connected, comparative analysis, whereas Ward's is less technical, more elaborate and descriptive, and, for Whitman, easier to comprehend. However, we shall take a passing look at one or two more passages from these pages that may have given him at least "surface impressions":

> The existence of soul is demonstrated by several arguments: "The assemblage of sensible objects is for another's use;" as a bed is for a sleeper, a chair for a sitter: that other, who uses it, must be a sensitive being; and the sensitive being is soul. . . . "There must be superintendence;" as there is a charioteer to a car: the superintendent of inanimate matter is soul. "There must be one to enjoy" what is formed for enjoyment: a spectator, a witness of it: that spectator is soul.[142]

This notion of the soul as the enjoyer, and of all nature, with its forms resulting from the multifarious combination of its three qualities, as "objects of apprehension and enjoyment"[143] can be heard in a characteristic Whitmanesque echo in these lines of his first drafts:

As of Forms.

Their genesis, all genesis,
They lost, all lost—for they include all.

The earth and everything in it,
The wave, the snake, the babe, the landscape, the human head,
Things, faces, reminiscences, presences, conditions, thoughts—
    tally and make definite a divine indistinct spiritual delight
    in the soul
Of the arts, as music, poems, architecture, outlines, and the
    rest, they are in their way to provoke the delight out of the
    soul.
They are to seek where it waits—for I see that it always
    patiently waits.[144]

Many more details contributing to Whitman's ideas of the soul, life and death, and immortality could easily have come from these pages. They insist on "a separate soul for each particular body" on the argument that "birth, death, and the instruments of life are allotted severally"; they speak of birth as "the union of soul with instruments, namely intellect, consciousness, mind and corporeal organs," not "a modification of soul, for soul is unalterable"; they regard death as the soul's "abandonment of them; not an extinction of it, for it is imperishable"; and they describe the soul, the "undiscrete" principle, as "causeless; eternal; all pervading; immutable, or unacted upon; single . . . unsupported (relying but on itself); uninvolvable . . . self-ruled."[145] Whitman's words, "Only the soul is of itself . . . all else has reference to what ensues,"[146] could be a reverberation of the last line. And, though, as will appear later on, Whitman collected his notion of the "uninvolved" soul, or "the ME myself," from Ward's more elaborate description, he might have gathered a fleeting suggestion of it in Colebrooke's brief account, where "the *Carica* affirms that 'soul is witness, bystander, solitary, and passive. Therefore, by reason of union with it, insensible body seems sensible: and, though the qualities be active, the stranger (soul) appears as the agent.' "[147]

The next two essays of Colebrooke appear to deserve little more than a passing glance. There are very few indications of their having supplied Whitman with anything of special significance, perhaps because of their extreme technicality. The first of these deals with what Colebrooke regards "as parts of one system . . . the dialectic philosophy of GÓTAMA," and the "atomical of CANÁDE," respectively called *Nyaya,* "reasoning," and *Vaiséshica,* "particular." Nyaya, "as its title implies, is chiefly occupied with the metaphysics of logic"; Vaiséshica, "with physics." They are essentially scientific in character, but the fundamental points of Hindu thought are never lost sight of, and the questions of "the soul's eternal existence separable from the body," the "final excellence," "transmigration," "Karma," and so on, come in for repeated attention. One of the passages in the essay speaks of the soul thus:

The individual soul is infinite; for whithersoever the body goes there the soul too is present. It experiences the fruit of its deeds, pain or pleasure. . . .[148]

Perhaps these words went into the making of Whitman's affirmation of the importance of the body, without which "mortality" there could be no "immortality," or, at least, into these lines of his first drafts:

As the shadow concurs with the body and comes not unless of the body, so the soul concurs with the body and comes not unless of the body. . . .[149]

For, in the same passage, the Nyaya school regarded the body "as the site of effort; of organs of sensation; and of sentiment of pain and pleasure . . . an ultimate compound; the seat of soul's enjoyment . . . associated with which, soul experiences fruition; . . . the site . . . of action tending to the attainment of what is pleasing, and to the removal of what is displeasing. . . ."[150]

The reciprocal relationship of body and soul that is one of Whitman's basic concepts, by which "the spirit receives from the body just as much as it gives to the body," is as much a condensed expression of the Karma doctrine as of this Nyaya thought:

Virtue and vice (*Dharma* and *Adharma*), or moral merit and demerit . . . are qualities of the soul; imperceptible, but inferred from reasoning.

The proof of them is deduced from transmigration. The body of an individual, with his limbs and organs of sense, is a result of a peculiar quality of his soul; since this is the cause of that individual's fruition, like a thing which is produced by his effort or volition. The peculiar quality of the soul, which does occasion its being invested with body, limbs, and organs, is virtue or vice. . . .[151]

The next essay of Colebrooke deals with the Mimamsa school, "the object of which is the interpretation of the Vedas," and which, as a result, merely relates "to works (*carma*) or religious observances," and "is not directly a system of philosophy; nor chiefly so," though it "incidentally touches upon philosophical topics." Very little of its contribution to Whitman's thinking can be evidenced, because the account is mostly a discussion of principles and an explanation of Vedic texts and terms. However, one small passage deserves some attention.

Bliss Perry has mentioned as one of Whitman's Oriental traits his habit of naming himself in his poems.[152] Whitman could have read of this Oriental practice anywhere in his wide readings, or found his cue in the following paragraph in which Colebrooke comments on Jaimini, who is "repeatedly named" in the *Sutras* of *Mimamsa* of which he was the author.

> It is no doubt possible, that the true author of a work may speak in it of himself by name, and in the third person. Nor, indeed, is that very unusual. A Hindu commentator will, however, say, as the scholiasts of *Menu's* or *Yajnyawalcya's* institutes of law do, that the oral instructions of the teacher were put in writing by some disciple; and for this reason, the mention of him as of a third person is strictly proper.[153]

Part IV of Colebrooke's survey discusses the heterodox schools of Indian philosophy, such as the Buddhist, the Jain, the Charvaka, and so on. A succinct account of the doctrines of these various systems is there, with an explanation of the original texts and the terms in which the tenets are enunciated. It looks as if, like the previous ones, even this essay has not yielded anything very substantial to Whitman. Nevertheless a few passages may be given some consideration.

Whitman's passion for "nakedness" has found frequent expression both in his poems and prose, and is, of course, the product of his religious adoration of the body as "sacred," and his belief "in the flesh." In his eagerness, described in "Song of Myself," to "undress" to have "a turn together" with the sea, or for "contact" with the "atmosphere," he does not merely look like a man who loves the "smoke of [his] own breath," his "respiration and inspiration," the "beating of [his] heart," and the "passing of blood and air through [his] lungs,"[154] but betrays a far deeper, philosophic conviction. That the foundations of this love of nakedness are more than a psychological whim, or a hygienic fad, is demonstrated by the passage in his "Specimen Days" where he pays a glowing tribute to the doctrine of Nakedness. He mentions the

Hellenic race, of course, but that does not seem to be the origin of his own feeling.

> As I walk'd slowly over the grass, the sun shone out enough to show the shadow moving with me. Somehow I seem'd to get identity with each and everything around me in its condition. Nature was naked, and I was also. It was too lazy, soothing, and joyous-equable to speculate about. Yet I might have thought somehow in this vein: Perhaps the inner never-lost rapport we hold with earth, light, air, trees, &c., is not to be realized through eyes and mind only, but through the whole corporeal body, which I will not have blinded or bandaged any more than the eyes. Sweet, sane, still Nakedness in Nature!—ah if poor, sick, prurient humanity in cities might really know you once more! Is not nakedness then indecent? No, not inherently. It is your thought, your sophistication, your fear, your respectability, that is indecent. There come moods, when these clothes of ours are not only too irksome to wear, but are themselves indecent. Perhaps he or she to whom the free exhilarating extasy of nakedness in Nature has never been eligible (and how many thousands there are!) has not really known what purity is —nor what faith or health really is. (Probably the whole curriculum of first-class philosophy, beauty, heroism, form, illustrated by the old Hellenic race—the highest height and deepest depth known to civilization in those departments—came from their natural and religious idea of Nakedness.)[155]

It certainly looks curious that Whitman does not refer here to India, though, as our evidence shows, he had repeatedly read of one of its sects, called the Jains, whose "nakedness," among all the nations and faiths of the world, is the nakedness of a religious principle. One of the peculiar tenets of the orthodox Jain order is the doctrine of nudity, symbolic of their freedom from the traditional authority of the *Vedas,* and also of the spirit's perfect detachment from the temporal world. They call themselves *Digambaras,* or, those whose clothes are the skies themselves, the "sky-robed." Nakedness to them is the complete freedom of their soul. Accounts of this sect and an explanation of this tenet are found in all the journals and books on India. It is possible that Whitman's fertile imagination was impressed by the suggestions of this concept, and in his characteristic way he molded it into his philosophy.

For his passion looks more like the gymnosophist faith of a Jain than the gymnastic religion of a Greek.

Colebrooke's essay has no elaborate explanation of the tenet, only a note that "the Jainas or Arhats, followers of JINA or ARHAT (terms of like import) are also denominated *Vivasanas, Muctavasanas, Muctámbaras,* or *Digambaras,* with reference to the nakedness of the rigid order of ascetics in this sect, who go 'bare of clothing,' 'disrobed' or 'clad by the regions of space.' "[156] Bearing in mind Whitman's power of fusing hints from his reading into his poetry, it is not difficult to trace the effect of this description in the following lines:

> The atmosphere is not a perfume. . . . it has no taste of the
>   distillation. . . . it is odorless,
> It is for my mouth forever. . . . I am in love with it.
> I will go to the bank by the wood and become undisguised and
>   naked,
> I am mad for it to be in contact with me.[157]

It is in his impatience with "houses and rooms . . . full of perfume," that he goes out into the purer, truer, open air. The "houses and rooms," and the "shelves" with their books of the world's wisdom, have only a "distillation"; it would "intoxicate" him but he "shall not let it." And clothes would only "disguise" him, whereas, in "undisguised" nakedness alone, as the implication of the passage is, lies true understanding, "the origin of all poems." Undoubtedly it is the nakedness of the spirit, like that of the Jain to whom clothes are an impediment to the liberation of the soul, or apprehension of truth, and who in his nakedness spiritually disrobes himself of the mere "distillation" of the old books of Vedic wisdom.

The Sankhya notion of the two "opposite equal" principles occurs again in the account of Jainism, though slightly modified, for Jaina philosophy, like Buddhism, is founded on the Sankhya.

According to the *Digambara Jainas,* the universe consists of two classes, "animate" and "inanimate" (jiva and ajiva). . . . These gymnosophists distinguish . . . 1st, *Jiva,* intelligent and sentient soul . . . endued with body and consequently composed of parts; eternal: 2d, *Ajiva,* all that is not a living soul; that is, the whole of . . . inanimate and unsentient substance. . . .[158]

And like the Vyseshicas, the Jains admit only four elements, earth, water, fire, and air, as the "modified compounds of homogeneous atoms," which they hold to be the "cause" of the world. Ether, the fifth element, "the ethereal fluid," admitted by Sankhya and other systems, is not recognized by them, and so probably Whitman's four elements in "A Song of the Rolling Earth," noted earlier, with the element "earth" becoming "soil" for obvious reasons, reflect the Vyseshica and Jaina, rather than the other schools.

Whitman's insistent philosophic respect for procreation that is as the soul,[159] may have had its contribution from the Jaina notion of "Ayushca," of which Colebrooke says:

> Otherwise interpreted, the four *carmas* of this second set, taken in the inverse order, that is, beginning with *áyushca,* import procreation, and subsequent progress in the formation of the person. . . .[160]

One of the points on which Jaina thought conforms to the orthodox Hindu philosophy is the "transmigration of the soul," mentioned in these pages with the words: "The thoughts, inclinations, and resolves of man . . . determine the future character, and regulate the subsequent place, in transmigration. As was his thought in one body, such he becomes in another, into which he accordingly passes."[161]

Kennedy made the observation that Whitman got his word "identity" (occurring so often) from Schelling, whose identitätsphilosophie teaches that there is one identical, indifferent, absolute, substratum both for nature and spirit.[162] He is apparently mistaken on both counts, because, as we have noticed elsewhere, unlike both Schelling and the Transcendentalists, Whitman uses the term "identity" to mean personal individuality. "I too had receiv'd identity by my body," says he in "Crossing Brooklyn Ferry." In this sense the word is used many times and explained in the *Transactions* as well as other accounts of Hindu thought. From the extracts that follow it can be seen that Whitman collected it in his Indian readings, along with many other suggestions that have been eroneously attributed to German sources. In the survey of the tenets of Buddhism by Colebrooke occur these lines:

. . . Other disciples of BUDDHA except internal sensation or intelligence (*vijnyána*) and acknowledge all else to be void. They maintain the eternal existence of conscious sense alone. . . .

Others, again, affirm the actual existence of external objects, no less than internal sensations: considering external as perceived by senses; and internal as inferred by reasoning.

Some of them recognise the immediate perception of exterior objects. Others contend for a mediate perception, through images, or resembling forms, presented to the intellect: objects they insist are inferred, but not actually perceived. . . .

Both [Sauntránticas and Vaibhásicas] think, that objects cease to exist when no longer perceived: they have but a brief duration, like a flash of lightning, lasting no longer than the perception of them. Their identity, then, is but momentary: the atoms or component parts are scattered; and the aggregation or concourse was but instantaneous. . . .

. . . The followers of CANÁDE . . . acknowledge some of their categories to be eternal and invariable, and reckon only others transistory and changeable; and . . . insist that identity ceases with any variation in the composition of a body, and that a corporeal frame, receiving nutriment and discharging excretions, undergoes continual change, and consequent early loss of identity. . . .[163]

Whitman's "curious sense of body and identity"[164] for which,

Something long preparing and formless is arrived and
  formed. . . .
. . . .
The threads that were spun are gathered. . . . the weft
  crosses the warp. . . . the pattern is systematic,[165]

is quite the "compound of homogeneous atoms" of the Jaina thought, fused with "Jiva, intelligent and sentient soul." He describes it most clearly in "A Song of Joys":

O the joy of my soul leaning pois'd on itself, receiving identity through materials and loving them, observing
characters and absorbing them,
My soul vibrated back to me from them, from sight, hearing,
touch, reason, articulation, comparison,
memory and the like,
The real life of my senses and flesh transcending my senses
and flesh,
My body done with materials, my sight done with my material
eyes,
Proved to me this day beyond cavil that it is not my material
eyes which finally see,
Not my material body which finally loves, walks, laughs,
shouts, embraces, procreates. . . .

Among the thoughts so superbly fused into these lines is the
notion of the two bodies, the "subtile" enduring, the "gross" perishable, the former naturally transcending the latter that is composed of "materials." It is possible, furthermore, that in the last
lines an interesting concept of the Nyaya school with regard to the
"five external organs" of sensation is subtly condensed.

The pupil of the eye is not the organ of sight (as the
Bau'ddhas affirm); nor is the outer ear, or opening of the
auditory passage, the organ of hearing; but a ray of light, proceeding from the eye toward the object viewed, is the visual
organ; and ether, contained in the cavity of the ear, and
communicating by intermediate ether with the object heard, is
the organ of hearing.[166]

The epistemological discussion of the Buddhist passages quoted
above, which also forms a large part of the subject of the Nyaya,
Vyseshica, and Mimamsa schools, all of which dwell upon "sources
of knowledge" as their chief issue, probably interested Whitman
in the questions of cognition and the reality of the external world,
and his emphatic affirmation of the latter may have gathered its
suggestion from these pages. In an early notebook he recorded:

I am the poet of reality
I say the earth is not an echo.
Nor man an apparition;
But that all the things seen are real.[167]

Confuting the sect of the Buddhists, referred to in the discussion, who hold the view of the "non-reality" of things, "the Vedantins argue, that 'the untruth or non-existence of external objects is an untenable position; for there is perception or apprehension of them: . . . and that, which actually is apprehended, cannot be unexistent. Nor does the existence of objects cease when the apprehension does so. Nor is it like a dream, a juggle, or an illusion; for the condition of dreaming and waking is quite different. When awake, a person is aware of the illusory nature of the dream which he recollects.' "[168]

The "identity" Whitman "received" is not the result merely of the gross body "born out of [his] mother," for before that "generations guided" him:

> Immense have been the preparations for me,
> Faithful and friendly the arms that have helped me,
> . . . .
> All forces have been steadily employ'd to complete and delight
>   me.[169]

There is a complex scientific imagery in the passage describing the "forces" employed in the evolution of his being, obviously "the subtile" portion of it, but yet it is possible that the basic suggestions of the lines came from the evolution of "the embodied being" according to the Buddhists:

> The seeming but unreal course of events, or worldly succession, external and mental, or physical and moral, is described as a concatenation of causes and effects in a continual round. . . .
> Earth furnishes solidity to the seed, and coherence to the germ; water moistens the grain; fire warms and matures it; air or wind supplies impulse to vegetation; ether expands the seed; and season transmutes it. By concurrence of all these, seed vegetates, and a sprout grows. . . .
> Likewise, in the moral world [or "personal"] . . . earth furnishes solidity to the bodily frame; water affords to it moisture; fire supplies heat; wind causes inspiration and respiration; ether occasions cavities; sentiment gives corporeal impulse and mental incitement. . . .
> ["Sentiment . . . or incipient consciousness" arises from "ignorance" and "passion" "concurring in the embryo with paternal seed and uterine blood."] From concurrence of [senti-

ment] with parental seed and blood, comes the rudiment of body; its flesh and blood; its name (náman) and shape (rúpa).[170]

To his notion of happiness as the end of all life and to his promise of joy, Whitman gives articulation all through his songs:

Do you see, O my brothers and sisters?
It is not chaos or death. . . . it is form and union and plan.
. . . it is eternal life. . . . it is happiness.[171]

The ideas of form, union, and plan are found plentifully in these pages, glimpses of which we have had in the extracts so far presented. The notions of eternal life and of happiness are also discussed. For instance, in the essay we are examining there is a long passage on this basic Hindu thought, portions of which are reproduced here:

Both these sects, like most others of Indian origin, propose for the grand object to which man should aspire, the attainment of a final happy state . . . .
All concur in assigning to its attainment the same term *múcti* or *móchsa.* . . . Many other terms are in use, . . . such as *amrita,* immortality; . . . *sréyas,* excellence. . . . But the term which the *Bauddhas* as well as *Jainas* . . . use is *nirvána.* . . . It is a condition of unmixed tranquil happiness or extasy (*ánanda*). . . . It is not annihilation, but . . . supreme felicity.[172]

Although Hindu thought is chiefly characterized by its spiritualism, there is one school which is essentially materialistic, and, like Whitman, worships the body. In a brief account of this system, called the *Charvaca,* Colebrooke comments:

The *Chárvácas* recognize four (not five) elements, *viz.* earth, water, fire and wind (or air); and acknowledge no other principles (*tatwa*).
The most important and characteristic tenet of this sect concerns the soul, which they deny to be other than body. . . . SADÁNANDA, in the *Védanta sára,* calls up for refutation no less than four followers of CHÁRVÁCA, asserting that doctrine

under various modifications; one maintaining, that the gross corporeal frame is identical with the soul; another, that the corporeal organs constitute the soul. . . .

"Seeing no soul but body, they maintain the nonexistence of soul other than body; . . . they affirm that an organic body (*cáya*) endued with sensibility and thought, though formed of . . . elements, is the human person.

"While there is body, there is thought, and sense of pleasure and pain; none when body is not; and hence, as well as from self-consciousness, it is concluded that self and body are identical."[173]

This concept of the identity of soul and body is the very foundation of Whitman's messianic philosophy, and for it, it appears, he did not need Hegel, as some critics affirm.

As the shadow concurs with the body and comes not unless
    of the body, so the soul
concurs with the body and comes not unless of the body.[174]

I have said that the soul is not more than the body,
And I have said that the body is not more than the soul.[175]

So says Whitman. The charvacas regarded the soul as "the principle . . . diffused through the body . . . inseparable from it.[176]

Apart from the "moon" passage, how much else of the last of Colebrooke's essays dealing with Vedanta[177] entered into Whitman's utterances cannot with equal definiteness be established on thought or verbal correspondences. However, there would be no doubt, even upon a casual examination of the essay, that the Vedanta school of Hindu thought had a deep influence on him, supplying him with his fundamental notions of Pantheism, the Concept of God as the Universal Soul, the divinity of all Creation, the Unity of God and Man's self, Love and Good and Happiness as the basic principles of life, and so on. We shall present a brief summary with a few significant extracts from it, echoes of which are easily heard in his poetry or prose.

Among all the expositions and discussions of this system of Hindu thought, extensive or fragmentary, found in the books available to Whitman in those early days, Colebrooke's was not only correct and authoritative, being based upon both the original texts themselves and their many commentators, but was also scholarly and elaborate. It contains, in addition, a brief history of the system and of the various writers on it, as well as of the different sects that later rose out of it. The *Vedanta* signifies "the conclusion of the Veda," and bears reference to the *Upanishads*. And so Colebrooke relies chiefly on the *Upanishads* themselves, quoting extensively from "*Chandógya, Caushítací, Vrihad-áranyaca, Aitaréyaca, Taittiríyaca, Cáthaca, Cathavalli, Múndaca, Prusna, Swetáswatara;* to which may be added the *Isa-vásya, Céna,* and one or two more," supplemented by *Brahmasutras,* and the commentary of Sankara and other writers. There are also a few passages quoted from the *Vedas,* and references to the *Bhagavad-Gita.*

The major part of the *Vedanta* concerns the nature of God, the soul of man, the world, death, and immortality; so the analysis opens with the inquiry "concerning God," the nature of His being and attributes, as postulated by the *Upanishads*. Selections of the quotations are reproduced here:

> He is the omnipotent creator of the world and the omniscient author of revelation (p. 10). The omnipotent, omniscient, sentient cause of the universe, is (*ánandamaya*) essentially happy. He is the brilliant, golden person, seen *within* (*antar*) the solar orb and the human eye. He is the *etherial* element (*ácásá*), from which all things proceed and to which all return. He is the *breath* (*prána*) in which all beings merge, into which they all rise. He is the *light* (*jyótish*) which shines in heaven, and in all places high and low, everywhere throughout the world, and within the human person. He is the *breath* (*prána*) and intelligent self, immortal, undecaying, and happy, with which INDRA, in a dialogue with PRATARDANA, identifies himself (p. 11).

Whitman's "Transcendent" in "Passage to India," and his concept of God in general have a noticeable resemblance to this account. Besides, like the *Upanishads,* he too regarded that "all [is] enfolded in Joy Joy Joy, which underlies and overtops the whole effusion";[178] sang of "a perfect world, all joy!" and of "joy in the ecstasy of life"; felt that it was "enough to merely be";[179] and declared:

The efflux of the soul is happiness, here is happiness,
I think it pervades the open air, waiting at all times,
Now it flows unto us, we are rightly charged.[180]

In section 2 of "Song of Myself," after repudiating "houses and perfumes," and establishing "undisguised and naked" contact with the atmosphere, Whitman expresses his joy of the senses, and catalogues them rhapsodically:

The smoke of my own breath,
Echoes, ripples, and buzzed whispers . . . . loveroot, silk-
  thread, crotch and vine,
My respiration and inspiration . . . . the beating of my heart
  . . . the passing of blood and air through my lungs . . . .[181]

He is celebrating his senses as part of the celebration of himself, which is the theme of the poem. And, apart from the identity he has recognized and is celebrating, of his soul with the Universal Soul, his body is also identified with his soul. So, the celebration of the body is an important part of the celebration of his self. The senses and organs, the body, the soul, and the Supreme Soul are all thus regarded in one single understanding. Though, as we shall see later on, the composition of the poem, as well as the position of these lines in it, received their inspiration elsewhere, this equalization of the bodily portion of his self and the soul, and their equation with the Supreme or Universal Self in one unified celebration, may have been affected by his reading of the passage that follows as Colebrooke's commentary on the Upani-shadic notion of God presented above:

The term *prána,* which is the subject of two of the sections just quoted . . . , properly and primarily signifies respiration, as well as certain other vital actions (inspiration, energy, ex-piration, digestion, or circulation of nourishment); and secon-darily, the senses and organs. But in the passages here referred to, it is employed for a different signification, intending the supreme *Brahmé.* . . . (p. 11)

Whitman is obviously celebrating or worshiping "prana" in its first and second significations, while, at the same time, like "INDRA," he has identified himself with it in its third meaning, although it was clearly said in the lines that followed that "it is not the embodied (saríra) and individual soul, but the supreme *Brahmé* himself, on whom devout meditation is to be fixed." (p. 12)

Whitman's pantheism, or recognition of God in the "materials" of the world, might have received encouragement from such passages as this, which in the same paragraph, declares: "This universe is indeed *Brahmé;* for it springs from him, merges in him, breathes in him; therefore, serene, worship him."

The analysis next dwells upon the "supreme spirit" and the "individual living soul" as "two occupying the cavity or ventricle of the heart . . . dwelling together in the worldly body, and tasting the fruit of good (or of evil) works."

So, in a dialogue, in which YÁJNYAWALCYA instructs UDDÁLACA "the internal check" (*antaryámin*) is the supreme being . . . "he who eternally restrains (or governs) this and the other world, and all beings therein . . . who standing in the earth is other than the earth, whom the earth knows not, whose body the earth is, who interiorly restrains (and governs) the earth: the same is thy soul (and mine)."

Again, in another dialogue, ANGIRAS . . . declares "there are two sciences . . . the superior . . . is that by which the unalterable (being) is comprehended, who is invisible (imperceptible by organs of sense), ungrasped (not prehensible by organs of action), . . . everlasting lord, present everywhere, yet most minute. Him, invariable, the wise contemplate as the source (or cause) of beings. As the spider puts forth and draws in his thread . . . so does the universe come of the unalterable."

"That on which heaven and earth and the intermediate transpicuous region are fixt, mind, with the vital airs (or sensitive organs), know to be the one soul (*atman*): reject other doctrines. This alone is the bridge of immortality." (pp. 12–14)

Apart from the description of the Supreme Being, and its identity with the individual soul, it is possible that the passage, with the simile of the spider and his thread, and the bridge of immortality, may have suggested Whitman's poem "A Noiseless Patient

Spider," in which, like the spider that "launch'd forth filament, filament, filament, out of itself," his own soul flung its "gossamer thread" to form "the bridge . . . to connect . . . the spheres"— obviously of life and death. Kennedy felt that the inspiration was W. R. Alger's "The Doctrine of a Future Life."[182]

Although Hindu thought is generally marked by an insistence on the insignificance of the body, liberation from which is the summum bonum of all philosophic inquiry, the body is nonetheless divine, being the abode of the Universal Being. Colebrooke's analysis of the *Vedanta* elaborates this point in the next paragraphs, and Whitman's religious respect for the body might well have received a suggestion from these too:

> In a passage descriptive of the lesser ventricle of the heart, it is said: "Within this body (*Brahmé-pura*) Brahme's abode, is a (*dahara*) little lotus, a dwelling within which is a (*dahara*) small vacuity occupied by ether (*ácása*). What that is which is within (the heart's ventricle) is to be inquired, and should be known." . . . The supreme being is here meant.
>
> "The sun shines not therein, nor the moon, nor stars: much less this fire. All shines after his effulgence (reflecting his light), by whose splendour this whole (world) is illumined." . . .
>
> In the dialogue between YAMA and NACHICÉTAS, before cited, occur the following passages. "A person (*purusha*) no bigger than the thumb abides in the midst of self;" and again, "the person no bigger than the thumb is clear as a smokeless flame, lord of the past (present) and future; he is today and will be tomorrow: such is he (concerning whom you inquire)." . . .
>
> Another passage of the same *upanishad* declares: "this whole universe, issuing from breath (*prána*), moves as it impels: great, terrible, as a clap of thunder. They, who know it, become immortal." . . .
>
> "The living soul (*samprasáda*) rising from this corporeal frame, attains the supreme light, and comes forth with his identical form." . . .
>
> "Ether (*ácása*) is the bearer (cause of bearing) of name and form. That, in the midst of which they both are, is BRAHME: it is immortality; it is soul." . . .
>
> In a dialogue between YÁJNYAWALCYA and JANACA, in answer to an enquiry "which is the soul?" the intelligent internal light within the heart is declared to be so. This likewise

is shown to relate to the supreme one, unaffected by worldly course. (pp. 15–16)

The thought of this passage reverberates in Whitman's "Inscription: to the Reader—at the entrance to Leaves of Grass," where he describes the "purport of his poetry," his gift:

> Such—and from where it lurks, indeed within yourself, for every apparition in this world is but to rout the real object up from sleeping in yourself, that something, to remind you, may appear, before your very feet, or under them—that fuses past and present and to-come in One, and never doubts them more.
> A little lowly thing, yet shining brighter than the sun, perfuming strange the hour that bathes you, the spot you stand upon, and every drop of blood that courses through your veins. Belief implicit, comprehending all,—may prove our journey's gift.[183]

One of the most profound of the Upanishadic discussions on the nature of the soul occurs in a "dialogue between YÁJNYAWAL-CYA and his wife MAITRÉYÍ," in which "soul and all else which is desirable, are contrasted as mutual objects of affection: 'it is for soul (atman) that opulence, kindred, and all else which is dear, are so; and thereunto soul reciprocally is so; and such is the object which should be meditated, inquired, and known, and by knowledge of whom all becomes known.' " (p. 17)

We have echoes of this thought throughout Whitman's poetry and prose. The "Song for Occupations," at first unnamed, essentially describes the primacy of the value of the soul, for which all else is meant, and for which the poet adds up "the sum of all known value and respect."

> All doctrines, all politics and civilization exurge from you,
> All sculpture and monuments and anything inscribed anywhere are tallied in you. . . .[184]

In "A Song of the Rolling Earth" he says again:

> Whoever you are! motion and reflection are especially for you,
> The divine ship sails the divine sea for you.

Whoever you are! you are he or she for whom the earth is
  solid and liquid,
You are he or she for whom the sun and moon hang in the
  sky . . . .

An important tenet of the *Vedanta,* that the supreme being is
the material as well as the efficient cause of the universe differen-
tiates it from the other schools, like Sankhya, that postulate two
principles as the cause of the universe. In refutation of that doctrine, the *Vedanta* dwells at length upon the unity of God:

> "The distinction relative to fruition, discriminating one who
> enjoys and that which is enjoyed, does not invalidate the single-
> ness and identity of BRAHME as cause and effect. The sea is
> one and not other than its waters; yet waves, foam, spray, drops,
> froth, and other modifications of it, differ from each other.
> "An effect is not other than its cause. BRAHME is single
> without a second. He is not separate from the embodied self.
> He is soul; and the soul is he. Yet he does not do that only
> which is agreeable and beneficial to self. The same earth exhibits
> diamonds, rock crystals, red orpiment, &c. . . .
> "As milk changes to curd, and water to ice, so is *BRAHME*
> variously transformed and diversified, without aid of tools or
> exterior means of any sort. In like manner, the spider spins his
> web out of his own substance. . . . Various changes are presented
> to the same dreaming soul. Divers illusory shapes and disguises
> are assumed by the same spirit.
> "BRAHME is omnipotent, able for every act, without organ
> or instrument . . . .
> "Unfairness and uncompassionateness are not to be imputed
> to him, because some (the gods) are happy, others (beasts and
> inferior beings) are miserable, and others again (men) partake
> of happiness and unhappiness. Every one has his lot, in the reno-
> vated world, according to his merits, his previous virtue or vice
> in a former stage of an universe, which is sempiternal and had
> no beginning in time. So the rain-cloud distributes rain im-
> partially; yet the sprout varies according to the seed." (pp.
> 20–21)

It is this Vedantic unity, surely, that Whitman describes in his
characteristic style, in an 1856 poem "On the Beach at Night
Alone":

A vast similitude interlocks all,
All spheres, grown, ungrown, small, large, suns, moons,
    planets,
All distances of place however wide,
All distances of time, all inanimate forms,
All souls, all living bodies though they be ever so different,
    or in different worlds,
All gaseous, watery, vegetable, mineral processes, the fishes,
    the brutes,
All nations, colors, barbarisms, civilizations, languages,
All identities that have existed or may exist on this globe or
    any globe,
All lives and deaths, all of the past, present, future,
This vast similitude spans them, and always has spann'd,
And shall forever span them and compactly hold and enclose
    them.

The passages that follow next in Colebrooke's analysis concern
the second of the topics of Vedanta discussion, the soul. Though
Whitman did not have to learn of the immortality and the divinity of his soul here, many of his utterances bear the impress of
the Hindu discussions on the subject, and probably these pages
played their role too.

". . . Evolution and re-absorption, or material birth and
death, cannot be affirmed of the soul. Birth and death are predicated of an individual, referring merely to his association with
body, which is matter fixed or moveable. Individual souls are,
in the *véda,* compared to sparks issuing from a blazing fire; but
the soul is likewise declared expressly to be eternal and unborn.
Its emanation is no birth, nor original production. . . .
"The soul is not of finite dimensions, as its transmigrations
seemingly indicate . . . but, on the contrary, being identified
with supreme BRAHME, it participates in his infinity.
"The soul is active. . . . Its activity, however, is not essential, but adventitious. As the carpenter, having his tools in hand,
toils and suffers, and laying them aside, rests and is easy, so the
soul in conjunction with its instruments (the senses and organs)
is active, and quitting them, reposes.
"Blind in the darkness of ignorance, the soul is guided in its
actions and fruition, in its attainment of knowledge and consequent liberation and bliss, by the supreme ruler of the universe,

who causes it to act conformably with its previous resolves: now, according to its former purposes, as then consonantly to its yet earlier predispositions, accruing from preceding forms with no retrospective limit; for the world had no beginning. . . .

"The soul is a portion of the supreme ruler, as a spark is of fire. The relation is not as that of master and servant, ruler and ruled, but as that of whole and part. . . . The soul, that animates body, is expressly affirmed to be a portion of him. He does not, however, partake of the pain and suffering of which the individual soul is conscious, through sympathy, during its association with body. . . ." (pp. 22–23)

These notions of the soul are basic to Whitman's philosophy and find expression in "Song of Myself" as well as in other poems carrying the heart of his message.

The next sections of the discussion of the nature of soul touch upon the corporeal element, and irresistibly put us in mind of Whitman's celebration of his senses and organs already referred to:

The corporeal organs of sense and of action, designated by the term *prána* in a secondary acceptation . . . have, like the elements and other objects . . . a similar origin, as modifications of BRAHME. . . . The precise number [of these] is, however, eleven: the five senses, sight, &c.; five active organs, the hand, &c.; and lastly, the internal faculty, mind, comprehending intelligence, consciousness, and sensation. . . . In its primary or principal signification, *prána* is vital action, and chiefly respiration. This, too, is a modification of BRAHME. . . . It is a particular vital act, and comprehends . . . respiration, inspiration, . . . a vigorous action, which is a mean between the foregoing two; . . . expiration, or passage upwards, as in metempsychosis; . . . digestion, or circulation of nutriment throughout the corporeal frame. . . . (pp. 23–24)

It is the supreme ruler, not the individual soul, who is described in passages of the *vedas* as transforming himself into diverse combinations, assuming various names and shapes, deemed terrene, aqueous or igneous, according to the predominancy of the one or the other element. When nourishment is received into the corporeal frame, it undergoes a threefold distribution, according to its fineness or coarseness: corn and other terrene food becomes flesh; but the coarser portion is ejected and the finer nourishes the mental organ. Water is converted into blood; the coarser particles are rejected as urine; the finer supports the breath. Oil or other combustible substance, deemed igneous, becomes marrow; the coarser part is deposited as bone, and the finer supplies the faculty of speech. (pp. 24–25)

Even if Whitman's note on the "soul or spirit" which,

transmits itself into all matter—into rocks, and can live the life of a rock—into the sea, and can feel itself the sea—into the oak, or other tree—into an animal, and feel itself a horse, a fish or bird—into the earth—into the motions of the sun and stars—[185]

did not arise from the passage quoted above, it is possible to suspect that he is speaking of that "vital act" of the "animating spirit" achieving "fruition" when he asks:

> Who goes there! hankering, gross, mystical nude?
> How is it I extract strength from the beef I eat?[186]

The succeeding sections of Colebrooke's essay deal with death and transmigration, and we have already noticed them as giving to Whitman the moon and sun figure to describe the infinity and immortality of his self. In the midst of this discussion there are some passages that again take up the question of the "nature and attributes of the supreme being," of which a brief extract is presented here:

". . . This luminous immortal being, who is in this earth, is the same with the luminous, immortal, embodied spirit, which informs the corporeal self, and is the same with the (supreme) soul. . . .

". . . The luminous sun, though single, yet reflected in water, becomes various; and so does the unborn divine soul by disguise in divers modes."

The *veda* so describes him, as entering into and pervading the corporeal shapes by himself wrought. "He framed bodies, biped and quadruped; and becoming a bird, he passed into those bodies, filling them as their informing spirit." (p. 26)

We may remember that, like this supreme being, Whitman's "Self" is "unitary," and yet says,

I resist anything better than my own diversity,[187]

while still possessing omnipresence, omniscience, and universal incorporation.

The supreme being, to Vedanta, "is imperceptible; yet during devout meditation is, as it were, apprehended by perception and inference, through revelation and authentic recollections. . . . Therefore is one, who knows the truth, identified with the infinite being; for so revelation indicates. . . . There is none other but he. . . . He is ubiquitary and eternal; for he is pronounced to be greater than ethereal space, which is infinite." (p. 27)

Whitman's entry in an early notebook is an echo of this passage:

All the vastness of Astronomy—and space—and systems of suns [blank] carried in their computation to the farthest that figures are able . . . then multiplied in geometrical progression ten thousand billion fold do not more than symbolize the reflection of the reflection, of the spark thrown off a spark, from some emanation of God.—Even these the greatest of the great men of the world, can in their best moments[188]

A large portion of the essay next relates "chiefly to devout exercises and pious meditation, the practice of which is inculcated as proper and requisite to prepare the soul and mind for the reception of divine knowledge," and to "the fruit and effect" of those practices. Certain parts of this have been cited earlier in our survey, describing the "journey of the soul" after its "retirement from body." There is, however, one more interesting passage in which the phenomenon of death, the "ascent of the soul, or mode in which it passes from the body," is described, that deserves notice.

Of a dying person the speech, followed by the rest of the ten exterior faculties (not the corporeal organs themselves), is absorbed into the mind, for the action of the outer organ ceases before the mind's. This, in like manner, retires into the breath, attended likewise by all the other vital functions, for they are life's companions; and the same retreat of the mind is observable, also, in profound sleep and in a swoon. Breath, attended likewise by all other vital faculties, is withdrawn into the living soul which governs the corporeal organs, as the attendants of a king assemble around him when he is setting out upon a journey; for all vital functions gather about the soul at the last minute when it is expiring. The living soul, attended with all its faculties, retires within a rudiment of body, composed of light with the rest of the five elements, in a subtle state. "Breath" is, therefore, said to withdraw into "light;" not meaning that element (or fire) exclusively; nor intending direct transition, for a traveller has gone from one city to another, though he passed through an intermediate town. (pp. 29–30)

The account of death as a journey of the soul, given thus in this and the other passages noticed, probably had a share in the making of Whitman's notion of "the exquisite transition of death,"[189] "the beautiful touch of Death, soothing and benumbing a few minutes, for reasons."[190] More significant, doubtless, is the contribution of the idea of "journey" that these pages have made to his poetic imagination. In a penetrating analysis, Allen has noticed how the "long journey" motif is "of the greatest importance in a study of the genesis of *Leaves of Grass,* in the interpretation of its message, and in understanding the psychology of Whitman's style."[191]

This fascination of Whitman with the idea of "journey of souls," which he uses with such profound connotations in both his poems and prose, can be traced to his readings in Hindu philosophy, because the notion of the soul as traveling through life, death, time, and the material universe to the ultimate liberation or absorption with the Supreme Being is basic to it, and is to be found in all accounts of it. Bliss Perry rightly regarded as one of his Oriental traits this concept of Whitman, of the "Universe as a Road for traveling souls."[192] The idea, undoubtedly, came to Whitman, with many other details, from such passages as the one we are examining, which repeatedly uses the metaphor. In addition to what is seen in the above extracts, there is a description of the souls that "proceed further on their respective paths" after departing from the body; of the liberated soul "proceeding directly to reunion with the supreme being"; of the heart that lightens "the passage by which the soul is to depart," by which passage, in virtue of "recollection of the meditated way," the soul "by that route" proceeds; of the "further progress of the soul . . . to its final destination"; of "intermediate stations" relating to "one uniform route . . . for the divine journey (*déva-yána*) which the liberated soul travels"; of "the intermediate stations," or "scenes of fruition to be visited in succession, or landmarks designated for the course and direction of the route"; of "the presiding deities or regents of the places or regions indicated, . . . guides to the soul, who forward it on its way"; of "the route . . . by a solar ray to the realm of fire; thence to the regents of the day, . . . and thence to the abode of gods . . . to air or wind, the regent of which forwards the journeying soul from his precincts, by a narrow passage . . . towards the sun; thence the transition to the moon, whence to the region of lightning, above which is the realm of VARUNA, . . . the rest of the way . . . by the realm of INDRA, to the abode of PRAJÁPATI or *Brahme*." (pp. 31–32)

The consequence of all this long journey of the soul "is single, not varying in degree and inducing different gradations of bliss, but complete and final happiness" (p. 28), because the soul "ascends to the supreme light which is *Brahme*." Whitman's message is,

> To know the universe itself as a road, as many roads, as roads
> for traveling souls.

> All parts away for the progress of souls,
> All religion, all solid things, arts, governments—all that was
> or is apparent upon this globe or any globe,
> falls into niches and corners before the pro-
> cession of souls along the grand roads of the
> universe.
> . . . .
> They go! They go! I know that they go, but I know not
> where they go,
> But I know that they go toward the best—toward something
> great.[193]

And when his own "eidólon yacht" was ready for his voyage "on really deep waters" in 1891, he cried:

(I will not call it our concluding voyage
But outset and sure entrance to the truest, best maturest;)
Depart, depart from solid earth—no more returning to these
    shores,
Now on for aye our infinite free venture wending,
Spurning all yet tried ports, seas, hawsers, densities, gravita-
    tion,
Sail out for good, eidólon yacht of me![194]

From the testimony of his friends like Bucke, Kennedy, and Carpenter, we gather that Whitman was personally a man of great
equanimity of spirit, of serenity of temper, cheerful, fearless, and
so on, though from Carpenter's account we also understand his
"contradictory, self-willed, tenacious, obstinate character, and
even extreme moods, united with infinite tenderness, wistful love,
and studied tolerance; also great caution . . . and a certain artfulness, combined with keen, penetrating and determined candour;
the wild-hawk look still there 'untamable, untranslatable,' yet,
with that wonderful tenderness at bottom."[195] Burroughs said,
"He is by far the wisest man I have ever met. . . . He loves everything and everybody," and yet noted, "Notwithstanding the beauty
and expressiveness of his eyes, I see something in them . . . that
almost makes me draw back. . . . It is as if the Earth looked at
me—dumb, yearning, relentless, immodest, inhuman. . . ."[196]
Bucke's biographical sketch describes how Whitman "would not
allow his tongue to give expression to fretfulness, antipathy, complaint and remonstrance . . . never complained or grumbled at the
weather, pain, illness or anything else . . . never spoke in anger . . .
never exhibited fear. . . ."[197] Helen Price regarded him as "a born
exalté," and "his *religious sentiment* or feeling" as his "leading
characteristic."[198]

From the element of contradiction in him, and the "artfulness"
and other evidences his life supplies, it looks as if a good deal of the
character he came to possess was "studied" and deliberate, consciously imposed upon the native elements of his true being in an
attempt to identify himself with the personality he imaginatively
created in his poetry. On later occasions we shall examine this
question at length, and show how both as a poet, the writer, and
as a man, personally, Whitman appears to have closely modeled

himself after the ideal man of Hindu thought, the yogi, or "liberated soul," who is one of the major themes of discussion in all systems. The account of "yoga" and the "yogi" appears in a more elaborate description in Ward's *View* and other books like the *Bhagvat-Geeta* to be noticed hereafter, but Colebrooke, combining the Yoga with the Sankhya system, as the theistical version of it, in a single essay, treated it succinctly, merely enunciating its philosophical tenets in a comparative study. His other essays make occasional references to it too, but none of them gives a picture of the "yogi" in detail. The Vedanta account likewise, toward the close, briefly alludes to the "liberated soul" of a yogi, presenting the following opinion of this condition.

[The liberated man,] JAIMINI maintained . . . is endued with divine attributes, omniscience, ubiquitary power, and other transcendent faculties. AUDULOMI insisted, that he becomes sheer thought, sentient intelligence. The author of the *Sútras* (BADARÁYANA) accedes to the last-mentioned opinion; admitting, however, the practical or apparent possession of divine faculties by one who has attained perfection of knowledge.

By certain devout exercises and meditation, a less perfect knowledge is acquired. . . . In that condition transcendent power is enjoyed. . . . The *pitris,* or shades of progenitors, may be called up by a simple act of the will; and other superhuman faculties may be similarly exerted. The possessor of these is independent, subject to no other's control. He may, at his option, be vested with one or more bodies, furnished with senses and organs, or be unincumbered with a corporeal frame. . . . In one case, the condition is that of a person dreaming; in the other case, as of one awake.

"Master of several bodies, by a simple act of his will, the Yogi does not occupy one only, leaving the rest inanimate, like so many wooden machines. He may animate more than one, in like manner as a single lamp may be made to supply more than one wick."

Such a *Yogi,* uncontrolled and independent as he has been pronounced to be, can exert every faculty and superior power analogous to that of the divinity's, which may be conducive to enjoyment; but he has not a creative power. His faculties are transcendent for enjoyment, not for action. (pp. 33–34)

If the young, troubled, depressed soul of Catel's Whitman
sought a means of exaltation, a release from diffidence and sense of
frustration, he might have found fascinating suggestions in the
yogi and the exercises that give such assurance and transcendence
to him.

Colebrooke ends his last essay with a recapitulation in which he
sums up "the principal and essential tenets of the Vedanta," and
some of them, partly on account of the additional remarks "in
which other authorities are likewise employed," stand clearer here,
such as God's being the "creator and nature, framer and frame,
doer and deed," and of being "one, sole-existent, secondless, entire,
without parts, sempiternal, infinite, ineffable, invariable ruler of
all, universal soul, truth, wisdom, intelligence, happiness"; and the
soul, "emanating from the supreme one," being "a portion of the
divine substance; and as such, infinite, immortal, intelligent, sentient, true." (p. 35)

The most significant of these clarifications concerns the idea of
many bodies investing the soul, and since it is one of the favorite
notions of Whitman, the passage is reproduced in full.

> The soul is incased in body as in a sheath, or rather in a suc-
> cession of sheaths. The first or inner case is the intellectual one
> (*vijnyánamaya*): it is composed of the sheer (*tan-mátra*), or
> simple elements uncombined, and consists of the intellect
> (*buddhi*) joined with the five senses.
>
> The next is the mental (*manómaya*) sheath, in which mind is
> joined with the preceding. A third sheath or case comprises the
> organs of action and the vital faculties, and is termed the organic
> or vital case. These three sheaths (*cósa*) constitute the subtile
> frame (*súcshma-saríra,* or *linga-saríra*) which attends the soul in
> its transmigrations. The interior rudiment confined to the inner
> case in the causal frame (*cárana-sarira*).
>
> The gross body (*st'húla-saríra*) which it animates from birth
> to death in any step of its transmigrations, is composed of the
> coarse elements, formed by combinations of the simple ele-
> ments. . . . The exterior case, composed of elements so combined,
> is the nutrimentitious (*annamaya*) sheath; and being the scene

of coarse fruition, is therefore termed gross body. (pp. 35–36)

And if Whitman accepted evil as part of the nature of things, even a principle of life as one portion of the Four-faced God of the "Square Deific," and yet reconciled it with his firm faith in God, so did the Vedanta account in Colebrooke:

> According to its predisposition for good or evil, for enjoined or forbidden deeds, it [the individual soul] is made to do good or ill, and thus has its retribution for previous works. Yet GOD is not the author of evil; for so it has been from eternity: the series of preceding forms and dispositions manifested in them has been infinite. (p. 35)

If all this Vedantic thought influenced Whitman, as our rough study of correspondences implies, it would seem that the famous "Maya" doctrine of the school should have found a significant place in his system. But Whitman is as much a poet of the body as of the soul, indeed, too much of it, a position to which another ardent body-worshiper like D. H. Lawrence "took off his hat," and said, "Whitman was the first heroic seer to seize the soul by the scruff of her neck and plant her down among the potsherds."[199] There are several answers to the question; one of them may be, as Colebrooke finally observes, that

> The notion, that the versatile world is an illusion (*máyá*), that all which passes to the apprehension of the waking individual is but a phantasy presented to his imagination, and every seeming thing is unreal and all is visionary, does not appear to be the doctrine of the text of the *Vedanta*. . . . The doctrine of the early *Vedanta* is complete and consistent, without this graft of a later growth. (p. 39)

For, truly, the doctrine of "maya or illusion," though of its signification Whitman gathered enough from all the Hindu material he read, from the periodicals to the *Gita,* to use it in his poems and in the "Democratic Vistas,"[200] does not deny the reality of matter altogether. As Sir William Jones, quoted in Colonel Vans Kennedy's essay on "the Vedanta System," the last of the articles we have to notice in the *Transactions,*[201] said:

The fundamental tenet of the *Vedanti* school, to which in a more modern age the incomparable SANCARA was a firm and illustrious adherent, consisted, not in denying the existence of matter, that is, of solidity, impenetrability, and extended figure (to deny which would be lunacy), but in correcting the popular notion of it, and in contending that it has no essence independent of mental perception; that existence and perceptibility are convertible terms; that external appearances and sensations are illusory, and would vanish into nothing, if the divine energy, which alone sustains them, were suspended for a moment. (pp. 414–15)

Kennedy's essay is primarily concerned with controverting Colebrooke's assertion that the "maya" concept is not part of the original Vedanta, but his elaborate discussion of the subject involves a considerable analysis of the Vedanta thought itself, besides ranging, in a comparative investigation, into Western schools of philosophy like those of Fichte, Schelling, Berkeley, Malebranche, and Descartes, with extracts and quotations from Mosheim, Cousis, and Tiedman. The sum of his argument is that "SANCARA, however, in general uses other terms than *maya,* but all imply the same meaning and convey the same doctrine, namely, that this universe is a mere illusion, and that man, even in this life, may become so enlightened by the acquisition of divine knowledge as to perceive that there is nothing real except the Supreme Soul, and *he* is that soul." The second point on which the argument is carried is that the Vedanta is a "spiritual" not "material" pantheism, as, in Kennedy's opinion, Colebrooke has suggested. In support of his contention, Kennedy quotes Sir W. Jones again, who says:

The *Vedanta* theologists asserted in a remote age "that all spirit is homogeneous, that the spirit of God is in kind the the same with that of man, though differing from it infinitely in degree, and that, as material substance is mere illusion, there exists in the universe only one generic spiritual substance, the sole primary cause, efficient, substantial, and formal of all secondary causes and appearances whatever." (p. 415)

The controversy apart, Kennedy's essay, in its survey of Western schools whose thought is brought in to substantiate or clarify

Vedanta notions, touches upon other questions of philosophical interest like cognition, the nature of reality, and the like, and could have been of considerable use to Whitman, as these few of his extracts from Fichte and Schelling will show:

"Egoism . . . is subject-objectivity, and nothing else whatever; the considering that the subject and its object, consciousness and conception are one and the same; and that there is absolutely nothing except this identity."

"Except God there is nothing real. . . ."

"God is essentially nature, and nature is essentially God."

"That which is, is reality, and reality is, that which is." (pp. 432–34)

5

A GODDESS NAMED SANTA SPIRITA

THE OTHER JOURNALS ON ORIENTAL RESEARCH NEED NOT HOLD
our attention at all. The larger part of the material they contain
is relative to political or historical affairs, and is in the form of
brief notices, and, even if some of the articles, as in the Journal
of the Royal Society of England and Ireland, concern the literature of India, like *the Puranas, Mahavamsa, Shabdakalpadruma,*
and so on, and so incidentally carry frequent philosophical suggestions, they cannot be considered to have given anything new to
Whitman. Bucke's list of magazine articles in Whitman's possession
mentions one called "Indian Mounds" (No. 537). Volume No. 7
Part I, of the Journal of the R. A. S., had an article entitled
"Mounds of Ashes in India," and it is possible that this was the
one Whitman had in his collection.

Examining the pages of the *Oriental Collections,* I and III,
1797–1799, by William Ouseley for any material on India, I was
particularly struck by the similarity of Whitman's verse line pattern to that of the "Persian Ode of Hafiz," which Ouseley translated on pages 277–278 of his first volume:

It is festival, and the season of the rose; boy, bring wine.—
Whoever saw, in the time of the rose, a cup placed down
without wine?
My heart shrinks from the malicious hypocrisy of affected
temperance: pour out the wine, boy, that my heart may be
expanded.
Him, who yesterday preached serious advice to lovers, I this

day beheld drunk, and his piety and solemnity given to the
wind.

For these two or three days to come, plunder the roses! and if
you are a lover, seek the delights of love in revelling with
beautiful damsels.

The rose is now departed! but why, my companions, do you
sit languid and inanimate without the sound of tabour and
flute, without a minstrel and a flask of wine?

. . . .

The *Oriental Collections,* which was available both in the Astor
and the Mercantile Libraries, has only a translation of a "Fragment from *Bhagavat Purana,*" and a list of Sanskrit works in Urdu
done into English, and all else is from the Arabic or Persian.

The Journal of the American Oriental Society, four volumes of
which both Astor and Mercantile possessed, has a long article in
its fourth volume on the "History of Vedic Texts" by J. Muir,
and likewise, scattered among the pages of the Asiatic Journal,
the Asiatic Annual Register, and the Journal of the Asiatic Society of Bengal, there are many articles that deal directly or indirectly with Hindu religious or philosophical thought. Since it
would be a tedious affair to examine all these scattered fragments,
we may pass over them as of inferior, if not of no importance.
Thomas Maurice's *Antiquities* and Cory's *Ancient Fragments* may
be similarly disregarded.

Sir William Jones's *Works,* however, deserves some attention as
one of the major sources of Oriental knowledge to the Western
world, and in particular to the Concordians. Jones was available
to Whitman both on the Mercantile and the Astor shelves. A good
part of the contents of the *Works* had first appeared in the *Asiatic
Researches* in our survey of which we have noticed a few of Jones's
articles. Therefore the rest of the *Works* may be dismissed with a
brief word. Among its contents not found in the *Researches,* the
significant ones are: the translation of *The Institutes of Menu*
occupying the whole of Volume III; the *Panchatantra* of which
the *Hitopadesha* is a part, Kalidasa's *Sacontala,* extracts from the
Vedas, and several hymns of Jones's own, to *Narayana, Ganga,
Pracriti, Indra, Cáma, Lakshmi, Saraswati* and *Surya,* all rooted
in Hindu philosophical thought, in volume VI.

Whether Whitman had read the *Works* also or not cannot be decided entirely on the basis of striking verbal correspondence or identity of expression; it rests mainly on the support of probability. He had read *Sakuntala* as we know from Carpenter's report. Astor library had also a separate edition of Jones's translation of *Sacontala: or the Fatal Ring,* and it is impossible to fix which of these he read, the independent edition or the one in the *Works,* or even, for that matter, Jones's or some one else's translation later. But from the circumstance that Jones is repeatedly referred to in the periodical articles as the source of much of their observations on India, with his *Sacontala* mentioned as well, and from Whitman's own reading in the *Researches,* which could hardly have failed to rouse his enthusiasm for the scholarly president of the society publishing those researches, it is reasonable to suppose that he read both Jones's *Sacontala* and the rest of his *Works.* Besides, as we have noticed, the *Laws of Menu* appears to have captured Whitman's imagination, but the articles of the *Whig Review* and the *Dial* had carried only a few extracts, and so, again, it is a fair presumption that he was interested enough to read Jones where he found the full text of *The Institutes.*

Addressing God as the "light of the light" in "Passage to India," section 8, Whitman prays:

> Bathe me O God in thee, mounting to thee,
> I and my soul to range in range of thee,

so that with "the seas all crossed, weather'd the capes, the voyage done," and "the Elder Brother found," "the Younger" might melt "in fondness in his arms."

How closely his prayer resembles one of the extracts of the *Vedas* in Jones may be observed.

> "May that soul of mine, which mounts aloft in my waking hours, as an ethereal spark, and which, even in my slumber, has a like ascent, soaring to a great distance, as an emanation from the light of lights, be united by devout meditation with *the* spirit supremely blest, and supremely intelligent."[202]

Another Vedic extract on the same page speaks of the Self thus:

"May that soul of mine, in which, as an immortal essence, may be comprised whatever has past, is present, or will be hereafter . . ."

Here are a few of Whitman's utterances on the soul:

The similitudes of the past and those of the future,
The glories strung like beads on my smallest sights and hearings . . .[203]

. . . You and your soul enclose all things.[204]

Such—and from where it lurks, indeed within yourself, . . . that something . . . that fuses past and present and to-come in One.[205]

A third extract in Jones hints at the spiritual unity of all beings:

May that soul of mine, which, *distributed in other bodies,* guides mankind, as a skilful charioteer guides his rapid horses with reins . . .

One wonders if this prayer lurked in Whitman's fancy, when, his new verse playing upon his cosmic identity as a being, and his ambition upon his messianic role as a poet, he wrote in his 1847 manuscript:

I will not be the cart, nor the load on the cart, nor the horses that draw the cart; but I will be the little hands that guide the cart.[206]

We may also remember that Lord Krishna of the *Bhagavadgita* was a charioteer when he uttered his song.

One of the personal characteristics of Whitman as described by his friends was his universal love and sympathy. ". . . So kind, sympathetic, charitable, humane, tolerant a man I did not suppose was possible. He loves everything and everybody," said Burroughs.[207] Bucke wrote: "He appeared to like all the men, women, children, he saw. . . . He never spoke deprecatingly of any nationality or class of men, or time in the world's history, or against any trades or occupations—not even against any animals, insects, or inanimate things, nor any of the laws of nature. . . ."[208] In the "self" of his poetry, too, the same universal charity and love breathe. "The meal" he sets, is set "for the wicked just the same as the righteous"; he "will not have a single person slighted or left away."[209] And in that infinite sympathy (which, incidentally, D. H. Lawrence so ungenerously belittles)[210] we remember that he makes "appointments with all," a "common prostitute" too; for he will not "exclude" her,—"not till the sun excludes her.[211] Now, this limitless benevolence is the result of the realization that, like him,

They show their descent from the Master himself.

Therefore,

Off the word I have spoken I except not one. . . . red white or black, all are deific. . . .[212]

Both this personal demeanor and this poetic attitude have a common foundation: they correspond to the man of true knowledge, the man of God, the philosopher, or Whitman's "Answerer." This is the man, we have suggested, that Whitman sought to be, and to picture in his poems. He found him throughout his readings in Indian philosophy, and, in Jones, in the following extracts from *Isavásyam,* an upanishad from *Yejurveda:*

"The man who considers all beings as existing even in the supreme spirit, and the supreme spirit as pervading all beings, henceforth views no creature with contempt."

"In him who knows that all spiritual beings are the same *in kind* with the supreme spirit, what *room can there be* for the delusion of mind, or what room for sorrow when he reflects on the identity of spirit?"

"That all-pervading spirit, that spirit which gives light to the visible sun, even the same *in kind* am I, though infinitely distant in degree."[213]

I should think that a reading such as this is sufficient "revelation" for the "knowledge" Whitman wrote of:

And I know that the hand of God is the elderhand of my own,
And I know that the spirit of God is the eldest brother of my
own,
And that all the men ever born are also my brothers. . . . and
the women my sisters and lovers.[214]

So if, as Gabriel Sarrazin said, Whitman "is the only man who has absolutely *known* that Man is an indivisible fragment of the Universal Divinity,"[215] the *knowing* does not seem to have necessitated a mystic vision.

The message of equality that Whitman gave to mankind, which, incidentally, is of the spirit; the philosophic identity with which

He says indifferently and alike, How are you friend, to the
President at his levee,
And he says Good-day my brother, to Cudge that hoes in the
sugarfield. . . ;[216]

and the spiritual pride in which he declares, "I cock my hat as I please indoors or out,"[217] all could have been born in the knowledge to which the next extract in Jones, a "Fragment," refers:

"In thee, in me, in every other, VISHNU resides; in vain art thou angry with me, not bearing my approach; this is perfectly true, all must be esteemed equal; be not, therefore, proud of a magnificent palace."[218]

Unlike the poems of most lyric poets, those of Whitman are not "spontaneous outbursts of powerful feeling," but slowly, patiently, painstakingly wrought expressions of thought. To this fact not only the testimony of his friends about his method of composition bears witness, but also the enormous mass of drafts that went into the making of a poem. "He wrote and rewrote," said Brinton, "with indefatigable industry. Every line, every phrase, every word, was patiently considered and reconsidered. The Prayer of Columbus, for instance, was rewritten about twenty times. The re-scripts are in existence. I have examined them."[219] From such a picture of the growth of a poem in Whitman's art, one gets the impression that his genius lay more in what may be called formation than in creation. This is not to deny the power in him, because even formation is, to a considerable degree, creation, and involves originality. However, the result of his prolonged and complex mode of constructing a poem is often that, in the shaping of a poem or even of its single lines, several inspirations, several details of varied origin, become fused and integrated.

One of Whitman's most profound poems, as well as beautiful from the viewpoint of artistic unity and workmanship, is "Chanting the Square Deific," a poem whose novelty of thought has been regarded as much a puzzle as its masterly expression a marvel. The desire from which it is to be taken to have sprung, namely, to create a new theological system, is understandable as part of his larger scheme of constructing "the New Bible." But it looks as if the inspiration for the particular idea of a Square Deific, apparently so original, like much less in him has an external source. George L. Sixbey has examined, as we have seen, the contribution of Bailey's *Festus* to the third of Whitman's Square.[220] The concepts of a Square and the fourth of the Square have in turn similar indications of originating in his readings in Hindu philosophy.

The concept of Trinity in Godhead is not foreign to Whitman's own native thought, and the first three of his Square are essentially drawn from the Christian doctrine, with which—to take into consideration Whitman's universal element—the Egyptian and the more well-known Hindu concept also correspond, at least in number. But a less well-known Hindu thought postulates a square godhead. Not, in fairness, to widen the field to include what Whitman possibly did not read, even in the limited area of what he has read this thought is frequently expressed. In Whelpley's article, as we have noticed, he ran into the description of *Brahme,* the Supreme Being, issuing into three gods, Brahma the creator, Vishnu the preserver, and Shiva the destroyer and regenerator. Frederick von Raumer's *Lectures on Ancient History,* also noticed earlier, had a similar thought. These, we must repeat, do not in all details correspond with Whitman's Square. Nor do the following, described in *The Vishnu Purana.* But the notion of a Square Deific is powerfully suggested in them:

These four—Pradhána (primary or crude matter), Purusha (spirit), Vyakta (visible substance), and Kála (time)—the wise consider to be the pure and supreme condition.

Thus Hari, the four-faced God . . . accomplished the creation.

By a fourfold manifestation does Janardhana operate in creation, preservation and destruction. In one portion, as Brahma, the invisible assumes a visible form; in another he . . . is the progenitor of all creatures; his third portion is time; his fourth is all beings: and thus he became quadruple in creation, invested with the quality of passion.

So in periods of creation and of dissolution (and duration) the four portions of the god of gods are equally essential. . . .

But his highest glory is detached from all qualities; for the fourfold essence of the Supreme Spirit is composed of true wisdom, pervades all things, is only to be appreciated by itself, and admits of no similitude. . . . Maitréya—But, Muni, describe to me fully the four varieties of the condition of Brahma. . . .
Parásara—[after describing them] . . . Those Yogis, who, by the annihilation of ignorance, are resolved into this fourfold Brahma, lose the seminal property.[221]

In the course of an explanatory footnote on a point concerning the Hindu Trinity, the translator quotes from Cudworth that "Orpheus, Pythagoras, and Plato have all of them asserted a trinity of divine hypostases."[222] If all the other philosophers of the world gave a trinity, Whitman probably felt he would give a quaternity.

Apart from the suggestion of a square, *The Vishnu Purana* appears to have played an important role in the fourth of the Square Deific, though here it shares its honour with others, principally Jones's *Works*. The fourth part of the Deific, in spite of Trowbridge's mistaken impression,[223] does not seem female by the accident of a philological error due to Whitman's bad knowledge of the Italian, but by the design of a philosophical assertion. Sixbey rightly affirms that in the fourth, "in a sense, is the progenitor of the gods—Gaea, the Earth Mother, the almost universal primitive symbol of the emergence of life," and that "the feminine Santa Spirita mystically resolves the eternal conflict with love and gives direction and form to the divine energies released as the life force."[224]

In the Harned Collection of Whitman material there is an item, No. 1980, which discusses the Indian Trinity. In its analysis it refers to "Devaki" as the "idea of feminine deity." Whitman writes in the margin of the piece: "Ingersoll's lecture."

Now, the concept of a feminine deity could have come to Whitman from the description of "*Maya, the Supreme Goddess*," in Jones's article on the "Gods of Greece, Italy and India," or from Wilford's, where the true meaning of the Sanskrit word "Ambá" was explained as referring to the "Universal Mother," or from "Bhavani, the all-generative nature," who, according to Frederick von Raumer's account, produced the gods of the Hindu trinity. These are slight hints, but the following passage from *The Vishnu Purana* appears to be one of the two major sources of inspiration from the Santa Spirita, the other being Jones, to whom we shall return shortly. The passage is an account of "the gods, invisible to mortals," celebrating Devaki's praises:

Thou (said the divinities) art Prakriti, infinite and subtile, which formerly bore Brahmá in its womb: then wast thou the goddess of speech, the energy of the creator of the universe, and the parent of the Vedas. Thou eternal being, comprising in thy substance the essence of all created things, wast identical with creation: thou wast the parent of the triform sacrifice, being the germ of all things: thou art sacrifice, whence all fruit proceeds: thou art the wood, whose attrition engenders fire. As Aditi, thou art the parent of the gods; as Diti thou art the mother of Daityas, their foes. Thou art light, whence day is begotten: thou art humility, the mother of true wisdom: thou art kingly policy, the parent of order: thou art modesty, the progenitrex of affection: thou art desire, of whom love is born: thou art contentment, whence resignation is derived: thou art intelligence, the mother of knowledge: thou art patience, the parent of fortitude: thou art the heavens, and thy children are the stars: and from thee does all that exists proceed. Such, goddess, and thousands more, are thy mighty faculties; and how innumerable are the contents of thy womb, O mother of the universe. . . . Thou art Swáhá; thou art Swádhá; thou art wisdom, ambrosia, light, and heaven. Thou hast descended upon the earth for the preservation of the world. Have compassion upon us, O goddess, and do good unto the world.[225]

This elaborate digression into *The Vishnu Purana* was required to make it clear how the entire poem perhaps came to be conceived, as well as the idea of the feminine portion of the Square Deific. We shall now return to the *Works* of Sir. W. Jones, whose hymns in Volume 6, particularly those touching upon the "feminine deity," could have added appreciably to Whitman's thought. We shall consider only two of them, and in fragments. One of these, the twin of the "Two Hymns to Pracriti," is called "Hymn to Bhavani"; the other is the famous "Hymn to Narayena" that inspired Emerson.

In an introduction to the "Two Hymns to Pracriti," presenting the argument of the poems, Jones offers an explanation of the concept:

> The *female* divinity, in the mythological systems of the East represents the active *power* of the *male*. . . ; this feminine character of PRAKRITI or *created* nature is so familiar in most languages, and even in our own, that the gravest of English writers . . . speak of *her* operations, as if *she* were actually an animated being. . . . The principal operations of nature are, not the absolute annihilation and new creation of what we call *material substances,* but . . . the *transmutation* of forms.[226]

The first, the third, and the ninth stanzas of the second of these Hymns, the one to "Bhavani," are reproduced here:

> When time was drowned in sacred sleep,
> And raven darkness brooded o'er the deep,
> Reposing on primeval pillows
> Of tossing billows,
> The forms of animated nature lay;
> Till o'er the wild abyss, where love
> Sat like a nestling dove,
> From heav'n's dun concave shot a golden ray.

The second describes the rising of the Lotus, Bhavani's "orient bed."

Mother of Gods, rich nature's queen,
Thy genial fire emblaz'd the bursting scene;
For, on th' expanded blossom fitting,
With sun-beams knitting
That mystick veil for ever unremov'd,
Thou badst the softly kindling flame
Pervade this peopled frame,
And smiles, with blushes ting'd, the work approv'd.
. . . .

Thus, in one vast eternal gyre,
Compact or fluid shapes, instinct with fire,
Lead, as thy dance, this gay creation,
Whose mild gradation
Of melting tints illu[m]es the visual ray:
Dense earth in springing herbage lives,
Thence life and nurture gives
To sentient forms, that sink again to clay.[227]

In the preface presenting the argument of the "Hymn to Narayena," Jones makes the following remarks:

> . . . The inextricable difficulties attending the *vulgar notion* of *material substances,* concerning which
>   "We know this only, that we nothing know,"
> induced many of the wisest among the Ancients, and some of the most enlightened among the Moderns to believe, that the whole Creation was rather an *energy* than a *work,* by which the Infinite Being, who is present at all times in all places, exhibits to the minds of his creatures a set of perceptions, like a wonderful picture or piece of musick, always varied, yet always uniform; so that all bodies and their qualities exist, indeed, to every wise and useful purpose, but exist only as far as they are perceived; . . . This *illusive operation* of the Deity the Hindu philosophers call MAYÁ or *Deception.*[228]

Whitman makes similar observations on the universe in his notes for "Lectures on Religion."

> . . . And what is the Universe, with all its shows? What is Life itself? but a Vestibule to something, in the future, we know not what—but something as certain as the Present is

certain. Nay, who that has reach'd what may be called the full
Vestibule but has had some strong suspicions that what we
call the Present, Reality, &c. with all its Corporeal shows,
may be the Illusion for reasons, & that even to this Identity of
yours or mine, the far more Permanent is yet unseen, yet to
come.[229]

The first stanza of the "Hymn to Narayena," to use the author's
own description, "represents the sublimest attributes of the Supreme Being, and the three forms, in which they most clearly appear to us, *Power, Wisdom* and *Goodness,* or, in the language of
ORPHEUS and his disciples, *LOVE:* the *second* [stanza] com-
prises the *Indian* and *Egyptian* doctrine of the Divine Essence
and Archetypal *Ideas.*" These two stanzas are reproduced here as
another possible source of inspiration and suggestion to Whitman's Square generally, and to Santa Spirita specifically:

Spirit of Spirits, who, through ev'ry part
    Of space expanded and of endless time,
    Beyond the stretch of lab'ring thought sublime,
    Badst uproar into beauteous order start,
        Before Heav'n was, Thou art:
Ere spheres beneath us roll'd or spheres above,
    Ere earth in firmamental ether hung,
    Thou satst alone; till through thy mystic Love,
    Things unexisting to existence sprung,
        And grateful descant sung.
What first impell'd thee to exert thy might?
    Goodness unlimited. What glorious light
    Thy pow'r directed? Wisdom without bound.
    What prov'd it first? Oh! guide my fancy right;
        Oh! raise from cumbrous ground,
        My soul in rapture drown'd,
    That fearless it may soar on wings of fire;
For Thou, who only knowst, Thou only canst inspire.

Wrapt in eternal solitary shade,
    Th' impenetrable gloom of light intense,
    Impervious, inaccessible, immense,
    Ere spirits were infus'd or forms display'd,
        BREHM his own Mind survey'd,

> As mortal eyes (thus finite we compare
>   With infinite) in smoothest mirrors gaze:
> Swift, at his look, a shape supremely fair
> Leap'd into being with a boundless blaze,
>   That fifty suns might daze.
> Primeval MAYA was the Goddess nam'd
>   Who to her Sire, with Love divine inflam'd,
>   A casket gave with rich *Ideas* fill'd,
> From which this gorgeous Universe he fram'd;
>   For when th' Almighty will'd,
>   Unnumber'd worlds to build,
>   From Unity diversified he sprang,
> While gay Creation laugh'd, and procreant Nature sang.[230]

There is, as we have said, no precise correspondence between these chants and Whitman's own, but that the basic thought came from these sources cannot be doubted. In Ward's *View,* again, is a brief account of this feminine aspect of Godhead: "This energy is said to have created the universe, and therefore this, as displayed in the grandest of the forms it assumes, is the object of worship. . . . This energy itself has been personified and worshipped . . . in the form of Bhagavati."[231]

In the subtle chemistry of Whitman's imagination all these issue into a shape of his own. But the major elements of that beautiful artistry were certainly contributed by his readings of the passages presented above. And like Parasara, the narrator of The *Vishnu Purana,* insisting that "the four portions of the god of gods are equally essential," Whitman also insists:

> . . . Out of the square entirely divine,
> Solid, four-sided, (all the sides needed,) . . . .

In his "Santa Spirita," described as "pervading all," "including all life on earth, touching, including God . . . and Satan," and "essence of forms," there is a perceptible portion of Devaki, Bhavani, Maya, and Bhagavati. And his "square deific, out of the One advancing," reminds us of the line from Menu, described by Whelpley, about the "three [gods] that emanated from Brehm, the Vast, ineffable, One."

Another lovely hymn of Jones, to Saraswati, the Hindu Goddess of Knowledge, "Queen of the flowery speech," entreats:

> . . . Oh, Joy of Mortal hearts,
>   Thy mystic wisdom teach,
> Expand thy leaves; and, with ethereal light
>   Spangle the veil of night.[232]

It is possible that Whitman's own metaphor of the leaves for the canticles or songs of a man whose "speech is the twin of [his] vision," and who, too, taught his "mystic wisdom," originated here.

Our remaining interest in the works of Sir William Jones concerns Volume three, where we have the entire text of the *Laws of Menu*. But the extracts of the *Laws* so far noticed in the other areas of Whitman's reading were adequate, as we have observed, to explain much of Whitman's Hindu thought, and it would be a wearisome business to subject the remainder of even the philosophic passages in Menu to a similar investigation. Therefore, we shall pass over them, except for a few very striking ones whose echoes are strong in Whitman.

In his poem "To Think of Time," the theme of which is immortality, the poet asserts:

> I swear I see now that everything has an eternal soul!
> The trees have, rooted in the ground. . . . the weeds of the sea
>   have . . . . the animals.[233]

This belief is more than a poetic fancy; it is, as we know, part of his philosophy, the faith in the community of all things in which "there is nothing but immortality." The notion is most clearly expressed again in "Song of the Redwood Tree," where the tree declares,

> (For I know I bear the soul befitting me, I too have consciousness, identity,
> And all the rocks and mountains have, and all the earth,)

and in "Song at Sunset,"

> (Surely there is something more in each of the trees, some living soul.)

Like his "law" that "cannot be eluded," of which the poem "To think of Time" speaks while on its theme of immortality, even this thought of a living soul in trees and weeds appears to have its roots in Menu, who says, in the chapter on Creation:

These *animals and vegetables,* encircled with multiform darkness, by reason of past actions, have internal conscience, are sensible of pleasure and pain.

All transmigrations, recorded *in sacred books,* from the state of BRAHMÁ, to that of plants, happen continually in this tremendous world of beings. . . .

Then too this vital soul *of created bodies,* with all the organs of sense and action, remain long immersed in *the first idea or in* darkness. . . .

When, being *again* composed of minute elementary particles, it enters at once into vegetable or animal seed, it then assumes a *new* form.[234]

Elaborate conceptions of the harmony and order of the physical universe might have come to Whitman from his readings in the scientific areas of the periodicals, but even the religious Menu had some notions of the kind:

With very minute transformable portions, called *mátras,* of the five elements, all this perceptible world was composed in fit order . . . .

Thus, having at once pervaded, with emanations from the Supreme Spirit, the minutest portion of six principles immensely operative, *consciousness and the five perceptions,* He framed all creatures . . . .

Thence proceeded the great elements, endued with particular powers, and Mind with operations infinitely subtile, the imperceptible cause of all apparent forms.

The *universe,* therefore, is compacted from the minute portions of those seven divine and active principles, *the great Soul,* or first emanation, *consciousness,* and *five perceptions; a* mutable *universe* from immutable *ideas.*

Among them each succeeding element acquires the quality of the preceding; and, in as many degrees as each of them is advanced, with so many more properties is it said to be endued.[235]

The following lines from "Song of Myself" describing the relations animals have with the poet's own self, seem to have their

roots in the last of the *Laws* quoted here, with all their suggestion
of the theory of evolution:

> They bring me tokens of myself, they evince them plainly in
> their possession.

> I wonder where they get those tokens,
> Did I pass that way huge times ago and negligently drop
> them?

> Myself moving forward then and now and forever,
> Gathering and showing more always and with velocity.[236]

He has gathered more and shows more, because, as man, "the
succeeding element" after animals, he is "endued" with "so many
more properties." But the "preceding" share their quality with
him; they have "tokens" of his dropped "huge times ago" when he
passed "that way." In another poem written in 1860, called "All
is Truth," one hears some verbal echoes of the above-quoted *Laws,*
when he affirms

> . . . that each thing exactly represents itself and what has
> preceded it,

and resolves to "celebrate anything" he sees or is, bemoaning having
been

> O me, man of slack faith so long,
> Standing aloof, denying portions so long,
> Only aware to-day of compact all-diffused truth.

6

OF GOD, MAN, AND SEX

THE *Vedas* OF INDIA ARE MENTIONED IN WHITMAN'S PROSE
writings more often than any other Hindu work. Astor library in
those days had Max Mueller's edition of the *Rig-Veda-Samhita,*
but since the only considerable portion of it is the English introduction, which is mostly in the nature of a commentary on the
text, we have to overlook it. Apart from that, Astor had J.
Stevenson's "Translations of the Samhita of Sama Veda," and
Roy's "Translations of several principal books, passages and texts
of the Veda, etc." Postponing the latter to a later occasion, we
shall bestow a fleeting glance on the "Sama Veda" translations of
Stevenson. From the point of view of philosophical thought, this
book cannot be said to have contributed much to Whitman beyond
vague suggestions and a profound religious feeling, but the Vedic
prayers could presumably have offered verbal hints. The principal
phraseology in which the prayers are uttered is of "celebration."
While, as we shall see by and by, the idea of "worshipping" the
self was suggested by another page of his reading, it is possible that
Whitman picked up the manner of worship here:

O my Voice, do thou celebrate the cloud-shaped divinity.
(p. 23)

We . . . celebrate thee; O Indra, in sacred hymns." (p. 29)

I celebrate with my voice . . . Indra. (p. 31)

Do not celebrate any other God. . . . Praise Indra. (p. 31)

I celebrate the tamer of multitudes of horses [Indra]. (p. 69)

. . . O Indra, . . . I celebrate thee in a song. (p. 150)

Probably, again, Whitman's habit of addressing his own soul in his poems, was the result of his reading such as these:

While the moon-plant sacrifice is in progress, do thou,
O my soul, in union with the other (chanters),
sing the happiness of Indra. (p. 23)

O my Soul, do thou, in songs of praise, extol Agni. (p. 9)

O my Soul, praise him, whom the gods have appointed to be giver of gifts. (p. 22)

(O my Soul), thou approachest, for thy protection, . . . Indra. (p. 31)

References to the sacred grass are frequently found in the chants:

Agni, the high priest . . . who sits on the sacred grass. (p. 9)

Let Mitra and Aryama, along with all the gods who come . . . sit down on the sacred grass during the sacrifice. (pp. 9–10)

Come, O Indra, . . . sit down on this our carpeting of sacred grass. (p. 112)

And of the Supreme Soul a chant said:

. . . Were there a hundred heavens, and a hundred earths, and in addition to them a thousand suns . . . they could not contain thee; for thou encirclest heaven and earth. (p. 51)

Reverend W. Ward's "A View of the History, Literature, and

Mythology of the Hindoos, including a minute Description of their Manners and Customs, and Translations from their Principal Works," is, true to its titular announcement, an exhaustive account of Hindu life and thought, though it is not always strictly authentic, and is often inaccurate and biased. There is tremendous research in its pages, and considerable scholarship, but there is also the prepossession of a Christian missionary, impatient of "pagan" thought, which frequently expresses itself in declamatory judgment. That overlooked, *A View* in two volumes makes a thorough and comprehensive source of information on its subject, rising to almost encyclopedic proportions in the range of its survey.

Whatever part the other books to which Whitman applied himself in his quest for philosophical knowledge played in his mental or moral equipment, it appears that Ward's book played a more vital, a more material, a more immediate role in the evolution of the first poems with which he ushered in his new career, as the following study will show. *A View,* we may remember, was available both on the Mercantile and the Astor shelves.

In asserting his egalitarian doctrine, the corresponding importance of body with soul, Whitman says in "Song of Myself,"

Clear and sweet is my soul, and clear and sweet is all that
is not my soul.
Lack one lacks both, and the unseen is proved by the seen,
Till that becomes unseen and receives proof in its turn. (Sec. 3)

Ignoring the last line, which has been regarded as absurd, and which may be explained as Whitman's fanciful working upon the thought of the preceding phrase (examples of this kind of verbal embroidering and extension of a fine thought, sometimes to the point of absurdity, are frequent in him), we notice that in that beautiful sentence, "the unseen is proved by the seen,"[237] the poet is offering an argument for affirming the existence of the soul. Now, this argument is not quite the product of Whitman's own philosophical speculation. One of the basic questions dealt with in all the six systems of Hindu philosophy as well as Buddhism and the rest, is that of knowledge and its many sources. With regard to the precise number of these, opinions are divergent, but all schools agree on Inference as one of the major sources or proofs of knowledge. The principle of inference has been explained, with illustrations, in Colebrooke's accounts, in words similar to Whitman's line. But the closest correspondence with it is found in the following passage in Ward's *View,* presenting the Nyaya School's discussion of the validity of knowledge to be derived from inference:

> That a first cause exists is inferred from the nature of things; and from the impossibility of an effect without a cause; hence things invisible are proved to exist from those which are visible.[238]

If we substitute the word "unseen" for "invisible," we have the same argument for almost the same logical situation.

Even the saying "Clear and sweet is my soul," like his other line in "The Sleepers," "The soul is always beautiful," could have come from Ward's *Sankhya,* where it was said:

Spirit is more lovely than anything. (p. 344)

Spirit is of itself lovely. (p. 345)

Spirit is lovely and is identified with love. (p. 345)

Again, if in his insistence, "clear and sweet is all that is not my soul," he is succinctly asseverating his doctrine elaborated elsewhere, that the body is as much a reality, and has as much validity, as the soul, and that identity is the composition of these two equal principles, even there he is not very original. For the Vysesika School, in Ward, emphatically asserted:

> I [personal identity] cannot be identified either with spirit or body separately . . . spirit separate from body does not use I, nor does (a dead) body separate from spirit; but in the use of I, both are necessary.[239]

In the same connection we might notice another vehemently asserted notion of Whitman, namely, the reality of the material world, for, in a way it is implied in the lines of "Song of Myself" that we are examining. At first sight the "materialism" of Whitman seems a strange bedfellow to the utter spiritualism of his philosophy. Not only does he, in accordance with a resolution recorded in his notes, "all through [his] writings preserve the equilibrium of the truth that the material world, and all its laws, are as grand and superb as the spiritual world and all its laws,"[240] but, poet of the "Soul" that he was, he insisted that he was also the "poet of the Body," and of "Reality," and declared that "the stars are not echoes," that "Space is no apparition," and that "all things seen or demonstrated are so":[241] real, valid, significant. Though he later playfully toyed with the Vedantic idea of illusion, he substantially remained a firm believer and champion of the material world. This attitude toward "all that is not . . . soul" again seems to be, not originally the offspring of Whitman's poetic fancy, but the offspring of his reading into the Vysesika thought in Ward, where,

> In reply to some who maintain, that all visible objects are shadowy, unsubstantial and worthless, Kanáda maintains, that material objects are not to be despised and rejected, since the most important future effects, as merit and demerit, arise out of them: we must therefore in this respect, consider them as equal to realities (sat).[242]

This idea that the material world is a means to a future spiritual end also reverberates in Whitman. For instance, in "To Think of Time," he says

> The domestic joys, the daily housework or business, the building of houses—they are not phantasms. . . . they have weight and form and location;
> The forms and profits and crops. . . . the markets and wages and government. . . . they also are not phantasms;
> The difference between sin and goodness is no apparition;
> The earth is not an echo. . . . man and his life and all the things of his life are well-considered.[243]

The following passage from "Crossing Brooklyn Ferry," perhaps most eminently exploits the idea of Kanáda, while at the same time playing with the Maya concept of Vedanta:

Appearances, now or henceforth, indicate what you are,
You necessary film, continue to envelop the soul,
About my body for me, and your body for you, be hung out
    divinest aromas,
Thrive, cities—bring your freight, bring your shows, ample
    and sufficient rivers,
Expand, being than which none else is perhaps more spiritual,
Keep your places, objects than which none else is more lasting.

You have waited, you always wait, you dumb, beautiful min-
    isters,
We receive you with free sense at last, and are insatiate hence-
    forward,
Not you any more shall be able to foil us, or withhold your-
    selves from us,
We use you, and do not cast you aside—we plant you perma-
    nently within us,
We fathom you not—we love you—there is perfection in you
    also,
You furnish your parts toward eternity,
Great or small, you furnish your parts toward the soul.

In fact, Whitman practically echoes Kanáda when he says in
the *Democratic Vistas:* "True, we must not condemn the show
[of the universe], neither absolutely deny it, for the indispensability
of its meanings."[244]
For his sense of the "all enfolded in Joy Joy Joy" likewise,
many passages in Ward could have offered further confirmation.
Here is just one from the account of the Shatwata sect:

From the divine form proceed rays of glory, so that God appears as a body of light. The deity is perfect joy. Creation
arose from his will; and the desire to create, from the energetic
joy which is essential to the divine nature.[245]

From Whitman's habit, instanced earlier, of incorporating little
pictures and scenes borrowed from others' accounts of them, I
suspected that the description in section 43 of "Song of Myself,"
of "dancing yet through the streets in a phallic procession," had,
like some other phrases of the same section, a possible source in the
pages he read. In none of the other books can an account be dis-

covered bearing upon a scene like that. And remembering that usually Whitman's fancy is more often stimulated by verbal suggestions, which might also be one of the reasons for his taking words along with the thoughts, as in the case of the battle scene in "Song of Myself," the source had to be one whose words came closest to Whitman's line. On both counts it appears Ward is the source, as this extract shows:

> In the open day, and in the most public streets of a large town, I have seen men entirely naked, dancing with unblushing effrontery before the idol, as it was carried in triumphant procession, encouraged by the smiles and eager gaze of the brahmins.[246]

That Whitman's procession is "phallic" is explained by the fact that earlier in the same elaborate account of the many gods and goddesses of common Hindu worship, the idol in reference, through an obvious misunderstanding, was explained thus:

> The worship of the Linga also, strongly resembles the worship of the phallus in honour of Bacchus.[247]

Perhaps the "fetish of the first rock or stump" of Whitman, in the same section, has an independent origin, or it may be from Ward's brief account of the "worship of stones" and "a log of wood," occurring close to that of the procession. And the phrase, "Drinking mead from the skull-cap," appears likewise to have come from a later page in Ward describing certain "impure orgies" performed by some sects, in which,

> The priest then offers to the goddess, an intoxicating beverage. . . . Next the priest gives to the women spirituous liquors, in cups made of cocoanut, or of human skulls. . . .[248]

And the other phrase, "rapt and austere in the woods," possibly grew from this passage:

> The ceremonies leading to absorption are called . . . tapasya. . . . Forsaking the world; returning to a forest . . . these, and many other austere practices, are prescribed, to subdue the passions, to fix the mind.[249]

Flimsy as the foregoing are to be regarded as clues to Whitman's reading of Ward's *View,* an examination of the pages of these volumes accumulates irresistible impressions of his having stuffed his mind and his poetic passages with their thought and phrases. In fact it seems that Ward was the one pasture in which Whitman's imagination grazed longest and most deeply. But since a complete and thorough scrutiny of these immense volumes is impossible, we shall notice only that portion of their contents that expressly deals with the religion and philosophy of India, and then only in selected extracts that bear closest resemblance to Whitman's thought and expression.

We shall begin with the second volume, because our interest in it is limited chiefly to the opening pages of its long introduction, and can be exhausted with brief attention. The volume, however, presents an elaborate account of the religious practices of the Hindus, their various gods and goddesses, their duties and ceremonies of different occasions, of their many sects and their doctrines, and so on. In the first four pages of the Introductory Remarks, there is a summary of Hindu religious thought from which alone could Whitman have forged the philosophy he postulated through his poetry. A few significant passages from those pages are reproduced here:

> The whole system of Hindoo theology is founded upon the doctrine that the Divine Spirit, as the soul of the universe, becomes, in all animate beings, united to matter; that spirit is insulated or individuated by particular portions of matter, which is continually quitting, and joining itself to new portions of matter; that the human soul is, in other words, God himself; that the knowledge of this . . . is the only means of being reunited to the divine nature; that this deliverance . . . if not obtained in one birth, is to be sought through every future transmigration till obtained.

A footnote, on "portions of matter," explains:

> There are two opinions among the Hindoos on this subject, some philosophers maintaining that it is one Soul which is united to sentient creatures, while others . . . affirm, that human souls must be emanations from the Great Spirit. . . . The Vedanta

philosophers teach, "that God exists in millions of forms, from the ant to Brahma, the grandfather of the gods, as one moon is seen at once in twenty different pans of water."

. . . The compiler of the "Essence of the Vedanta" says, "Brahma and life are one: that which, pervading all the members of the body, gives to them life and motion, is called jiva, life: that which pervading the whole universe, gives life and motion to all, is Brahma; therefore these two are one. Every kind of matter is without life; that which is created cannot possess life: therefore all life is the creator, or Brahma: God is the soul of the world. This is the substance of the Vedanta philosophy."

Not only is God thus declared to be the soul of the world, but . . . that the world itself is God—God expanding himself in an infinite variety of forms: "All things past, present and to come; all that is in the earth, sky, &c. of every class and description, all this is Brahma, who is the cause of all things, and the things themselves. . . . The principle of life is Brahma; that which is animated is the work of Brahma, who directs everything, as to the charioteer directs the chariot. Brahma is everlasting and unchangeable; the world, which is his work, is changeable."

The Vedanta writers add, that at certain revolutions of time, Brahma, awaking from [his] repose, unites to himself his own energy, and creates the universe; that as soon as souls are united to matter, they become impressed, according to their destiny, with more or less of three qualities. . . . The character is formed, and the future destiny regulated, by the preponderance of any one of these qualities. . . .

The soul then, by these writers, is considered as separated from the source of happiness when it takes mortal birth, and as remaining as miserable wanderer in various births and states, till it regain its place in the divine essence. . . .

In consonance with these ideas, a system of devotion has been formed to enable men to emancipate themselves from the influence of material objects, and thus to prepare them for absorption. In the first place, the devotee is to acquire the right knowledge of Brahma, namely, that God and matter are the same; that Brahma is the soul of the world. . . . The person possessed of these ideas of God is called the "wise man," *Brahmagnani*.[250]

It is these "ideas of God" that Whitman came to possess when he wrote his poems, and in that acquisition of the "right knowledge," he also came to be "Brahmagnani," the wise man, or yogi, or, in his own context, the Answerer, the Poet of the Preface, the "I" of his poetry. He wrote the *Leaves,* as he said, to "rout" that something lurking within the reader's self, which "fuses past and present and to come,"[251] evidently the "Brahma" of the Hindu thought. The Vedantins regarded the "Great Spirit" as the "charioteer [who] directs the chariot" of the universe; Whitman, as we have seen, proposed to "be the little hands that guide the cart."[252] If the Hindus considered the soul as a "wanderer," Whitman's self declared,

> I tramp a perpetual journey,[253]

and was certain to "regain its place in the divine essence," for after all

> Our rendezvous is fitly appointed . . . God will be there and wait till we come.[254]

Of the "destiny" regulated by "qualities," "To Think of Time" speaks as the "law" that "cannot be eluded"; and of the matter to which souls are "united," and of the qualities with which they become "impressed" in such a union, the following experimental lines carry an undeveloped suggestion:

> . . . vast unknown matter and qualities lying inert
> —much doubtless more than known matter and qualities.[255]

A detailed description of the "Brahmagnani" follows the passages cited above in Ward, and a large part of it is presented in extracts from the *Bhagvat-Geeta* of Wilkins's translation, where Krishna delineates the picture of a yogi. There is a whole page and a half of these extracts, a few of which are given here, partly because, as has been suggested, Whitman modeled both his personality and the author of his poetry after the Hindu yogi (and probably Ward's account offered its share of intimations), and partly because our later examination of the *Gita* as Whitman's source of thought will be lighter.

A man is said to be confirmed in wisdom, when he forsaketh every desire which entereth into his heart, and of himself is happy, and contented in himself. His mind is undisturbed in adversity, he is happy and contented in prosperity, and he is a stranger to anxiety, fear and anger. Such a wise man is called a sage. The wisdom of that man is established, who, in all things, is without affection, and having received good and evil, neither rejoiceth at the one, nor is cast down by the other. His wisdom is confirmed, when, like the tortoise, he can draw in all his members, and restrain them from their wonted purpose. . . . The wise neither grieve for the dead, nor for the living. . . . The wise man to whom pain and pleasure are the same, is formed for immortality. . . . The heart, which followeth the dictates of the moving passions, carrieth away the reason, as the storm·the bark in the raging ocean. . . . The man whose passions enter his heart as waters run into the unswelling placid ocean obtaineth happiness. . . . Even at the hour of death, should he attain it, he shall mix with the incorporeal nature of Brahma. . . . The man who may be self-delighted and self-satisfied, and who may be happy in his own soul, hath no interest either in that which is done, or that which is not done. . . . The learned behold Brahma alike in the reverend brahmin perfected in knowledge, in the ox, and in the elephant; in the dog, and in him who eateth the flesh of dogs. . . . Those whose minds are fixed on this equality, gain eternity even in this world. They put their trust in Brahma, the eternal, because he is everywhere alike free from fault. . . . To the yogi, gold, iron, and stones, are the same. . . . He is recluse, of a subdued mind and spirit. The man whose mind is endued with this devotion, and looketh on all things alike, beholdeth the supreme soul in all things, and all things in the supreme soul. . . . He my servant is dear unto me who is unexpecting, just, and pure, impartial, free from distraction of mind . . . who neither requireth, nor findeth fault, who neither lamenteth, nor coveteth, and being my servant, hath forsaken both good and evil fortune; who is the same in friendship and in hatred, in honour and dishonour, in cold and in heat, in pain and in pleasure; who is unsolicitous about the events of things; to whom praise and blame are as one; who is of little spirit, and pleased with whatever cometh to pass;

who owneth no particular home, and who is of a steady mind.
. . . Wisdom is exemption from attachments and affection for
children, wife, and home; a constant evenness of temper upon
the arrival of every event whether longed for or not.[256]

Forgetting for the present the larger question of how much of all
this Whitman attempted to be in his own life, we might notice
how much of this thought and these phrases enters into his own
writings, often, to use the only term that fits the description,
Whitmanized, but sometimes in bodily rendering. We shall again
ignore the doctrinal element, that is, notions like equality, the acceptance of evil, the identification of the world with God, and so
on, that this description contributed to his philosophical system.
The processes by which the ideas and phrases of the extracts have
been shaped into his own lines are illustrated in the following,
which—needless to point out—is also a study in his basic technique,
the very making of his poems.

The wise man of the *Gita* is "of himself happy," "contented in
himself," "self-delighted," "self-satisfied," "happy in his own
soul," and the like. And Whitman, playing upon this idea of
"soul-centered-ness," teases it into this shape:

No one can realize anything unless he has it in him . . . or
    has been it.
It must certainly tally with what is in him . . . otherwise
    it is all blank to him.
The animals, the past, light, space—if I have them not in me,
    I have them not at all.
The future is in me as a seed or nascent thought—
If the general has a good army in himself he has a good
    army . . . otherwise he has no army worth mentioning.
If you are rich in yourself you are rich . . . otherwise you are
    wretchedly poor.
If you are located in yourself you are well located . . . you
    can never be dislodged or moved then.
If you are happy out of yourself you are happy . . . but I tell
    you you cannot be happy by others any more than you can
    beget a child by others . . . or conceive a child by others.[257]

Such a "sage" of the *Gita* "hath no interest either in that which is done, or that which is not done"; this description becomes the slightly absurd

> What will be will be well—for what is is well,
> To take interest is well, and not to take interest shall be
>   well.[258]

The wise man receives "good and evil, neither rejoiceth at the one, nor is cast down by the other"; and Whitman declares:

> What blurt is it about virtue and about vice?
> Evil propels me, and reform of evil propels me. . . . I stand
>   indifferent,
> My gait is no fault-finder's or rejecter's gait.[259]

In the same lines again he echoes Krishna; for the sage not only hath "forsaken good and evil fortune," but "neither requireth, nor findeth fault," and is "impartial." Whitman is no "fault-finder" or "rejecter." "The wise," according to Krishna, "neither grieve for the dead, nor for the living . . . neither lamenteth." Whitman says,

> All has been gentle with me. . . . I keep no account with
>   lamentation,
> What have I to do with lamentation?[260]

The extracts from the *Bhagvat-Geeta* were introduced by Ward with this remark:

> Krishna, in his conversation with Arjuna, makes the perfection of religion to consist in subduing the passions, in perfect abstraction from all objects of the senses, and in fixing the whole mind on Brahma.[261]

The object of all Hindu philosophical knowledge, frequently explained in our survey so far, is the emancipation or abstraction of the soul from material objects; and Krishna's "dear . . . servant" is one who has achieved "exemption from attachments," and a "constant evenness of temper upon the arrival of every event whether longed for or not." The following lines in Whitman, despite their verbal alteration and decoration, seem, beyond a shadow of doubt, to have emerged from here:

Perfect serenity of mind.

To take with entire self-possession whatever comes.
What is this small thing in the great continuous volumes everywhere?
This is but a temporary portion—not to be dwelt upon—not to distress—not to have prominence

Superior nonchalance
No fumes—no ennui—no complaints or scornful criticisms.
To find how easily one can abstract his identity from temporal affairs.[262]

Krishna's sage is a "recluse," "whose business is in the restraining of passions" that "carrieth away the reason," and who can "draw in all his members, and restrain from their wonted purpose." Two of the virtues of Whitman's "Answerer" are "law of reason" and "withdrawness," refined from the first draft just quoted. And the wise men "put their trust in Brahma, the eternal, because he is everywhere alike free from fault." Whitman sings of the faultless perfection of the universe in "The Sleepers," and in "To Think of Time":

The universe is duly in order. . . . everything is in its place,
What is arrived is in its place, and what waits is in its place.[263]

How perfect the earth, and the minutest thing upon it!
What is called good is perfect, and what is called bad is just as perfect.
The vegetables and minerals are all perfect, and the imponderable fluids perfect.[264]

The list of echoes given above is sufficient to show that, for all the care Whitman took to cash the thought into his own currency, a good many foreign coins managed to slip into his coffers.

Connected with the description of the yogi in Ward's introduction to the second volume is an account of the famous exercises of Yoga, but since the same occurs in volume 1 in the exposition of the Yoga school of Hindu philosophy, we may ignore it here with the rest of the introductory remarks analyzing the religious aspects of Hindu Culture. In fact the entire second volume, as we have said, concerns itself chiefly with the religious practices of the Hindus and has very little to do with actual philosophical thought, except in indirect and incidental references to the ideas underlying certain customs and ceremonies. What little direct discussion of philosophical notions is there, such as in the chapter on the "Doctrines of Hindu Religion," or in the accounts of the Bouddhas, the Jains, and so on, is already familiar to us through the other works we have gone through, and could not have been of any significant use to Whitman. However, before we pass on to the first volume, we may briefly notice the likelihood that these pages supplied Whitman with another well-known Hindu belief, along with one or two other interesting suggestions.

In "By Blue Ontario's Shore," Whitman makes the following startling assertion:

Have you thought there could be but a single supreme?
There can be any number of supremes—one does not counter-
    vail another any more than one eyesight
    countervails another, or one life countervails
    another.

In this poem, once called "Poem of Many in One," which sings the patriotic lay, he applies the idea of many supremes to the individual states composing the American nation; elsewhere, in what in all probability is an earlier composition, for its echoes are heard in the 1847 notebooks too, the thought stands for the divinity or godhood of all individual men. In other words, it has first been conceived in a religious or philosophical connotation. In his notes for "Lectures on Religion" he recorded:

The new theologies bring forward man—there is nothing in the universe more divine than man. All gathers to the worship of man—How awful, how beautiful a being—How full of Gods is the world—There are none greater than these present ones—

why has it been taught that there is only one Supreme?—I say there are and must be myriads of Supremes. I say that that is blasphemous petty and infidel which denies any immortal soul to be eligible to advance onward to be as supreme as any—I say that all goes on to be eligible to become one of the Supremes—[265]

The idea that man, divine in essence, attains to godhood through prescribed spiritual exercises, or acquisition of the right knowledge of Brahma, or devotion, has been found frequently reiterated in Whitman's readings. All the yoga accounts dwell on it, and the "Sketch of Buddhism" in the *Transactions* reported a Buddhist scholar explaining that "Buddha . . . is one of the names which we give to God. . . . Neither Ádi Buddha nor any of the Pancha Buddha Dhyani ever made a descent . . . but certain persons of mortal mould would have by degrees attained to . . . Bodhignana."[266] However, whether it was gathered as an independent thought, or logically developed from the concept of the divinity of man and of himself as a man, which idea has already saturated his thoughts as early as 1847, the notion of many gods runs all through Whitman's poetry. And it is not merely a philosophic concept of the divinity of all beings and things, but a downright recognition of the worshipable, that is, the religious divineness of certain things, that symbolizes his attitude to Godhead. It is this aspect of Whitman's faith to which Bliss Perry refers in the words: "Monist as he [Whitman] was in philosophy, he was polytheist in practice; he dropped on his knees anywhere before stick or stone, flesh or spirit, and swore that each in turn was divine."[267] It is needless to say how accurately these words describe the Hindu on whose philosophical monism is raised his religious polytheism, a practice for which Max Mueller had to coin a new term, Henotheism or Kathenotheism. A poem that Whitman wrote in 1870, "Gods," most eminently illustrates this facet of his faith, which regards as God not only the "Lover divine and perfect comrade," and "the Ideal Man," who is "fair, able, beautiful, content, and loving," but all that he sees, conceives, or knows.

O Death, (for Life has served its turn,)
Opener and usher to the heavenly mansion,
Be thou my God.

Aught, aught of mightiest, best I see, conceive, or know,
(To break the stagnant tie—thee, thee to free, O soul,)
Be thou my god.

All great ideas, the races' aspirations,
All heroisms, deeds of rapt enthusiasts,
Be ye my Gods.

Or Time and Space
Or shape of Earth divine and wondrous,
Or some fair shape I viewing, worship,
Or lustrous orb of sun or star by night,
Be ye my Gods.

The yearning "to break the stagnant tie" in order "to free" the
soul, is undeniably the Hindu thought of the liberation or emancipation of the soul from earthly or material bondage. One may
notice, incidentally, that the Vedantic element appears to grow
stronger in Whitman's poems as he grows older, and to overcome
the earlier materialism as well as the arrogance, shaped under
what might be regarded as a relatively hurried and superficial comprehension of the philosophical thought he had gathered or developed out of his readings. However, this worship of the sun, the
stars, the earth, death, all that is best in sight, conception, or
knowledge, is a habit he decidedly learned from the Hindu—the
Hindu whose death is a god called Yama (Whitman read of him
in the Savitri episode), whose earth is Prithvi or Amba (so did the
Researches describe), whose sun is Surya, "saluted" every morning
and worshiped as the symbol of Brahma, the Supreme Light, and
who is even laughed at in Ward for his "honoring the gods":

The Hindu mythology [says the Reverend Ward] . . . presents us with gods of every possible shape, and for every possible
purpose (*even to cure the itch!*), but most of them appear to
refer to the doctrine of the periodical creation and destruction;—
the appearances of nature,—the heavenly bodies,—the history of
deified heroes,—the poetical wars of the giants with the gods,—
or to the real or imagined wants of mankind.
It cannot be doubted from . . . the vedas . . . that the PRI-
MARY ELEMENTS, fire, air, water, earth, and space, with
the HEAVENLY BODIES, and AERIAL BEINGS, were

the first objects of worship among these people.

The worship of the *primary elements* possibly originated in the doctrine of the vedas respecting the eternity of matter, for we find in these writings the elements deified, and called by appropriate names. . . .

The worship of the *heavenly bodies* may probably be attributed to the astronomical notions of the Hindoos. . . . They . . . worshipped the host of heaven . . . believed the stars to have . . . a mighty and immediate influence on their destiny here and hereafter. In the prayers of the vedas, the name of Indra is found, who was probably considered as a personification of the heavens . . . his body, covered with stars, might easily be supposed to resemble "the spangled heavens."

The worship of *aerial* beings, under the general name of spirits, is easily accounted for from the proneness of mankind to superstitious fears respecting invisible existences, and from the notion found in the Hindoo writings, that every form of animated existence has its tutelar divinity presiding over it.[268]

Referring to the underlying concept of these polytheistic practices, Ward also said at the commencement of the passage that "the gods, the heavens collectively, the sun and moon, as well as the stars, the sea, the mighty rivers, and extraordinary appearances in nature, receive the adorations of the Hindoos. . . . The universe being full of divine majesty, a deity has been consecrated as the regent of every element.[269]

Since we are not interested in the concept, we may ignore Ward's interpretation of it, but the closeness of Whitman's poem to this passage deserves attention. He too would worship "Earth," "space," "sun," and "stars"; and if the Hindus adore "extraordinary appearances," deify "heroes" of history, worship "wants of mankind," and have "gods of every possible shape," Whitman reverences "aught of mightiest," "all heroisms," "the races' aspirations," and all the best seen or conceived or known. We may also remember that he has a whole poem like a Vedic chant to the sun in "Thou Orb Aloft Full-Dazzling," that he calls upon the "sacred moon" in "Look Down Fair Moon" to "pour down [her] unstinted nimbus," and that he utters several chants to the Earth.

If the Hindus have "superstitious fears respecting invisible existences" in the air, Whitman, too, believes in

Living beings, identities now doubtless near us in the air that
we know not of.[270]

To this superstition of his concerning "invisible existences," the
1856 poem, "Song of the Open Road," bears most eloquent testimony:

You air that serves me with breath to speak!
You objects that call from diffusion my meanings and give
them shape!
You light that wraps me and all things in delicate equable
showers!
You paths worn in the irregular hollows by the roadsides!
I believe you are latent with unseen existences, you are so
dear to me.[271]

Even this line from his "Song at Sunset" echoes Ward:

Illustrious what we name space, sphere of unnumbered
spirits . . .

In a word, Whitman is quite "the Hindoostanee with his
deities," chanting, saluting, "carolling" his "myriads of Supremes,"
and I wonder if Ward's minute account of these gods and goddesses
of Hindoostan was the source of that phrase, too.

On a later page, Ward describes the Hindus as urging "that
the moving cause of every action, however fictitious, is God; that
man is an instrument upon which God plays what tune he
pleases."[272] In his "Mystic Trumpeter," Whitman says,

O trumpeter, methinks I am myself the instrument thou
playest. (sec. 7)

Whitman's use of the word "sudra" to describe the "face" of
Satan, the third of his "Square Deific," is curious. Considering
how packed and compact with deep meanings are the words in the
line, as well as in the whole poem, the adjective "sudra" must have
been employed to signify a specific virtue of that portion of the
"Deific." The various other meanings in which that word could

have come to Whitman from Whelpley's or others' accounts of the
Sudra class of the ancient Hindu society are exhausted in the other
epithets used to describe the Satanic Element, namely "despised,"
"a drudge," "ignorant," or even "black," and "worn brow." For
the Sudra class in all these accounts was the lowest of the social
order, underprivileged, laboring for the comfort of the other three
classes, uneducated, and dark in complexion, being mostly Dravid-
ian, unlike the fair Aryans in the higher strata. Thus the precise
connotation of its use in the line eluded me until I came upon the
following passage in Ward touching upon the Brahmins and the
Sudras:

> The sacred writings of the Hindoos encourage the brahmins
> to despise the great body of the people, and teach them, that
> the very sight and touch of a sudra renders them unclean. To
> be contented in ignorance, is the duty of a sudra, as well as to
> drink with reverence and hope the water in which the brahmin
> has dipped his foot. The services too and the hopes held forth
> by this religion, are most exclusively confined to the brahmins.
> The sudra is supposed to be born to evil destiny; and the only
> hope he can indulge is, that after a long succession of trans-
> migrations he may probably be born a brahmin.[273]

From the suggestion of the association of "evil destiny" with the
"sudra," and of the "despised" nature of his being, as well as
of his "ignorance," found all at once in these lines, it seems probable
that Whitman remembered Ward in using that word, rather than
Menu or Whelpley or some other source. The fact that he does
not use the word "evil" at all directly in connection with Satan,
seems to suggest that "sudra" is made to do duty for that quality.
A few pages later on, Ward speaks of the "poor sudra" and mentions "the very circumstances of his degradation." An elaborate
account of the caste occurs in the first volume of his *View*.

One of the most jarring notes in all the melody Whitman makes
as a poet is heard in the early experimental lines recorded in the
1847 notebook, where he regards himself as a "curse" and "in-
voke[s] Revenge to assist" him, wrathfully calling upon "Fate to

pursue"—presumably his foes.[274] The following fragment, a later development, works upon the same idea, subsequently supplying lines to his published poems:

> Topple down upon him, Light! for you seem to me all one
>   lurid curse;
> Damn him! how he does defy me,
> This day or some other I will have him and the like of him
>   to do my will upon,
> They shall not break the lids off their coffins but what with
>   pennies on their eyes I will have them,
> I will tear their flesh out from under the graveclothes.
>
> I will not listen—I will not spare—I am justified of myself:
> For a hundred years I will pursue those who have injured me
>   so much;
> Though they hide themselves under the lappets of God I will
>   pursue them there,
> I will drag them out—the sweet marches of Heaven shall be
>   stopped with my maledictions.[275]

For a prophet of love and sympathy, for a poet of compassion who made "appointments with all, . . . the wicked just the same as the righteous," this note of vengeful ire appears blasphemous. And it is curious that the wrathful prayer to "Fate to pursue" his foes is uttered at about the same time that he looked upon himself as equally "for sinners and the unlearned," and even identified himself with "Christ" to "remember my crucifixion and bloody coronation."[276] Both the 1847 passage and the fragment are of course experimental, and such a loud note of utter malediction is never struck in his final composition. At first, trying to explain the nature of the thought on which his experimental verse is playing in these frightful lines, I considered them as offshoots of his imaginative exercise on the idea of evil, or an extension of the thought of the following rejected passage, which, toned down and truncated, entered into section 6 of the 1855 "Sleepers," only to disappear in the final edition of the poem, probably being regarded as discordant with his religion of joy:

I am a hell-name and a curse

Black Lucifer was not dead
Or if he was I am his sorrowful, terrible heir;
I am the God of revolt—deathless, sorrowful vast; whoever
    oppresses me
I will either destroy him or he shall release me.

Damn him, how he defiles me!
Hoppler of his own sons, breeder of children and trader of
    them—
Selling his daughters and the breast that fed his young,
Informer against my brother and sister and taking pay for
    their blood.

He laughed when I looked from my iron necklace after the
    steamboat that carried away my women.[277]

The complex way in which Whitman's thoughts and lines evolve themselves is noticeable in this case also. Among the several layers of thought that have, as in a palimpsest, gone into the lines just quoted, is the very early thought of the poem "Blood-Money" too. From these to the later Satan section of the "Square Deific" there is an easily traceable link. It is also evident that there is an affinity between this passage and that of the 1847 notebook, which, in fact, appears to be the root of all the subsequent development and modification. The underlying stimulus of this violent emotion, as it is first expressed in the supremely bitter words of the notebook, makes an interesting inquiry. Again, on a superficial first look, it could possibly be considered as having sprung from the feeling of bitterness due to sex-frustration, or deprivation of the pleasures of sex. The fact that the previous lines ecstatically dwell upon the "touch" of the sex act supports such an assumption. Perhaps, in the lyricism of poetic imagination, he is releasing the pent-up personal anger at his disappointment, and cursing those, whoever they are, who refuse to return his love. In an 1860 poem called "Sometimes with One I Love," he does suggest such a rage:

Sometimes with one I love I fill myself with rage for fear I
    effuse unreturn'd love,

> But now I think there is no unreturn'd love, the pay is certain
>   one way or another,
> (I loved a person ardently and my love was not return'd,
> Yet out of that I have written these songs.)

But that was many, many years afterwards, and before this wonderful sublimation occurred, by which the man in him, so to speak, could accept the poet's "pay" that is "certain one way or another," it is possible that in the year 1847 the poet accepted the man's demand, and mourned in rage the "unreturn'd love." However, even granting the personal derivation of the feeling, the poetic utterance in those maledictory lines may yet have a different explanation, at least as far as their "revengeful passion" is concerned. Without insisting it is so, I would make the suggestion that, like many of his passages both of the early experimental writing and of the final composition, even these arose out of his readings. A considerable number of the early prayers in the *Vedas* seek from the gods "destruction of foes." Whitman read of them in the *Researches,* the *Transactions,* the *Sama Veda* translation of Stevenson, and other accounts of the *Vedas.* A few specimens of these prayers are given here, for the sake of convenience, from Ward, though Whitman might have read him later than the others:

"O Agni! make dumb the mouth and words of this my enemy.

"O Agni! fasten with a peg the tongue of this my enemy. . . . O Agni! fill with distraction the mind of this my enemy. . . . O Agni! confound the speech of the friends of this my enemy. . . . O Agni! destroy the senses of this my enemy. . . .

"O Lamp! as the insect, attracted by thee, falls into the blaze, so let my enemy be overthrown in the seat of judgment.

"O Agni! thou who art the mouth of all the gods, as the smoke entering the eyes renders them dim, so do thou destroy the wisdom of my enemy.

"O Agni! thou who by digesting their food, nourishest mankind, reduce to ashes this my enemy.

"Destroy, O sacred grass, my foes; exterminate my enemies; annihilate all those who hate me, O precious gem!

"O Agni! thou who receivest the clarified butter, and art always glorious, reduce to ashes our enemies, who are constantly injurious and spiteful.

"O Indra! destroy all our covetous enemies, and cherish our bountiful friends."[278]

These "Extracts from the Vedas" were presented by Ward in his first volume, with the closing remark that "the Atharva has been called the anathematizing veda, since it is acknowledged that a considerable portion of it contains incantation of enemies." In the second, which we are examining now, the following observation is made in explanation of some passage in the same Veda:

The Atharva Veda contains many prayers for the destruction of enemies; and gives a list of offerings proper to be presented to Bhagavati, that she may be induced to assist in the gratification of revengeful passions: among the rest, the worshipper is to make a paste image of a man, cut off its head, and offer the head to the goddess, with a burnt-sacrifice, etc.[279]

Whether or not Whitman did poetically imagine foes, "those who have injured [him] so much" (for there is no record of any personal enemies at that point of his career), the violent incantations uttered and the lyricization of vengeful passion in the passages we have noticed may have been the experimental operations of poetic fancy upon suggestions supplied by such readings as the above, though he is in those lines, as in all his early poetry, less the person praying than the deity prayed to.

Advanced upon the same foundation of probability rather than conviction is the following explanation for the metaphysical (to use Dr. Johnson's term) conjunction of the sexual element with the religious, which forms the basis of Whitman's poetry and philosophy, specifically affirmed in that famous passage in section 5 of "Song of Myself," where, through the "sexual" union of body and soul, the "peace and joy and knowledge that pass all the art and argument of the earth" are declared to have come to the poet. Such a meaningful insistence on sex in that passage; the rhapsodic celebration of it in a special section of poems, "Children of Adam," as well as elsewhere in verse and prose; the pointed affirmation found in many places that sexual ecstasy and profound mystic apprehension of life have a vital relationship all imply a far more logical conviction than the mere poetic adoration of the raptures of sex. In this understanding of the violent combination of the poet of sex and the poet of soul in one, to whom the supreme knowledge came from the body, the senses, and the sex act, and who was so much unlike the other mystic poets of the world, whose love, for the woman or for the wine, never rose (or descended) to the extreme physicality of his poetry, it looks as if the source of this passion is neither the frustrated sex of his personal life, nor the relatively innocent suggestions of the Vedanta thought which regarded the body as an equal emanation of the Divine Being, nor even the simple desire to be a philosopher of the inclusive wisdom to which materialism and spiritualism were only two parts of one truth.

There may have been, in the sensitive psychology of Whitman's poetic mind, a slightly excessive sexual element, aggravated by the complicated nature of his homosexual propensities and by the unfortunate circumstance of dissatisfaction, ending up in the silent "perturbations" of his journal or in the more eloquent, less repressed, outbursts of "Calamus," while at the same time generally flooding his lyrical consciousness, thus creating the emotional basis of some of the "erotic," or "autocrotic" passages of his tentative or finished compositions. In these passages, found in the early notebooks or among the rejected fragments that were later skillfully incorporated into "Song of Myself," we notice a lyric orgy of sexual emotions, but also an underlying assertion that in the ecstasy of "touch" is the supreme wisdom attained. In other words he does more than glorify sexual emotion poetically; he is poetically indulging it, or reveling in it as if to seek the exalted state it is believed to reach to. Examine these lines from the 1847 notebook:

A touch now reaches me a library of knowledge in an instant.
It smells for me the fragrance of wine and lemon-blows.
It tastes for me ripe strawberries and melons,—
It talks for me with a tongue of its own,
It finds an ear wherever (wherein?) it rests or taps.[280]

The rest of the passage issues into a frenzy of the erotic state of

mind, but the declaration that the sex "touch" leads to a heightened
condition of consciousness in which all the five senses are endued
with extraordinary power is clear. From this to the more profound suggestion of the section of "Song of Myself" where the
great revelation occurs to the poet in a sexual union, is an easily
noticed step. At any rate the primary roots of the profoundly phi-
losophized sex of his later poems are here in these lines. A similar
fragment in which, leading Bucke to a prophetic interpretation, he
spoke of the "touch," making him "awake for the first time" from
what had been "a mean sleep," has already been noted.

The passages in which Whitman's fancy, probably achieving
poetry's vicarious satisfaction, indulges in the delight of the sex
act, often, as it were, in the act itself, are many in the early notebooks and among the rejected or first drafts. Take this fragment,
which for all its artistic cunning, is an account of the sex act:

> My hand will not hurt what it holds and yet will devour it,
> It must remain perfect before me though I enclose and divide
> it.
>
> Only one minute, only two or three sheathed touches,
> Yet they gather all of me and my spirit into a knot,
> They hold us long enough there to show us what we can be,
> And that our flesh, and even a part of our flesh, seems more
> than senses and life.
> What has become of my senses?
> Touch has jolted down all of them but feeling;
> He pleases the rest so everyone would swap off and go with
> him,
> Or else she will abdicate and nibble at the edges of me.[281]

This is obviously a revision of the lines of the 1847 notebook,
in its turn revised and whittled down into the 28th chant of "Song
of Myself," to be combined with other similarly treated experimental fragments. Here are a couple more of such rhapsodies of
the sexual:

> Living bulbs, melons with polished rinds smooth to the reached
> hand
> Bulbs of life, lilies, polished melons, flavoured for the mildest
> hand that shall reach.

Common things—the trickling sap that flows from the end of the manly maple.

One no more than a point lets in and out of me such bliss and magnitude,
I think I could lift the girder of the house away if it lay between me then and whatever I wanted.[282]

Elsewhere the image changes, but the frenzy remains:

> Yet I strike and dart through. . . .
> I think I could dash the girder of the earth away
> If it lay between me and whatever I wanted.[283]

The entire section 28 of "Song of Myself" dwells upon the sex emotion; the Adamic poems and the "Calamus" poems harp upon the same string. Note the following lines, too, from the 1847 notebook, which, in fewer words but with greater power, were subsequently put into section 40 of "Song of Myself":

> Where is one abortive, mangy, cold
> Starved of his masculine lustiness?
> Without core and loose in the knees?
> Clutch fast to me, my ungrown brother,
> That I may infuse you with grit and jets of life
> I am not to be scorned (?) :—I compel;
> It is quite indifferent to me who (you) are.
> I have stores plenty and to spare
> And of whatsoever I have I bestow upon you.
> And first I bestow of my love.[284]

All these extracts are taken from writing earlier than the 1855 poems, in order that the later mystic dignity they achieve through a cunning verbal modification and an adroit positioning of them in the poems should not interfere with our comprehension of the basic mood out of which they sprang. The basic mood is visibly one of emotional revelry, in poetic fancy; for the intensity and the minute physical relish with which poetic fancy is drawn upon to work, and the frenzied violence with which the sexual feeling is lyricized in them, do not suggest just the faith of a man who "knows[s] that procreation is just as divine as spirituality," and therefore is resolved that "this which [he] know[s] [he] put freely in [his] poems,"[285] nor just the unconscious or conscious attempt of a personally frustrated sex impulse or excessive eroticism to find vent for "pent up aching rivers." If it were the former alone, it would stay from the crude, detailed, emotional masturbation, and if it were the latter alone, it would lack the courage of its philosophical convictions, which we cannot deny to be the only grace that saves his sex from downright imbecility. His attitude of acceptance of sex is one thing, and may be said to be the gift of the first; his actual treatment of it is another. The question is, was it the answer the poet gave to the "perturbed" man, with the assurances of philosophic faith coming in for support?

Our examination of Ward's *View* seems to offer an explanation for this phenomenal poetic sex-indulgence of Whitman. It is of course possible that many of these sex passages had each an independent origin in different inspirations, verbal or of thought. For instance, as suggested earlier, the sexual foundation of the transcendental knowledge received by the poet in section 5 of "Song of Myself" may appreciably be the result of reading in Menu the description of how the Supreme Being is apprehended in the body of the devotee. And the reassuring readiness of the last of the extracts to "infuse" the impotent "with grit and jets of life" may have been a fanciful development of the thought of the following chant in Atharva Veda, though I cannot discover evidence of his having read it:

The Brahmachari scatters his virile power on the ridge of the earth,
And by this live the four quarters.

But that does not explain the larger foundations of sex in him. However, the orgiac element as well as the philosophic conviction respecting sex in *Leaves of Grass* could, in their remarkable unification, be explained in terms of some religious sects of India, accounts of which Ward gives in elaborate detail in his second volume. *A View,* we may remember, was available in the Mercantile Library in the 1840s. References to these sects are also briefly to be found in *Asiatic Researches.* These sects are called the

Tantric sects, and their philosophy is known as Tantric philosophy. These people and their doctrines, as Ward remarks, are chiefly confined to a province in India, where their beliefs and practices, corrupted offshoots of basic Hindu thought, often issue into "the most abominable rites," described by Ward with understandable righteous indignation. A few significant extracts from his frequent and detailed descriptions are given here (Appendix II, a), enough to indicate the essence of the Tantric thought.

From these accounts came, as I have suggested, Whitman's phrase, "Drinking the mead from a skull cap," and it is likely that his philosophy of the senses, and the passion of sex through a free acceptance and unrestrained enjoyment of which an exalted understanding of life's truths is attained, as well as the ardent worship of the body, were also suggested by them. His own adoration of the "Body Electric," where with exquisite relish his lyric enthusiasm dwells on the smallest "parts and poems of the body," declaring that "these are the soul," has an uncanny resemblance to the worship the Tantric sect offered to the bodies of men and women, regarding them as the abode of divinity. Like the vamacharees, he adores the sex; he declares:

Without shame the man I like knows and avows the deliciousness of his sex,
Without shame the woman I like knows and avows hers.[286]

Whitman's sex is more meaningful, but the physical overtones of his treatment of it suggest the probability of an inspiration of this kind.

7

THE BIRTH OF A POEM

THE FIRST VOLUME OF WARD'S *View* CONTAINS AN EXTENSIVE
account of the history of the Hindus, based on their *puranas* and
mythological works, and a minute study of their social institutions
and religious and domestic manners, together with brief notices,
substantiated with illustrations, of their achievement in various
creative and speculative realms of activity. But the main body of
the book concerns their philosophical thought, and here "the author
has . . . endeavoured to supply something from all these schools
[the six systems of Hindu philosophy] with the view of enabling
the reader to form an opinion of what was taught by these philosophers."[287] Added to this are extracts from the *Vedas* and the
Upanishads, and brief individual sketches of the many Hindu
thinkers with a summary of their teachings. We shall, however,
for obvious reasons, confine our attention exclusively to the philosophical accounts and ignore what else Whitman might imaginably
have learned about the Hindus from the rest of the book.

The volume is prefaced with quite elaborate "Introductory Remarks," in the course of which the author "attempt[s] a comparison of the Hindu philosophy with the systems which obtained
among the Greeks and other nations."[288] In this section are presented the thoughts of the various Hindu philosophers under
different heads of discussion, and though it is, to a certain degree,
a repetition of what the other accounts have generally said, the
systematic and perspicuous statement of these pages deserves notice,
because if Whitman had not read another page else on philosophy

these alone could have supplied almost the entire philosophical background of his poems. Therefore some of the Hindu teachings under each of these classifications are reproduced in an appendix (Appendix II, b). The selection is limited to those only that have a direct bearing on Whitman's ideas.

How much such a systematic "summary" of "the most distinguished parts of the Hindoo philosophy" was able to contribute to the philosophical foundations of Whitman's writings, it is hoped, can be imagined even in the truncated version given. Yet, as our evidence has shown, Ward's is not the only book on Hindu philosophy that Whitman read, and much of the same thought is likely to have been obtained from the other sources. All the same, while a precise estimation of the role of *A View* in the philosophical education of our poet is not possible, the probability of its cooperation in the composition of the great message he formed for his mission cannot be underrated.

The story, however, of the actual accounts of the six schools of Hindu philosophy, given in the body of the book, is different: their role in the evolution of his poems can be directly perceived and precisely evaluated. These accounts, in fact, translations of treatises enunciating the doctrines of the various systems, though in the case of one school, the Vedanta, the treatise is of doubtful authenticity, are found in Part II of the volume, which undertakes a very elaborate survey of the "Literature of the Hindoos," from the *Vedas* and the *Upanishads* through poetry and drama and ethics to medical and scientific works, specimens of each of which are presented in the author's translation, sometimes with the original Sanskrit passages. Part I deals with the history and social life of the Hindus, and, passing this by, we shall examine the second.

Preparatory to the study of the schools of Hindu thought, the Reverend Ward, an author whose thoroughness of investigation and extensive scholarship more than compensate for the general Christian impatience with the pagan thought he is examining, which, as he himself is aware, often forces him into remarks "harsh and overcoloured,"[289] presents individual accounts of fifty-nine "of the Hindoo sages, and a summary of their philosophical opinions."[290] One of these sages is called Lokakshee, who "taught, that the true shastra substantiated its own legitimacy, and needed not

foreign proof; that the works of philosophers were full of contradictions. . . ." And Ward, in his account of him, cites "a celebrated verse, often quoted by the Hindoos, but difficult to be
understood," which "is ascribed to Lokakshee":

The vedas are at variance—the smritees are at variance.
He who gives a meaning of his own, quoting the vedas, is no
    philosopher;
True philosophy, thro' ignorance, is concealed as in the fissures
    of a rock;
But—the way of the Great One—that is to be followed.[291]

The famous claim of self-contradiction Whitman makes in
"Song of Myself" may appear to be the verbal echo of an Emerson-
ian passage, as Kennedy has noted,[292] but it is more likely that its
inspiration lay less in the love of a well-expressed thought than in
the self-conscious apology resulting from an awareness that he had
attempted to weld the stuff of his poetry from the reading of
divergent and often mutually conflicting teachings of the Hindus,
who were, as Ward, repeatedly insisting, said, "incessantly con-
tradicting each other,"[293] and whom Lokakshee endeavored to
correct in his teaching. The influence of the above account, however, can with greater ease be seen on another passage in the same
poem. In section 31 of the "Song," Whitman's Cosmic Soul claims:

In vain the speeding or shyness,
In vain the plutonic rocks send their old heat against my ap-
    proach,
In vain the mastodon retreats beneath its own powdered bones,
In vain objects stand leagues off and assume manifold shapes,
In vain the ocean settling in hollows and the great monsters ly-
    ing low,
In vain the buzzard houses herself with the sky,
In vain the snake slides through the creepers and logs,
In vain the elk takes to the inner passes of the woods,
In vain the razorbilled auk sails far north to Labrador,
I follow quickly. . . . I ascend to the nest in the fissure of the
    cliff.[294]

In the lines preceding these, as Miller observes, "the poet shows an awareness of self as the product of a long, evolutionary development,"[295] but what he wants to show in these is slightly "difficult to be understood." It cannot be merely that his powers of motion are greater, and so, by "follow[ing] quickly," he can outdistance all of them. Nor does the thought of these lines look like the product of his characteristic verbal embroidering of a basic idea, here, that of his self's evolution, though, for all we know, the apparent similarity of these lines to the previous ones may have forced them into the same "envelope." The true clue to what he means here seems to be in the fourth line of the passage: "In vain objects stand leagues off and assume manifold shapes." In vain do all these things, objects, qualities, creatures, do what they do, for the poet is resistless, and can "call anything again" when he desires it. And this he does, if we accept the connection of thought with the other, the opening, passage of the section, to find the evidence of his belief that "a leaf of grass is no less than the journey-work of the stars," or, in other words, to discover the truth of all objects, whose being he "find[s]" he "incorporate[s]." The involved fashion in which Whitman's words and thoughts travel from inspiration to composition, and from the "slips" of composition again through a tortuous route to the ultimate poetic position on the printed page, defeats the strongest detective imagination of research. But when we remember how ardently he sought to be a "true" philosopher himself, and how enthusiastically he assumed "the way of the Great One," and offered to lead "each man and woman" of the world along "that road," it is not hard to see that he understood the "celebrated verse" of Lokakshee enough to "ascend to the nest in the fissure" of a rock, where the Hindu philosopher mystically announced "true philosophy" to lie concealed.

Immediately preceding the section "of the Six Darshanas," or systems of philosophy, in Ward, are the extracts from the *Vedas* and the *Upanishads,* one of them containing passages from different *Upanishads* all bearing on the subject of the creation. A good deal of this early Hindu thought has already been noticed, but I shall here reproduce a few lines, not quoted before, suggestion of which can easily be seen in Whitman.

Formerly this world (Brahma) was in the form of a male. He, reflecting, saw nothing but himself. He first uttered the sound I: from hence his name became I. Therefore, to the present time people first say I, and then mention any other name. . . . He enjoyed not pleasure alone; therefore at present men enjoy not pleasure alone. He wished for another. He divided his body into two parts like the lobes of a seed of pulse, and one became a male and the other a female. . . . First, was created vacuum, from vacuum, air, from air, fire, from fire, water, from water, earth, from the earth, food; from food, man. . . . Some persons regard . . . that the body is the whole of man; others . . . contend for the existence in the body of an immaterial spirit. The writer then adds another comparison; two birds having perched on a tree, one (param-atma) eats not of the fruit; the other (the animal spirit) partakes of the fruit of works. The seed of the tree is delusion; the fruit, religion and irreligion; the roots, the three gunas; . . . its eight branches, are the five primary elements, the reasoning faculty, personal identity, and wisdom. . . . As a house forsaken by its occupant becomes dark, so the body, when forsaken by the deity, is filled with darkness; therefore should this divine guest be always retained.[296]

We may not be able to insist that Whitman gathered the cosmic connotations of his "I" here in this passage; or the doctrine of the male and female principles in creation; or the notion of the final evolution of man from vacuum through the earth; or the "personal identity," which is one of the principles of being, but it is surely this "divine guest" without whom the body is "filled with darkness" of whom he speaks in "To Think of Time":

It is not to diffuse you that you were born of your mother and
    father—it is to identify you,
. . . .
Something long preparing and formless is arrived and formed
    in you,
. . . .
The threads that were spun are gathered . . . . the weft crosses
    the warp . . . . the pattern is systematic.
. . . .

The guest that was coming . . . . he waited long for reasons
. . . . he is now housed,
He is one of those who are beautiful and happy.[297]

Even the qualities of the guest he praises have been found in the
pages we have noticed. "Spirit is lovely," said Kapila; "the Deity
is perfect Joy," said the Shatwatas. And, again, a few paragraphs
later in Ward, in another specimen of the *Upanishads* dealing
with "absorption, or emancipation," Brahma, the Supreme Being,
whom the soul obtains, is described as "the happy refuge of souls;
the giver of joy to the mind; the fountain of joy; and the immortal."[298]

As another proof of his wonderful power of transformation of
borrowed ideas, the following passage from Whitman's "Song of
the Universal" may be cited:

> Over the mountain-growths disease and sorrow,
> An uncaught bird is ever hovering, hovering,
> High in the purer, happier air.

The "uncaught bird," the reader can see without much difficulty,
is the "param-atma," or the Supreme Soul, of the Upanishadic
passage quoted above, which, perched on the tree of life with the
other bird—the individual, animal spirit—yet "eats not of the
fruit."

Introducing the six schools of Hindu philosophy, Ward makes
two remarks:[299] one is, that "in the different darshanas various
opposite opinions are taught, and these clashing sentiments appear
to have given rise to much contention, and to many controversial
writings." Whitman could by himself certainly have realized this
element of divergence and mutual opposition in the teachings of
the Hindu sages, but it is possible that Ward's warning increased
his consciousness of the same in him. For, after all, he knew that he
was, to use our old metaphor, like a bee gathering his mint and
marjorum from the flowers of these gardens. And it is also likely
that any intellectual qualms he might have had about such a task
of weaving a pattern from discordant strands were considerably
relieved by the second of Ward's remarks, which said:

Among those who profess to study the darshanas, none at

present maintain all the decisions of any particular school or sect. Respecting the Divine Being, the doctrine of the vedanta seems chiefly to prevail among the best informed of the Hindoo pandits; on the subject of abstract ideas and logic, the nyaya is in the highest esteem. On creation, three opinions, derived from the darshanas, are current: the one of that of the atomic philosophy; another that of matter possessing in itself the power of assuming all manner of forms, and the other, that spirit operates on matter, and produces the universe in all its various appearances. The first opinion is that of the vysheshika and nyaya schools; the second is that of the sankhya, and the last that of the vedanta. . . . Most of the darshanas agree, that matter and spirit are eternal. The works point out three ways of obtaining emancipation, the knowledge of spirit; devotion; and works.

In a rough way this is exactly what Whitman, as a "pandit", maintains. Respecting the Divine Being, he is a Vedantin, and on creation, he readily combines all the "three opinions, derived from the darshanas." The logic of the Nyaya school enters into his own inference, as we have seen, to prove the "unseen." With the last two details, of the eternity of matter and spirit and of the modes of emancipation, we have an equally perceptible correspondence in his thought.

Of the accounts of the six philosophical systems given by Ward, the one that appears to have made the strongest impression on Whitman's mind is that of the Sankhya school, the first in the series. Ward's account is a "translation of the Sankhya-sara, written by Vignana-bhikshuka." "The best text of the *Sanchya,*" as Colebrooke observes, "is a short treatise in verse, which is denominated *Carica,*"[300] the acknowledged author of which is Iswara-Krishna. Yet the *Sankhya-sara* of Vignana-bhikshuka—one of the many writers on the system who compiled the doctrines taught by the founder of the school, Kapila—presents the essence of it with commentary and discussion, and in nontechnical phrase, which might explain how this exposition came closer to Whitman's understanding than that of Colebrooke, or than, if he read that too, the *Sankhya-Karika* itself.

Whatever part the other books, over which Whitman's avid and inquisitive imagination brooded, played in the formation and fertilization of the mental soil out of which *Leaves of Grass* sprouted, the indications are that in the actual efflorescence of the 1855 poems, these pages, setting forth the essential thought of the Sankhya school, have played a vital role. In fact, the most important of all his poems, one that is the very heart and soul of his poetry and philosophy, namely, "Song of Myself," seems to have its major physical roots among these pages, many of its portions actually appearing to be an exquisite versification of the prose passages of the account. Upon the evidence that follows, it is even possible to maintain that if Whitman had not even read the *Bhagvat-Geeta,* which, as we shall see later, supplied him the final persuasion for the metaphysical foundations of the self on which his lyric "I" so magnificently revolves, the "Sankhya-sara" rendering of Ward alone could explain the "Song of Myself." Yet, as we concentrate our attention upon the energies these pages provided Whitman for his poetic utterances, their gift of philosophic thought cannot be overlooked. Therefore, in our analysis, we shall briefly notice the latter too, especially because, being a discussion rather than a mere exposition, the treatise ranges beyond the Sankhya thought to include the ideas of other schools for a comparative examination. Avoiding thoughts and notions noticed elsewhere already, and expressions similar to the ones found in other writers, here is the account in a severe abridgement.

The "Sankhya-sara"[301] opens with the question of "emancipation," which, as all Hindu philosophy insists, "is procured by the wisdom which discriminates between matter and spirit," and examines the nature of this wisdom: "This discrimination will destroy the pride of imaginary separate existence (that is, that the human spirit is separate from the divine); as well as passion, malevolence, works of merit and demerit. . . . Works of former births . . . will cease . . . transmigration is at an end . . . the person obtains emancipation. . . . He who desires God, as well as he who desires nothing, though not freed from the body, in the body becomes God. . . . When all the desires of the heart are dismissed, a mortal becomes immortal, and here obtains Brahma . . . Passion, hatred, &c. arise from ignorance, and . . . ignorance gives birth to works of merit and demerit. . . . The fire of wisdom destroys all works. . . . False ideas, selfishness, passion, and other evils are extinguished so soon as a person obtains discriminating wisdom."

The second section describes "the connection between spirit

and that which is not spirit. . . . Thus also the veda: Spirit is not this, is not that: it is immeasurable; it cannot be grasped (therefore) it is not grasped; undecayable, it decays not; incapable of adhesion, it does not unite; it is not susceptible of pain; it is deathless. . . . Spirit is not matter, for matter is liable to change. . . . When all things, from crude matter to the smallest object produced by the mutation of matter, are known in their separate state, discriminating wisdom is perfected. . . . Clear knowledge of spirit arises from yoga, or abstraction of mind; and this leads to liberation; but not immediately. . . . Error is removed, first, by doubts respecting the reality of our conceptions, and then by more certain knowledge. . . . The Geeta says, The person who, with the eye of wisdom, distinguishes between soul and body, obtains the Supreme. . . . By this wisdom the person at length attains to such perfection, that he esteems all sentient creatures alike, and sees that spirit is everything. . . . Establishment in the habit of discrimination is thus described in the Geeta: O Pandava, he who has obtained a settled habit of discrimination, neither dislikes nor desires the three qualities which lead to truth, excitation, or stupefaction. . . . By [the] mode of inferring one thing from the other, the understanding is proved to be distinct from the things discovered by it. . . . Spirit is distinct from that which it discovers . . . and also . . . is omnipresent, unchangeable, everlasting, undivided, and wisdom itself."

The argument of the third section is "what then is matter?"; and here the author enunciates the fundamental Sankhya doctrine that "it is divided into twenty-four parts, viz. crude matter, the understanding, consciousness of personal identity, the qualities of the five primary elements, the eleven organs, and the five primary elements." An extensive analysis follows in which the nature of each of these twenty-four principles is discussed, along with the doctrine of the three gunas, or qualities, constituting the "natural state itself." There is also an account of the three bodies investing the soul, or "three states of body": the "archetype," the "atomic," and the "gross." It is finally declared: "Narayana is the spirit of all sentient creatures. . . . All living creatures, with their organs, proceeded from the body of that being (Narayana thus clothed with matter). . . . The four-faced God was unfolded from . . . this god."

The fourth section's theme is "spirit, as the first cause (purusha), and distinct from matter. The common concerns of life are conducted by this one idea 'I am' (that is, by identifying spirit with matter) ; but by the true knowledge of God it is made clear, that he is eternal, omnipresent, &c. . . . He is the cause of every operation of the understanding, and of every creature produced by the mutations of matter." The discussion of the nature of the "spirit and of that which is not spirit" progresses into the rest of the account, and in the next six sections dwells upon "the distinction between them," "the intellectual nature of the spirit," "the happiness of the spirit," "discrimination," "the method of celebrating" yoga to achieve "discrimination," and finally, "the properties of the man who obtains liberation in this life." Though much from all these sections has entered into the general background of Whitman's thought, only three of these, namely the seventh, the eighth, and the ninth, need be noticed in any elaborateness.

Section seven "proceeds to describe the happiness of spirit," and, declaring that the word "happiness is figuratively applied," maintains that "Spirit is neither joyful nor joyless." The idea of spirit that the Sankhya thought insists on here is this: "By this sentence of the veda, Spirit is more lovely than anything, the beauty of spirit is intended to be set above happiness," "of spirit as identified with love"; "therefore spirit (self) is the most beloved object; there is nothing so beloved as this. . . . Spirit is lovely; and is identified with love. Hence, in reality, spirit is the object of love. . . . Love to spirit is constant; for spirit is styled the eternally happy. If the understanding be well settled, and perceive the entire loveliness of spirit, will it not bathe in a sea of happiness? In common affairs, the understanding enjoys happiness when anything pleasant is presented to the sight; from hence we infer, that supreme happiness must arise from a view of that which is supremely lovely. The exciting cause to love is always spirit—spirit is of itself lovely. . . . The happiness arising from the sight of the beloved object, spirit, and which can be represented by no similitude, is enjoyed by the wise (who are) emancipated, even in a bodily state."

Clearly this well-settled "understanding," bathing in a "sea of happiness" through a perception of "the entire loveliness of spirit," is the heart of Whitman's mystic adoration of life and the very pulse of his utterances. If we rely on the testimony of his friends and admirers who spoke of his own joy of life and spirituality, he was one of those "wise emancipated," enjoying supreme happiness "even in a bodily state." "I am a man preoccupied by his own soul," said he in "Assurances." The burden of his songs is this intense love for the soul, reverberating over all his poetry. "The soul is always beautiful" ("The Sleepers"); the "guest," that is spirit, now "housed" in the body, "is one of those who are beautiful and happy," "one of those that to look upon and be with is enough" ("To Think of Time"); "Clear and sweet is my soul" ("Song of Myself"); and hence it is that he could declare, "All seems beautiful to me" ("Song of the Open Road"). And his own constant "love to spirit" bursts forth into insistent announcements in his later songs. "O the joy of my spirit," he exclaims in "A Song of Joys," and in "Passage to India" asserts, "O soul thou pleasest me":

> O we can wait no longer,
> We too take ship O soul,
> Joyous we too launch out on trackless seas,
> Fearless for unknown shores on waves of ecstasy to sail,
> Amid the wafting winds, (thou pressing me to thee, I thee to
>   me, O soul,)
> Caroling free, singing our song of God,
> Chanting our song of pleasant exploration. (Sec. 8)

And when his own life's true ship approaches the unknown shores of death, he still shouts, "Joy, Shipmate, Joy."[302] It is the same "supreme happiness" that is at the root of his self-love, of which he speaks so ecstatically in "Song of Myself."

> I dote on myself. . . . there is that lot of me, and all so
>   luscious,
> Each moment and whatever happens thrills me with joy.[303]

The "body" that enters into this "lot of me" in the passage, is after all the result of the identity of spirit with matter that is part of Brahma; and so is the physical language in which the spiritual love of his "beloved object" expresses itself. It is "with laugh and many a kiss" that the soul pleases him.[304] As

> The satisfier, after due long-waiting now advancing,
> Yes here comes my mistress the soul.[305]

In "Song of the Open Road," the same sexual language serves for
the spiritual sentiment, when he speaks of "the fluid and attaching
character" that rises from the happiness that is "the efflux of the
soul"; but, cruelly reduced as it is to "amative" love, which is one
half of his message, it is still the product of the love that is the
identity of spirit. And in a prose fragment he wrote: "We know
that sympathy or love is the law over all laws, because in nothing
else but love is the soul conscious of pure happiness, which appears to be the ultimate resting place, and point of all things."[306]
Thus there is no doubt that what Bucke ascribed to a mystic revelation and others to a subjective intuition is but the outcome of a
literary inspiration. To put it less reverently, Whitman read these
pages of Ward "in June, such a transparent summer morning"
bathing the streets around the Mercantile or the Astor Library;
and perhaps he "settled" the book "athwart" his "hips and gently
turned over" the pages, drew the pen from his "bosom" pocket,
"plunged" the nib on the "bare" sheets, and made notes till
"Swiftly arose and spread around [him] the peace and joy and
knowledge that pass all the argument of the earth . . . that a
kelson of the creation is love."[307]

The central thought of the eighth section of Vignana-bhikshuka's
discussion of Sankhya is the relation of the spirit to the material
universe. According to Sankhya, the spirit, though all-pervading,
is detached, unassociated, and uninvolved. These ideas are set
forth in detail in this section, but because this concept of the Unaffected Nature of the Spirit is the distinguishing and fundamental
doctrine of the system, references to it occur in the other sections
dealing with the nature of spirit in general. But let us first notice
the passages and the thought in Whitman that arose from these
discussions.

Trippers and askers surround me,
People I meet . . . . the effect upon me of my early life . . . .
    of the ward and city I live in . . . . of the nation,
The latest news . . . . discoveries, inventions, societies . . . .
    authors old and new,
My dinner, dress, associates, looks, business, compliments,
    dues,
The real or fancied indifference of some man or woman I love,
The sickness of one of my folks—or of myself . . . . or ill-

doing . . . . or loss or lack of money . . . . or depressions
or exaltations,
They come to me days and nights and go from me again,
But they are not the Me myself.

Apart from the pulling and hauling stands what I am,
Stands amused, complacent, compassionating, idle, unitary,
Looks down, is erect, bends an arm on an implacable certain
rest,
Looks with its sidecurved head curious what will come next,
Both in and out of the game, and watching and wondering
at it.[308]

Me imperturbe, standing at ease in Nature,
Master of all or mistress of all, aplomb in the midst of irra-
tional things,
Imbued as they, passive, receptive, silent as they. . . .[309]

That shadow my likeness that goes to and fro seeking a livelihood, chattering, chaffering,
How often I find myself standing and looking at it where it
flits,
How often I question and doubt whether that is really me.[310]

In these passages, Whitman is asserting the distinction between
the external phenomenal self and the true identity, the internal,
real, soul. To that extent, it is a thought that the meagerest
imaginative sensibility could achieve in common apprehension, unassisted by any profound aid from philosophic studies. The concept of these two selves in him, making, together with the body, a
"trio," is constantly expressed in his other poems. But the idea
dwelt upon here, particularly in the first of the passages from
"Song of Myself," is the transcendental, unattached, unaffected
nature of his inner self, though in his voluminous asseveration of
the minute involvement of his soul in the affairs of all beings and
things of the universe, nowhere is this aloofness suggested. In fact,
unless we insist upon a different foundation for this portion of
"Song of Myself," with its indifference to "the sickness of one of
my folks," the incongruity becomes glaring with the later operations of the poet's self, which was "the man" and "suffered," and
"was there."[311] For, manifestly, in the same cosmic identity could

Whitman claim, "All these I feel and am," in which he claims the real "Me," because the "Me" that is a poet and "chant[s] a new chant of dilation or pride,"[312] is, according to the implications of the argument, "not the Me myself," but only "the shadow my likeness that goes to and fro seeking a livelihood." Nevertheless, he is all these as and when, it appears, the "slips" manage to find a resting-place in the "envelope." And we might grant that liberty to a poet who insisted that he was a "law" unto himself. However, the thought of this "slip" is not the gift of "personal intuition," as can be seen in a comparison with the following extracts from Vignana-bhikshuka, from which it will also appear that the passage in Whitman rose out of the mere love of a beautiful idea:

> When we speak of spirit, as the sovereign, we mean, that it presides over the operations of the understanding as the receiver, as a shadow is received by the mirror. ([Footnote by Ward:] According to the Sankhya, spirit is not considered . . . as really receiving the fruit of actions; this reception being only in appearance in consequence of union to matter, and not more, in reality, than as a mirror suffers or enjoys, from the image reflected on it.)

> All desires, &c. arise in the understanding, and not in the spirit. . . . In the understanding only . . . pleasure and pain, exist. . . . Spirit receives pleasure, &c. as a wall the shadow; but that which enjoys or suffers is the understanding.

> (Spirit) . . . enjoys not pleasure, he endures not pain, he is pure spirit.[313]

The foregoing are lines scattered in the previous sections of the "Sankhya-sara." The main body of the thought is in section eight, from which selections are reproduced here.

> . . . The great sages, using the comparisons of the ether and the lotus, untouched by earth and water, have declared, that spirit is not tangible, is *unassociated,* and *unaffected.* . . . *The bodily organs naturally collect all articles of enjoyment for the sovereign (spirit),* and deliver them to the chief minister, the understanding. The understanding, charged with all the arti-

cles of enjoyment, presents them to the *spirit; the spirit, as lord of all, enjoys them, like a king, by merely looking on them.* . . . He, *undivided* and *uniform* . . . is known only to himself. . . . Enjoyment (bhoga) does not belong to the immutable spirit. . . . Spirit, without assistance, sees the operations of the understanding, and is therefore called the testifier for the understanding; and because it sees in itself everything free from change, it is called the universal *testifier. The manifestations imparted by spirit are temporary, for it retains the images of things only for a time.* . . . The understanding charges all the *faults* of the objects of sense on spirit, the *perceiver,* but falsely, for it is free from impurity, as the mirror or the pure ether. . . . Spirit, on account of its *uniformity,* is called The Unchangeable. . . . Spirit is *indivisible.* . . . Let the wise, by these and other ways pointed out by teachers, books, their own experience . . . distinguish between spirit and that which is not spirit. . . . (Italics added)

From the next section are a few lines bearing on the same idea:

The operations of the understanding resemble a jar, and spirit the vacuum in the jar; they are (in their union) subtile and indestructible. In reality, spirit . . . is unchangeable, unassociated, and undecayable. . . . *Spirit is distinct from these miseries (these operations), yet sees them without a medium.* . . . *Filled with joy, grief, fear, anger, desire, infatuation, inebriation, envy, self-importance, covetousness, sleep, indolence, lust, and other marks both of religion and irreligion: in short, full of joy or misery,* the understanding exhibits itself as spirit (when a person says *I* am sick, *I* am happy, &c. [original italics]). . . . I (spirit) am . . . *pacific,* . . . pure, . . . *unmixed,* . . . *untroubled,* . . . the mirror in which all is seen, and, through my union to all souls, the displayer of all things. . . . If the reflection of the operations of the understanding falls upon me as on a mirror, the fault . . . is not mine. . . . That the spirit is in chains, and subject to sensations . . . appears to be false as soon as the mirror, spirit, is inspected. . . . The testifier (spirit) is not subject to the three states, wakefulness, repose, and profound sleep. I, the sun-like spirit, am perfect; I neither rise nor set. . . . As nothing adheres to space, neither does anything adhere to me. . . . *My birth,* and *all its consequences, are as false* as the visions of religion and irreligion, birth and death, pleasure and pain, &c. appear when a person awakes. . . . *As the clouds, whether they conceal the sun or not, do not approach that luminary, so do I (spirit) see the evil dream-like train of existence, birth, death, and the momentary operations of the understanding, without being affected by them.* . . . (Italics added)

This concept, however, as we have seen, has briefly appeared elsewhere in Whitman's readings, as, for instance, in the *Transactions,* where both the Sankhya and the Vedanta variations of it were suggested by Colebrooke. But the close verbal correspondence of Whitman's passage to this, as the italics indicate, is remarkable, though it does not prove that this account was the only source. The "joy or misery" of Vignana-bhikshuka, becomes his "depressions or exaltations"; the "faults" his "illdoing"; the "indivisible" and "undivided" form his "unitary"; the "pacific" is turned into his "complacent"; the kingly unconcern suggests his "idle"; the phrase, "my birth and all its consequences" has given rise to his "effect upon me of my early life"; the "temporary" or "momentary" association of the spirit, has inspired the line: "They come to me days and nights and go from me again"; and the "anger," "love," "sick[ness]," in short, almost the whole list of "miseries (these operations)" reappears in him, understandably "impressed" with his own "masterly identity." His self "looks," like the "perceiver," and is "both in and out" like the "vacuum in the jar," and like the "testifier," the actual word for which, as we found in his other readings, is "witness," he declares in the same section of "Song of Myself" "I witness and wait," and in a later one, "I am he attesting sympathy."[314] Elsewhere, again, like the "luminary" "unaffected" by the "visions" of the "evil dream-like train of existence, birth and death, &c.," his self "witness[es] the corpse with its dabbled hair," witnesses "arrests of criminals, slights, adulterous offers," and all else of the myriad forms of life in the universe and their activities, merely "mind[ing] them or the show or resonance of them," because it just "come[s] and depart[s]."[315]

In his illuminating study of Whitman in the light of Vedantic mysticism, Chari observes that this "Not the Me myself" thought of Whitman is Vedantic and not Sankhya.[316] Perhaps it is, and Whitman, in spite of his verbal similarity to the Sankhya account of Vignana-bhikshuka, was impressed more by the qualified detachedness of spirit he found in Colebrooke's Vedanta account, or in the *Bhagvat-Geeta*. Or perhaps the consistency with his other Vedantic notions that this Sankhya doctrine has come to have in the power of containing "multitudes," is just part of the marvel of his achievement as a poet. But the point, in the light of the evidence this study has unearthed as to the way in which Whitman became the "maker of poems," who alone "begets," while "the singers do not beget,"[317] appears rather irrelevant, because, far from being able to claim in happy admiration that "Whitman has, by means of his intuitive vision, penetrated to the spiritual center within himself and discovered the true glory and independence of his self,"[318] the present writer is in the uncomfortable position of having to assert that, if Whitman was one of the "wise" described by the philosopher in the passage quoted above "who distinguish between spirit and that which is not spirit," and thus obtain "discriminating wisdom," he was not so from his "own experience" but "by . . . ways pointed out by . . . books."

Two more brief thoughts of these pages demand our attention before we pass on to the next section. One of them is on the nature of the state of sleep, and it has already been suggested that Whitman's "Night-Poem," or "The Sleepers," is not inspired by the mere fancy of poetic imagination. This is what "Sankhya-sara" said on the subject:

> We learn from the veda, that the distinction between the operations of the understanding on visible objects, and spirit, is mostly clearly seen during the time of profound sleep, when spirit, as the manifester, appears as light. . . . Though the body and faculties in waking time appear not to be different from spirit, yet during a dream, spirit is clearly seen to be different from both. In a dream, all bodies different from spirit appear in the spirit. . . . In a dream, they are the immediate objects of perception, because they are ideal. In waking hours, they are the objects of perception by the instrumentality of the organs. . . . As a person dreaming, sees everything in spirit, so in his waking hours (not withstanding the omnipresence of spirit, through the individuation of his ideas, he fancies) he sees it confined in one place (body). Profound sleep, then, shews simple spirit (rather than its state of embodied existence). . . .[319]

It is hard not to think that this and similar passages found frequently in the Hindu philosophical writings roused Whitman's

poetic eagerness with which to "wander all night in [his] vision,"
and see the ideality of all objects and their spiritual unity.

Probably the most startling of all Whitman's messianic utterances is his insistence that

Nothing, not God, is greater to one than one's self is.[320]

And that there is no God any more divine than Yourself. . . .[321]

In fairness to Whitman, it must be admitted that this belief of his
was not only for preaching but for his own practice too. For the
obvious Godhood he himself assumed breathes aloud in all his
poems, though those of his old age pierce this mythical shell he so
ardently built around him; where once the gigantic assurances
thundered full-throatedly, the later poems are filled with humility,
doubt, pain, and even fear, which demand much from faith. But if
his own convictions of being God failed him so, it might have been
of some satisfaction to him that there was at least one man among
his disciples who, as we have noticed, unhesitatingly accepted him
as God. With regard to his message, perhaps an equally unhesi-
tating acceptance is possible, as far as it comes to us in the poetic
intimation, where the underlying concept of the divinity of the
individual soul, consubstantial with God, philosophically clarifies
and defines it. But in the fragmentary, inconsequential, and abrupt
fashion in which the thought glares at us on the prose pages of his
early notebook, apparently as a private personal feeling, its amazing
egotism takes our breath away. In 1847, years before he finally
emerged into the lines of his poetry as the Cosmic Being, he
recorded:

Who is the being of whom I am the inferior?— . . . I never
yet knew how it felt to think I stood in the presence of my superior.—If the presence of God were made visible immediately
before me, I could not abase myself.—How do I know but I
myself [thought incomplete].

If I walk with Jah in Heaven, and he assume to be intrinsically greater than I it offends me, and I shall certainly withdraw from heaven. . . .

Not even God, (that dread?) is so great to me as Myself is great to me.—Who knows but I too shall in time be a God as pure and prodigious as any of them?[322]

We must first of all recognize that this is a lot more than the normal pride of a young man, and more, too, than the mere political or social independence of an American, "voices . . . by [Whitman's poetic] me clarified and transfigured,"[323] in other words, thoughts natural to the young, proud, American that Whitman was then; or God would not be the obvious point of reference. Nor could we ascribe it to the consciousness of the "dangerously high"[324] self-esteem in his character, because that phrenological self-discovery occurred in July 1849. Nor again, despite the abnormality of his personal character, could it be conveniently suggested that it all arose from a delicate fancy inspired by the following notes he made "Of Insanity" in his "Preparatory Reading and Thought":

> Of Insanity—Some are affected with melancholia, in these the organ of cautiousness will be found large; some fancy themselves the Deity, in these self-esteem predominates; some are furious, in these destructiveness, or more likely, combativeness. But a small organ may become diseased and often does so.[325]

These notes, as Shephard suggests,[326] were obviously made from Fowler's phrenological chart, in which both Cautiousness and Combativeness are rated 6, the same as Self-esteem and Destructiveness, 5 to 6. But the reference to melancholia in his notes, and their general title "Insanity," are curious indeed, the former because he was both a poet and a man of joy, and the chart rated his Mirthfulness as 5, which indicates the "full" degree of development; and the latter because we can hardly imagine him to have regarded his own qualities as related to insanity.

However, none of these can explain the deliberate equality with God with which he chooses to assert his self-respect. In other words, it is not the social self-esteem of a proud man he is speaking of in the early notebook, but the philosophical self-esteem, the greatness of the Myself he later poetically celebrates. This consciousness of self is not the result of self-consciousness, if the pun be permitted, but of such utterances as the following from "Sankhya-sara," on which, obviously, his fancy was working when he wrote those thoughts:

> The immutable one [spirit] has no lord to whom he owes obedience. . . . The yogi, viewing the glory of spirit, which is beyond all comparison, and free from alloy, values the glory of (the god) Brahma no higher than a blade of grass.

> Vishnu and the other principal deities who possess great glory, do not enjoy more than I (the yogi) do. . . . When a person sees another in qualities and actions greater than himself, he labours to become his equal; but I see no one greater than myself: nor do I consider myself as less than others, that I should, through fear of being beaten, worship the gods. . . . There is no distinction between governer and governed; therefore there is nothing greater than myself. . . .[327]

It may be noticed that almost the same words, "there is nothing greater than myself," are used by Whitman both in his prose notes and his message. With what scrupulous fidelity he carries out the instructions of the foregoing can be seen in section 20 of "Song of Myself":

> I cock my hat as I please indoors or out.
> Shall I pray? Shall I venerate and be ceremonious?

Indeed, he did not have to, because the yogi, said the account of Sankhya a little later, "resembles a king. He who in the body has obtained emancipation is of no cast, of no sect, of no order, attends to no duties, adheres to no shastras, to no formulas, to no works of merit; he leaves the net of secular affairs as the lion his toils; . . . he is glorious as the autumnal sky; he flatters none; he honours none; he is not worshipped; he worships not. Whether he practise the ceremonies, and follow the customs (of his country) or not, this is his character."[328] Again, it is not only fidelity to the thought, but to the word itself, that surprises us here. And since the yogi need not have to "follow the customs," "conformity goes to the fourth remov'd"[329] for Whitman.

All these instances show how little of "own experience," or, to use Allen's words, "his own psychology, which enabled him to intuit some of the oldest spiritual truths in human experience,"[330] there is in the making of Whitman's poems, although the marvel of his making of them remains undimished. But of all these discoveries that dethrone him from the divine pedestal on which he mysteriously ensconced himself to the delight and amazement of the critical world, none surprises us more than the ninth section of "Sankhya-sara," of which the "Song of Myself" has all the indications of being an extended paraphrase, on which rough sketch a magnificent picture was raised, with colors and lines worked into in later impulses.

In this section, after having previously "defined discrimination, for its further manifestation," Vignana-bhikshuka "briefly relate[s] the method of celebrating raja-yoga"; instructing, however, that "he who is not able to perform the raja-yoga, may attend to that called hatha-yoga," or "the common yoga," as a footnote explains.

    . . . In the celebration of the raja-yoga, the exercise of the understanding is required. In the hatha-yoga, the suppression and expression of the breath, and a peculiar posture in sitting, are the two principal things required; other things are to be attended to according to the strength of the yogi. . . . To the yogi spirit manifests itself, when, with an unwavering mind, he thus meditates, "I am that which manifests the operations of the understanding, I am the eyewitness of the understanding, I am different from the understanding, I am the all-pervading, I am the unchangeable, I am the ever-living." . . . I . . . am all-pervading, pacific, the total of pure spirit, pure, the inconceivable, simple life, pure vacuum, undecayable, unmixed, boundless, without qualities, untroubled, unchangeable, the mirror in which all is seen, and, through my union to all souls, the displayer of all things. Not being different in nature, I am every living creature, from Brahma, Vishnu, Maheswara, down to inanimate matter. I and all other living creatures are one (in essence) like the vacuum, we are life; therefore we are taught in the veda to meditate on spirit as one, and as expressed by the particle I. Seeing this, the yogi worships . . . all living creatures. The veda says, that in this manner *the sankhya yogis worship spirit or (self). He who worships spirit (self) viewing himself equally in all beings and all equally in himself, ascends to his own heaven. Menu calls the worship of (self) spirit, the method of obtaining divine knowledge. . . . The yogi, who views all on an equality with himself, desires not the pleasures enjoyed by Brahma, Vishnu, Siva, &c. Therefore, let the yogi meditate on equality.* How can desire exist in the mind of him who, in production and dissolution, in all states and times, sees everything the same. . . . *From Brahma even to the people in hell, the yogi loves all as himself, even as parents love their children.* . . . From men's (false) conceptions of the undivided one, viz that such a one is sovereign, that these are subjects, that this is best, that this is the worst, the fear of death arises. The various shades of existence . . . appear in the one vacuum-formed spirit as non-entities, or like shadows on a chrystal pillar. In the operations of the understanding, the one spirit appears multiform, as a juggler who personifies a number of animals by clothing himself with their skins. Maya (illusion), in various forms, embracing formless spirit, dances, and thus brings the understanding into a state of infatuation. The idea of a plurality of spirits arises from variety in the operations of the understanding: this may be illustrated by the appearance of many suns in different pans of water, and many skies as seen through different apertures in a jar, &c. "Therefore, attend! I am pure, wise, free, all-pervading, undecayable": the wise, thus judging, treat as false the distinctions of I and thou, friend and enemy, &c. . . . The distinctions of good, middling, evil, arising from illusion, are false. . . . *He, to whom I am is applied, is spirit, imperishable, ever-living; the same in the body as in other places;* with this single difference, that he is perceived within, but not without. . . . Profound repose (death) is my beloved wife, for she destroys all my misery; but the wife of the ignorant, that is, the understanding, is unbeloved and unchaste. . . . Notwithstanding the diversity of created forms, I am always the same, whether I enjoy or not my appointed spouse who seeks not another. Whether clothed or unclothed, since I resemble the purity of a mirror, of ether, and of simple knowledge, I (spirit) am the same. . . . *Neither confinement nor liberation belongs to me. . . . I* the sun-like spirit, *am perfect;* I neither rise nor set. As the face in a glass, so the universe, through the understanding, is realized in me as a reality. . . . *I am eternal. . . . All is in me as in space;* and *I, like space, am everywhere. . . . The great sages call the universe wisdom itself, for matter and spirit, as milk and water, are inseparable. The universe is mine, because the pleasures, &c. of the body belong to me; yet as they are mine, so they belong to others.* . . . As vacuum is everywhere, evident in some places and exceedingly confined in others, so is it with spirit, whether clothed with the understanding, or confined by gross matter. . . . *The sage with his mind exclusively fixed on spirit, thus meditates, and obtains the vision of spirit.* (Italics added)

To the foregoing may be added a few extracts from the last section of the treatise which "clearly point[s] out the properties" of the yogi "who obtains liberation in this life":

> *To a yogi, in whose mind all things are identified as spirit, what is infatuation?—what is grief? He sees all things as one.* He is a wise man who is destitute of affections, who *neither rejoices in good, nor is offended with evil.* . . . The wise man never forgets what he has learned of spirit . . . *is never elevated nor depressed, whose face shines both in pleasure and pain,* and . . . is always the same. He is free even in this life, who *is awake* (to his spiritual nature) *though asleep* (in reference to sensible objects). . . . A woman whose affections are placed on a gallant, though actively engaged in the business of her house, still continues to dwell on the pleasures derived from her criminal amours; so a wise man, having found the excellent and pure Brahma, delights in him, even though he is engaged in other things. *The yogi who, however clothed, however fed, and wherever placed, is always the same, who is entire spirit, and is always looking inwards, who is happy, profound, benign, who enjoys happiness undisturbed as a lake in a mountain, who though he may have cause for the highest joy, remains unaffected, and (is pleased with himself, or) enjoys spirit in spirit, who rejects all his works, is always cheerful and free from pain, and who is not absorbed either in works of merit and demerit; nor in anything besides*—this man resembles a king. . . . These are the true characteristics of him . . . in whom desire, anger, sadness, infatuation, covetousness, &c. diminish every day. He who has found rest in the fourth state (spirit), having crossed the sea of this world, has no occasion for the delusions promised . . . upon the performance of works of merit . . . enters into unembodied liberty, and remains like the unruffled wind. . . . When spirit does not look upon (is not united to) those visible objects which are connected with mine and thine, it (like the mirror) remains alone. If it be allowed that spirit is clothed, still it is everlasting, undecayable, good, without beginning, without con-

tinuance, without support, immutable, without disease, without vacuum, without form, not an object of sight, not sight, something undescribable and unknown. [Italics added]

Here, among these words, are the "illumination," the "cosmic sense" that "suddenly" came to Whitman; "the mental power, the moral elevation, and the perennial joyousness which are the characteristics of the state to which he attained";[331] and the "wit and wisdom" with which he dazzled Emerson; here also are the "vision of [the] spirit" that "swiftly arose and spread the peace and joy and knowledge" which he undertook to teach to mankind that had long "dream'd contemptible dreams";[332] and "the convictions as to the nature and destiny of his soul," which Allen was forced to owe to "no literary or philosophical convention," but to his own "experience";[333] and here, most importantly, is the genesis of the "great visionary"[334] poem, "Song of Myself," the first product of his "remarkable accession of power."[335]

Take these instructions of Vignana-bhikshuka: "The Sankhya yogis worship spirit or (self). He who worships all equally in himself, ascends to his own heaven. Menu calls this worship of (self) spirit, the method of obtaining divine knowledge." In place of the word "worship," borrow the synonymous "celebrate" from the chants of the *Samaveda,* noticed earlier, and we have the American yogi composing his poetic meditation on spirit thus:

I celebrate myself,
And what I assume you shall assume,
For every atom belonging to me as good belongs to you.
   (Sec. 1)

Even the second half of this opening passage is a mere adaptation of the sentence in Vignana-bhikshuka:

The universe is mine, because the pleasures, &c., of the body are mine; yet as they are mine, so they belong to others.

The meditation of the sage obtains for him "the vision of spirit," and through that vision, "divine knowledge"; Whitman's celebration of self also issues into a vision of the spirit, or "soul," as he calls it, and the consequent acquisition of the "peace and joy and knowledge that pass all the art and argument of the earth," both of which are described in section 5 of "Song of Myself." The yogi views "himself equally in all beings and all equally in himself"; so,

> In all people I see myself, none more and not one a barleycorn less,
> And the good or the bad I say of myself I say of them. (Sec. 20)[336]

And since "I and all other living creatures are one," he declares in "One's-self I sing":

> One's-self I sing, a simple separate person,
> Yet utter the word Democratic, the word En-Masse.

The yogi must "meditate on equality"; so Whitman does:

> I am the poet of Equality.[337]

> I do not call one greater and one smaller,
> That which fills its period and place is equal to any. (Sec. 44)

> I acknowledge the duplicates of myself under all the scrape-lipped and pipe-legged concealments. (Sec. 42)

In the last of the above can be heard an echo of the line: "As vacuum is everywhere, evident in some places and exceedingly confined in others, so is it with spirit, whether clothed with the understanding, or confined by gross matter." The yogi "loves all as himself, even as parents love their children." Says Whitman:

> . . . all the men ever born are also my brothers. . . . and the women my sisters and lovers. . . . (Sec. 5)

> For me all that have been boys and that love women,
> For me the man that is proud and feels how it stings to be slighted,
> For me the sweetheart and the old maid . . . . for me mothers and the mothers of mothers,

For me lips that have smiled, eyes that have shed tears,
For me children and the begetters of children. (Sec. 7)

The spirit "is deathless . . . it receives birth and absorption with
the utmost ease,"[338] and "confinement" does not belong to it. So
Whitman declares,

I am deathless. (Sec. 21)

I pass death with the dying, and birth with the new-washed
babe, . . . and am not contained between my hat and boots.
(Sec. 7)

The distinctions "that this is best, that this is the worst," are,
according to Vignana-bhikshuka, "(false) conceptions"; the yogi
transcends them in his divine knowledge of the "undivided one,"
the "spirit." So does Whitman:

Showing the best and dividing it from the worst, age vexes age,
Knowing the perfect fitness and equanimity of things, while
they discuss I am silent, and go bathe and admire myself.
(Sec. 3)

"This is an abstract view of pleasure and pain; there is no need
of further enlargement,"[339] said the "Sankhya-sara." Whitman
says,

To elaborate is no avail. . . . learned and unlearned feel that
it is so. (Sec. 3)

"The great sages call the universe wisdom itself, for matter and
spirit, as milk and water, are inseparable" (Vignana-bhikshuka).
Whitman insists,

Lack one lacks both. (Sec. 3)

The insignificant is as big to me as any. (Sec. 30)

The earth [is] good, and the stars good, and their adjuncts
all good. (Sec. 7)

I have said that the soul is not more than the body,

And I have said that the body is not more than the soul. (Sec.
48)

The moth and the fisheggs are in their place,
The suns I see and the suns I cannot see are in their place,
The palpable is in its place and the impalpable is in its place.
(Sec. 16)

The "pleasures" of the "body" belong to the spirit; Whitman
believes "in the flesh and the appetites," and is "the poet of the
body," too, each "particular thing" in which he "worship[s]" (Sec.
24). Since "they belong to others" also, the others "shall assume
what [he] assume[s]."

I speak the password primeval. . . . I give the sign of democracy,
By God! I will accept nothing which all cannot have their
counterpart of on the same terms. (Sec. 24)

All I mark as my own you shall offset it with your own.
(Sec. 20)

The yogi is declared to be "awake" when aware of his "spiritual
nature," though "asleep" in reference to "sensible objects." Whitman appears to have realized this when he wrote those misconstrued
lines we have noticed:

. . . I am awake for the first time, and all before has been a
mean sleep.[340]

Whitman's real "What I am" is described as having an "implacable certain rest," on which it "bends an arm" (Sec. 4);
apparently it has, like the yogi, "found rest in the fourth state."
And the spirit being "something undescribable and unknown,"
Whitman's soul, for all its eloquence, will not explain itself:

My final merit I refuse you. . . . I refuse putting from me
the best I am.
Encompass worlds but never try to encompass me,
I crowd your noisiest talk by looking toward you.

Writing and talk do not prove me,

I carry the plenum of proof and everything else in my face,
With the hush of my lips I confound the topmost skeptic.
(Sec. 25)

It is in the kingly dignity of the yogic spirit that he proclaims,

That I eat and drink is spectacle enough for the great authors
and schools. (Sec. 24)

We may remember that the passages that inspired the "not
the Me myself" portion of "Song of Myself" are also part of the
same meditation on self that Vignana-bhikshuka is celebrating in
this section. How much else of the poem merely develops the contents of "Sankhya-sara" could be easily seen by a similar juxtaposition of the prose of Ward's pages and the verse of Whitman.
The entire sections 15 and 16 of the "Song," cataloguing the
"contralto," who "sings," "the carpenter" who "dresses his plank,"
"the married and unmarried children" who "ride home," the "pilot"
who "seizes the king-pin," the "farmer" who "stops by the bars,"
and all the innumerable different beings and things that

. . . one and all tend inward to me, and I tend outward to
them,
And such as it is to be of these more or less I am,

are manifestly nothing more than an elaboration of the thought
that "He, to whom I am is applied, is spirit, imperishable, ever-
living; the same in the body as in other places," and so, "not being
different in nature, I am every living creature, from Brahma,
Vishnu, Maheswara, down to inanimate matter." And it is in the
consciousness of the "all-pervading" self that, vacuum-like, has the
entire "space," or universe, in itself, that Whitman's soul could
"peeringly view" all life's multiform motion, see the "suicide"
(Sec. 8), and be there and help the harvester with an unseen
hand (Sec. 9), and "take part" and "see and hear the whole" of
what happened in the "fort's bombardment" (Sec. 33).

In me the caresser of life wherever moving. . . . backward as
well as forward sluing,
To niches aside and junior bending. (Sec. 13)

In the same yogic wisdom, again, he realizes that the "distinctions of good, middling, evil, arising from illusion, are false," and so does "not decline to be the poet of wickedness also":

What blurt is this about virtue and about vice?
Evil propels me, and reform of evil propels me. . . . I stand
　indifferent. (Sec. 22)

The spirit is "free" and "unaffected," for the miseries of existence are only of the understanding with which it is "clothed." Whitman declares, "Agonies are one of my changes of garments" (Sec. 33). Perhaps even the use of the "I" in "Song of Myself," without which a philosophical poem on the glory of his self could have been written, has its support in these words of Vignanabhikshuka: "The pronoun I is expressive of sovereignty; . . . therefore the wise express spirit by the sign I."[341] And, aware of the "undecayable" "ever-living" nature of the spirit, which transcends "production and dissolution," Whitman declares, using even the very word:

My foothold is tenoned and mortised in granite,
I laugh at what you call dissolution,
And I know the amplitude of time. (Sec. 20)

The spirit, we read in an earlier section, is like the sovereign to whom "the understanding," as the "chief minister," offers all the "articles of enjoyment" collected by the "bodily organs" from the world of inanimate objects; and it is "immutable," "without support," and "without disease." Whitman turns the description into these lines:

And I know I am solid and sound,
To me the converging objects of the universe perpetually flow,
All are written to me, and I must get what the writing means.
　(Sec. 20)

The yogi, said Vignana-bhikshuka, "wherever placed, is always the same," "always looking inwards," "profound, benign," "enjoys happiness undisturbed," is "pleased with himself," and "is always cheerful." Whitman announces,

I exist as I am, that is enough,
If no other in the world be aware I sit content,
And if each and all be aware I sit content.

One world is aware, and by far the largest to me, and that is
    myself,
And whether I come to my own today or in ten thousand or
    ten million years,
I can cheerfully take it now, or with equal cheerfulness I can
    wait. (Sec. 20)

If he says "I know I am august" (Sec. 20), so did "Sankhya-sara" tell him: he was "glorious as the autumnal sky," for the spirit was "sovereign." In another line he declares: "I too am of one phase and of all phases" (Sec. 22). Similarly was the spirit described in "Sankhya-sara": "When spirit received the operations of the understanding, it is many, and when distinct from these operations, it is one"; "Spirit is one when we apply to it discriminating wisdom; and many when united to matter."[342] Even the phrase, "partaker of influx and efflux" (Sec. 22), echoes another description of the spirit in the same:

By the letter [hum] breath goes forth, and by the letter [sa] it enters again; on account of this ingress and egress of the animal soul, spirit is called [humsa] a duck [swan].[343]

Speaking of his own message, Whitman says in section 23 of the "Song":

Endless unfolding of words of ages!
And mine a word of the modern. . . . a word en-masse.

A word of the faith that never balks,
One time as good as another time. . . . here or henceforward
it is all the same to me.

Truly is this "modern" word of his a mere "unfolding of words" from Vignana-bhikshuka, who extracted "that which is written in the veda and smritees respecting the marks of the wise and of emancipating wisdom . . . to strengthen the faith of a yogi"[344] who "in all states and times, sees everything the same."[345] The perfection he sees in the nature of things reminds us that "the universe is wisdom itself":

> I believe a leaf of grass is no less than the journey work of
>   stars,
> And the pismire is equally perfect, and a grain of sand. . . .
>   (Sec. 31)

Even the acknowledging of

> The sharphoofed moose of the north, the cat on the housesill,
>   the chickadee, the prairie-dog. (Sec. 14)

in all of whom and himself he sees "the same old law," is but a lyric chanting of the thought that "in the operations of the understanding, the one spirit appears multiform," and so "let a person collect around him living animals . . . and honour them . . . and thus think on spirit."[346] (Ward's footnote: "Agreeable to which doctrine, some mendicants may be seen making a companion of a dog.") For in all these is one spirit like a "juggler who personifies a number of animals by clothing himself with their clothes," for it is "the same in [one's] body as in other places." It is the same "pure" spirit, "clothed with understanding," and "confined by gross matter," that is the "mystical, nude" within the "hankering grass" in Whitman (Sec. 20). The readiness with which he would set the "meal equally" for all, "the wicked just the same as the righteous," making "appointments with all" (Sec. 19), is but an answer to the Sankhya commentator who insisted that "from Brahma even to the people in hell, the yogi loves all."

Though a poet of the Soul, Whitman has a "word of reality": shouting "hurrah for positive science" and "exact demonstration," he accepts "the lexicographer," "the chemist," "the geologist," and the like—those whose work reveals the material universe:

> Gentlemen I receive you, and attach and clasp hands with you,
> The facts are useful and real. . . . they are not my dwell-
>   ing. . . . I enter by them to an area of my dwelling.
>   (Sec. 23)

He regards them so because they deal with "property or qualities," whereas he, with his vision of spirit, is "the reminder of

life." The world and the facts of "the understanding" are not
real realities; the true reality, or entity, is of the spirit. Now,
this is one of the ideas on which Vignana-bhikshuka lingered elaborately:

> Spirit is not matter. . . . He who knows, that spirit, separate
> from the body and its members, is pure, renounces in a measure
> the changes of matter. The works of nature are connected with
> the operations of the understanding. . . . Spirit is distinct. . . .
> what then is matter? . . . It is divided into twenty four parts. . . .
> In these . . . are included quality, action and kind. In all these
> parts of matter, the abstract idea is that of the materiality of all
> things. . . . The satwa, raja, tama, are *qualities of matter* in its
> natural state. . . . I have mentioned individuality as a *property of
> matter.* . . . [And, following an elaboration of the principles
> of matter:] Thus the twenty four principles (of things), and
> the production of the world. . . . Standing aloof . . . [is] the
> spirit. . . . He is called sut (the existent) because he exists of
> himself. . . . When we speak of the world as possessing entity and
> non-entity, we lie under a mistake: (still, as real impressions
> are produced by it on the mind, we may say) this world is sut
> (substance) and asut (unreal); to believe that this world is a
> substantial good, is a real mistake. . . . Spirit is real entity. . . .
> This error-formed world is like a bubble on the water: we can
> never say that it does not exist, nor that it does. . . . The happi-
> ness enjoyed by spirit which dwells within, is genuine. . . .
> Secular persons desire happiness, but, like a householder who
> seeks pleasure by looking through the windows, instead of look-
> ing for it within, they seek it by looking through the senses. . . .
> Spirit . . . is perceived within, but not without (pp. 322–351).

The italics are mine, to show that Whitman has taken not only
the thought of these pages but the words too. With one more
example we may close our study of "Sankhya-sara." In section 25
of the "Song" Whitman says:

> Dazzling and tremendous how quick the sunrise would kill
>   me,
> If I could not now and always send sunrise out of me.
>
> We also ascend dazzling and tremendous as the sun,
> We found our own my soul in the calm and cool of the day-
>   break.

In a later section occurs the following:

Flaunt of the sunshine I need not your bask. . . . lie over,
You light surfaces only. . . . I force surfaces and the depths
    also. (Sec. 40)

"Sankhya-sara" said, "I, the sun-like spirit, am perfect," and
a little earlier, discussing the identity of spirit and the nature of
the world, declared: "Wherever, in any form, that omnipresent,
omnipotent, universal, all-inspiring, self-existent being, is visible,
there, in these forms, this agitated world . . . appears extended in
him like the reflected rays of the sun. . . . This visible world was
spread out by the mind of the self-existent."[347] And, in Colebrooke's essay "On the Religious Ceremonies of the Hindus,"
noticed earlier, was a prayer, in explanation of which it was said:

The greatest of lights which exists in the sun, exists also as
    the principle of life in the hearts of all things. It shines ex-
    ternally in the sky, internally in the heart. . . . The thinking
    soul is light alone; it shines with unborrowed splendour.[348]

8

THE GROWTH OF A POEM

IF THUS, AS THE FOREGOING ILLUSTRATIONS DEMONSTRATE, "SONG of Myself" was born, and naturally received its first nourishment at the same time in the express instructions of Vignana-bhikshuka, the account of the "Patanjala philosophy" which follows appears to have played the wet-nurse in its subsequent growth. In fact, it even seems to hold the key to another of the puzzles in the "Song" on which critical attention has worked long and hard, namely, the structure of the poem. There are critics who have violently championed a coherent structure, whatever be the divergence we find in them with regard to the principle of it; and there are those who have with equal vehemence asserted the unprincipled, incoherent, and rambling nature of the poem. Roy Harvey Pearce,[349] in his analysis of the structure of the poem, observes that the "Song" has no structure of "an internal-external sense of necessity," that is, "a scheme by which we may decide that a given section should or should not have begun where it begins and ended where it ends, or contain what it contains." All that the poem has is a "movement," not a "form," a "movement of sensibility" comparable to the process of "hypnogogic meditation, controlled not by rules or method but by the intensely personal pulsations and periodicities of the meditative act."

Among those who "have proclaimed their discoveries of obscure or hidden formal elements"[350] in the "Song," is James E. Miller, who maintains that "Whitman's poetry was not formless but sensitively ordered,"[351] and demonstrates that "Song of Myself" is "the dramatic representation of a mystical experience," "not necessarily a transcript of an actual mystical experience, but rather a work of art in which such an experience conceived in the imagination, is represented dramatically, with the author assuming the role."[352] Analyzing the entire poem on this basis, Miller discovers that it "conforms in framework remarkably well" to the five stages of the Mystic Way as described by Evelyn Underhill in her valuable study *Mysticism,* but with some "significant differences from the traditional mystical concepts or attitudes." The differences Miller speaks of are the attitudes of Whitman toward sex, the body, the senses, the material world, the personal self, and so on, in the insistence on the importance of which he had to "deny some of the basic traditions" of mysticism. As a result, while of the mystical experience "the form is adhered to," "its substance is transfigured." Miller also observes[353] that "Whitman knew that the 'frenzied fit' never resulted in poetry," and so "conceived the process of writing a poem as the strategy of a game of chess"; though, unable to find, like the other critics, how Whitman came to put the "I" into his poems with so much drama around it, he regards that Whitman "had a highly developed dramatic sense, . . . his plays are poems; he is the protagonist," and in them "he was not stating philosophical truths so much as he was dramatizing himself and his life of imagination." The form, then, into which (with such a conception of poetry, and being "master of his material") Whitman ordered his "Song of Myself" is, according to him, an "inverted" mystical experience, to which it corresponds "step by step," the incongruities being a deliberate "departure from reality, . . . justified in the requirements of a work of art."[354]

Despite the exactness with which he shows this qualified correspondence of the "Song" to the mystical experience of tradition, Miller does not claim an actual experience of the kind for the poem, which is not a "religious document" but a "work of art," in which the poet represents "such an experience, conceived in the imagination." Nor does he claim, like Malcolm Cowley, that the poem was "largely based on the ignorance of the mystical tradition," or suggest that "Whitman, of course, had never heard of this purely anonymous or transpersonal state" of the mystics, which he repudiates "in the dangerous phase of self-inflation"[355] that went into the composition of the poem. However, from the following analysis it will be clear that Whitman did not have to trouble himself about conceiving such an experience; that, far from being ignorant of it, he actually drew both the pattern of his song and much of its material from his reading of it; that the poem is less the product of self-dramatization than of "lyricization" of the experiences of a yogi given in Ward's account of the Patanjala school of Hindu philosophy; and that the representation of the experience is developed in stages roughly corresponding to the order of progression through which the yogic exercises are achieved. In other words, the right clue to the puzzle seems to be that the self-celebration that started the poem in the yogic discipleship of Vignana-bhik-shuka continued it along the lines of the yoga account.

In all of this, as we shall see, he merely versifies the words of his reading or its thought, or his embellishment or extension of it, subsequently inserting passages of similar composition—all on the subject of that multifaced self of his—wherever a traceable relation in phrase or mood to the basic fragments was found, and creating, wherever necessary or wherever he could, adhesive links one to the other. For apart from the fact that, in innocent poetic expansion or arrogant personal egotism (or even, possibly, a deliberate artistic design to tease the original thought into an unrecognizable shape in order to hide the borrowing), he confounds the metaphysical self of the Hindu teaching by "meditating" on his Manhattan, American, authorial, and individual "selves" in one ill-assorted exercise of imagination, "Song of Myself" explains both its contents and its form when regarded as the extended lyricization of the teachings of "Sankhya-sara" in the direction suggested by the instructions of Patanjala, presented by Ward through the commentary of Bhojadeva.[356]

The restraining of the mind, and confining it to internal meditations, is called yoga. When the mind is thus confined within, it becomes assimilated to the Being whom it seeks to know; but when the mind is secularized, this Being takes the form of secularity. In the first case, the mind is singly and irrevocably fixed on God. In the second, it is restless, injurious, and voluptuous. . . . In the former, the person, into a well-regulated mind, constantly brings the Being upon whom he wishes to meditate. In performing the latter, the person, by realizing the

unsubstantial nature of everything included in visible objects . . .
delivers his mind from subjection to these things, and subjects
his senses to his mind. . . . The proper objects of meditation are
two, matter and spirit. Matter assumes twenty-four forms;
spirit is one . . . Sampragnata [one of the two phases of yoga]
is of four kinds, 1. Meditation on the distinction between sound
and substance in reference to the deity as a visible being, until
the yogi, by continued meditation, arrives at the non-distinction
between sound and substance in reference to god.—2. Meditation on the deity in reference to his form, as well as to time and
place, till the yogi is able to fix his meditations without regard
to form, time, or place.—3. Meditation on the deity, till the
mind, in which the satwa guna prevails, is filled with joy, and
till the powers of the understanding become abstracted, so that
the distinction between matter and spirit is no longer recognized, and spirit alone is seen; in which state, the yogi is videha,
that is, he is emancipated from that pride of separate existence
which is connected with a secular or bodily state.—4. Meditation till the yogi becomes so far delivered from pride, that it
exists only as a shadow in his mind, and the divine principle
receives the strongest manifestation. This state is called absorption. . . . At length the yogi attains what is called asampragnata
[the second phase], in which, if he be perfect in his abstraction,
the very shadow of separate existence will be destroyed; visible
objects will be completely extinguished, and spirit alone become
manifest. . . . By thus looking constantly inward . . . he is
brought to resemble God. . . .

[He must find] a suitable place for his yoga. . . .

Fixedness of mind on him who is the only and genuine reality,
leads to liberation. . . . The yogi must, in the next place, attend
to pranayama, that is, to the gradual suppression of breathing,
since the animal soul and the mind act in conjunction; in this
work, he must endeavor to fix the understanding by some act of
the senses, that is, he must place his sight and thoughts on the
tip of his nose, by which he will perceive smell; then bring his
mind to the tip of his tongue, when taste will be realized; and
afterwards fix his mind at the root of his tongue from which
sound will be perceived. . . . He who meditates on God, placing
his mind on the sun, moon, fire, or any other luminous body, or
within his heart, or at the bottom of his throat, or in the centre
of his skull, will, by afterwards ascending from these gross
images of the deity to the glorious original, secure fixedness of
mind. . . .

Before proceeding with the rest of the account, let us notice how the "Song" follows the pattern of thought so far. The first long paragraph quoted above is a description of the nature of yogic meditation, and, apart from having many suggestions that form the general background of the poem, it also gives a direction to its thought. The opening passage in "Song of Myself" announcing the self-celebration of the poet is this yogic meditation on the spirit. And since the yogi must find a "suitable place" for his yoga, Whitman then decides to find, to use Miller's words,[357] "surroundings congenial to the experience," and so, discarding "houses and rooms," declares, "I will go to the bank by the wood and become undisguised and naked." All "man-made objects—houses, rooms, clothes—" are forsaken in his poetic emulation of the yogi, whose mind becomes "restless, injurious, voluptuous" in the midst of these "visible objects," and who therefore must abstract himself from "illusion." Having found his right place on the river bank, Whitman next lets his poetic fancy operate on the senses, whose importance "to the anticipated experience is suggested in the catalogue in the middle of section 2 in which the poet expresses delight in and implies unqualified acceptance of each of the senses: of taste ('the smoke of my own breath') ; of sound ('echoes, ripples, buzz'd whispers') ; of odor ('the sniff of green leaves and dry leaves') ; of touch ('a few light kisses, a few embraces') ; of sight ('the play of shine and shade on the trees).' "[358] He does more, too: he dwells upon his "respiration and inspiration," "the beating of [his] heart," "the passing of blood and air through [his] lungs," the "streets," the "fields," the "full-noon" and the "sun." All this is his poetic "pranayama" by which to "fix the understanding" through the "act of the senses," perceiving smell, taste, and sound, and afterwards placing the mind on the "gross images of the deity," the "sun," "his heart," "his throat," or "any other luminous body."

To return to the instructions of Bhojadeva: "The yogi, having brought his mind to a fixed state, will not be subject to present things, whether his mind be employed on the most subtile or the most gross objects; and he will, by these means, deliver himself from all error, and be filled with the effects of satwa guna." Not "subject to present things" himself now, Whitman too is filled with satwa guna, and wisely steps up to deliver others "from all error":

Have you reckoned a thousand acres much? Have you reckoned
   the earth much?
Have you practised so long to learn to read?
Have you felt so proud to get at the meaning of poems?

For he has realized true knowledge, and possessed "the origin
of all poems," "the good of the earth and sun," not "at second or
third hand," because that is the stage when, fixing his mind on the
"Being," he has ascended from the "gross images of the deity to the
glorious original" who is "the only and genuine reality." Sections
3 and 4, with "further hints" of that real knowledge, composed,
as we have seen, of thoughts from his other readings, are his account of the state in which "the distinction between matter and
spirit is no longer recognized (there is only a 'knit of identity'),
and spirit alone is seen," which is the real "what I am," "free
from the fruit of works, that is . . . from the increase or decrease
of life and from enjoyment or suffering as the consequence of actions."[359]

In section 5, as Miller observes, "the soul materializes and is
invited to loaf on the grass," and "the poet then portrays his entry
into the mystical state of consciousness,"[360] and then we have "the
peace and joy and knowledge" spread around him. How does all
this translate into Whitman's idiom, the contents of Bhojadeva?
"Into a well-regulated mind" Whitman brings the "Being upon
whom he wishes to meditate." And that Being is after all the
spirit which Vignana-bhikshuka so ardently described as "lovely,"
the "object of love," and "the most beloved object." The manner
of Whitman's seeking "the sight of the beloved object, spirit," need
not frighten us, for that is perhaps his way of perceiving "the entire
loveliness of spirit." That granted, the rest is merely an imaginative rendering of the next paragraphs in Ward:

He [the yogi, after the fixed state of abstraction is achieved]
thus becomes identified with deity, that is, visible objects, the
operations of the understanding, and personal identity, become
absorbed in the Being contemplated . . . and God is realized in
the mind as pure light; and to this succeeds a state of mind
similar to self-annihilation. . . . God will shine forth in complete
splendour, the mind of the yogi will become completely absorbed
in him, and he will possess universal prescience. He whose abstraction continues imperfect, obtains complete knowledge by the

assistance of reflection, &c. and by degrees ascends to the unassisted knowledge of universal nature, and identity with the
spirituality and perfection of God.

Though he would have none of that "state of mind similar to
self-annihilation," it is this "universal prescience," or "knowledge
of universal nature" and of the "perfection of God" that Whitman's vision brought him, when his mind was "filled with joy"
and the "spirit" was seen. The rest of the poem is merely a description of that "complete knowledge by the assistance of reflection,
&c."; reflection, in its turn, assisted by all the philosophical school-
ing he had in his other readings regarding the nature of self,
reality, life, death, and so on.

In this subsequent reflection that develops the initial celebration
of self, the next pages of Bhojadeva's commentary, which elaborate the preliminary survey of the nature of yoga presented in the
first chapter—and our foregoing extracts were cited from that—
have played a considerable role, guiding the course of the poem's
thought as well as supplementing the thought itself. The second
chapter points out "the method in which a secular person should
perform ceremonial yoga" that helps in "the more perfect yoga
and in victory over pain (or the cause of pain) which are of five
kinds." These sources of pain are overcome by "turning the
thoughts inward, which will secure meditation on God," and by
"fixing the mind on God, and by cultivating benevolent feelings
towards men in every condition of life." In the discussion of the
fifth cause of pain, called "love of life," are these comments:

This desire of life is to be attributed to a latent impression on
the mind respecting the misery following death, and the delay in
rising to life, during former transmigrations. This is illustrated
by seed cast into the earth, which remains for months till it
appears to be assimilated to earth itself, but at the appointed
season, receiving the accustomed rain springs to life. . . . The
impress of actions is to be attributed to illusion, and is discovered
either in this or in a future birth. Actions performed under the
influence of illusion are followed by eight millions of births in
connection with some cast, with an appointed period of life, and
subjection to the fruit of actions: from works of merit result
excellent cast, existence and many enjoyments; from evil actions
arise degraded cast, unhappy life, and great misery. . . . This

illusion is destroyed by discriminating wisdom in reference to the divine nature: this discrimination leads to deliverance from sorrow arising from transmigrations, and to the reception of truth (God).

Whitman's vision is in section 5, and the central theme of section 6, unfolding the first element of his new knowledge, with the imagery of the grass, is immortality:

They are all alive and well somewhere;
The smallest sprout shows there is really no death,
And if ever there was it led forward life, and does not wait at the end to arrest it,
And ceased the moment life appeared.

The doctrine of the "impress of actions," the meritorious ones making for "many enjoyments" and the evil ones for "great misery," enters briefly into his other poem, "To Think of Time," and elaborately into the Preface and the later "Song of Prudence."

From the deathlessness of all beings, the poet's thought turns immediately, in section 7, to his own immortality and other qualities:

I pass death with the dying, and birth with the new-washed babe
. . . . and am not contained between my hat and boots,
And peruse manifold objects . . .

I am not an earth nor an adjunct of an earth,
I am the mate and companion of people, all just as immortal and fathomless as myself.

Similarly, Bhojadeva's commentary continues into thoughts like these:

The origin or source of birth is the union or vicinity of spirit with the understanding, in which the former is the partaker and the latter the thing enjoyed; or, in other words, the one displays and the other is the thing displayed. . . . The elements form the objects of participation; the senses, &c. are the partakers; but the elements, senses, &c., are to be considered as united to spirit in the work of participation. . . . If we speak of him who is light, or the male power, we say he is simple life; life is not an adjunct of his nature; he is pure or perfect, and seeks not association with material subjects. . . .

For all the changes in development, Whitman appears to have built that thought on this passage; only, where the yogi, described as "the eye of the body," sees "that every earthly thing is unstable," Whitman "peruse[s] manifold objects," finding "everyone good"; but the verbal echo is remarkable in his not being "an adjunct of an earth."

There is another striking sentence in the same passage of Bhojadeva: "He [spirit] is therefore the receiver, that is, he receives, through the understanding, the impression of visible objects, and then becomes identified with them." We cannot determine whether Whitman had read Tennyson's "Ulysses" before 1855, but the line, "I am a part of all that I have met," could hardly be imagined to have inspired his poem "A Child Went Forth," in which

There was a child went forth every day,
And the first object he looked upon and received with wonder
    or pity or love or dread, that object he became. . . .

The "child" ascribed to the "requirements of a work of art," it can be clearly seen that Whitman is developing the spirit's identification with visible objects the philosopher spoke of in the sentence quoted.

If Whitman in this section does not disregard "manifold objects," as a yogi ought to do, he is not doing anything strange at all, because the next paragraph in the yoga account says:

If visible objects exist merely as objects of reception by spirit, it may be asked, what further use is there for them when the yogi has passed through whatever was allotted to him as the fruit of works? To this it is replied, that visible objects are not wholly dismissed till discriminating wisdom is perfected. And even after this, when the yogi becomes perfect spirit, . . . in consequence of his connection with creatures, he appears as though he took an interest in visible objects.

At the end of this analysis, the philosopher returns to the "discriminating wisdom" which destroys the sources of pain. "These destroyed, the understanding is turned inward, and becomes fixed on spirit as reflected on itself." If we examine Whitman's "Song" we find that section 8 initiates a long unfolding of the nature of his "self," into which, poetically, is gathered all that he has read and mused about. Bhojadeva next examines the "eight parts of yoga" necessary for the "discriminating wisdom:" This part has not offered much to the poem, but since it contains a description of the yogic exercises and thereby proves that Whitman was familiar with them, I shall present it in a brief summary.

The eight parts of yoga are: yama, niyama, asana, pranayama, prityahara, dharana, dhyana, and samadhi. . . . In *yama,* there are five divisions, 1. freedom from the desire of injuring others; 2. truth in reference both to words and to the mind; 3. freedom from the least appropriation of the property of another . . . ; 4. the subjection of the members for the sake of extirpating desire; and 5. the renunciation of all pleasure. . . . . *Niyama* includes five divisions, viz. 1. purity of body . . . and purity of mind, through the exercise of friendly and benevolent affections; 2. cheerfulness in every condition; 3. religious austerities; 4. the repetition of incantations; and 5 . . . causing all the formularies of worship and all its benefits to terminate in God. . . . *Asana* includes eighty four modes of sitting at yoga; but to be complete, the posture must be quite easy, neither painful nor attended with agitation. That a rigid posture may become easy . . . and that he may be happy in these circumstances, he must raise his mind to the wonders of the heavens, and not confine it to the body. . . .[361] Perfection in the yoga-posture prepares the person for perfection in *pranayama,* or, in the suppression of the inspiration and respiration of breath. Vital air is either stationary in the body, or received into it, or thrown from it. . . .[362] In *prityahara,* by withholding the mind from wandering, the organs are turned from their accustomed objects inward, and become subject to the yogi. . . . The fixing of the mind . . . is called *dharana,* in which the yogi purifies his mind by benevolence; practises the duties connected with yama and niyama; perfects himself in the yoga-postures; regulates the ingress and egress of the animal soul; and . . . subdues all his members, and all the power of the elements over him. *Dhyana,* or meditation, implies, that the person thus employed is endeavouring to fix his mind on the deity, agreeably to the forms of *dharana;* so as to secure a constant stream of thought towards him, and exclude all worldly tendencies. In *samadhi,* the understanding, carried along by an uninterrupted current of thought towards the deity, or towards that which is the reflection of spirit upon the understanding, becomes nearly extinguished. Dharana, dhyana, and samadhi, for the sake of brevity, are distinguished by one name *samyama,* that is, the restraining of the mind from all visible objects.—To the person who is able to perfect himself in samyama, the infinitely abstracted God, discovered by perfect discrimination, and identified with light, becomes manifest.

This technical exposition is followed by an elaborate description of the benefits accruing from the yogic exercises. The sections of "Song of Myself" that delineate the nature of the "Self" Whitman has discovered through the vision of his, grow by the development of some of this description, with the stuff of his other readings built on and around it.

"After the yogi has fixed his mind on the deity, it occasionally wanders, but at length he contemplates God only in himself, so that the divine spirit is seen equally in the mind and in visible objects." The "grass" to Whitman is the "handkerchief of God," and the refrain of the poem is the perception of the divine spirit everywhere. "The yogi . . . obtains a knowledge of the past and the future"; and omniscience is one of the virtues of Whitman's "Self." "If he apply samyama to sounds, . . . he will possess, from mere sound, universal knowledge." Whitman resolves,

> I think I will do nothing for a long time but listen,
> And accrue what I hear into myself . . . . and let sounds
>   contribute toward me. (Sec. 26)

"He will obtain a knowledge of the events of preceding transmigrations." Whitman obtains it too:

> Rise after rise bow the phantoms behind me,
> Afar down I see the huge first Nothing, the vapour from the
>   nostrils of death,
> I know I was even there. . . . (Sec. 44)

The yogi "will know the hearts of all." Whitman can "understand the large hearts of heroes" (Sec. 33), and "remove the veil" covering the "many long dumb voices," and through him even "forbidden voices" are "clarified and transfigured" (Sec. 24). "He will be able to render his body invisible." Invisibly it is that Whitman can "peeringly view" the objects he describes in section 8, and be the "unseen hand" that "passed over" the swimmers' "bodies" in section 11. "He . . . will become acquainted with the time, and place, and causes of his death." But since the immortal spirit of Whitman will never "mention . . . death inside a house" (Sec. 47), he knows only that he will "proceed to fill [his] next fold of the future" (Sec. 51). "He who applies samyama to that compassion which has respect to the miserable, will secure the friendship of all." Whitman's compassion is eloquently expressed for the "impotent," "the despairer," "the descending man," "the drudge of the cotton fields or emptier of privies" (Sec. 40), and, because he is such a "friendly and flowing savage," "wherever he goes men and women accept and desire him" (Sec. 39). "He who according to these rules, meditates upon the strength of the powerful, so as to identify his own strength with theirs, will acquire the same strength." Whitman has meditated upon the strength of the Most Powerful, and so he has "stores plenty and to spare" (Sec. 40), can "troop forth replenished with supreme power" (Sec. 38), and, regarding what the "old cautious hucksters" had to "offer for mankind and eternity [as] less than a spirit of [his] own seminal wet," can take himself "the exact dimensions of Jehovah" (Sec. 41). "He who meditates, in the same manner, on the sun, as perfect light, will become acquainted with the state of things in every place. Similar meditation on the moon, procures a knowledge, from mere sight, of the union, progress, and influence of the planets; similar contemplation applied to the polar star, will enable the yogi to distinguish between the stars and planets, and observe their motions." Whitman applies his contemplative fancy to the "dazzling and tremendous" sunrise, and "with the twirl of [his] tongue [he] encompass[es] worlds and volumes of worlds" (Sec. 25). Though he does not specifically touch the moon, because he "ascend[s] from" it, he hears the "whispering there" of the "stars of heaven," and "suns" (Sec. 49) ; and, by opening his "scuttle at night," sees

> the far-sprinkled systems,
> And all I see, multiplied as high as I can cipher, edge but the
>   rim of the farther systems. (Sec. 45)

The yogic account says, "By the application of samyama to the
centre of the bowels at the navel, he will become acquainted with
the anatomy of the human body." The poet applies his samyama to
the center of his bowels, too, in section 24, where, in "worship
. . . of the spread of [his] body," he gives us a detailed acquaintance with his anatomy, from "the brain" with its "occult convolu-
tions" to the "timorous pond-snipe" with its "trickling sap of
maple." "By meditation on the basilar suture, he will be capaci-
tated to see and converse with the deified spirits who range through
the aerial regions." Apart from traversing the aerial regions himself, with his "palms over continents," and "through the clear
atmosphere" "stretch[ing] around on the wonderful beauty" of
the "globe" (Sec. 33), Whitman sees and converses with aerial
beings too:

> Eleves I salute you,
> I see the approach of your numberless gangs . . . . I see you
>   understand yourselves and me. . . . (Sec. 38)

He even has a brief monologue with a "listener up there":

> Listener up there! Here you . . . . what have you to confide
>   to me?
> Look in my face while I snuff the sidle of evening,
> Talk honestly, for no one else hears you, and I stay only a
>   minute longer. (Sec. 51)

"He will become acquainted with his own thoughts and those of
others, past, present, and future," says the account. So does Whitman "understand" "the courage of present times and all times"
(Sec. 33), and moving "backward as well as forward" (Sec. 13),
absorb all for his song, "not a person or object missing."[363] If "by
meditation on the state of the yogi, who has nearly lost all consciousness of separate existence, he will recognize spirit as unassociated and perfect existence," Whitman too, after a long
meditation on his self, turns his attention to the state of his own
yogi-like exercise:

Swift wind! Space! My Soul! Now I know it is true what I
  guessed at;
What I guessed when I loafed on the grass. . . . (Sec. 33)

"After this, he will hear celestial sounds, the songs and conversation of the celestial choirs; he will have the perception of their
touch in their passage through the air; his taste will become refined,
and he will enjoy the constant fragrance of sweet scents." To the
"Song" of Whitman these "sounds contribute," for his hearing
too is "refined":

I hear the bravuras of birds . . . . the bustle of growing wheat
  . . . . gossip of flames . . . . clack of sticks cooking my meals.

I hear the sound of the human voice . . . . a sound I love,
I hear all sounds as they are turned to their uses . . . . sounds
  of the city and sounds out of the city . . . . sounds of the
  day and night;

. . . .

I hear . . . the echo of sunset.

I hear the chorus . . . . it is a grand-opera . . . . this indeed is
  music!
A tenor large and fresh as the creation fills me,
The orbic flex of his mouth is pouring and filling me full.
  (Sec. 26)

I hear and behold God in every object . . . . (Sec. 48)

I hear you whispering there O stars of heaven,
O suns . . . . O grass of graves . . . . O perpetual transfers
  and promotions. . . . (Sec. 49)

The early manuscript readings of the passage he put into section 26
clearly show that he was working on the notion of "celestial
sounds":

A soprano heard at intervals over the immense waves,
Audible these from the underlying chorus,
Occupants and joyous vibraters of space.

Never fails the combination,
An underlying chorus, occupant and joyous vibrater of space.
A clear transparent base that lusciously shudders the universe,
A tenor strong and ascending, with glad notes of morning—
    with power and health.[364]

There is, however, very little of the "fragrance of sweet scents" in
Whitman's song, except "the scent of these arm-pits" (Sec. 24).
"The collected power of all the senses is called the animal soul,
which is distinguished by five operations connected with the vital
air, or air collected in the body. The body of the yogi who . . .
meditates on the air [in the body] will become light as wood, and
he will be able to walk on the fluid element . . . becom[ing]
glorious as a body light." Whitman writes,

Alone far in the wilds and mountains I hunt,
Wandering amazed at my own lightness. . . . (Sec. 10)

The yogi "will hear the softest and most distant sounds, as well
as those uttered in the celestial regions and in the world of the
hydras." Whitman even hears the "bustle of growing wheat,"
"gossip of flames," and "sounds out of the city" (Sec. 26). "He
. . . will be able to ascend into the air . . . will . . . be transformed
into these [subtile] elements . . . become as rarified and atomic as
he may wish, and . . . proceed to the greatest distance; in short,
he will be enabled to realize in himself the power of deity." Whitman does all this:

Speeding through space. . . . speeding through heaven and the
    stars,
Speeding amid the seven satellites and the broad ring and the
    diameter of eighty thousand miles,
Speeding with tailed meteors . . . . throwing fire-balls like the
    rest,
Carrying the crescent child that carries its own full mother in
    its belly:
Storming enjoying planning loving cautioning,
Backing and filling, appearing and disappearing,
I tread day and night such roads. (Sec. 33)

As to the realization in himself of the "power of deity" there is testimony throughout the poem.

"When the yogi has gained victory over the gunas . . . he triumphs over illusion . . . exterminates the very root error (the cause of birth) and obtains liberation"; this, in other words, is the Vedantic wisdom by which the soul of the yogi transcends the moon, from which other unenlightened souls return to the earth for further births, and obtains the "supreme light." Whitman, in his victory over illusion, does "ascend from the moon" and "from the night" and "debouch to the steady and central" (Sec. 49). "The local deities will assail such a yogi, and will endeavour to divert him from the religious abstraction which he has attained, by bringing before him sensual gratifications, or by exciting in his mind thoughts of personal aggrandizement, but he should partake of these gratifications without interest." Whitman's response (if we can call it so) to this passage is quite an imaginative marvel. He has his distractions and diversions, too; perhaps the leader of the local deities that assail him is the "treacherous tip of [him]," which he so ardently worshiped in the divine temple of his "flesh and blood," now "playing out lightning, to strike what is hardly different from [himself]," assisted by the "prurient provokers stiffening" his limbs, who have "all come to the headland to witness and assist against" him. So he cries, like a betrayed yogi:

I am given up by traitors;
I talk wildly. . . . I have lost my wits. . . . I and nobody else
    am the greatest traitor,
I went myself first to the headland . . . . my own hands carried
    me there. (Sec. 28)

Bhojadeva's description of the yoga closes with these words:

The yogi passes through four stages: in the first, he . . . enters on the work of abstraction and the subjection of the senses. In the next stage . . . he acquires perfect knowledge. In the third, the advance towards perfection is that which has been just described. . . . In the fourth, he loses all personality, and all consciousness of separate existence . . . and spirit alone remains. . . . He who attained this is called . . . the discriminator. The knowledge which is the fruit of discrimination is called the saviour, for it is this which delivers the yogi from the bottomless sea of the world. This knowledge brings before the yogi all visible objects at once, so that he does not wait for the tedious process of the senses.

Applying the mystic phenomenon, Miller discovers five stages in "Song of Myself," though he divides it into seven parts. (Others, by a different arrangement of the fifty-two sections into which Whitman himself finally divided the poem, have given it a structure of eight, nine, and ten parts.) Perhaps by a further combination and repatterning of the sections, the poem may even be reduced to four stages. Yet all this might possibly be an act of critical ingenuity that surpassed the poetic genius itself, finding a better order in the tranquility of explanation than the one the artist put in the heat of creation. However, of the knowledge that is acquired by the yogi without the "tedious process of the senses," Whitman speaks repeatedly:

"The real life of my senses and flesh transcending my senses
    and flesh,
My body done with materials, my sight done with my material
    eyes,
Proved to me this day beyond cavil that it is not my material
    eyes which finally see. . . ."[365]

"From the eyesight proceeds another eyesight, and from the hearing proceeds another hearing, and from the voice proceeds another voice, eternally curious of the harmony of things with man."[366]

"There is apart from mere intellect, in the make-up of every superior identity . . . a wondrous something that realizes without argument . . . an intuition of the absolute balance, in time and space, of . . . *the world;* a soul-sight of that divine thread which holds the whole congeries of things . . ."[367]

And the same sense-transcending intuition is affirmed when he writes about

"that unspeakable something in my own soul which makes me
know without being able to tell how it is that I know. . . ."[368]

The rest of the yoga account involves a discussion of some of the
doctrines underlying the system, and Whitman appears to have
gathered a few hints from it. Among the "perfect ascetics" who
"attained in the preceding birth perfection in samadhi," and therefore are "perfect at their (present) birth" are mentioned "the
winged tribes, &c." Whitman, in his "Song of Myself," fancies
"the wood-drake and wood-duck" that "rise" and "slowly circle
around," and declares he "believe[s] in those winged purposes"
(Sec. 13). "To others the last touch of perfection was given by
some sacred prescription prepared by a perfect ascetic." Whitman
plays the part of the perfect ascetic and gives the "touch of perfection" to the "boys and girls" of the world, and will "wash the
gum" from their eyes (Sec. 46). In the final version of the "Song,"
he inserts an explanatory passage in the first section, and says:

> I permit to speak at every hazard,
> Nature without check with original energy.

In spite of the reshaping of the words, it looks as if the inspiration
of these lines is in the following, which occurs at the end of an
argument maintaining that "Nature is the source of all" and that
"meritorious actions may remove the obstructions arising out from
demerit in the progress of nature":

> For, even in the yogi, in whom nature, or illusion, is re-
> duced to a shadow, when tempted by the local deities, and
> again immersed in illusion, nature displays its energy.

One of the challenges that Miller had to answer, in his identification of the structure of "Song of Myself" with the pattern of
mystical experience, was Whitman's treatment of the senses. His
explanation is as follows:

> Throughout sections 1–5 of the poem, the senses have been
> defiantly accepted and even celebrated, with the suggestion that
> they are to have a significant part in the approaching union with
> the soul. This attitude toward the senses constitutes the basic

paradox in the poem. Where as normally the mystical state is achieved only through a mortification of, or escape from, the senses, the poet of "Song of Myself" asserts that it is *through* the transfigured senses that he reaches mystical consciousness.[369]

The challenge, the defiance, the paradox, all disappear when we realize the real origin of this celebration of the senses in Whitman, and that may well be in the next words of the discussion:

> Yet the yogi, when united to a new body, necessarily feels the force of the five senses; though this is not connected with visible objects, but it leads to God. And thus, as his mind is free from the sources of pain, so is his conduct spiritual.

A little later on these words occur:

> Spirit is identified with life, is independent and unconnected. ... Amongst all material objects, the most excellent is the body; those parts which are most excellent in the body are the senses; that which is more excellent than the senses, is mind under the influence of the satwa guna; after this, and separate from this, is spirit, which is identified with life, and in consequence is separate from all material objects. (p. 394)

Whitman recognizes the excellence of all these, and so is both "the poet of the Body" and "the poet of the Soul." Apart from that, it may be observed that he verbally echoes the first of the passages just quoted, in another poem, "Proud Music of the Storm":

> (Such led to thee O soul,
> All senses, shows and objects, lead to thee,
> But now it seems to me sound leads o'er all the rest.) (Sec. 5)

"The effects of actions," says Bhojadeva next, "are of two kinds, recollection and species. He who at death loses the human form, and . . . is born among irrational animals, or the forms of brute matter, loses, during those transmigrations, the impressions received in the human state, but when he is again born in this state, all the impressions of humanity are revived. Though during these transmigrations he may have been often born, and in many shapes, and, as a wild beast, may have traversed many distant regions, still as species and recollection are inseparably united, the impressions of humanity are always revived when he springs to human birth." Frightening, and incomplete in its treatment of the Hindu concept of transmigration as this passage is, Whitman imaginatively turns it, with the help of his other sources of information, into the beautiful account of what resembles the theory of evolution in section 32 of "Song of Myself," where he celebrates "the animals [which] are so placid and self-contained." But it is with the ideas of "recollection" and "species" and the underlying "transmigration" that his fancy is playing there:

> So they show their relations to me and I accept them;
> They bring me tokens of myself . . . . they evince them plainly
>   in their possession.

> I do not know where they got those tokens,
> I must have passed that way untold times ago and negligently
>   dropt them.

The remaining part of Bhojadeva's discussion echoes familiar thoughts, and, so, ignoring all that, we shall notice just one more sentence at the close of it:

> Throughout universal nature, whatever exists by the conjunction of various causes, exists not for itself but for another; as therefore the operations of the understanding are regulated by the three gunas, the understanding must exist, not for itself but for another, and that other spirit.

In Whitman we have this thought frequently expressed:

> To me the converging objects of the universe perpetually flow,
> All are written to me, and I must get what the writing
>   means.[370]

> Keep your places, objects . . .
> . . . .
> Great or small, you furnish your parts toward the soul.[371]

The soul is of itself,
All verges to it. . . .[372]

Each is not for its own sake.[373]

All tends to the soul. . . .

Of countless germs waiting the due conjunction, the arousing
   touch,
Of all these tending fluidly and duly to myself. . . .[374]

The verbal closeness of the last two extracts to the passage in
Bhojadeva is remarkable.

9

THE MAKING OF A WISE MAN

THUS IT SEEMS TO ME THAT "SONG OF MYSELF," ASIDE FROM ITS enlargement through the processes of imaginative extension and addition of material evolved out of similar suggestions, stands explained almost completely as to its original inspiration, content, and form, in the Sankhya and Yoga accounts of Ward's pages. The doctrinal value of these accounts, being the work of commentators, may be doubtful, but after all Whitman was not a philosophic disciple seeking intellectual instruction, but a poetic aspirant prospecting for matter for imaginative treatment. He found his gold in this little stream flowing in a distant, unknown corner, away from the regular haunts of his compeers, and he kept the secret well. He was also lucky, comparatively speaking, because he found a gold that needed very little processing to remove its alloy and coarser parts. Yet, over years of patient, passionate labor, melting and remelting, shaping and reshaping, enriching the little bits in amalgamation with the ore he discovered along the other streams of the same hidden area, he endlessly molded them all into the final shape of a strange, skillfully wrought, and monstrously costly, statue.

But beneath all the diligent enrichment and craftsmanly shaping of the later years there is unmistakably visible the inspiration of these accounts for the first poem with which he startled America into awareness of the sudden descent of a new Moses from the poetic Sinai. These accounts explain the "wit and wisdom" of the most "extraordinary piece"; they explain even the little unwisdom —if we may call it so from the philosophical viewpoint—that has

303

been fused into the wisdom, namely, the hard-to-explain challenges in what has all the appearance of a mystic song. Further, not only does "Song of Myself" owe a great deal to these pages; even the other little poems of philosophic nature in the 1855 edition do too. "A Child that Went Forth," with its theme of the soul-world identification, was born here. The interest in the profound state of sleep, the concept of the immortality and divinity of the human soul, and the sense of the "excellent body," that inspired "Sleepers," "To Think of Time," "A Song for Occupations," and "I Sing My Body Electric," respectively acquired their "sprouts" here. Considering that the total poetry of Whitman's life-long achievement is, from the standpoint of philosophical thought, a mere superstructure on the first building of 1855, the role played by these accounts should not be minimized as relevant only for the first poems.

Aside from all this, these accounts, especially the latter, have another significance for our understanding of the poet who "contain[ed] multitudes." It has been frequently suggested in the course of this study that Whitman, both poetically and personally, assumed the character of a yogi, and if there was any pose in him, in Esther Shephard's sense, it was this. The "Answerer" from whose pedestal Whitman's philosophic gifts—that is, his poems—issue for mankind, the magnetic personality with which, as a man, he amazed his disciples were skillful modifications of the "sage," the "muni," the "wise man," and the "jivan-mukta" of the Hindu philosophers, which he assumed and imitated just as any individual fashions himself after some model—a hero of history or of acquaintance, or even an ideal man partly concocted of imagination. There is nothing in such an act for censure or condemnation, whether on the poetic or the personal side, for, even as "every man who lifts pen to write is assuming a poetic pose,"[375] so do men in normal life assume poses. It is no hypocrisy, nor, if it is, is it to be regarded as reprehensible, as long as, to use a legal phrase, there is no intent to defraud. A man, as the law permits, might assume another name for honest reasons. But there is a difference between calling oneself George Washington in enthusiasm for the great hero, even fashioning one's character after him, and actually claiming the virtues and accomplishments of the man. While in real life the falsity of such an arrogation would be obvious, in that world of imaginative activity where poets have their abode it would not be difficult to persuade others into a willing suspension of disbelief. The history of literature has more testimony to such a phenomenon than Macpherson. The question, therefore, is not of moral but of psychological validity. The world can accept any identity an individual assumes, accept him in any mask he would wear, as long as the identity covers all his being and actions completely, and the mask, his face. Identity is a matter of congruity and harmony, the unification of the elements that go into the composition of things. It is in this unity that things are apprehended and evaluated. But any incongruity between the shape or color of the face and the mask, or between the identity one assumes and the things one does, disturbs our understanding and judgment, and, if the mask cannot be taken as a mask, our reactions end up in psychological confusion. This is precisely what happens in our acquaintance with Whitman.

Let us consider the personal side first. What he showed himself to be as a man is quite clear from the recorded description of those who saw him, and admired him for what they saw. In essence, he was another Buddha, Paul, Mohammed, or Christ, and, for Harned, God Himself; all this not as one who taught, but as one who was. Maybe this excess was not of his seeking, and in reality he would have been content with the non-deific glory of a man of wisdom, or a man of God, which every great teacher of mankind personally is. But, literally interpreting his poetic description of himself, the inordinate admiration of the "hot little prophets" applied the account to the man himself, and gave him a divine throne to sit upon. The natural reaction of excessive ambition that could ill resist the adulation so flatteringly offered in reward for his labors, or a real belief in his own deific nature, as suggested by his philosophical readings about the human soul—one of these, or both together, might have persuaded him to occupy the seat of worship. And, if he had any qualms about it, he might have consoled his conscience by recognizing how close the seat of honor the world gives to a yogi or a Messiah is to the seat of worship he was virtually forced to adorn. Seated on it, it was incumbent on him to belong to it. Honor is a growth of human endeavor, and has no reason to be ashamed of its labor and its insignificant, even unflattering, beginnings. Shakespeare stole a deer and did not bother to destroy the evidence; Mohammed ran away from his enemies, a frightened man, but God-visited, he never tried to hide the shame. But worship is different; it needs miracles. (Great prophets had to resort to miracles in order to win the minds of men to God.) It needs an immaculate birth; a supernatural paraphernalia; mystery; an event not traceable or calculable by ordinary human standards. And we know with what ardor Whitman labored to supply all these in his attempt to belong to that seat of worship. He could not, for all his ingenuity, invent a manger and a star and the wise magi for his life history, but he did give it the Christ-mystery of the pre-preaching years and, for good measure (without questioning the charity in the service), the Christ-compassion of a "Wound Dresser." And yet he caught hold of a cat that was bothering him by its tail, and threw it out of the window; quarreled over the money he borrowed; uttered a falsehood just to impress Emerson; bewailed his poverty and neglectedness, appealed for help, and denied the receipt of money given in help; was ashamed of being unmarried, and to cover his sexual disorder invented six grandchildren; ill-treated his housekeeper and drove her to a court of law for financial redress; and finally entombed himself in a five-thousand-dollar grave.

That is the incongruity that confuses us, an incongruity that was bound to result from the wearing of a robe too big for a mortal man. But this confusion of the private personality of his assumption pales into insignificance before that of his poetic assumption. It is true, as Miller has said, that all writers assume a pose; but the question is slightly complicated in the case of Whitman, who is a lyric poet singing of himself. For, whereas the pose assumed by a writer of (to use a cliché) objective literature is just the viewpoint from which to apprehend, evaluate, and judge life, the one assumed by a poet who is subjective is more than a standpoint of vision; it becomes the very subject-matter of his art. (In both cases, a psychological as well as an artistic necessity, it is a superior pose.) Whitman is a singer of the self; the philosophical matter apart, the entire *Leaves of Grass* is one complex "Song of Myself." Whitman himself said, "The volumes . . . were intended to be most decided, serious, *bona-fide* expressions of an identical individual personality—*egotism,* if you choose. . . . They proceed out of, and revolve around, one's self, myself, an identity, and declaredly make that self the nucleus of the whole utterance. . . . (Carlyle said, 'there is no grand poem in the world but is at bottom a biography—the life of a man.')"[376] Therefore the question of what Whitman assumes in his poetry goes beyond the limits of Miller's argument, because, writing so many poems all about one's self, his own self, he is not merely assuming an imaginative experience to "attempt diligently to palm [it] off . . . as an 'actual' experience,"[377] but a different self altogether, whatever its qualities be. And in celebrating that different self he comes to lyricize its sensibilities, or dramatize its experiences.

The central theme of all the poems being "ONE'S SELF, that wondrous thing," it would not be so much correct to say, "his poems are plays; he is the protagonist,"[378] thus implying a distinct separation of one from the other, as to consider, in recognition of his own repeated assertion, that they are all so many scenes of one immense drama of the self he celebrates. They are not the dramatic monologues of a Browning in which the poet, like "a juggler who personifies a number of animals by clothing himself with their skins," imaginatively incorporates himself in the different characters of his creation and dramatizes their experiences, that is to say, by going out of himself and becoming them. Whitman does not go out of himself; he is always in himself, having assumed a self of vast proportions, and if there are others involved in his poetry, he speaks for them, not of them.

This self so celebrated is recognizably not just his simple self as an individual, nor even the more than ordinary self of a richly endowed poet; nor is it just the typical self of humanity with which a genius identifies himself for his artistic operations; nor, again, is it only the absolute self of philosophical speculation which one learns of in metaphysical writings. The self he unfolds in his poetry is a compound of all these; his "I" has an identity whose dimensions range from the simple to the absolute: the animal of sex, the man of society, the poet of imagination, the universal man, and God Almighty, are all there, not as several impersonations of one imaginative genius in different poems, but in one "Myself" of the "Song." The self of the poet is all inclusive. Besides, the "I" that is the subject of the "Song," is also, under artistic necessity, the maker of the song, and of the other songs. It watches the "Sleepers," is the "Answerer," the "Child that Went Forth," and the owner of the "Body Electric"; in short, it is at once the chanted and the chanter.

In thus assuming an all inclusive "I" for his poetic purposes, Whitman achieves only a motley, a violent physical assemblage of the skins of various creatures on one person. He sounds like a ventriloquist who collects the notes of many different animals in one frenzied cry. A poet is a man, and, as a man, is a beast, a rational animal, an imaginative soul, the symbol of humanity, and God, and is all these perhaps all at once; but he cannot be all these all at once as a poet. An actor can play the role of a king, a queen, a villain, and a beggar on the same stage at different times, even, possibly, in succession, if his is a solo performance. But he cannot in one single speech articulate the minds of all of them, or in one role represent the wealth and regality of the king, the sweetness and charity of the queen, the craft and villainy of the rogue, and the poverty and obsequiousness of the beggar. A poet's assumption of an identity for the role of a singer, or a novelist's for that of a story-teller, is under the same principle. Autobiographical or mere mode of technique, the "I" is the unifying principle in a work of art, and if in presenting an experience it changes its identification, it creates the chaos of a dream or the confusion of madness. It is in art, as it is in life, one single unified consciousness, not a thread upon which many consciousnesses are hung. Even with the cosmic or deific foundations on which such an identity can be built, as obviously Whitman attempts to do, it is just a matter of enlargement—a more powerful lens or a bigger telescope, but not a multiplication of different lenses.

The "I" of *Leaves of Grass,* or the eye with which Whitman sees himself and the world—and, as he sees, presents them to our sight—is a strange contraption that combines a telescopic lens that perceives distance and a microscopic lens that sees minuteness. For the "I" that chants the anatomy of the "body electric" and the agonies of a "Calamus" "perturbation," is conjoined to the "I" within which "latitude widens, longitude lengthens."[379] The "I" that lived in the "City of Orgies,"[380] the "I" that was all the sides of the "Square Deific," the "I" greater than whom God was not, the "I" that was a "batter'd, wreck'd old man"[381] praying to God, the "I" that was God, the "I" that "shrivel[led] at the thought of God"[382]—all these "I's" are there in the one "vision" the poet is "afoot" with.[383] This multiplicity of point of view disturbs the unity of *Leaves of Grass* and makes for a philosophic multitudinousness. Even a mystic poet has a unity of vision, a consistency of standpoint which is the first principle of art. No philosopher in his work can look at life and its truths as a reporter, as a suffering man, as a dispassionate observer, as the general mind of humanity, and as God, all in one understanding, and create an evaluation that is coherent and consistent. The experience of God, if we can imagine it beyond mere exaggeration of the human, is not the experience of man; the philosopher's is not the poet's; the body-worshiper's is not the soul-worshiper's; and the prophet's is not the humble sinner's. And Whitman was a philosopher-poet claiming to be a teacher more than a maker of songs.

The key to this confusion seems to lie in the unfortunate circumstance that he made the first poem of his ambitious career out of the printed words of philosophical pages. The metaphysical concept of self and the personal or lyrical form of its expression that he bodily gathered and developed into "Song of Myself" from the Sankhya and Yoga accounts—further supplemented, as we shall see, by similar exercises—gave him an identity which he decided to assume seriously for himself as a philosophical poet, without realizing that the self of those printed pages was not the self that sings in a poet or suffers in a man, and that, while it would be fine subject-matter for a poem it was not a convenient instrument for his own suffering, singing, poetic view of life. The success of the initial assumption (one wonders what might have happened to his later career if Emerson had not so rapturously applauded him) appears to have persuaded him, and he clung to it for its literary profitability as he clung to the yogic character in private life for the social profit it brought him, regardless of the underlying contradiction involved in both cases. If his first poems had sprung from genuine emotional experience, or deep cogitation, though stimulated by reading, and not, as we have seen, from an artificial transformation of borrowed words, or imitation, he would have been a poet (as a man) chanting his sorrows and joys, or a prophet (as a philosopher) chanting his wisdom, or God (as the Universal Soul or as the Unknown Absolute) chanting His revelations. But the poet of *Leaves of Grass* is all these in one. The self he assumed from the Sankhya thought gave him an identity with which as a god to reveal; the self he gathered from the Yoga account contributed an identity as a yogi to preach; added to them, as we shall see, was what he found in the self of God of the *Bhagvat-Geeta*. Further, the self of his poetic character gave him an identity with which to represent mankind; and then there was the other identity, the true, basic one, the gift of the native self, "born here of parents." Whitman assembles them all into one unnatural and inartistic combination. In one gigantic complex, he is the autobiographical man, the universal poet, the prophetic teacher, and the revealing God. Thus we hear in one mouth many different voices; and he chants his songs in all these discordant identities simply because he *is* all these at once, as he delineated himself in "Song of Myself." It is the self of the "Song" that is the author of all the songs of *Leaves of Grass*. And since that self is actually an ill-integrated, ill-integratable conjunction of many different selves, what it later comes to sing has sometimes the private voice of the mortal man, sometimes the general voice of the universal poet, sometimes the messianic voice of the prophet, and sometimes the awesome voice of God Almighty.

To give to this fanciful conglomeration of different selves in the "Myself" of Whitman the explanation generally offered and call it the Cosmic Self does not resolve the confusion. For the Cosmic Self is not a physical aggregate of individual selves, including God, but the total spiritual principle. If Whitman as a poet played the mouthpiece for this "Kosmos," he would hardly be able to speak of the "suns [he] cannot see,"[384] of being "born out of [his] mother,"[385] and of being "Walt Whitman, an American, one of the roughs,"[386] worship the "spread of [his] body,"[387] tell what happened "in Texas in [his] early youth,"[388] and so on. But he is and does all this, because his imitative meditations on his self go beyond the philosophical limits of the original which set him on to the poetic exercise. Poetic imitation, not philosophic meditation, being the source of his "Song"—for all the splendor of imagination and the skill of art to be found in it—an unmistakable philosophical absurdity underlies the poem as a whole.

Binns, who noticed the strong mystical element in Whitman, rightly regarded it as of a purely sensuous nature, and said, "it is clearly not the mysticism which is completed in . . . meditation and ecstasy."[389] In other words, Whitman as a poet is not the

mystic who captured a vision of life in an ecstatic frenzy of imagination, but a writer of remarkable verbal skill, in fancy creating
the vision of a mystic. And having created it in the poem—on the
model, and with the material, of the yogi's meditation found in his
reading—he perpetually assumes, as a poet, the character of the
vision. It is significant, in this connection, that his resolution to
"make *the Works,*" and the plan of "the Great Construction of
the New Bible," were made in "1856" and "June '57" respectively,
after he had assumed the new role.

Not only does Whitman thus artistically recreate the "discriminating wisdom" of a yogi, but he even creates the impression
of having actually acquired it in the way the yogi is said to acquire
it—in meditation and exercises. Furness observes in his introduction to *Walt Whitman's Workshop,* referring to an entry in
a "notebook filled with material showing the complete genesis of
a poem":

He records in a working notebook the conception of a poem
in a state psychologically comparable to the ecstasy attained
through mystic meditation: "a trance, yet with all the senses
alert—only a state of high exalted musing—the tangible and
material with all its shows, the objective world suspended or
surmounted for a while, & the powers in exaltation, freedom,
vision—yet the *senses* not lost or counteracted."[390]

One of the fragments collected in *Notes and Fragments* obviously
refers to the yogic exercise, and also carries a self-direction:

? Outlines of a lecture. I imagining myself in that condition.
You must do the work—you must think.
To you. First of all prepare for study by the following self-
teaching exercises. *Abstract* yourself from this book; realize
where you are at present located, the point you stand that is now
to you the centre of all. Look up overhead, think of *space*
stretching out, think of all the unnumbered orbs wheeling safely
there, invisible to us by day, some visible by night; think of
the *sun* around which the earth revolves; the *moon* revolving
round the earth, and accompanying it; think of the different
planets belonging to our system. Spend some minutes faithfully
in this exercise. Then again realize yourself upon the earth, at

the particular point you now occupy. Which way stretches the north, and what country, seas etc.? Which way the south? Which way the east? Which way the west? Seize these firmly with your mind, *pass freely over immense distances.* Turn your face a moment thither. Fix definitely the direction and the idea of the distances of separate sections of your own country, also of England, the Mediterranean sea, Cape Horn, the North Pole, and such like distant places.[391] (Italics added.)

Commenting on this passage, Furness says, "The similarity of this practice to the methods of meditation recommended in modern mystical and occult treatises is striking. . . . Whitman's knowledge of studies in occult religion is noteworthy. . . ."[392] Whether Whitman actually practised these "self-teaching exercises" is a matter of doubt, but his knowledge of the "occult" method of meditation is undoubted, and the source of it is obviously what his "Song of Myself" grew from, namely, the Yoga account of Bhojadeva, where the objects of meditation, upon which, after *abstraction,* the mind is to be *fixed,* were the *sun,* the *moon,* the *polar star,* the *vacuum,* the stars and *planets,* and the five primary elements, meditating upon which the yogi could "proceed to the greatest distance." He is only "imagining" himself in the condition of a yogi, just as he imagined himself the yogi in "Song of Myself," though Furness, apparently carried away by his references to it, says that "he made a conscious goal of 'meditation, the devout ecstasy, the soaring flight.' "[393] Of the fact that, far from being a philosophic votary seeking the "devout ecstasy" through the discipline of such exercises, he was only an imaginative poet who found in the concept so much grist to his artistic mill, further proof can be found in the manuscripts in the collection of Mr. Milton I. D. Einstein, studied by Furness. These notebooks show "the complete genesis of a poem":[394]

The title for the projected poem was to be *Penitenzia.* This is written in red ink on the covers of both notebooks. Then the unworked raw material follows. "For part in L of G. Collect the good portraits. Kurtz's head with eyelids drooping. Tarisse's head. Make poems to match. Veil (?) Mask with the lids thine eyes, O soul! . . . Retire within thyself. Mask with the lids thine eyes, O soul. Droop—droop thine eyes O soul. Be not abased. I sing the unaccomplished—I sing the vast dark unknown. . . .

Then chant (celebrate) the unknown, the future hidden spiritual world the real reality."

A second notebook, probably merely a collateral or alternative place for jotting fragments, which he may have reserved for the more detailed formulation of the material for this poem, contains general directions for the composition of the piece, and its first tentative draft. "Sentiment of the piece: Abstraction, Meditation; Penitence. ? qu.—three (or more) stanzas of interrogatory character. For portrait with hat. Behind (Under) that mask of shade? heavy shade. Veil with the lids. Eyes, droop thy lids. O penitence. Repentance (It.) Penitenzia? The drooping of the eyelids generally accompanies humility—indicates penitence—see the Roman Catholic devotees—& specimen pictures of the saints, &c. On the portrait. Photo by Mr Tarisse. As apostrophising the depths. Look out from the shadows. Thou who—(? qu) Lookest out from the shadows on. . . ."

Then appears the poem itself. . . .

Mask with their lids thine eyes, O Soul
Pass to the unaccomplished, over the vast unknown
Droop, droop thine eyes O Soul
Exalt thyself to musing—speed thy flight—thy slough dropt
   from thee
The objective world behind thee leave
The standards of the light and sense shut off
To darkness now retiring
Aloof inward to thy abysms (?)
How curious then appears the world,
Thy comrades, life and this thy visage, passive each
The objective world behind thee left.

The image of the soul with its "slough dropt from" it, is an echo of "Sankhya-sara," which said that he who knows the spirit "renounces the world" and "becomes like the serpent when he has cast off his skin."[395] Apart from that, the light that the foregoing sheds on Whitman's art of making poems is significant. The process is of manipulation, assemblage, and formulation. The abstraction-thought is teased into "penitenzia"; bits gathered from reading are assembled with fragments of imaginative extension; and all, word by word, are formulated into a strange mystic synthesis. The only meditation behind or under the poem is verbal meditation, not meditation of thought; the magic of a poet, not the vision of a prophet, of which he said: "Only to the rapt vision does the seen become the prophecy of the unseen."[396] Elsewhere, again, the yoga description is just so many words to weave a song with: "I am a look—mystic—in a trance—exaltation";[397] a verbal experience, if experience it is.

To the impact that the character of the yogi and his exalted experience, which he read so much about in all the Hindu writings, had upon Whitman's imagination, though not necessarily upon his personal character, the following passage from *Democratic Vistas* carries further testimony:

> Personalism fuses this, and favours it. I should say, indeed, that only in the perfect uncontamination and solitariness of individuality may be the spirituality of religion positively come forth at all. Only here, and on such terms, the meditation, the devout ecstasy, the soaring flight. Only here, communion with mysteries, the eternal problems, whence? whither? Alone, and identity, and the mood—and the soul emerges, and all statements, churches, sermons, melt away like vapours. Alone, and silent thought and awe, and aspiration—and then the interior consciousness, like a hitherto unseen inscription, in magic ink, beams out its wondrous lines to the sense. Bibles may convey, and priests expound, but it is exclusively for the noiseless operation of one's isolated Self, to enter the pure ether of veneration, reach the divine levels, and commune with the unutterable.[398]

One of the ways in which Whitman's "literatus" is to aid America is by "a strong mastership of the general inferior self by the superior self."[399] Adapted to his requirements as it is, it is the condition of a yogi he describes thus:

> In that condition the whole body is elevated to a state by others unknown—inwardly and outwardly illuminated, purified, made solid, strong, yet buoyant. A singular charm, more than beauty, flickers out of, and over, the face—a curious transparency beams in the eyes, . . . —the temper partakes also. Nothing that happens—no event, recontre, weather, etc.—but it is confronted—nothing but is subdued into sustenance—such is the marvellous transformation from the old timorousness and the old process of causes and effects. Sorrows and disappointments cease—there is no more borrowing trouble in advance. A man realizes the venerable myth—he is a god walking the earth, he

sees new eligibilities, powers and beauties everywhere; he himself has a new eyesight and hearing. The play of the body in motion takes a previously unknown grace ... All the beforehand gratifications, drink, spirits, coffee grease, stimulants, mixtures, late hours, luxuries, deeds of the night, seem as vexatious dreams, and now the awakening;—many fall into their natural places, wholesome, conveying diviner joys.[400]

Of the yogic wisdom, of the Vedantic attitude to the material world—the concept of Maya or illusion, and of the ultimate reality of spirit—and even of Kanada's qualified acceptance of the material reality, which the pages of his reading have unfolded, we have echoes all at once in another passage of *Democratic Vistas,* in which (to use Furness's summary),

he explains the "completion of material births and beginnings" in the light of the "prophecy of those births, namely, spiritual results." At moments of the highest exaltation he seems almost to approximate the Hindu conception of *Maya* in his attitude toward "the seen." He believes that there is a "conviction brooding within the recesses of every envision'd soul" that the "intellect, demonstrations, solid perpetuities, facts" and so forth, of the visible world are but "illusions! apparitions! figments all!" "Migrate in soul to what we can already conceive of superior and spiritual points of view, and palpable as it seems under present relations, it all and several might, nay certainly would, fall apart and vanish." Yet, with the solid practicality which usually characterizes his final judgments, he cautions that "we must not condemn the show, neither absolutely deny it, for the indispensability of its meanings."[401]

That, as we find, is Whitman, whose words, to adapt his own phrase, "are made in the spirit that comes from the study of pictures of things—and not from the spirit that comes from the contact with real things themselves."[402] Perhaps the only originality there is in him is the one of his own description, the one that must "show itself in new combinations and new meanings."[403]

The Vedanta account in Ward's *View,* sandwiched between the Sankhya and the Patanjala, presents a very thin picture of the system, being based on an unauthoritative text, and therefore it

could be ignored as source of any valuable information on the
subject, particularly because the thoughts of this branch of Hindu
philosophy have been obtained by Whitman from a more authentic
study of it in the *Transactions*. However, one aspect of Vedanta
thought, namely, the doctrine of Maya, which Colebrooke did not
supply, is discussed in Ward's translation of "Vedanta-sara," as
well as in his accounts of the other schools generally, and it is
likely that Whitman's knowledge of it—evidenced in the passage
of *Democratic Vistas* noticed above, and in the poems, "Of the
Terrible Doubt of Appearances," "Are You the New Person
Drawn Toward Me?" and "Crossing Brooklyn Ferry"—had
its origin here. His reaction to the concept, in the early days at
any rate, seems to be less of serious belief than of purely imaginative interest, and he appears to have been fascinated more by the
charm of the thought than by the philosophy of the doctrine. His
use of the term, limited to signify false knowledge (which is
basically what it stands for), is seen in the following lines:

Are you the new person drawn toward me?
To begin with take warning, I am surely far different from
    what you suppose;
. . . .
Do you see no further than this façade, this smooth and toler-
    ant manner of me?
Do you suppose yourself advancing on real ground toward a
    real heroic man?
Have you no thought O dreamer that it may be all maya,
    illusion?[404]

The same distinction between appearance and reality, with a
keener philosophical feeling, in spite of the same personal, "Calamus" associations, is struck in the poem "Of the Terrible Doubt of
Appearances":

Of the Terrible doubt of appearances,
Of the uncertainty after all, that we may be deluded,
That may-be reliance and hope are but speculations after all,
That may-be identity beyond the grave is a beautiful fable
    only,
May-be the things I perceive, the animals, plants, men, hills,
    shining and flowing waters,

The skies of day and night, colours, densities, forms, may-be
these are (as doubtless they are) only apparitions, and the
real something has yet to be known,

....

May-be seeming to me what they are (as doubtless they indeed
but seem) as from my present point of view, and might
prove (as of course they would) nought of what they appear
or nought anyhow, from entirely changed points of view. . . .

These words were written in 1860. In his notes for the "Sunday
Evening Lectures," "written in the late sixties or very early seven-
ties," he uses the very words of the last section, in discussing the
"finale," the "inquiry" that "has the most important bearing upon
metaphysics":[405]

What we realize as truth in the objective and other Natural
worlds is not the absolute but only the relative truth from our
existing point of view; in other terms, . . . this is what we realize
of the objective world by our present imperfect senses and cog-
nizance and . . . what we realize would be entirely changed and
perhaps overthrown and reversed if we were advanced to superior
development and points of view.

That is how he elaborates what he calls "Kant's tremendous
and unquestionable point," but "the hands of 'Esau" only write,
as Bucke describes it, and "the voice is always the voice of Jacob—
Whitman himself." In other words, the phraseology is his own,
from the early poem, which he is echoing in his later prose. Kant,
therefore, or, Hedge, whose book was the source of these notes,
was not the origin of Whitman's knowledge of the relative truth
of the "imperfect senses" that "would be entirely changed" by
superior "points of view," which are acquired in the soul whose
"laws repel the inconsistent and gravitate forever toward the absolute, the supernatural, the eternal truth. . . ."[406]

Of the description of the concept of Maya in Ward, only a few
brief extracts from "Vedanta-sara" and "Sankhya-sara" are given
here:

We cannot call illusion entity, for as soon as a person obtains
discriminating wisdom, illusion is destroyed; nor can it be
called non-entity, for the universe which is an effect of this

illusion, is an object of sight. . . . This illusion resembles the temporary blindness under which the owl and other creatures labour, so that they can see nothing after the sun has risen. . . . It is not merely the absence of wisdom; but, as being opposed to the true knowledge of Brahma, is called agnana. . . . This illusion . . . assumes an endless variety of deceptive forms, similar to real ones, yet no more real than when a cord, a cane, the edge of a river, &c. are feared under the illusive appearance of a serpent. . . . This illusion possesses the power of concealing an object, and of deception: a small cloud darkening the sight of the person looking at the sun, appears to hide this immense luminary.[407]
A wise man, desirous of that which is truly substantial, having tried the objects of sense, those airy nothings, rejects them all. . . . Maya (illusion), in various forms, embracing formless spirit, dances, and . . . brings the understanding into a state of infatuation. . . . Spirit is real entity, but not so the visible world. . . . An ignorant person sees in the world only cities, houses, mountains, elephants, and other splendid objects; he has no idea of that which is spiritual. . . .[408]

Not much by way of serious philosophical thought may be assumed to have come to Whitman from the remaining three accounts, but a few more utterances of his appear to be indebted to these pages than the ones already traced to them. Among the first drafts in *Notes and Fragments* is this tentative piece, obviously intended for a poem:

Poem of existence.

We call one the past and we call another the future,
But both are alike the present.

It is not the past, though we call it so—nor the future though
    we call it so,
All the while it is the present only.[409]

The lines seem to have been inspired by the following in Gautama's Nyaya philosophy:

Time gives birth to all things, and in it all is comprehended. It divides the past and the future, and is indivisible; the divisions of time are mere accidents. . . . The objector . . . maintains that present time is a non-entity: we can never say Time is; while we are uttering the words it is gone. Gautama contends, that if present time be not admitted, neither the past nor the future can be maintained, for they belong to each other; and the very idea of anything being present or visible necessarily belongs to present time.[410]

In fact Whitman echoes almost the very phrase of the first of the above extracts in section 2 of "Song of the Answerer" when he says:

Time, always without a break, indicates itself in parts. . . .

One of the evidences of facts Gautama insists upon in his system is that of the senses:

The five senses apprehend the forms of things, also of scents, tastes, sounds, and contact. . . . The senses were created to give the knowledge of objects. . . . Gautama admits, that the understanding is the most proper witness; but still contends, that the senses, as supplying proof of things, must be admitted also as witnesses. The objector now urges . . . the imperfection of the evidence of the senses . . . their testimony not being self-sufficient. Should it be maintained, he continues, that the senses alone are competent to supply sufficient evidence of things, might I not affirm, that there is no need to search for evidence, things having their own evidence in themselves? Gautama says, the evidence which relates to objects is of two kinds, that which needs support, and that which is in itself decisive: a lamp depends upon the sight of others for manifestation, but the eyes are possessed of an inherent energy, so that other assistance is unnecessary. . . . It is further objected . . . the senses depend upon union to spirit for the power they possess. . . . Gautama admits, that the union of spirit is necessary, but this does not affect the argument, since spirit is necessary to every action, as well as space and time; but spirit merely assists in forming general ideas; the senses individuate objects. . . . Each sense has its separate office, but spirit is served by them all. . . . The understanding, in its operations, uses all the five senses for the different purposes of life.[411]

Whitman's attitude toward the senses, both as a poet and a philosopher, is clearly too similar to this to need any demonstration.

We may note, however, the verbal echoes in his poetry of the line about "things having their own evidence in themselves." In "A Song of the Rolling Earth," section 1, he insists that "the truths of the earth . . . are not so conceal'd either," "all things conveying themselves willingly," and, in "Song of Myself," section 30, he says: "All truths wait in all things. . . . They do not need the obstetric forceps of the surgeon." In an experimental line of the latter passage, he is obviously closer to the source:

A test of anything!
It proves itself to the experience and senses of men and
    women.[412]

Gautama says, "the pious man is everywhere honoured; he is never despised."[413] Whitman's "Answerer" has a "welcome [that] is universal."[414] The beautiful poem "This Compost," dealing with the chemistry of the earth, appears to have its inspiration in the following:

Gautama now engages the Vedantis, some of whom maintain . . . that the universe is a form of Brahma (Parinama). "This word [as a footnote says] conveys the idea of change, such as that in which vegetables become manure, which afterwards undergoes a change, and becomes vegetables, and which are again converted into animal substance, &c."[415]

Speaking of the principle of action and result, Gautama says:

Some actions give rise to immediate consequences, as reading produces immediate knowledge; but the cultivator receives the fruit of his labours at a future period; and in the same manner, the fruits of religious or wicked actions are to be reaped in a future state. Against this sentiment a person rises up and maintains, that as actions do not resemble a seed, but vanish as soon as committed, it is not possible that they should produce future misery. Gautama says, from actions arise merit and demerit, and though the actions may not be permanent, the invisible fruits are so. . . . Both the shastra and mankind use this form of speech, *good* actions and *evil* actions; for though actions in themselves are neither good nor evil, yet merit and demerit arise out of them, and hence they are thus designated.[416]

This briefly is the Hindu theory of Karma; Whitman found it in Menu, in Vishnu Sharma, in Jones, in the *Transactions,* and in the *Researches,* in a word, in all his Hindu readings; possibly Gautama gave it only a verbal clarification. "Song of Prudence," which announces that "Not one word or deed. . . . But has results beyond death as really as before death" and "To Think of Time," which, in section 7, speaks of the "law of heroes and good-doers" and "the law of drunkards, informers, mean persons," may have used this clarification.

The account of the Mimamsa philosophy also dwells upon the senses, and the law of actions, as follows:

> From the evidence of things which God has afforded, especially the evidence of the senses, mistakes cannot arise respecting secular or religious affairs: by this evidence all secular and religious actions are perfected. If it were otherwise, then the whole economy of things respecting both worlds would be destroyed. Where there may exist error in this evidence, it will diminish,˙ but it cannot destroy the nature of things. If there be an imperfection in seed, the production may be imperfect, but its nature will not be changed. If it be then asked respecting the seat of error and inattention, we affirm, that they are found in the reasoning faculty, and not in the senses. . . .[417]
>
> From one law, according to the dispositions and actions of those who are subject to it, a great variety of consequences arise. Works give birth to invisible consequences, propitious or unpropitious according to their nature; and, besides works there is no other sovereign or judge. These consequences, ever accompanying the individual *as the shadow the body,* appear in the next birth, according to the time in which the actions were performed in the preceding birth.[418] (Italics added)

The Vysheshika account carries the following footnote on the same doctrine, linking it up with transmigration:

> The Hindoos believe, that the dispositions of a person in a new transmigration . . . are regulated by the preceding actions . . . that millions and millions of actions unexpiated or unenjoyed are laid up for and against every individual, and that the fruits of only a few actions are enjoyed or endured in one birth: so that

every person not an ascetic lies under almost infinite arrears, and his transmigrations appear interminable.[419]

In the first tentative fragment in which he was organizing his concept of "Prudence," and the "law" that "cannot be eluded,"[420] by which a man's "real body" carries, "item for item," what "has accrued to it from the moment of birth to the moment of death,"[421] Whitman even used the simile italicised above:

As the shadow concurs with the body

. . . .

As craft, lies, thefts, sarcasm, greed, denial, avarice, hatred, gluttony, so the soul,
As the types set up by the printers are faithfully returned by their impression, what they are for, so a man's life and a woman's life is returned in the soul before death and interminably after death.[422]

10

OF SOUL AND NATURE

AN EXAMINATION OF *Sankhya Karika* AS A SOURCE OF PHIL-osophical knowledge to Whitman is apparently unnecessary, considering that we have found its thoughts reflected in two different and elaborate accounts. But one of the most important doctrines of Sankhya, of which we have a very strong echo in Whitman, is not brought into clear relief in either of them—clear enough to have captured his imagination. He almost verbally repeats the original utterance of *Sankhya Karika,* which persuades us to believe that he read that book too. The doctrine in question is respecting Nature, i.e., the material world, and its relation or importance to the soul. The thought is briefly summed up in Colebrooke, and is only implicit in Ward, whose account is not quite authentically derived, but the *Sankhya Karika* dwells upon it with emphasis, and Whitman's phrases are closer to it. Here are some of his utterances on the Nature and Soul relationship:

> One's Self—you, whoever you are, pour'd into whom all that you read and hear and what existent is in heroes or events, with landscape, heavens, and every beast and bird, becomes so only with play and interplay. *For what to you or me is the round universe . . . except as feeding you and me?* May-be indeed it is by us created in winking of our eyes. Or maybe *for preparing us,* by giving us identity—then *sailing us* with winds o'er the great seas, the apparent known, *steadily to the harbors of the really great unknown. . . .*

323

I . . . chant materials, emanating spirituality—and the human form surcharged through all its veins the same.

As I behold the Universe the things of Nature the least as well as largest item ever inexplicable, I think the things of *Nature,* as in the main suggestive and gymnastic—*not great because of objects or events themselves but great in reference to a human personality* and for identity and needful exercise. Such is the hint that comes (in whispers to me—and out of it I chant the following poems.) (Italics added.)

. . . Nature is not great with reference to itself, but great with reference to a human personality.

Every apparition in this world is but to rout [rouse?] the real object up from sleeping in yourself.[423]

The entire section 5 of "A Song for Occupations" versifies the same idea, as do many other poems of his, especially portions of "Starting from Paumanok," where "having look'd at the objects of the universe [he] find[s] there is no one nor any particle of one but has reference to the soul."[424] All this, one can see in spite of Whitman's claim, did not come to him "in whispers," but from the following stanzas and extracts of the accompanying commentary, found in the *Sankhya Karika* :[425]

"This evolution of nature, from intellect to the special elements, is performed for the deliverance of each soul respectively; done for another's sake as for self."
COMMENT: The object of nature's activity is here said to be the final liberation of individual soul. Nature is properly inert, and its activity, its "motion" or evolution, takes place only for the purpose of soul, not for any object of its own. . . . This [evolution] is the spontaneous act of nature: it is not influenced by any external intelligent principle, such as the Supreme Being or a subordinate agent; as BRAHMÁ, it is without (external) cause. . . . The work is done for a special purpose, the liberation of individual soul. . . . The activity of nature [is] for the purpose of accomplishing soul's object. . . .

"As it is a function of milk, an unintelligent (substance), to nourish the calf, so it is the office of the chief (principle) to liberate the soul."

COMMENT: The intuitive or spontaneous evolution of nature, for soul's purpose, is here illustrated. . . ."

"As people engage in acts to relieve desires, so does the undiscrete (principle) to liberate the soul."

"As a dancer, having exhibited herself to the spectator, desists from the dance, so does nature desist, having manifested herself to the soul."

"Generous nature, endued with qualities, does by manifold means accomplish, without benefit (to herself) the wish of ungrateful soul, devoid as he is of qualities."
COMMENT: . . . Nature labours for the benefit of soul as if for self, but not for any advantage.

"Nothing, in my opinion, is more gentle than nature; once aware of having been seen, she does not again expose herself to the gaze of soul."
BHASHYA: . . . It . . . declares Îswara (God) to be the cause of the world. . . . Others say, spontaneity is cause. . . .[426]
COMMENT: Nature being once properly understood by soul ceases to act.

An earlier verse, presenting the same idea, also touches upon the Sankhya notion of creation:[427]

"For the soul's contemplation of nature, and for abstraction, the union of both takes place, as of the halt and blind. By that union a creation is framed."
COMMENT: . . . "Contemplation" . . . is considered to comprise "fruition". . . . For the fulfilment . . .—the fruition of nature, and liberation of soul—their mutual co-operation and combination are essential. . . . These results cannot be attained without the evolution of the products of nature . . . For both purposes, therefore, the world must exist, as developed from its material cause.

The "bhashya" on this, or, the commentary of Gaurapada, carries an explanation of the latter part of the verse as follows, and Whitman's use of the sexual symbol for creation loses much of its strangeness when we realize that he is merely echoing both the thought and the image of the explanation:

... Again, *By that,* by that union, *a creation is framed.*—As the birth of a child proceeds from the union of male and female, so the production of creation results from the connection of nature and soul. . . .[428]

In the comment on verse No. 8, a discussion refers to the concept of Maya thus:

> The Vedantis . . . maintain that all that exists is but the *vivarttas,* literally the "revolutions"—the emanations from, or manifestations of, one only universal spirit. . . . The popular form of Vedantism asserts, indeed, that nothing exists but cause, and that its effects, or all that appears to exist, are unrealities, illusions, the phantoms of a dream: but the commentator . . . declares that the doctrine of *maya,* or "illusion," is modern, and is contrary to the Vedas. . . .[429]

It may be noticed how close to the second of these sentences the utterance of Whitman in *Democratic Vistas,* quoted earlier, about "illusions! apparitions! figments all!" comes in phrase.

"Agonies are one of my changes of garments," says Whitman in "Song of Myself," section 33. The comment on verse 17 of *Sankhya Karika* has these lines:

> Birth is defined to be the association of soul with body; death, its detachment: soul being always existent, and not in itself subject to birth or death. . . . "Life is the combination of soul with the pains incident to body, &c.; not any modification of soul. Death is the abandonment of those bodies, &c.; not the destruction of soul." . . . But though manifold, as individualized, this individual soul is one and unchanged, through all its migrations into various forms. . . . It is the disguise which is changed, not that which wears it. . . .[430]

And Whitman read of the nature of the real "what I am" very clearly here, thus:

> And from that contrast (before set forth) it follows, that soul is witness, solitary, bystander, spectator, and passive.[431]

11

AT THE FEET OF A GREAT MASTER

The Vishnu Purana: A System of Hindu Mythology and Tradition, translated by H. H. Wilson, contains more than Hindu mythology and tradition. In its vast encyclopedic sweep, it presents the religious and philosophical thought of Hindu beliefs and practices too, because the principal object of all the *puranas* was "religious instruction," as Colonel Vans Kennedy has observed.[432] The religion of the *Vedas,* the philosophy of the *Upanishads,* the doctrines of the six systems of Hindu thought, the "laws" of Menu, are all here in a narrative "plainly and unpretendingly told," with elaborate discourses on "the divine nature and creation," "descriptions of the universe," and "argumentative and metaphysical discussion."[433] *The Vishnu Purana* was one of the major sources of Hindu thought for the Concordians, especially Emerson, whose "Hamatreya" was inspired by the Song of the Earth in Book IV, and it is possible that such a knowledge had something to do with Whitman's reading it when he found it in the Oriental collection of the Astor Library. His own passionate ridicule of the "madness of owning things" in the 1847–8 manuscript notebook has a remarkable closeness of expression to the words chanted by the Earth:

> How great is the folly of princes . . . to cherish the confidence of ambition, when they themselves are but foam upon the earth. . . . "Thus," they say, "will we conquer the ocean-circled earth;" and, intent upon their project, behold not death, which is not far-off. . . . It is through infatuation that kings desire to

327

possess me, whom their predecessors have been forced to leave, whom their fathers have not retained. . . . Foolishness has been the character of every king who has boasted, "All this earth is mine—everything is mine—it will be mine in my house for ever"; for he is dead. . . . When I hear a king sending word to another by his ambassador, "This earth is mine; immediately resign your pretensions to it;" I am moved to violent laughter at first, but it soon subsides in pity for the infatuated fool.[434]

The narrator of *The Vishnu Purana,* commenting upon the Earth's chant, said:

He who has heard [of the kings that are no more to possess the earth], will learn wisdom, and forbear to call either children, or wife, or house, or lands, or wealth, his own. . . . Aware of this truth, a wise man will never be influenced by the principle of individual appropriation; and regarding them as only transient and temporary possessions, he will not consider children and posterity, lands and property, or whatever else is personal, to be his own.

Whitman wrote in his notebook:

But the wisest soul knows that no object can really be owned by one man or woman any more than another.—The orthodox proprietor says This is mine, I earned or received or paid for it,— and by positive right of my own I will put a fence round it, and keep it exclusively to myself. . . . Yet—yet—what cold drop is that which slowly patters . . . on the skull of his greediness . . . ? —that dismal and measureless fool not to see the hourly lesson of the one eternal law, that he who would grab blessings to himself, as by right, and deny others their equal chance—and will not share with them everything that he has.

He cannot share his friend or wife because of them he is no owner, except by their love, and if anyone gets that away from him, it is best not to curse, but quietly call the offal cart to his door and let physical wife or friend go, the tail with the hide.[435]

But these words were written, according to the evidence, sometime around 1847 or '48, and Astor came to have its copy of *The Vishnu Purana* in December 1851. Though Whitman's contempt tor riches has a native and early origin, the thought of this note and its pattern bear a strikingly close resemblance to the passage in *The Vishnu Purana* quoted above, and to Emerson's "Hamatreya," which verbally follows it. But Emerson's Earth does not call its "hot owner" an "infatuated fool," nor does Emerson, like Parasara, continue the chant into the positive description of a wise man. Whitman calls the "orthodox proprietor" a "dismal and measureless fool," and develops the thought into references to "wife" and personal ownership, or "individual appropriation," like the narrator of *The Vishnu Purana*. However, since the other libraries did not possess a copy of *The Vishnu Purana*, and no evidence of his reading it before 1847 is discoverable, the only inference seems to be that the first thoughts of the note were roused from reading Emerson's poem, upon which he imaginatively raised the rest of his sentiments.

Both because Whitman had not possibly read *The Vishnu Purana* prior to 1851, before which time, as we have seen, the foundations of his poetic experiment were already laid, and because the ideas that would deserve our attention in the book have been found in other sources so far examined, the part it played in the making of the poet of *Leaves of Grass* will not be given as much notice as it would otherwise have merited. A few important passages, however, have already been shown as having supplied Whitman with suggestions toward a Deific Quaternity and "Santa Spirita," the fourth of the quaternity. Ignoring, therefore, the profounder philosophical thought in it, in which we merely have a reverberation of Sankhya, Vedanta, and other systems, we shall glance at some passages that are unique in manner of expression, if not in content, to this book alone, because of which Whitman's indebtedness to it can easily be established.

In "A Song for Occupations" Whitman asserts:

> Strange and hard that paradox true I give
> Objects gross and the unseen soul are one.[436]

Indeed, this is the refrain of his message, reverberating all through his poetry and prose. But his doctrine of integration does not stop here. As Allen observes, "the primary stress, however, is on the unity of the Kosmos (Whitman's spelling), the oneness of time, nature, and of soul and body.[437] As his songs "draw to a close" he declares that that is what "underlies the precedent songs"—the aim to sing the "entrance of man,"

> Through Space and Time fused in a chant, and the flowing
>   eternal identity,
> To Nature encompassing these, encompassing God—to the
>   joyous, electric all . . . .[438]

And in the *Democratic Vistas* he says: "The spirit and the form are one, and depend far more on association, identity and place, than is supposed."[439]

Though this concept of unity could have been formed from his readings in Vedanta thought, it is probable that the following passage in the Preface, in which Wilson summarizes the contents of the book, had its share to offer:

> The course of the elemental creation [the theme of Book I of *The Vishnu Purana*] is in the Vishnu, as in other Puranas, taken from the Sankhya philosophy; but the agency that operates upon passive matter is confusedly exhibited, in consequence of a partial adoption of the illusory theory of the Vedanta philosophy, and the prevalence of the Pauranik doctrine of Pantheism. However incompatible with the independent existence of Pradhana or crude matter, and however incongruous with the separate condition of pure spirit or Purusha, it is declared repeatedly that Vishnu, as one with the supreme being is not only spirit, but crude matter; and not only the latter, but all visible substance, and Time. He is Purusha, "spirit"; Pradhána, "crude matter;" Vyakta, "visible form;" and Kála, "time."[440]

The most captivating passages in *The Vishnu Purana* are those in which the nature of God or the Divine Spirit is described in innumerable prayers addressed to Vishnu, whose glories are the theme of the narrative. The contents of many of Whitman's poems that dwell on God, or the Universal Spirit, can be traced to them. The "Electric All," encompassing time, nature, form, and spirit, is described by "On the Beach at Night Alone," as "a vast similitude" that "interlocks all," "spheres," "distances of space," "distances of time," "all souls, all living bodies," "all gaseous, watery, vegetable, mineral processes, the fishes, the brutes," "all identities," "all lives and deaths, all of the past, present, future," "compactly" holding them and enclosing them. In "You Tides with Ceaseless Swell" he speaks of it as the "unseen force centripetal, centrifugal, through space's spread,/Rapport of sun, moon, earth, and all the constellations," "the pulse," "the boundless aggregate of all," "holding the universe with all its parts as one." In "A Voice from Death," he addresses it as:

> Thou that in all, and over all, and through and under all, incessant!
> Thou! thou! the vital, universal force resistless, sleepless, calm. . . .

"A Persian Lesson" declares:

> Allah is all, all, all—is immanent in every life and object,
> . . . .
> Latent the same in subject and in object, without one exception.

Elsewhere he calls Him "lighter than light," the "essence of forms" "the general soul" ("Chanting the Square Deific"), "Light of the light," "centre" of the "universes," "moral spiritual fountain," "affection's source," "the motive of the stars, sun, systems" ("Passage to India"), "light rare untellable, lighting the very light," "beyond all signs, descriptions, languages" ("Prayer of Columbus"), and so on. *The Vishnu Purana* praises God thus:

> The world was produced from VISHNU: it exists in him: he is the cause of its continuance and cessation: he is the world . . . the support of all things . . . the smallest of the small . . . is in all created things. He is the liberator (tára), or he who bears mortals across the ocean of existence: he is both single and manifold . . . [footnote]. They who know true wisdom . . . behold this whole world as one with divine knowledge, as one with thee, oh god. We glorify him who is all things; the lord supreme over all . . . unperceived, indivisible . . . in whom are all things, from whom are all things . . . who is all beings . . . the soul of all embodied substance . . . who is both cause and

effect; who is the cause of cause, the effect of effect . . . the enjoyer and thing to be enjoyed; the creator and thing to be created; who is the agent and the effect . . . supreme being . . . lord of all, great soul of all, asylum of all. . . . From thee is all this universe, all that has been, and that shall be: and all this world is in thee, assuming this universal form. . . . The whole universe is comprehended in thee as its germ. As the Nyagrodha [Indian fig tree] germinates from the seed . . . so the created world proceeds from thee, and expands into magnitude. . . . Thou, imperishable . . . art in all, the element of all; thou art all, assuming every form; all is from thee. . . . I salute thee, universal soul . . . who is primeval light . . . one with time, whose first forms . . . are day and evening and night . . . the life of all living things, who is the same with the moon, one with the sun . . . with earth, all-pervading . . . water . . . the seed of all living beings . . . identical with fire . . . one with air . . . identical with the atmosphere . . . the direction of the faculties of sense . . . one with the senses, both subtle and substantial, the recipient of all impressions, the root of all knowledge. He is the infinite . . . and . . . both as every object and agent, preserves the universe. Thou, Achyuta, art the gods . . . goblins, evil spirits, men, animals, birds, insects, reptiles, plants, and stones, earth, water, fire, sky, wind, sound, touch, taste, colour, flavour, mind, intellect, soul, time, and the qualities of nature: thou art all these, and the chief object of them all. Thou art knowledge and ignorance, truth and falsehood, poison and ambrosia. . . . The universe is thy intellectual form. . . . I glorify the supreme deity Vishnu, the universal witness, who seated internally, beholds the good and ill of all . . . in whom everything is warped and woven (or rather 'woven as the warp and woof' [footnote]). . . . Glory, again and again, to that being to whom all returns, from whom all proceeds; who is all, and in whom all things are: to him whom I also am; for he is everywhere; through whom all things are from me. I am all things: all things are in me, who am everlasting. I am undecayable, ever enduring, the receptacle of the spirit of the supreme. Brahma is my name; the supreme soul, that is before all things, that is after the end of all. (pp. 6–142 passim).

The last of these prayers was uttered by Prahlada (in whose story it occurs), who,

thus meditating upon Vishnu, as identical with his own spirit, . . . became as one with him, and finally regarded himself as the divinity: he forgot entirely his own individuality, and was conscious of nothing else than his being the inexhaustible, eternal, supreme soul; and in consequence of the efficacy of this conviction of identity, the imperishable Vishnu, whose essence is wisdom, became present in his heart, which was wholly purified from sin. As soon as, through the force of his contemplation, Prahlada had become one with Vishnu, the bonds with which he was bound burst instantly asunder . . . and again he hymned . . . Purushottama . . . : "Om! glory . . . to thee, lord, who are subtile and substantial; mutable and immutable; perceptible and imperceptible . . . minute and vast; . . . hideousness and beauty; ignorance and wisdom; . . . comprehending all that is good and evil. . . . Oh thou who art large and small, manifest and hidden; who art all beings. . . ."[441]

Though Whitman, as we have seen, fashioned the "Song of Myself" and the "Myself" of the "Song" after the more elaborated character of the yogi in Ward's pages, it is possible that he found additional support and encouragement in the conduct of Prahlada, who "became as one with" God's Absolute Self. We have in him the same mystical identification of himself with the Absolute.[442] That apart, from among these descriptions of the nature of the Supreme Soul, much seems to have gone into his thought. Malcolm Cowley, speaking of the ideas in *Leaves of Grass,* says: "In some ways this God of the first edition resembles Emerson's Oversoul, but he seems much closer to the Brahman of the *Upanishads,* the absolute, unchanging, all-ending Consciousness, the Divine Ground from which all things emanate and to which all living things may hope to return. And this Divine Ground is by no means the only conception that Whitman shared with Indian philosophers, in the days when he was writing 'Song of Myself.'" Among these other conceptions, Cowley mentions the notion that "true knowledge is to be acquired not through the senses or the intellect, but through union with the Self," and that "this true knowledge is available to every man and woman, since each conceals a divine Self." He adds, "Such parallels—and there are dozens that might be quoted—are more than accidental. They reveal a kinship in thinking and experience. . . ."[443] Speaking of Whitman's Pantheism, Gabriel Sarrazin remarks:

For him, Nature and God are one. God is the universe, or, to speak more exactly, the mystery at once visible and hidden in the universe. . . . Living in happy harmony with all the aspects of the Cosmos, even the most sombre, he exclaims at the close of 'Leaves of Grass,' his great collection of poems: 'And henceforth I will go and celebrate anything I see or am . . . and deny nothing.' And then in effect, he says: God being in all things and everywhere, how can I help loving Him in all things and everywhere. . . .

. . . From this flows that mighty and sacred joy which laughs through the whole work . . . from this . . . his worship of forms and of colours . . . [and] his adoration of the body. . . . When all is full of the Spirit, when all is divine, what evil is there in the fact that the source of life lies in bubbling passion and frenzy. . . . In the light of thought all things are necessary, because divine—all, even vice and crime.[444]

The conceptions that Cowley describes in Whitman, and the Pantheism, the adoration of the universe, even of the evil in it, that Sarrazin speaks of, are all in the extracts quoted above from *Vishnu Purana,* which appear to have given him many another suggestion besides. One of the major images that recur in his poetry is that of the sea and the ship. His *Leaves of Grass* is a "lone bark cleaving the ether," "full of faith," spreading her "white sails," "athwart the imperious waves" ("In Cabin'd Ships at Sea"). His soul is a "shipmate," his life a "ship"; "clear at last" "at death," "she swiftly courses from the shore" ("Joy, Shipmate, Joy!"); it is a "Voyager" bidding a "finale to the shore" of this world, to "depart upon" the "endless cruise" of eternal life ("Now Finale to the Shore"). As a "batter'd, wreck'd old man," he is "thrown on this savage shore, far, far from home" ("Prayer of Columbus"). The concept of life as an ocean and the soul as a ship is particularly the theme of "Aboard at a Ship's Helm":

But O the ship, the immortal ship! O ship aboard the ship!
Ship of the body, ship of the soul, voyaging, voyaging, voyaging.

In "As I Ebbed with the Ocean of Life" he clearly calls life an ocean. In "Yet, Yet, Ye Downcast Hours" he calls upon the sea which he is "quickly to sail" to come and tell him "where [he is] speeding" and where is his "destination." "As a ship on the waters advancing," is "the voyage of the soul," of which he will sing in "Gliding O'er All." And one of the favorite analogies of Hindu speculation for life is the ocean: God, as in the extracts above, is "he who bears mortals across the ocean of existence." Prahlada elsewhere again speaks of "this ocean of the world, this sea of many sorrows."[445]

The prayers also praised God as "the universal witness, who seated internally, beholds the good and ill of all." In all probability this description inspired Whitman to write his "I Sit and Look Out":

> I sit and look out upon all the sorrows of the world, and upon
>   all oppression and shame,
> . . . [A list of the sorrows he hears and sees:]
> All these—all the meanness and agony without end I sitting
>   look out upon,
> See, hear, and am silent.

And it is the same "universal witness" in all, "seated internally," that he speaks of in "Tests":

> All submit to them where they sit, inner, secure, unapproach-
>   able to analysis in the soul. . . .

In a passage quoted early in this study was the notion of the fourfold aspects of God, from which the inspiration for Whitman's "Square Deific" was suggested to have come. The twenty-second chapter of Book I of *The Vishnu Purana* deals with this theme at length. This discussion of "the fourfold essence of the supreme spirit" that "is composed of true wisdom, pervades all things, is only to be appreciated by itself, and admits of no similitude," appears to have supplied something more. Here, in part, is the description of "the four varieties of the condition of Brahma," and of "the supreme condition":

> . . . The third kind is the ascertainment of the identity of the end
> and the means, the rejection of the notion of duality. The last
> kind is . . . contemplation of the true essence of soul. The
> supreme condition of Vishnu, who is one with wisdom, is
> the knowledge of truth; which requires no exercise; which is not
> to be taught; which is internally diffused; which is unequalled;

the object of which is self-illumination; which is simply existent, and is not to be defined; which is tranquil, fearless, pure;
which is not the theme of reasoning; which stands in need of no
support.[446]

A footnote explains, with the original Sanskrit terms:

The epithets of Jnyana, "wisdom," here employed, are taken
from the Yoga philosophy. "Requires no exercise," . . . is explained, "without the practice of abstract contemplation," &c.
. . . "Not to be taught" . . . "not capable of being enjoined." . . .
"Internally diffused," . . . means "mental identification of individual with universal spirit." . . . "Simply existent" . . . is said to
mean, "being unmodified by the accidents of happiness," &c . . .
consequently it is not to be defined. So the Yoga Pradípa explains Samadhi, or contemplation, to be the entire occupation
of the thoughts by the idea of Brahma, without any effort of
the mind. It is the entire abandonment of the faculties to one
all-engrossing notion. . . . "Tranquil," . . . is, "being void of
passion," &c. . . . "Fearless;" not dreading agitation or perplexity by ideas of duality. . . . "Pure;" "undisturbed by external objects." . . . "Not the theme of reasoning" . . . is, "not
to be ascertained by logical deduction." . . . "Standing in no
need of support" . . . [is] "not resting or depending on perceptible objects."

That is the nature of wisdom which is the knowledge of truth,
according to Yoga. Whitman echoes all this, thus offering incon-
trovertible proof of his reading *The Vishnu Purana:*

Here is the test of wisdom,
Wisdom is not finally tested in schools,
Wisdom cannot be pass'd from one having it to another not
    having it,
Wisdom is of the soul, is not susceptible of proof, is its own
    proof,
Applies to all stages and objects and qualities and is content,
Is the certainty of the reality and immortality of things, and
    the excellence of things. . . .[447]

Logic and sermons never convince,
The damp of the night drives deeper into my soul.[448]

The greatest of thoughts are never put in print. They are not susceptible of proof like a sum in simple multiplication.

There is in the soul an instinctive test of the sense and actuality of anything. . . . Let the test of anything proposed in metaphysics be this instinct of the soul—this self-settling power. . . .[449]

There is . . . in the make-up of every superior human identity . . . a wondrous something that realizes without argument . . . an intuition . . . a soul-sight. . . .[450]

In Metaphysical points, here is what I guess about pure and positive truths. I guess that after all reasoning and analogy, and their most palpable demonstrations of anything, we have the real satisfaction when the soul tells and tests by its own alchemic power—superior to the learnedest proofs. . . .[451]

In these passages, especially the first, which catalogues the virtues of wisdom, we have almost every one of the "epithets" with which it was described by *The Vishnu Purana*. In the extract quoted above from "Carlyle from the American Points of View," we may notice that the poet of the "divine average" mentions "superior human identities"—obviously poets and great men who have "a soul-sight" that others lack. I wonder if the following words in the same chapter of *The Vishnu Purana* influenced that thought:

The blaze of fire burning on one spot diffuses light and heat around; so the world is nothing more than the manifested energy of the supreme Brahma: and inasmuch, Maitreya, as the light and heat are stronger or feebler as we are near to the fire, or far off from it, so the energy of the supreme is more or less intense in the beings that are less or more remote from him. . . .[452]

The Vishnu Purana also told Whitman that "every man reaps the consequences of his own acts;"[453] and so,

The song is to the singer, and comes back most to him,
The teaching is to the teacher, and comes back most to him,
The murder is to the murderer, and comes back most to him,
. . . .

The gift is to the giver, and comes back most to him—it cannot fail.[454]

For, said *The Vishnu Purana*, "Created beings, although they are destroyed (in their individual forms) at the periods of dissolution, yet, being affected by the good or evil acts of former existence, they are never exempted from their consequences."[455] "Death or immunity, prosperity or adversity, are in this life the inevitable consequences of conduct in a prior existence: no man can suffer a penalty which his vices in a preceding state of being have not incurred, nor can he avoid it if they have."[456]

It is true that the doctrine of Karma, which this is, has been gathered by Whitman from the other sources we have noticed, but he is very close to this when he insists in "To Think of Time" that "the law of heroes and good-doers" and of "informers and mean persons cannot be eluded."

Explaining the yoga that seeks "mystic union" with the Supreme Being, a footnote says: "This great Yoga, or union, is to have its relation or dependance . . . , which is Vishnu . . . ; and its seed . . . mystical ejaculations."[457] It is possible that this instruction lies behind the ejaculations that mark "Song of Myself," especially section 33 of it, in which, as we have observed, he is basically reproducing the yogic experience.

Even the famous passage that inspired Emerson's "Brahma" contributes something to Whitman: "What living creature slays, or is slain? [answered Prahlada,] what living creature preserves, or is preserved? Each is his own destroyer or preserver, as he follows evil or good."[458] Whitman in "A song of the Rolling Earth," section 2, says:

Each man to himself and each woman to herself, is the word
   of the past and present, and the true word of immortality;
No one can acquire for another—not one,
Not one can grow for another—not one.

Prahlada's story appears to have fascinated Whitman. In answer to his father's questions regarding "the marvellous powers" he was "possessed of," Prahlada says: "Whatever power I possess, father . . . is no more than that which is possessed by all in whose

hearts Achyuta abides. . . . I wish no evil to any, and do and
speak no offence; for I behold Kesava in all beings, as in my own
soul. . . . Love, then, for all creatures will be assiduously cherished
by all those who are wise in the knowledge that Hari is all
things."[459] So does what belongs to Whitman belong to all, and
his message is that "whoever walks a furlong without sympathy
walks to his own funeral drest in his shroud."[460]

If Whitman's account of true wisdom that is "of the soul" so
faithfully echoes the description of it in *Vishnu Purana,* his de-
preciation of the men of "positive science," whose "facts are useful" but are not the "dwelling"[461] of the soul, appears to have been
encouraged by a similar assessment Prahlada makes in reporting
his educational progress to his father, the king:

> It is true that I have been instructed in all these matters
> [viz. "science of polity," "administration of Government,"
> kingly conduct towards "friends or foes" etc., "principles of the
> science" of politics and so on,] by my venerable preceptor, and
> I have learnt them, but I cannot in all approve them. . . . The
> divine Vishnu is in thee, father, in me and in all everywhere
> else; and hence how can I speak of friend or foe, as distinct
> from myself? It is therefore waste of time to cultivate such
> tedious and unprofitable sciences, which are but false knowl-
> edge, and all our energies should be dedicated to the acquire-
> ment of true wisdom.[462]

Prahlada's explanation of that true wisdom is this: "That is
active duty, which is not for our bondage; that is knowledge,
which is for our liberation: all other duty is good only unto weariness; all other knowledge is only the cleverness of an artist.
Knowing this, I look upon all such acquirement as profitless."
Whitman describes his words as "reminders . . . of life untold,
and of freedom and extrication,"[463] a clever use of synonymous
terms. Teaching "the supreme truth" than which "nothing else is
fit to be regarded," Prahlada a little earlier said: "This, then, is
what I declare unto you . . . call to your minds Vishnu, the liberator from all bondage. . . . Verily I say unto you, that you shall
have no satisfaction in various revolutions through this treacherous
world, but that you will obtain placidity forever by propitiating
Vishnu, whose adoration is perfect calm."[464] Whitman, who, in-

cidentally, teaches the same supreme truth of the deathlessness of
soul, offers in place of a "liberator" an "Answerer," who alone
"indicates satisfaction," while "books, friendships, philosophers,
priests, action, pleasure, pride, beat up and down seeking to give
satisfaction."[465] Prahlada's wisdom, again, lies in this thought:
"He who cares not for dominion, he who cares not for wealth,
shall assuredly obtain both in a life to come."[466] Whitman's "Song
of Prudence" assures that of "all self-denial that stood steady and
aloof on wrecks, and saw others fill the seats of the boats," "the
interest will come round"; and elsewhere he preaches:

> You shall not heap what is call'd riches,
> You shall scatter with lavish hand all that you earn or achieve,
> You but arrive at the city to which you were destin'd, you
>   hardly settle yourself to satisfaction before
> you are call'd by an irresistible call to depart,
> . . . .
> You shall not allow the hold of those who spread their
>   reach'd hands toward you.[467]

There are echoes in these lines of more than Prahlada's thought,
but they are of related things, namely, of the transitoriness of life
on earth and of the unprofitability of attachment to the possessions
of this world, from which the perpetually journeying soul has to
depart. And that is a notion with which all the Hindu writings
Whitman read were full, particularly *The Vishnu Purana,* as will
be seen later. In fact, the next words of Prahlada touch on that
too: "All men, illustrious prince, are toiling to be great; but the
destinies of men, and not their exertions, are the cause of greatness. Kingdoms are the gifts of fate. . . . Let him therefore who
covets the goods of fortune be assiduous in the practice of virtue:
let him who hopes for final liberation learn to look upon all
things as equal and the same. Gods, men, animals, birds, reptiles,
are all but forms of one eternal Vishnu, existing as it were detached from himself. By him who knows this, all the existing
world, fixed or movable, is to be regarded as identical with himself, as proceeding alike from Vishnu, assuming a universal form.[468]
With a slight extension of meaning to relate it to the true
spiritual greatness of individuals, the first part of the foregoing
becomes the following in Whitman's "By Blue Ontario's Shore":

It is not the earth, it is not America who is so great,
It is I who am great or to be great, it is You up there, or any
   one. . . . (Sec. 15)

Underneath all, Nativity,
I swear I will stand by my own nativity, pious or impious so
   be it. (Sec. 16)

All things, "gods, men, animals," though "forms of one eternal"
God, existing "as it were detached from himself," Whitman describes with synonymous words:

The simple, compact, well-join'd scheme, myself disintegrated,
   everyone disintegrated yet part of the
   scheme. . . .[469]

Next to the sea, the road is Whitman's favorite image, recurring
frequently in his writings, and being, symbolically, the theme of
"Song of the Open Road," in which he regards "the universe itself
as a road, as many roads, as roads for traveling souls." The symbol
of the journey, and the notion of life as the eternal progress of the
soul in its long travel toward final union with God, are common to
Hindu speculations and have been noticed in the other sources of
Whitman so far surveyed. They occur repeatedly in the *Bhagvat-
Geeta,* as we shall observe later on, and are to be found in *The
Vishnu Purana* too. It is possible that the following passage, with
its attractive phrase, stimulated the poem of the "Open Road,"
though the notion may have been formed elsewhere:

Rishabha, having ruled with equity and wisdom . . . resigned
   the sovereignty of the earth to the heroic Bharata, and . . .
   adopted the life of an anchoret . . . until, emaciated by his
   austerities, . . . he put a pebble in his mouth, and naked went
   the way of all flesh. ("The great road," or "road of heroes."
   . . . The pebble was intended either to compel perpetual silence,
   or to prevent his eating.)[470]

Whitman is not naked on his "open road," but he warns that
the journey may involve "spare diet," at any rate.[471] The idea of
the world as a road "for traveling souls" is found in many pages.
For instance:

Travelling the path of the world for many thousands of births, man attains only the weariness of bewilderment, and is smothered by the dust of imagination. When that dust is washed away by the bland water of real knowledge, then the weariness of bewilderment sustained by the wayfarer through repeated births is removed. When that weariness is relieved, the internal man is at peace, and he obtains that supreme felicity which is unequalled and undisturbed. This soul is (of its own nature) pure, and composed of happiness and wisdom.[472]

In addition to such passages, there are, scattered through the book, phrases like "the road of the Pitris," "the path of the gods," "the splendid, celestial path of Vishnu," and, most significantly, "the path of the Vedas,"[473] which people have to follow.

And it is of the "internal man" of the passage quoted above that Whitman speaks in his "Song of the Open Road":

No husband, no wife, no friend, trusted to hear the confession,
Another self, a duplicate of everyone, skulking and hiding it goes. . . . (Sec. 13)

Even the image of the "city" where his disciples "arrive" only to be "call'd by an irresistible call to depart,"[474] though charged with a deeper meaning, seems to have been taken from the description of the "wandering mendicant" who must "reside but for one night in a village, and not more than five nights at a time in a city; and . . . so abide, that good-will, and not animosity, may be engendered . . . and . . . call nothing his own."[475] There is also, in another chapter, the story of a sage who said, propagating heretic doctrines: "If you are desirous of final emancipation . . . attend to my words, for you are worthy of a revelation which is the door to ultimate felicity. The duties that I will teach you are the secret path to liberation . . . by following them you shall obtain either heaven or exemption from future existence."[476] Whitman's, however, is not a "secret path" but an "open road"; and, as he declared in "Myself and Mine," he will "give nothing as duties."

Whitman's interest in astronomy and his use of astronomical imagery are obvious in his works. In fact he has sprinkled "his writings, poetry and prose, with references to and observations of

the planets, stars, and constellations." While the genuineness of the
enthusiasm, and the more scientific origin of some of this knowledge are probably beyond doubt, the fact cannot be ignored that
the Hindu writings which have supplied him his philosophical
thought also contain a great deal of astronomical thought, for
cosmogony and theogony are bound up in their speculations. His
concept of "evolution," which "to him meant principally cosmic
evolution," need not be particularly ascribed to astronomy, or, in
other words, to the scientific works, as with Allen, because the
notion of cosmic evolution is there in the Hindu discussion of
creation, as, for example, the stanzas of Menu noticed earlier in
our study indicate. Even his "belief in the cyclic processes of creation, disintegration, and recreation, something like Kant's concept of a universe perpetually winding up and unwinding itself,"[477]
is to be found in the verses of Menu, describing how "that immutable Power, by waking and reposing alternately, revivifies and
destroys in eternal succession the whole assemblage of locomotive
and immovable creatures," and "cause[s] them by the gradations of
birth, growth, and dissolution, to revolve in this world."[478] In
The Vishnu Purana it is said that the "four forms" of God "are
the causes of the production of the phenomena of creation, preservation, and destruction," and that "the deity as Time is without
beginning, and his end is not known; and from him the revolutions
of creation, continuance, and dissolution unintermittently succeed."[479] The Sankhya thought, described in the other accounts
surveyed, and reflected in *The Vishnu Purana,* maintains the notion of creation, primary and secondary, "the first explaining how
the universe proceeds from Prakriti, or eternal crude matter; the
second, in what manner the forms of things are developed from the
elementary substances previously evolved, or how they reappear
after their temporary destruction."[480] This "temporary destruction" occurs when Brahma goes to sleep, or, as *The Vishnu Purana*
describes, "the Supreme reposes. . . . He wakes after a season, and
again, as Brahma, becomes the author of creation."[481] The
"Absurd Chronology of the Hindus," a paper-clipping Whitman
possessed,[482] gave statistical details of "the day of Brahma," which
is the period of the universe's existence before it is dissolved for
further creation. The third chapter of Book I of *The Vishnu
Purana* has these statistics and may have been the source of that

article, too. Thus, scientific phraseology apart—words like tril-
lions, quadrillions, sextillions, and so on, with which he expresses
distances in time or space—the sense of the majestic infinity of
creation that astronomical thought produces in him as a lyric
poet, was, along with cosmic symbols suggesting the eternity of
life, presumably raised upon his reading of the Hindu accounts of
creation. One of the passages with an astronomical touch in "Song
of Myself," in which his poetic fancy is seen "Speeding through
space . . . . speeding through heaven and the stars," is, as we have
discovered, only a verbal imitation of the yogi's thought, with a
slight detail added from scientific journals about Saturn's "broad
ring and the diameter of eighty thousand miles." (Sec. 33) Of
the other significant passage in the same poem, namely section 44,
where (in some confusion, the I that is the uncreated Self becomes the physical Cosmos or Earth that was created), he describes his evolution cosmically, some words were from scientific
treatises, but again the thought was essentially from the philosophical pages of the Hindus. In an early notebook he records his astronomical thought in this vein:

> All the vastness of Astronomy—and space—and systems of
> suns [blank] carried in their computation to the farthest that
> figures are able . . . then multiplied in geometrical progression
> ten thousand billion fold do not more than symbolize the re-
> flection of the reflection, of the spark thrown off a spark, from
> some emanation of God.[483]

The notion of the universe as an emanation of God he had learned
in Menu, who said "all creatures" were "emanations from the
supreme spirit." The "Song of Creation" in *Aitareya Aranya,*
which he read in Colebrooke's essay "On the Vedas," described
"these (various) worlds" God created. And the idea of the indescribable glory of God, greater than His creation, which is Whitman's thought here, is the very burden of Hindu philosophy.

Aside from the notion of the cyclic processes of creation, dissolution, and recreation, which it shares with the other Hindu works,
The Vishnu Purana has a large amount of astronomical thought,
presented with figures though not scientifically accurate. There is a
whole chapter on "the extent and situation of the seven spheres,

viz. earth, sky, planets" and so on, with an "account of the situations and distances of the planets." Other chapters, whatever their mythological fancy, deal with the "planetary system," the sun and its path, the moon and various cosmic phenomena. A few extracts will be given here to show that Whitman's notions of the cosmic principles like expanse, compactness, wasteless economy, progression, ultimate good, and the like, which he repeatedly emphasizes in his chants of the Earth, have their roots in his philosophical readings:

> The sphere of the earth . . . extends as far as it is illuminated by the rays of the sun and moon; and to the same extent, both in diameter and circumference, the sphere of the sky . . . spreads above it. . . . The solar orb is situated a hundred thousand leagues from the earth; and that of the moon an equal distance from the sun. . . . Budha (Mercury) is two hundred thousand leagues above the lunar mansions. . . . (Venus) is at the same distance from Mercury [and so on]. The sphere of the Seven Rishis (Ursa Major) is a hundred thousand leagues above Saturn. . . . Such . . . is the elevation of the three spheres (Bhur, Bhuvar, Swar). . . . [Then follows the account of the other four.] These seven spheres together with the Patalas [netherlands or spheres of Hell] form . . . the extent of the whole world.[484]

In addition to the sense of the vastness of the universe, this description could have suggested the "spheres" that Whitman's soul visits "to look at the product" of their "orchards," though the word "quintillion" and the notion of the yet "green" spheres may have come from astronomical speculations.[485] In "Song at Sunset" he calls space the "sphere of unnumber'd spirits." *The Vishnu Purana* has a description of the other "locas" or "spheres" where "saints," "pure-minded sons of Brahma," "the deities," and so on, live.[486]

In "A Song of the Rolling Earth" is the following splendid passage:

> Tumbling on steadily, nothing dreading,
> Sunshine, storm, cold, heat, forever withstanding, passing, carrying,

The soul's realization and determination still inheriting,
The fluid vacuum around and ahead still entering and
    dividing,
. . . .
The divine ship sails the divine sea. (Sec. 1)

The "divine ship" is of course the earth, sailing the "divine
sea" of time and space to achieve the realization of the soul. The
sense of the divinity of the earth may have nothing special about it
in a poet who sang of the divinity of everything. But yet both the
divinity of the earth and the imagery of its sailing along "the fluid
vacuum around and ahead" seem to have been suggested by *The
Vishnu Purana,* in which there is the story of the Goddess Earth
(Prithvi) praising the Lord, upon which "the supreme, being
thus eulogized, upholding the earth, raised it quickly, and placed it
on the summit of the ocean, where it floats like a mighty vessel."[487]
And in the chapter we are examining at the moment is a further
description of the world:

> The world is encompassed on every side and above and below by
> the shell of the egg of Brahma. . . . Around the outer surface of
> the shell flows water, . . . [finally] encircled by the chief
> Principle, Pradhana [or Nature], . . . within [which] resides
> Soul, diffusive, conscious, and self-irradiating. . . . Nature
> (Pradhana) and soul (Puman) are both of the character of
> dependants, and are encompassed by the energy of Vishnu,
> which is one with the soul of the world, and which is the cause
> of the separation of those two (soul and nature) at the period
> of dissolution; of their aggregation in the continuance of things;
> and of their combination at the season of creation.[488]

"Within Pradhana [Nature] resides Soul." Whitman has his
"Me imperturbe, standing at ease in Nature," "aplomb in the midst
of irrational things" with qualities like "passive," "receptive,"
"silent," "self-balanced," and so on, just as the Sankhya and the
Vedanta accounts describe the soul.[489]

The notion of the wasteless economy in creation, of the principle of evolution, and of the final realization of God, are all in these
lines:

As a tree, consisting of root, stem, and branches, springs from a primitive seed, and produces other seeds, whence grow other trees analogous to the first in species, product, and origin, so from the first unexpanded germ (of nature, or Pradhana) spring Mahat (Intellect) and the other rudiments of things; from them proceed the grosser elements; from them men and gods, who are succeeded by sons and the sons of sons. In the growth of a tree from the seed, no detriment occurs to the parent plant, neither is there any waste of beings by the generation of others. In like manner as space and time and the rest are the cause of the tree (through the materiality of the seed), so the divine Hari is the cause of all things by successive developments (through the materiality of nature). As all the parts of the future plant, existing in the seed . . . , spontaneously evolve when they are in approximation with the subsidiary means of growth (or earth or water), so gods, men, and other beings, involved in many actions (or necessarily existing in those states which are the consequences of good or evil acts), become manifested only in their full growth, through the influence of the energy of Vishnu.

This Vishnu is the supreme spirit (Brahma), from whence all this world proceeds, who is this world, by whom the world subsists, and in whom it will be resolved.[490]

Whitman regards the universe as a "compact, well-join'd scheme" ("Crossing Brooklyn Ferry"); does "not see one imperfection in the universe" ("Song at Sunset"); holds that "what is prudence is indivisible . . . in the unshakable order of the universe" ("Song of Prudence"); believes that "in this broad earth of ours . . . nestles the seed perfection," of which "every life" has "a share or more or less," and "the partial to the permanent" flows ("Song of the Universal"); and with "All, all toward the mystic ocean tending," ("As Consequent, Etc.") is convinced of the "rendezvous" "appointed" with God waiting there ("Song of Myself").

Whitman's knowledge of the concept of Maya, or illusion, has come to him from each one of the Hindu sources he read. He seems to have been more seriously affected by the notion toward the end of his life when the yogic certainties he had ardently imposed on himself begin to wear thin, and he begins to doubt even his messages:

  A vague mist hanging 'round half the pages:
  (Sometimes how strange and clear to the soul,
  That all these solid things are indeed but apparitions,
    concepts, non-realities.)[491]

And "divine" as things are, they are "deceitful ones," for their
"glamour" is only "seeming."[492] But in the first words with which
he was playing with the idea in the 1860 poem "Of the Terrible
Doubt of Appearances," quoted partly earlier, he is echoing the
following admonition of Parasara:

  You must conceive therefore mountains, oceans, and all the
  diversities of earth and the rest, are the illusions of the apprehension. . . . For what is substance? . . . How can reality be
  predicated of that which is subject to change . . . ? . . . Say, is
  this reality? though it be so understood by man, whose self-
  knowledge is impeded by his own acts. Hence, Brahman, except
  discriminative knowledge, there is nothing anywhere or at any
  time, real. . . . Knowledge single and eternal—is the supreme
  Vasudeva [God], besides whom there is nothing. . . . That
  knowledge . . . is truth; from which all that differs is
  false. . . .[493]

To Whitman's thought of equality the following passage from
the story of Bharata, a "wise man," appears to have made an
interesting contribution. Carrying the palanquin of a proud king
who asks if he has become weary, the learned Brahmin philosophically replies:

  The assertion that you behold the palankin borne by me, or
  placed on me, is untrue. . . . This body which is seated in the
  palankin is defined as Thou; thence what is elsewhere called
  This, is here distinguished as I and Thou. I and thou and
  others are constructed of the elements; and the elements, following the stream of qualities, assume a bodily shape. . . . The
  pure, imperishable soul tranquil, void of qualities, prominent
  over nature (Prakriti), is one, without increase or diminution,
  in all bodies. . . . That which is the substance of the palankin is
  the substance of you and me and all others, being an aggregate
  of elements, aggregated by individuality.[494]

Whitman opened his "Song of Myself" by saying: "Every atom belonging to me as good belongs to you."

In the poem "Of the Terrible Doubt of Appearances," Whitman said:

> May-be seeming to me what they are (as doubtless they indeed
> but seem) as from my present point of view, and might
> prove (as of course they would) nought of what they
> appear, or nought anyhow, from entirely changed points
> of view.

The gift of these further words of Bharata to Whitman's line can easily be recognized:

> . . . Who are you? who am I? . . . The thing which in the
> world is called a king, the servant of a king, or by any other
> appellation, is not a reality; it is the creature of our imagina-
> tions: for what is there in the world, that is subject to vicissi-
> tude, that does not in the course of time go by different names.
> Thou art called the monarch of the world; the son of thy
> father; the enemy of thy foes; the husband of thy wife; the
> father of thy children. . . . Now then, rightly understanding
> the question, think who I am. . . .[495]

"Who are you? who am I?" asked the wise man, and thus continued his explanation:

> Thou art a king; this is a palankin; these are the bearers; these
> the running footmen; this is thy retinue: yet it is untrue that all
> these are said to be thine. The palankin on which thou sittest is
> made of timber derived from a tree. What then? is it denom-
> inated either timber or a tree? People do not say that the king
> is perched on a tree. . . . The vehicle is an assemblage of pieces
> of timber, artificially joined together. . . . Again; contemplate
> the sticks of the umbrella, in their separate state. Where then is
> the umbrella? Apply this reasoning to thee and to me. A man,
> a woman, a cow, a goat, a horse, an elephant, a bird, a tree, are
> names assigned to various bodies which are the consequences of
> acts. Man ('Pumán'—'used generically' [footnote]) is neither
> a god, nor a man, nor a brute, nor a tree; these are mere
> varieties of shape, the effects of acts. . . .

A little earlier, in answer to the King's question, "Who are you?"
Bharata had said, "Who I am it is not possible to say: arrival at
any place is for the sake of fruition; and enjoyment of pleasure, or
endurance of pain, is the cause of the production of the body. A
living being assumes a corporeal form to reap the results of virtue
or vice."[496] All this discussion has a condensed echo in Whitman's
"Song of Myself":

> What is a man anyhow? What am I? what are you?
> All I mark as my own you shall offset it with your own,
> Else it were time lost listening to me. (Sec. 20)

"Fruition," for which the soul of man arrives "at any place," or
condition of existence, is "soul's realization and determination"
that the "divine ship" inherits in "A Song of the Rolling Earth";
and it is as the Universal Man (Puman) who assumes the "various
bodies," "varieties of shape," of a goat, a horse, an elephant and
so on, quite as much (if it must be so regarded) as the Darwinian
Man, that he remembers "having passed that way" of the animals
"untold times ago" to be able to accept "their relations" to him and
recognize the "tokens" of himself they have "plainly in their
possession."[497]

The dialogue between Bharata and the King in the next chapter
turns upon the question of "the most desirable object" in life, "the
best of all things." Bharata replies:

> You, again, ask me what is the best of all things, not what is the
> great end of life. . . . Hundreds and thousands of conditions may
> be called the best; but these are not the great and true ends of
> life. . . . Wealth cannot be the true end of life . . . [nor] a
> son. . . . Final and supreme truth, therefore, would not exist in
> this world, as in all these cases those objects which are so de-
> nominated are the effects of causes, and consequently are not
> finite. . . . Acquisition of sovereignty . . . [or] the objects to be
> effected by sacrificial rites . . . any effect which is produced
> through the causality of earth partakes of the character of its
> origin, and . . . must itself be of but temporary efficacy. The
> great end of life (or truth) is considered by the wise to be
> eternal; but it would be transient, if it were accomplished
> through transitory things. If you imagine that this great truth
> is the performance of religious acts, . . . it is not so; for such

acts are the means of obtaining liberation, and truth is (the end), not the means. Meditation on self, again, is said to be for the sake of supreme truth; but the object of this is to establish distinctions (between soul and body), and the great truth of all is without distinctions. . . . What the great end of all is, you shall, monarch, briefly learn from me. It is soul: one (in all bodies), pervading, uniform, perfect, preeminent over nature (Prakriti), exempt from birth, growth, and decay, omnipresent, undecaying, made up of true knowledge, independent, and unconnected with unrealities, with name, species, and the rest, in time present, past, or to come. The knowledge that this is spirit, which is essentially one, is in one's own and in all other bodies, is the great end, or true wisdom, of one who knows the unity and the true principles of things.[498]

The wisdom in Whitman that "knows the unity" of things, the one soul of all bodies, and even the great truth that is "without distinctions," is too freely attested by all his writings to need any illustration here. But his use of the other parts of this exhortation may be specially noticed. His "Song of the Open Road," as we observed earlier, works upon the idea that wealth is not the end of life. In section 9 of the same poem, he nearly sums up the entire advice of Bharata when he says:

Allons! We must not stop here,
However sweet these laid-up stores, however convenient this
    dwelling we cannot remain here,
However shelter'd this port and however calm these waters
    we must not anchor here,
However welcome the hospitality that surrounds us we are
    permitted to receive it but a little while.

In the Preface to the 1855 edition of *Leaves of Grass,* he urged: "American bards . . . shall not be careful of riches and privilege. . . . The most affluent man is he that confronts all the shows he sees by equivalents out of the stronger wealth of himself."[499] For the gifts of the earth are of "but a little while," or "transient," and, like Bharata, he knows that "the eternal real life to come" is that to which the "soul" must be shaped;[500] and like him, again, he has a contempt for "religious acts," "rites or sacrifices," for he cries:

Allons! from all formules!
From your formules, O bat-eyed and materialistic priests.[501]

The "soul" is "preeminent over nature," said Bharata: Whitman
declared in the Preface that the soul does "tread master here and
everywhere, Master of spasms of the sky and of the shatter of the
sea, Master of nature."[502]
At the end of "Song of Myself," Whitman announces:

I depart as air. . . . I shake my white locks at the runaway sun,
I effuse my flesh in eddies and drift it in lacy jags.
. . . .
You will hardly know who I am or what I mean,
. . . .
Failing to fetch me at first keep encouraged,
Missing me one place search another,
I stop somewhere waiting for you.

A simple poetic fancy working on the parting words of the invisible, universal self, could of itself create such thoughts as these.
Yet it is possible that behind them lay the memory of what was said
by another sage called Ribhu, who, in a story told by Bharata,
instructs his disciple Nidagha in "perfect knowledge":

For your three other questions, Where I dwell? Whither I
go? and Whence I come? hear this reply. Man (the soul of
man) goes everywhere, and penetrates everywhere, like the
ether; and is it rational to enquire where it is? or whence or
whither thou goest? I neither am going nor coming, nor is my
dwelling in any one place; nor art thou, thou; nor are others,
others; nor am I, I.

And having taught "the ultimate truth," the sage, in reply to an
insistent enquiry from his disciple as to who he was, finally answers: "I am Ribhu, your preceptor, come hither to communicate
to you true wisdom; and having declared to you what that is, I
shall depart."[503]
In another story that follows, an ancient verse is quoted, which
teaches: "Desire is not appeased by enjoyment. . . . No one has
ever more than enough of rice, or barley, or gold, or cattle, or

women: abandon therefore inordinate desire. When a man finds neither good nor ill in all objects, but looks on all with an equal eye, then everything yields it pleasure."[504] It is these objects of desire "who spread their reach'd hands toward" us that Whitman warns against in his "Song of the Open Road"; and it is with this "equal eye" that he could sing the "Song of Joys" for "manhood, womanhood, infancy," "common employments," "old age," "death," in a word, "everything yields [him] pleasure."

> Whoever you are! motion and reflection are especially for you,
> The divine ship sails the divine sea for you,

Whitman mystically announces in "A Song of the Rolling Earth." "Motion" certainly carries the sense of the eternal journey of the soul, or the endless process of cosmic evolution in which the human being is involved, "the voyage we pursue." The word "reflection" is obviously of an equally profound meaning, and that seems to be the one in which the following passage in *The Vishnu Purana* uses it:

> It should therefore be the assiduous endeavour of wise men to attain unto god. The means of such attainment are said, great Muni, to be knowledge and works. Knowledge is of two kinds, that which is derived from scripture, and that which is derived from reflection. Brahma that is the word is composed of scripture; Brahma that is supreme is composed of reflection. . . . (Brahma is of two kinds: Sabda-Brahma, spirit or god to be attained through the word, that is, the Vedas and the duties they prescribe; and Para-Brahma, spirit or god to be attained through reflection.)[505]

Works, hearing the word, and reflection all attain unto god, or "the soul's realization." Though Whitman does not speak of "works," he seems to have had this in his mind when he wrote his lines, for in the same context he says:

> The true words do not fail, for motion does not fail and reflection does not fail,
> Also the day and night do not fail, and the voyage we pursue does not fail.

Even the word "motion" was probably suggested by the same passage describing a wise man as "one who knows the origin and end and revolutions of beings."[506]

Of the "condition" in which Whitman thought of "imagining" himself, namely, the yogic exercise, and of "the benefits of the Yoga," *The Vishnu Purana* has an elaborate account in a long chapter, but this subject has been given ample notice already. However, a couple of items in the accompanying discussion deserve attention.

The poet of the soul who was also the poet of the body, the poet who worshiped the senses, Whitman wrote in 1860 a poem of "Says," short aphorisms that put us in mind of the "Heetopades of Veeshnoo Sarma." One of these wise "says" is:

> I have said many times that materials and the Soul are great
>   and that all depends on physique;
> Now I reverse what I said ....
>   ....
>
> And I affirm now that the mind governs—and that all depends
>   on the mind.[507]

And in the same affirmation he wrote in *Democratic Vistas:*

> We have again pointedly to confess that all the objective grandeurs of the world, for highest purposes, yield themselves up, and depend on mentality alone. Here, and here only, all balances, all rests. For the mind, which alone builds the permanent edifice, haughtily builds it to itself. By it . . . are convey'd to mortal sense the culminations of the materialistic, the known, and a prophecy of the unknown. . . . We must not say one word against real materials; but the wise know that they do not become real till touched by emotions, the mind.[508]

Apart from the echo in the above lines of the Sankhya thought that intellect or mind collects the knowledge of the senses and communicates it to soul, whose intercourse with the material world is through the instrumentality of intellect alone, the importance accorded to mind in both the rejected poem and the prose passage appears to have been the product of his reading what the philosophical pages of the Hindus said about it. In an earlier account we discovered that the restraining of the mind and fixing it on internal meditation was called Yoga. The discussion we are now examining says: "The mind of man is the cause both of his bondage and his liberation: its addiction to the objects of sense is the means of his bondage; its separation from objects of sense is the means of his freedom. The sage who is capable of discriminative knowledge must therefore restrain his mind from all the objects of sense. . . . Contemplative devotion is the union with Brahma, effected by that condition of mind which has attained perfection through those exercises which complete the control of self."[509]

In the explanatory footnotes are some very interesting statements:[510]

The term Yoga . . . in its literal acceptation signifies "union," "junction," from (yug) "to join:" in a spiritual sense it denotes "union of separated with universal soul." . . .

When the mind has attained the state [through the yogic exercises] then the union with Brahma, which is the consequence, is called Yoga. . . . Union with Brahma is the abstraction that proposes the identity of the living with the supreme spirit. . . .

There are various postures in which the Yogi is directed to sit when he engages in meditation. In the Bhadrásana he is directed to cross his legs underneath him, and to lay hold of his feet on each side with his hands.

In the body of the discussion of Yoga, it is said:

The meditating sage must think (he beholds internally the figure) of Vishnu, as having a pleased and lovely countenance, with eyes like the leaf of the lotus, smooth cheeks, and a broad and brilliant forehead . . . a broad breast . . . a belly falling in graceful folds, with a deep-seated navel . . . and firm and well-knit thighs and legs, with well-formed feet and toes. . . . When this image never departs from his mind, whether he be going or standing, then he may believe his retention to be perfect. . . . This process of forming a lively image in the mind . . . constitutes Dhyána, or meditation . . . and when an accurate knowledge of self, free from all distinction, is attained by this mental meditation, that is termed Samadhi. . . . (When the Yogi has accomplished this stage, he acquires) discriminative

knowledge . . . [described a little earlier (pp. 654–655) as
"true knowledge, or knowledge of Brahma, *which recognizes no
distinctions,*" namely, "spirit is one thing, and the universe is
another," and "objects" are "distinct and various;" which "contemplates only simple existence, which is undefinable by words,
and is to be discovered solely in one's own spirit"; and which
realizes that the winds . . . the suns, stars, planets . . . men,
animals, oceans, rivers, trees, all beings, and all sources of
beings, all modifications whatever of nature and its products,
whether sentient or unconscious . . . all these are the sensible
form of Hari," and that] there is no difference between it (individual and) supreme spirit. (Italics added)

That is an abridgement of the yoga taught by Keshidhwaja to
Khandikya. When we juxtapose it to the famous section 5 of
"Song of Myself"—which so hopelessly drove Bucke (and many an
other critic) into seeing in it the record of a mystic experience that
made Whitman another Christ, Buddha, or Paul—and leave a
slight margin for the verbal freedom of a poetic imagination, it
will not be difficult to perceive that, like much else in Whitman's
first bid for literary glory, the magnificent description of the so-
called mystic experience is after all a very clever verse paraphrase
of the passages reproduced above. There is the "union" or "junction"; whether the other party invited to join him "on the grass"
is given the fairer sex, or, in consonance with the "robust American
love"[511] "of manly attachment"[512] that he preached and practised
in life, he was, in poetic fancy, content with the "lovely" figure of
Vishnu. In other words, whatever the specifications of sex (which,
incidentally, is irrelevant for understanding the passage), the details of the act of the "union of [the] separated with [the] universal soul" are there mere verbal extensions of Bhadrasana, the
posture of yogic union. It may be the phrenological "springs of
courage"[513] or the self-consciousness of the feminine proclivity of
his sexual discord[514] that rearranged the gestures of the parties to
the union, but the act of holding the feet is there. And the "true
knowledge" that is acquired after the union is also there, almost in
all its details.

Much as "Song of the Universal" is worked upon in our study,
we shall return to it just once more to show that the chapter in
The Vishnu Purana we are noticing shaped its opening section
about the "seed perfection" nestling "in this broad earth of ours,"

of which "every life [has] a share or more or less," for "none born it is born, conceal'd or unconceal'd the seed is waiting." Said Kesidhwaja:

> All this universal world, this world of moving and stationary beings, is pervaded by the energy of Vishnu, who is of the nature of the supreme Brahma. . . . The energy . . . is characterized by different degrees of perfection in all created beings. In things without life it exists in a small degree: it is more in things that have life, but are (without motion) : in insects it is still more abundant, and still more in birds; it is more in wild animals, and in domestic animals the faculty is still greater: men have more of this (spiritual) faculty than animals, and thence arises their authority over them.[515]

"Supreme truth cannot be defined, for it is not to be explained by words," said the same passage (p. 659). Whitman says: "I swear to you there are divine things more beautiful than words can tell" ("Song of the Open Road"), "The best of the earth cannot be told anyhow" ("A Song of the Rolling Earth"), and "I am charged with untold and untellable wisdom" ("Of the Terrible Doubt of Appearances").

From the many legends and myths in *The Vishnu Purana* that veil metaphysical ideas in allegorical representation, and the copious footnotes with their explanatory comment on the doctrinal element of the pages, Whitman can be seen to have received a considerable amount of the philosophical emotion that marks his poetic fancy, as well as tiny details of phrase and thought, which he works with skill into the body of his poems. It would be a wearisome affair to make an exhaustive study of all these diffuse and fragmentary contributions of the book to his pages. Only a few, therefore, are mentioned here.

In a chapter dealing with the measure of time from a day of the mortal earth to that of Brahma, it is declared "that Time is a form of Vishnu," or God (p. 22). There is the notion of evolution in Chapter 5 of Book I, which describes "the stages of creation [which] are seven," from "the immovable things," "the mineral and vegetable kingdoms," "the solid earth, with its mountains and rivers and seas . . . already prepared for their reception," "the animal creation," and so on, to the "creatures [that] were mankind" (pp. 35–36, nn.). Elsewhere it is said: "The various stages of existence, Maitreya, are inanimate things, fish, birds, animals, men, holy men, gods, and liberated spirits; each in succession a thousand degrees superior to that which precedes it: and through these stages the beings . . . are destined to proceed, until final emancipation be obtained" (p. 210). "This Earth," says another page, "the mother, the nurse, the receptacle, and nourisher of all existent things, was produced from the sole of the foot of Vishnu" (p. 105). With regard to the "peopling of the earth," it is explained that "from that period forwards [of Daksha, a patriarch] living creatures were engendered by sexual intercourse," formerly being "propagated" by the will, by sight, by touch, and so on (pp. 115–116). In another page, "the commencement of production [of creatures] through sexual agency is . . . described with sufficient distinctness" (n., p. 51). "Amongst them of old [Rishis and sages, possessing divine wisdom, and "not perplexed" by the law that "birth and death are constant in all creatures"] there was neither senior nor junior" (p. 116). One of the duties of a householder is: "Having risen, he must offer adoration to the sun . . . and with a lively faith worship the gods," the prayer to the sun beginning with "salutation" (pp. 300–303). There are frequent references to the "sacred grass": "holy grass, for the worship of the deity" (pp. 245–243). And the definition of "Nakedness" is "secession": "naked (seceder)"; "Those who have seceded from their original belief are said to be naked, because they have thrown off the garment of the Vedas" (p. 341).

More significant than all this is the fact that the poem "Salut au Monde!" or "Poem of Salutation" as it was first called, in which Whitman's spirit passes "in compassion and determination around the whole earth" and views "all the haunts and homes of men" to "salute all the inhabitants" thereof, is inspired by Book II of *The Vishnu Purana*,[516] the second to the fourth chapters of which give "a description of the earth: how many are its oceans and islands, its kingdoms and its mountains, its forests and rivers and the cities of the gods, its dimensions, its contents, its nature, and its form"—of the earth "that is the mother and nurse of all creatures, the foundation of all worlds"—the earth where, in "his universal form," "Vishnu resides," "for Hari pervades all places: He, Maitreya, is the supporter of all things; he is all things."

Chapter II has an account of "the seven great insular continents," which are "surrounded severally by seven great seas," "the boundary mountains," and "their ranges," the "rivers," the "cities of gods," and "the agreeable forests and pleasant cities" "peopled by celestial spirits."[517] Chapter III describes "Bhárata-Varsha [India]: extent: chief mountains: nine divisions: principal rivers and mountains of Bhárata proper: principal nations." The "topographical lists," added from the *Mahabharata,* catalogue "mountains and rivers" and "people and countries."[518] Chapter IV has an "account of kings, divisions, mountains, rivers, and inhabitants of the other Dwipas [or continents] . . . of the oceans separating them: of the tides: of the confines of the earth."[519] And this "detail of the geographical system"[520] terminates with the usual reminder that the "supreme spirit . . . from whence all this world proceeds . . . is the world, in [him] the world subsists, and . . . will be resolved,"[521] thus explaining even Whitman's "incarnation of geography"[522] in his poem.

Curiously enough, not only do "these flights [in which] the poet visualizes the steamships, railroads, harbors, canals, and highways around the globe," and in which "the history of the race comes alive on the projection screen of his fantasy,"[523] closely parallel those of Parasara who described the "orb of the earth" and "enumerated its oceans, mountains, continents, regions and rivers," but even the dialogic form of the original is imitated in Whitman. There is, however, this difference: he plays both the teacher who asked: "What else do you wish to hear?" and the disciple who requested: "I am now desirous to hear from you a description of the earth," while being, at the same time, the supreme spirit of "Song of Myself." Maitreya, the disciple, asks: "How many are its oceans and islands, its kingdoms and its mountains, its forests and rivers . . . ?" In the opening section of his poem, Whitman becomes the Inquirer:

What waves and soils exuding?
What climes? what persons and cities are here?
. . . .

What rivers are these? What forests and fruits are there?
What are the mountains call'd that rise so high in the mists?
What myriads of dwellings are they fill'd with dwellers?

Even the word "fruits" echoes the source of his inspiration,
which describes "the apples of that tree [the Jambu-tree]." "Soil,"
too, is taken from the sentence: "The soil on the banks of the river,
absorbing the Jambu juice . . . becomes the gold termed Jam-
bunada." The "mountains" that "rise so high" resemble the
"boundary mountains" of the original, "two thousand yojanas in
height."[524]

Then, in section 2, Whitman becomes the Answerer, and says:
"Asia, Africa, Europe, are to the east—America is . . . in the
west." Parasara said: "The country of Bhadráswa lies on the east
of Meru, and Ketumala on the west."

The term "Answerer" that Whitman coined to describe the
prophet-poet who

What can be answered . . . answers, and what cannot be
answered . . . shows how it cannot be answered[525]

may have been suggested to him by *The Vishnu Purana* too, in
which what "is equal in sanctity to the Vedas" was narrated by a
"holy teacher" to a disciple. The latter, eager for "acquirement of
knowledge," asks him: "Master . . . I am now desirous, oh thou
who art profound in piety! to hear from thee, how this world was,
and how in future it will be? what is its substance, oh Brahman,
and whence proceeded animate and inanimate beings? . . . how
were the elements manifested? whence proceeded the gods and
other beings? What are the situation and extent of the oceans and
the mountains, the earth, the sun, and the planets? . . . All these
things I wish to hear from you."[526] And all through the narration
he keeps up the questioning, in answer to which the learned sage
propounds "the most excellent of all holy writings," and then says:
"If there is anything else you wish to hear, propose your question,
and I will answer it."[527] For, "the invariable form of the Puranas
is that of a dialogue, in which some person relates its contents in
reply to the inquiries of another."[528] Whitman was probably working on this thought when he wrote the following experimental

fragment from which later the full-grown "Answerer" emerged:

> See'st thou?
> Know'st thou?
> The Three of the Three—
> There is on the one part—
> Between this beautiful but dumb earth, with all manifold
>   eloquent but inarticulate shows and objects,
> And on the other part the being Man, curious, questioning
>   and at fault,
> Now between the two comes the poet the Answerer.[529]

A curious feature of *Leaves of Grass* is the declaration of its intentions at the commencement (made in the section of "Inscriptions") and of its achievement at the close (made in "Songs of Parting" and "Good-bye My Fancy"). Not content, like other poets, with saying what he has been given to say by the "call," or the "flash [that] started [the] endless train of all,"[530] Whitman must say that he is going to say something and announce it in outline, and afterwards say in recapitulation that he has said it. "Starting from Paumanok," declaring what he "will sing" or "show" or "make," and pointing out what the readers are to "see," and "L. of G.'s Purport" or "So Long," declaring what he has "pressed through" or "sung" or "suffered," illustrate this peculiar detail, which might have been a conscious emulation of the Hindu practice by which the narrator of *The Vishnu Purana* announces at the start of the narrative: "I will relate to you the whole, even all of you have asked," and at the end sums it all up, saying: "I have related to you this Purana. . . . In this have been described . . . [the many subjects treated in it]." And, almost as if he were establishing his credentials as a teacher, Whitman, in his act of announcement, declares:

> I conn'd old times,
> I sat studying at the feet of the great masters,
> . . . .
> Dead poets, philosophs, priests,
> Martyrs, artists, inventors, governments long since,
> Language-shapers on other shores,
> . . . .
> I have perused. . . .[531]

Similarly, the "excellent sage" who narrated *The Vishnu Purana* "was versed in traditional history, and the Puranas . . . was acquainted with the Vedas, and the branches of science dependent upon them; and skilled in law and philosophy," and he was only narrating "all that was told [him] formerly by Vasistha, and by the wise Paulastya."[532]

Whitman's mystic adoration of America that is especially the "stage" on which "is acted God's calm annual drama," the "envy of the globe," the "miracle,"[533] and "the beautiful world of new superber birth" which shall "soar toward the fulfilment of the future," namely, "the soul, its destinies, the real real,"[534] appears to have borrowed a little of the enthusiasm with which the narrator of *The Vishnu Purana* regards Bhárata-varsha or India among all the countries of the world:

> Bhárata . . . is the land of works, in consequence of which men go to heaven, or obtain emancipation. . . . From this region heaven is obtained. . . . [Then follows a description of the land, and of the activities of its people "all for the sake of another world."] . . . Bhárata is therefore the best of the divisions of [the earth], because it is the land of works: the others are places of enjoyment alone. It is only after many thousand births, and the aggregation of much merit, that living beings are sometimes born in Bhárata as men. The gods themselves exclaim, "Happy are those who are born, even from the condition of gods, as men in Bhárata-varsha, as that is the way to the pleasures of Paradise, or the greater blessing of final liberation. Happy are they who . . . obtain existence in that land of works, as their path to him ["the supreme and eternal Vishnu"]. . . . We know that those men are fortunate who are born with perfect faculties in Bhárata-varsha."[535]

For the Hindu philosopher who chanted *The Vishnu Purana,* Bhárata was the "path" to the Eternal, the final abode of all. The American poet who chanted the Purana of his "Self," the "democratic individual,"[536] declares in his praise of America, "Thou Mother with Thy Equal Brood":

> The paths to the house I seek to make,
> But leave to those to come the house itself. (Sec. 1)

Offering "rough new prizes" to those who travel with him on the "Open Road," Whitman warns against settling in "the city" because they will soon have "an irresistible call to depart," and by departing, he says:

> You shall be treated to the ironical smiles and mockings of those who remain behind you. . . .[537]

After describing how a certain sage, "possessed of all true wisdom," "embued with the knowledge of self," and beholding "the gods and all other beings as in reality the same," was indifferent to the ways of the world, as a result of which "he was treated with contempt by all the people," Parasara instructs his disciple thus:

> Regard for the consideration of the world is fatal to the success of devotion. The ascetic who is despised of men attains the end of his abstractions. Let therefore a holy man pursue *the path of the righteous,* without murmuring; and though men condemn him, avoid association with mankind. . . . (Italics added)

The food of that sage "was raw pulse, potherbs, wild fruit, and grains of corn. Whatever came in his way he ate."[538] He who goes with Whitman on his "road" goes "often with spare diet, poverty."[539]

Another of his admonitions to those who would travel with him is this:

> Allons! yet take warning!
> He traveling with me needs the best blood, thews, endurance,
> None may come to the trial till he and she brings courage and health,
> . . . .
> No diseas'd person, no rum-drinker or venereal taint is permitted here.[540]

But he forgets that a little earlier in the same poem he had generously announced that on his open road was "the profound lesson of reception, nor preference nor denial," and that even "the felon, the diseas'd . . . are not denied," nor "the drunkard's stagger";

there are "none but are accepted, none but shall be dear to [him]."[541] He also forgets that a similar assertion had been made in "Song of Myself":

I will not have a single person slighted or left away,
The kept-woman and sponger and thief are hereby invited
    . . . . the heavy-lipped slave is invited . . . . the venerealee
    is invited,
There shall be no difference between them and the rest.
    (Sec. 19)

This self-contradiction is strange, even when the restriction imposed is regarded as a way of insisting upon the importance of physical health, which is one of the "words" of his poems, because the "open road" was one where "They pass, I pass, everything passes, none can be interdicted."[542] The explanation seems to be that, among the "multitudes" he tried to "contain,"[543] he was echoing in that warning the following sentence on transmigration that he had read in *The Vishnu Purana*:

A crippled or mutilated person, or one whose organs are defective, cannot at once obtain liberation; his merits must first secure his being born again perfect and entire.[544]

I am he that walks with the tender and growing night;
I call to the earth and sea half-held by the night.

With these words Whitman describes one of the many things that he is and does in "Song of Myself," and then follows an account of how as a "lover" he is "press[ed] close [by] barebosomed night," makes love to the "voluptuous cool-breathed earth"; and has "a turn together" with the "sea of the brine of life."[545] The making of his Cosmic Spirit to do all this has already been explained in our study; the image and the thought of this "doing" are similarly traceable not to an original exercise of imagination, but to a skillful fancy operating upon the suggestions of certain passages he read. One of them is a description of the man of "true wisdom" given by the *Bhagvat-Geeta*:

Such a one walketh but in that night when all things go to rest, the night of *time*. The contemplative Moonee sleepeth but in the day of *time,* when all things wake.[546]

Whitman walks not *in* the night but *with* it; the night is his love, as the earth is his love, and as the sea is his love. *The Vishnu Purana* describes Sri, the bride of Vishnu, "the mother of the world," thus:

Vishnu is meaning; she is speech. . . . Sri is the earth; Hari the support of it. . . . He is desire; Sri is wish. Govinda is the ocean; Lakshmi its shore. She is the night; [he] is the day. He . . . is the bridegroom; [Sri] is the bride. . . . Govinda is love; and [she], his gentle spouse, pleasure. . . . Hari is all that is called male: Lakshmi is all that is termed female.[547]

Considering Whitman's habit of turning into verse whatever attracted him in his reading and of later skillfully putting it into position in his poems, it is not unlikely that the following passage in "Song of Myself" was so created:

Sit awhile wayfarer,
Here are biscuits to eat and here is milk to drink,
But as soon as you sleep and renew yourself in sweet clothes
     I will certainly kiss you with my goodbye kiss and open the
     gate for your egress hence. (Sec. 46)

He had first worked this thought in prose.[548] The mystic depth these lines have in the poem is the result of the suggestion of the surrounding lines that he is the great teacher just guiding the truthseeker to a wisdom that is superior to the "contemptible dreams" he has dreamed so long. But basically it is the thought of hospitality that is in them, a virtue on which all the Hindu works he had read, from the *Laws of Menu* to *The Vishnu Purana,* insisted thus:

Satisfying . . . guests with hospitality . . . the householder is to them a constant refuge and parent: it is his duty to give them a welcome, and to address them with kindness; and to provide them, whenever they come to his house, with a bed, a seat, and food. . . . [The guests spoken of in this context are the religious "mendicants" who "wander over the world."] . . . The householder is . . . to await the arrival of a guest. Should such a one arrive, he is to be received with a hospitable welcome; a seat is to be offered to him, and his feet are to be washed, and food is to be given him with liberality, and he is to be civilly and kindly spoken to; and when he departs, to be sent away by his host with friendly wishes.[549]

It may be noticed that in the final version of the lines the word "wayfarer" becomes "dear son" and Whitman plays the role of "parent" too. And the "sweet clothes" he offers to his guest may also be the result of Parasara's insistence that one must eat food "dressed in clean clothes, perfumed." Parasara also said, "Let a householder who has a knowledge of Brahma reverence a guest, without inquiring . . . his practices, or his race."[550] Whitman asserts in "Song of Myself," "I do not ask who you are, that is not important to me."[551] Again, in the same passage, it is declared: "He who feeds himself, and neglects the poor and friendless stranger in want of hospitality goes to hell. . . . For he who eats his food without bestowing any upon a guest feeds only upon iniquity. . . . [So] having given a portion to his hungry companions, let him take food."[552] These precepts "are of the same tenor as those given by Menu on the subject of hospitality . . . but more detailed."[553] Whitman, as we have seen, had read the *Laws of Menu* very fondly in his preparatory years. It is certainly possible, therefore, that the impassioned passage on hunger and hospitality in his 1847 notebook was inspired by the Hindu law-giver:

I am hungry and with my last dime get me some meat and bread and have appetite enough to relish it all—But then like a phantom at my side suddenly appears a starved face, either human or brute, uttering not a word—Has my heart no more passion than a squid or clam shell has [?] . . . What is this that balances itself upon my lips and wrestles as with the knuckles of God . . . follows the innocent food down my throat and turns it to fire and lead within me?—And what is it but my soul that hisses like an angry snake, Fool! Will you stuff your greed and starve me?[554]

In *Notes and Fragments* is preserved the following piece:

Yet far sweeps your road, O martial constellation! ever adding
    group! stretches far your journey!
For the prize I see at issue is the world;
All its ships and shores I see interwoven with your threads,
    spotted cloth.
Dreamed, again, the flags of kings, highest borne, to flaunt
    unrivall'd?
O hasten blue and silver! O with sure and steady step, passing
    highest flags of kings,
Walk supreme to the heavens, mighty symbol—run up above
    them all
Dense starr'd bunting.[555]

This wild assemblage of words and phrases, possibly the gathering of "raw material" to be patiently shaped to the needs of whatever place it could later "fall into" in a poem, appears, as it stands, to be the working of his fancy on the immense future of the star-spangled banner, the "spotted cloth." And interspersed with this is another line of thought about a "prize," and a "dream" of something "highest borne," "passing highest flags of kings."

The meaning of this apparent rigmarole, which, incidentally, did develop into the mystic magnitude of most other passages in his poetry becomes clearer and more intelligible, at the same time throwing considerable light upon the technique of his verse-making, when we realize that the fancy operating in these lines was roused by the reading of a story in *The Vishnu Purana* about a young prince called Dhruva. Dhruva was the son of a king by a second wife, and, because the principal queen's son was claimed as the true heir to the throne, he was denied even the simple joy of sitting on "his father's lap." Passionately returning to his mother, he resolves to "obtain such elevated rank, that it shall be revered by the whole world," and "honours . . . such as even [his] father [the king] has not enjoyed." And then, going to the wise sages, he asks them: "I aspire to such a station as no one before me has attained. Tell me what I must do to effect this object; how I may reach an elevation superior to all other dignities." Told that "Indra, having worshipped the lord of the world, obtained the dignity of king of the celestials," and that "anything, child, that the mind covets . . . may be obtained by propitiating Vishnu, even though it be the station that is the most excellent in the three worlds," he performs "penance," prays to God, and solicits "of the support of the universe [Vishnu] an exalted station, superior to all others, and one that shall endure for ever." Moved by his devotion, Vishnu grants the boon: "A station shall be assigned to thee, Dhruva, above the three worlds; one in which thou shalt sustain the stars and the planets; a station above those of the sun, the moon, Mars . . . and all the other constellations; above the regions of the seven Rishis [The Great Bear], and the divinities who traverse the atmosphere."556 An explanatory footnote adds: "The station or sphere [granted to Dhruva] is that of the north pole, or of the polar star."

This beautiful legend obviously stirred Whitman's imagination: his "martial constellation" is probably a compound of the account's "Mars" and "constellations"; Dhruva's aspiration to the reverence of "the whole world" is his "prize"; he dreams, too, of the "highest borne" to "flaunt unrivalled"; and the station of Dhruva, above "those of the sun, the moon" and all the other groups of stars, suggested his, "Walk supreme to the heavens, mighty symbol— run up above them all." From a further account, in which it is described that "all the celestial luminaries are in fact bound to the polar star by aerial cords," because of which "as Dhruva revolves, it causes the moon, sun and stars to turn around also,"557 is taken his "threads" with which the "ships and shores" (though of the world) are "interwoven" and also of the line in section 24 of "Song of Myself" that speaks of "the threads that connect the stars."

Explaining the intentions of *Leaves of Grass,* Whitman wrote in the 1876 preface:

To the highest democratic view, man is most acceptable in living well the practical life and lot which happens to him as ordinary farmer, sea-farer, mechanic, clerk, laborer, or driver— upon and from which position as a central basis or pedestal, while performing his labours, and his duties as citizen, son, husband, father and employ'd person, he preserves his physique, ascends, developing, radiating himself in other regions—and especially where and when . . . he fully realizes the conscience, the spiritual, the divine faculty, cultivated well, exemplified in all his deeds and words, through life . . .—a flight loftier than any of Homer's or Shakespeare's—. . . namely, Nature's own, and in the midst of it, Yourself, your own Identity, body and soul (All serves, helps—but in the centre of all, absorbing all, giving, for your purpose, the only meaning and vitality to all, master or mistress of all, under the law, stands Yourself.) To sing the song of that law of average Identity, and of Yourself, consistently with the divine law of the universal, is a main intention of those "Leaves".[558]

A brief analysis of this confusing wilderness of words shows the several strands of thought that are woven into it. The "Yourself" standing "in the centre of all," in "the midst" of Nature, is the "Purusha" of Sankhya thought. In the subsequent "Yourself" there is something of the individual soul of Vedanta that is part of the divine Universal. Ignoring these subtle differences, we have an "Identity" which the "Leaves" sing of. This was the identity he had gained for himself in the strange exercises that, as we have seen, produced the first poem of 1855, "Song of Myself." Applying this as freely to others as he did to himself, he "meant 'Leaves of Grass' as published, to be the Poem of average Identity, (of *yours,* whoever you are, now reading the lines.)"[559] And when, elsewhere, he says his aim was to create "INDIVIDUALITY,"[560] it becomes the identity of the "Individual" he obviously conceived ideally. All this fantastic appropriation of what belongs only to the metaphysical soul and the Supreme Spirit aside, we have another confusion in that tortuous, ill-united mass of memories that makes the long sentence of the above passage, between whether it is an "Identity" attained after "the flight loftier than Homer's," or one that is already possessed in "living well the practical life" before man "ascends" to radiate "in other regions." That is because the part in which he tries to describe the "good life" is composed, for his "democratic view," out of what was described for the "philosophic view" of the Hindu writings. *The Vishnu Purana,* for instance, said:

A man who observes the institutions of caste, order, . . . follows the duties prescribed . . . conforms to the duties enjoined by scriptural authority for every caste and condition of life, is he who best worships Vishnu. . . . [The brahmin has his duties, the man of the warrior tribe has his, and so have those

of the occupations of commerce and agriculture and the sudra.]
. . . Besides these their respective obligations, there are duties
equally incumbent upon all . . . [such as] the acquisition of
property, for the support of their families; cohabitation with
their wives, for the sake of progeny; tenderness towards all
creatures, patience, humility, truth, purity. . . . These are also
the duties of every condition of life. [As a householder, the
individual must] discharge to the best of his ability the duties
of his station. . . . Let him . . . abstain from wrong, in act, word,
or thought. . . . The sage [who thus lives an ordered life] by
means of his spiritual fire . . . proceeds to his own proper
abode . . . the sphere of Brahma.[561]

This is Whitman's "living well the practical life and lot," and
"performing" one's "labours" and "duties," by which a man "ascends" to "other regions"; and the "conscience" "exemplified" in
"deeds and words"; to all of which is added the description of the
"Soul" reposing "in Pradhana (Nature)."

In instances such as this, Whitman's habit of using words and
ideas from the Hindu philosophical speculations for the explication
of his message should be noticed. His imagination has been saturated
with the thoughts of the sages whom he so ardently emulated, and
naturally they become the idiom in which he communicates his
thoughts. To give but one more example: when he speaks of "our
America," in the same Preface, as a "vast seething mass of *materials*
. . . to be used to carry towards its crowning stage, and build
for good, the great ideal nationality of the future, the nation of
the body and soul," and describes how "the United States" has
built the "basis" of life "upon scales of extent, variety, vitality,
and continuity, rivaling those of Nature,"[562] he is only using the
Sankhya concept of Nature, whose materials the soul utilizes for
its fruition, in the same way that he converted another philosophical thought to patriotic ends in "Thou Mother With Thy Equal
Brood."

Finally, I cannot resist the temptation of wondering if the total
plan of *Leaves of Grass* as a book—a plan conceived, as all the
evidence indicates, after the unexpected success of the first edition
through Emerson's praise, and not, as Whitman maintained, before,

or "at the age of thirty-one to thirty-three"—[563] does not owe something to *The Vishnu Purana,* which, for all its varied material, is basically the story of Vishnu, or the Supreme Spirit; whose themes are creation, the universe and its nature, life and the natural and spiritual and social laws governing it, death, immortality, and the history and geography of the earth, which is the region of human action; whose principal object is moral instruction; whose many myths, legends, allegories, and stories of kings and wars and sages, and whose discussions of social duties, and so on, are all designed to give the knowledge that is the means of attaining "the great end of life"; and which presents all this as part of the basic theme, namely, the identity of the Supreme Spirit, or the Universal Soul, called, for purposes of the narrative, Vishnu. For, if *The Vishnu Purana* is the story of the Supreme Self, *Leaves of Grass* is the song of "One's-self" none the less supreme: like it, it narrates the glorious history of that Self; it has, or, as Kennedy put it, is, "a Drama of Creation";[564] it chants songs of death and immortality; it glorifies its own land; propagates a path to wisdom; its " 'leaves,' all and several, surely prepare the way for, and necessitate morals, and are adjusted to them";[565] and like it, it announces intentions and closes with valedictions and prophecies. We may add that the authors of both of them are teachers who learned at the feet of great sages, both narrate at the instance of some wise seer,[566] and both are answerers.

12

THE LARGE UTTERANCE
OF AN EARLY GOD

FROM EMERSON TO MALCOLM COWLEY, THE ONE BOOK THAT MANY readers and critics of *Leaves of Grass* have been put in mind of, whether as a possible source of inspiration to "Song of Myself" or as one with which Whitman's entire work had remarkable parallels, is the *Bhagavadgita,* or *Bhagvat-Geeta* as it was spelt in the first English translation by Charles Wilkins in 1785, the "arrival" of which in Concord was an "event,"[567] and of which Christy, in *The Orient in American Transcendentalism* said: "No one Oriental Volume that ever came to Concord was more influential than the *Bhagavadgita.*"[568] Emerson described it "as the first of books; it was as if an empire spake to us, nothing small or unworthy, but large, serene, consistent, its voice of an old intelligence which in another age and climate had pondered and thus disposed of the same questions which exercise us."[569] Alcott regarded it as "superior to any of the other Oriental scriptures, the best of all reading for wise men."[570] Thoreau, into whose "consciousness," as Henry S. Canby said, the Gita "went deep down . . . and gave him a new birth,"[571] reacted to it with passionate enthusiasm; and, finding it remarkable "for its pure intellectuality," said: "The reader is nowhere raised into and sustained in a higher, purer, or *rarer* region of thought than in the *Bhagvat-Geeta,*" and "beside the vast cosmogonal philosophy of the Bhagvat-Geeta, even our Shakespeare seems youthfully green and practical merely."[572]

Running into raptures about the philosophy it represented,

Thoreau further wrote in *A Week on the Concord and Merrimack Rivers:* "I would say to the readers of scriptures, if they wish for a good book, read the Bhagvat-Geeta. . . . Ex Oriente Lux may still be the motto of the scholars, for the western world has not yet derived from the East all the light which it is destined to receive thence."[573] It would be a profitless question to ask if Whitman had already read Thoreau's book before he came to possess a copy of it through the author's gift in 1856, and so was influenced by his enthusiasm for the *Bhagvat-Geeta,* but it is curious that, almost as if he had carried out the suggestion of Thoreau and exhausted all "the light" to be derived from the East, he declared to Edward Carpenter, who remarked that the West probably had "much to learn from India": "I do not myself think there is anything more to come from that source. . . . We must rather look to modern science to open the way. Time alone can absolutely test my poems."[574] The reference to his own poems in the same breath is very suggestive. A note of natural pride is hardly the explanation; it is more probably a subconscious feeling that he had discovered and brought home to the West all that could be derived "from that source." And the words of Thoreau seem to be always there in the back of his mind whenever, in prose or poetry, he speaks of the great task of the American poet, which is

> After all not to create only, or found only,
> But to bring perhaps from afar what is already founded,
> To give it our own identity.[575]

He had done the task superbly well, too, so that he could justifiably exclaim: "Comrade Americanos! to us, then at last the Orient comes."[576]

Emerson's dream of a Poet for America he had brought into reality. Margaret Fuller's prophecy had come true in him. And he does not seem to have slighted Thoreau's wish: "It would be worthy of the age to print together the collected scriptures or sacred writings of the several nations, the Chinese, the Hindoos, the Persians, the Hebrews, and others, as the Scripture of Mankind. . . . This would be the Bible, or Book of Books."[577] For, his becoming a Christ, both in his own and his "hot little prophets' " thoughts, followed after "The Great Construction of the New

Bible," and it was purely in the ambition of a poet directed by such words as Thoreau's that he planned "the principal object—the main life work,"[578] because the "very early note" in which he resolved to "enter into the thoughts of the different theological faiths . . . Egyptian . . . Greek . . . Hindoo . . . Kooboo . . . Catholic . . . Turk,"[579] reproduces Thoreau's desire almost word for word. Whether he did make the "Book of Books," the "Scripture of Mankind," is another question, but that that was the intention behind *Leaves of Grass* can hardly be denied in the face of the repeated assertions of it in his notes, prefaces, and comments.

If the evidence so far discovered in this investigation did not explain how "Song of Myself" came to be written, it would look, in the light of the following pages, as if Whitman did precisely what the recipient of a letter from Emerson was told: "And of books there is another which, when you read, you shall sit for a while and write a poem—the 'Bhagvat-Geeta,' but read it in Charles Wilkins' translation." And, though "Emerson was one of the few Americans to own a copy of the work,"[580] it was available to Whitman, in the very translation of Emerson's insistence, both in the New York Society Library and the Astor Library, years before he said to Thoreau: "tell me about them."

It may be remembered at this point that, while the Concordians went to such rapturous lengths in praising this "one Oriental volume," in all the voluminous pages of Whitman—prose, poetry, or private record, or in his conversation, so scrupulously recorded by his admirers—there is not one single reference to it, direct or implicit. And yet he did own a copy of it in the 1855 translation of J. Cockburn Thomson, given as a "presentation" to him "(by Thomas Dixon) of Sunderland, Dec. 1875,"[581] and he read and annotated it.

If that presentation copy was the only one that Whitman read, though still his reticence about it is nonetheless surprising, the part played by the *Bhagavadgita* in his poetry would be understandably negligible, because it came to him, according to the evidence, in December 1875. But, as a matter of fact, whether he had another copy of his own earlier or not, he had read the *Gita* in 1865 when he wrote:

I see behind each mask that wonder a kindred soul,
O the bullet could never kill what you really are, dear friend,
Nor the bayonet stab what you really are;

The soul! yourself I see, great as any, good as the best,
Waiting secure and content, which the bullet could never kill,
Nor the bayonet stab O friend.[582]

For, this bit of "New York Herald" is merely "how little the
New after all, how much the Old, Old World!"[583] of the
"Bhagvat Ghita," where Krishna said:

> O *Arjoon,* resolve to fight. The man who believeth that it is
> the soul which killeth, and he who thinketh that the soul may be
> destroyed, are both alike deceived; for it neither killeth, nor is it
> killed. . . . It is ancient, constant,. and eternal, and is not to be
> destroyed in this its mortal frame. . . . As a man throweth
> away old garments, and putteth on new, even so the soul, hav-
> ing quitted its old mortal frames, entereth into others which are
> new. The weapon divideth it not, the fire burneth it not, the
> water corrupteth it not, the wind drieth it not away; for it is
> indivisible, inconsumable, incorruptible, and is not to be dried
> away: it is eternal, universal, permanent, immoveable; it is in-
> visible, inconceivable, and unalterable.[584]

But, to be fair, in a footnote explaining a philosophic observation in *The Vishnu Purana* the words of the above passage are
quoted in the editor's own translation: "Weapons wound it not;
fire doth not consume it; water cannot drown it."[585] The fact,
however, that the *Gita* alone has the context of the battlefield—
Whitman's poem is about "the ranks returning worn and sweaty"
—and also the notion of the garment of body the soul wears, like
the "mask" of Whitman, suggests that the brief and inconspicuous
footnote is not the source.

Five years earlier, in 1860, Whitman published, as "a prefatory
poem in *Chants Democratic*" (and "dropped in 1867"), a poem
called "Apostroph," and as part of it ("published separately in
1867" and finally "dropped in 1881"), another, called "O Sun
of Real Peace."[586] Both now are among the rejected poems.
"Apostroph" is an immense catalogue of things and ideas envisaged
in a vision:

> O mater! O fils!
> O brood continental!
> O flowers of the prairies!
> O space boundless! O hum of mighty products!

Apostrophizing thus, he sweeps over lands, nations, people, doctrines, present, future, life, death, and so on, and exclaims:

> O so amazing and so broad! up there resplendent, darting and
>   burning;
> O prophetic! O vision staggered with weight of light! with
>   pouring glories!
> . . . .
> O my Soul! O lips becoming tremulous, powerless!
> . . . .
> O heights! O infinitely too swift and dizzy yet!
> O purged lumine! you threaten me more than I can stand!
> O present! I return while yet I may to you!

"O Sun of Real Peace" carries on this incantation, and, as a separate poem, repeats:

> O sun of real peace! O hastening light!
> O free and extatic! . . .
> O the sun of the world. . . .
> O so amazing and broad—. . .
> O vision prophetic, stagger'd with weight of light! with pouring glories!
> O lips of my soul, already becoming powerless!
> . . . .
> O heights too swift and dizzy yet!
> O purged and luminous! you threaten me more than I can
>   stand!
> (I must not venture—the ground under my feet menaces me
>   —it will not support me:
> O future too immense,)—O present, I return, while yet I
>   may, to you.

In this "vision" and frenzied utterance, he is, to use the only expressive term, Whitmanizing the role of Arjun in the *Bhagvat-Geeta,* to whom is granted a vision of the Supreme Spirit thus:[587]

"Behold, O *Arjoon,* my million forms divine, of various species, and diverse shapes and colours. Behold [the various gods or regents of the universe]. Behold things wonderful, never seen before. Behold in this my body, the whole world animate and inanimate, and all things thou hast a mind to see. But as thou art unable to see with these thy natural eyes, I will give thee a heavenly eye, with which behold my divine connection."[588]

SANJAY.

The mighty compound and divine being . . . having . . . thus spoken, made evident unto *Arjoon* his supreme and heavenly form; of . . . many a wondrous sight . . . anointed with heavenly essence; covered with every marvellous thing; the eternal God, whose countenance is turned on every side! The glory and amazing splendour of this mighty being may be likened to the sun rising at once into the heavens, with a thousand times more than usual brightness. The son of *Pandoo* [Arjun] beheld within the body of the God of Gods, standing together, the whole universe divided forth into its vast variety. He was overwhelmed with wonder, and every hair was raised an end. He bowed down his head before the God, and thus addressed him with joined hands.

ARJOON.

"I behold, O God! within thy breast, the *Dews* [the gods] assembled, and every specific tribe of beings [a list of what was seen]. . . . I see thee . . . a mass of glory, darting refulgent beams around. I see thee, difficult to be seen, shining on all sides with light immeasurable, like the ardent fire or glorious sun. Thou art the Supreme Being . . . the prime supporter of the universal orb! . . . the sun and moon thy eyes; thy mouth a flaming fire, and the whole world shining with thy reflected glory! . . . [A list of all creatures, who "glorify" the Supreme.] Thus as I see thee, touching the heavens, and shining with such glory . . . I am disturbed within me . . . and I find no rest. . . . I know not which way I turn! I find no peace! Have mercy then, O God of Gods! . . . The world is filled with thy glory, as thy awful beams, O *Veeshnoo,* shine forth on all sides!"

Arjun is disturbed because, in addition to God's "power" and "glory," he has also seen the future in Krishna as Time, and so, his "mind . . . overwhelmed with awful fear," he beseeches Krishna to return to his original "placid human shape," having beheld which, he subsequently says: "I am again collected; my mind is no more disturbed, and I am once more returned to my natural state."

The same passage is in Whitman's mind when he writes the long section 33 of "Song of Myself," where

> My ties and ballasts leave me. . . . I travel. . . . I sail. . . . my
> elbows rest in the sea-gaps,
> I skirt the sierras. . . . my palms over continents,
> I am afoot with my vision.

But, having assumed the Yogic identity of God, it is the role of Krishna he plays this time, presenting in the entire section a cosmic identification in the manner of the *Gita* where Krishna makes Arjun acquainted with the infinite extent of His nature, detailing the fact that He is "the soul which standeth in the bodies of all beings . . . the seed of all things in nature; and there is not anything, whether animate or inanimate, that is without" Him.[589]

A considerable portion of this revelation by Krishna of his Supreme Self has been noticed in the early periodical articles in which Whitman probably had his first knowledge of this wonderful book that "had the greatest influence upon [the] literature of the west."[590] The influence it had upon the literature of Whitman is equally great, notwithstanding the fact that his philosophical foundations, the prophet's thoughts he uttered in his poetry, came from many another page, as we have observed. For one thing, though "Song of Myself" was not perhaps inspired by the *Gita* originally, and the cosmic identity he poetically assumed in it is not basically indebted to Krishna, the title of the poem may have been inspired by it (the *Bhagvat-Geeta* being described by Warren Hastings in the introductory letter as "the Geeta of 'Bhagvat,' which is one of the names of Kreeshna"),[591] assuming, that is, that Whitman could realize, despite his ignorance of Sanskrit, that the word "Geeta" meant "song." The earliest suggestion of his thinking of a term like "Myself" is in the 1847 manuscript notebook, where in company with words like "The highway" and "road," he records the phrase: "(Criticism on *Myself*)."[592] But it hardly looks like a word thought of as the title of a poem; it is more probably a self-direction toward developing his poetic meditations on the "Myself" he had assumed under the instructions of Vignana-Bhikshuka, or a comment on those already developed. The presumption of his finally calling the mass of meditations, achieved over years of celebrating his Self, after the "Geeta, or Song, of Bhagvat, or Krishna," recognizing that they were after all very similar, being self-revelations, is supported by the many ways in which he has attempted to make his self and its song correspond to Krishna's self and its song. In other words, even as he composed the first group of passages of "Song of Myself," initially through a very adroit versification of Ward's pages, so he did many more from the *Gita,* which, too, offered an extraordinary facility to the act, inasmuch as Krishna said the same kind of things in precisely the same manner as he himself had so far done in his yogic arrogations. The swollen sheaves of "slips" were after all held together in a single "envelope" marked for the "spinal idea" of "self."

The name of "Vyasa," the "compiler" or "arranger" of *Mahabharata,* occurs many times in Whitman's scrapbooks, his "storehouse of information,"[593] and almost always spelled so, for that was how it was generally written in all his sources. Besides, as the entries show, he was accurately informed in regard to "Vyasa—[author of] Mahabharata."[594] But yet in one of these fragments he records a query: "Indian epic poetry—who was Veias?"[595] It is not the question so much as the spelling of the name in it that should interest us, because the only source that spelled the name in that fashion was the *Bhagvat-Geeta* of Charles Wilkins, where, while the translator spells it "Vyās," Warren Hastings in his introductory letter spells it "Veiâs."[596]

The impact of Hasting's letter on Whitman is not limited to this and to the phrase, noted earlier, "the Hindoo teaching his favorite pupil," in the poem "Salut au Monde!"[597] He seems to have studied the letter as diligently as the body of the work itself. If he was not, as is claimed in Bucke's biography, a systematic reader, he was certainly avid when his fancy was captured, and read even better than a systematic reader, though it looks as if he were often content with verbal gleanings. But whatever his keen mind gathers he turns into tokens of his own transactions—words, phrases, images, symbols. For instance, Hastings, after a full-hearted praise of the *Bhagvat-Geeta,* extracts "from every reader the allowance of obscurity," because he is aware in recommending "this production for public notice," that "many passages will be found obscure, many will seem redundant . . . some elevated to a track of sublimity . . . difficult to pursue. . . . Something too must be allowed to the subject itself, which is highly metaphysical, to the extreme difficulty of rendering abstract terms . . . in words expressing unsubstantial qualities."[598] Whenever Whitman introduces his "works" he makes a similar admission of obscurity and vagueness. "In certain parts in these flights," says he, in his 1876 Preface, "or attempting to depict or suggest them, I have not been afraid of the charge of obscurity. . . . Poetic style, when address'd to the soul, is less definite form."[599] Elsewhere he writes: "A certain vagueness . . . is in a few pieces or passages; but this is apparently by the deliberate intention of the author."[600] It is not to be claimed that such utterances are the result themselves of fond imitation, because the obscurity he advertises is very much there in his poetry, but it is not impossible that the quality itself was the result of design, as the second of his statements concedes, under the persuasion that a subject "metaphysical" and dealing with "unsubstantial qualities" should be treated in a style of "half-tints, and even less than half-tints."[601]

Whitman's knowledge of the Yoga practices and its source among the many books of his reading have already been traced. The concepts of the philosophy of Yoga are part of the teachings of Krishna in the *Gita,* but of the physical aspects of that "spiritual discipline, not, I believe, unknown to some of the religious orders of Christians in the Romish Church,"[602] an interesting description is given by Hastings in the same letter. Whitman's manuscript workings on the "projected poem" to be called "Penitenzia," noticed earlier, have the appearance of being stimulated by this description:

This [discipline] consists in devoting a certain period of time to the contemplation of the Deity. . . . It is required of those who practise this exercise, not only that they divest their minds of all sensual desire, but that their attention be abstracted from every external object, and absorbed, with every sense, in the prescribed subject of their meditation. I myself was once a witness of a man employed in this species of devotion. . . . His right hand and arm were enclosed in a loose sleeve or bag of red cloth, within which he passed the beads of his rosary, . . . repeating with the touch of each . . . one of the names of God, while his mind laboured to catch and dwell on the idea of the quality which appertained to it, and shewed the violence of its exertion to attain this purpose by the convulsive movements of all his features, his eyes being at the same closed, doubtless to assist the abstraction.

Hastings then describes how the Hindus, through "the daily habit of abstracted contemplation" were led to "the discovery of new tracks or combinations of sentiment." The closing of the eyes, the "Roman Catholic devotees," the passing into the "unknown," and the discovery of the "real reality," of Whitman's record, are all here, "Kurtz" obviously being the name of the man *he* will witness in the exercise.[603]

"With the deductions, or rather qualifications," of obscurity, and so on, Warren Hastings does "hesitate not to pronounce the Geeta a performance of great originality; of a sublimity of conception, reasoning, and diction, almost unequalled; and a single exception, among all the known religions of mankind, of a theology accurately corresponding with that of the Christian dispensation, and most powerfully illustrating its fundamental doctrines."[604] In all probability such a strong recommendation as this, if nothing else, confirmed Whitman's enthusiasm for the book and its contents.

Whitman's use of physical, often sexual, imagery for the communication of loftier spiritual meanings, has been one of the major points of criticism. How far the following observation of Hastings on the *Gita* went into that poetic style of his, is an interesting question:

> One blemish will be found in it, which will scarcely fail to make its own impression on every correct mind . . . I mean, *the attempt to describe spiritual existences by terms and images which appertain to corporeal forms.* . . . Defective as it may first appear, I know not whether a doctrine so elevated above common perception did not require to be introduced by such ideas as were familiar to the mind, to lead it by a gradual advance to the pure and abstract comprehension of the subject. This will seem to have been, whether intentionally or accidentally, the order which is followed by the author of the Geeta; and so far at least he soars far beyond all competitors in this species of composition. Even the frequent recurrence of the same sentiment, in a variety of dress, may have been owing

to the same consideration of the extreme intricacy of the subject, and the consequent necessity of trying different kinds of exemplification and argument, to impress it with due conviction on the understanding.[605] (Italics added)

We may also notice such "frequent recurrence of the same sentiment" in Whitman, namely, his repetitions of thought.

One of the things that reading the *Bhagvat-Geeta* gave Whitman's "Song of Myself" and *Leaves of Grass* in general, may be said to be the position of dialogue in which Whitman makes his self-revelation and his philosophical pronouncements, for, as the Translator's Preface observed, the *Gita* "is a dialogue supposed to have passed between *Kreeshna,* an incarnation of the Deity, and his pupil and favourite *Arjoon."*[606] And the words in which his last-minute admission of acquaintance with Oriental works was made also appear to have come from the same source. He said he had read "the ancient Hindoo poems";[607] Wilkins' Preface starts thus: "The following work, forming part of the Mahabharat, an ancient Hindoo poem.[608] In further explanation of the work Wilkins observes:

It seems as if the principal design of these dialogues was to unite all the prevailing modes of worship of those days; and, by setting up the doctrine of the unity of the Godhead, in opposition to idolatrous sacrifices, and the worship of images, to undermine the tenets inculcated by the *Veds;* for although the author dared not make a direct attack, either upon the prevailing prejudices of the people, or the divine authority of those ancient books; yet, by offering eternal happiness to such as worship *Brahm,* the Almighty, whilst he declares the reward of such as follow other Gods shall be but a temporary enjoyment of an inferior heaven, . . . his design was to bring about the downfall of Polytheism; or, at least, to induce men to believe *God* present in every image before which they bent, and the object of all their ceremonies and sacrifices.[609]

In section 43 of "Song of Myself" Whitman does precisely the same:

My faith is the greatest of faiths and the least of faiths,
Enclosing all worship ancient and modern, and all between
  ancient and modern.

And in section 41:

Magnifying and applying come I,
Outbidding at the start the old cautious hucksters,
. . . .
Taking myself the exact dimensions [of all the gods of the
  world] . . . .
. . . .
Admitting they were alive and did the work of their day.

And after thus "uniting all the prevailing modes of worship," in
section 48 he induces "men to believe *God* present in every image":

I hear and behold God in every object. . . .
. . . .
I find letters from God dropped in the street, and everyone is
  signed by God's name.

Not failing to offer "eternal happiness" too, he says in section 50:

Do you see O my brothers and sisters?
It is . . . .
. . . eternal life. . . . it is happiness.

And if the author of the *Gita* does "not make a direct attack . . .
on the divine authority of those ancient books," Whitman performs his teaching, "Not objecting to special revelations" (Sec.
41), and "Accepting the gospels" (Sec. 43).
  The Preface further observes:

The most learned *Brahmans* of the present times are Unitar-
ians according to the doctrines of *Kreeshna;* but, at the same
time that they believe but in one God, an universal spirit, they
. . . perform all the ceremonies inculcated by the *Veds* such as
sacrifices, ablutions, &c. They do this, probably, more for the

support of their own consequence, which could only arise from the great ignorance of the people, than in compliance with the dictates of *Kreeshna* . . . as the superstition of the vulgar is the support of the priesthood in many other countries.[610]

Combining with the wisdom of the Supreme Spirit the human charity of Wilkins, Whitman assures his readers: "I do not despise you priests," and even "perform[s] all the ceremonies inculcated by the *Veds*" or "gospels" of the world: "all the idolatrous sacrifices, and the worship of images," with all "the prejudices of the vulgar"; though in that performance he withdraws necessarily into the Universal Spirit he has identified himself with:

> Waiting responses from oracles . . . . honoring the gods . . . .
>   saluting the sun,
> Making a fetish of the first rock or stump . . . . powowing
>   with sticks in the circle of obis,
> Helping the lama or brahmin as he trims the lamps of the
>   idols,
> Dancing yet through the streets in a phallic procession . . . .
>   rapt and austere in the woods, a gymnosophist,
> Drinking mead from the skull-cap . . . . to shasta and vedas
>   admirant . . . . minding the koran,
> Walking the teokallis, spotted with gore from the stone and
>   knife—beating the serpent-skin drum,
> . . . .
> To the mass kneeling—to the puritan's prayer rising—sitting
>   patiently in a pew. (Sec. 40)

13

ANOTHER UTTERANCE
EQUALLY LARGE

IT WOULD BE A TEDIOUS REPETITION TO INQUIRE INTO THE PHIL-
osophic contribution of the *Bhagvat-Geeta* to Whitman's prophetic
message, for the *Gita* is essentially a condensed account of the doctrines and notions that he had patiently and diversely collected
from the many sources of Hindu thought that we have already
examined. But in the making of his poems, especially "Song of Myself," the part played by the "Song of Krishna" cannot be ignored.
The following study of the process by which, as he did with the
rest of what he read, he fed from the pages of the *Bhagvat-Geeta*
more grist to his verbal mill, will clearly show how he used the
Gita as a model for his "Song," Krishna for his "Myself," and the
profound teachings of "Bhagvat" as the basis of his fancy's
"flights."

One of the aspects of Whitman's use of the *Bhagvat-Geeta* as
a model may be the final sectioning of the long "Song of Myself,"
which was merely an accumulation of the skillful paraphrasings of
his readings in many a book, and of the fancies stimulated by them
over a period of years. It was probably the awareness that, because
of the multiplicity of its thought sources, the "Song" obviously
lacked the natural unity or organization of a poem, however long,
whose origin is in the sustained operation of an internal emotion,
though externally caused, which made Whitman realize that the
only way of achieving a relationship among the diversely composed
fragments assembled into one large piece was to number them into

sections, thereby avoiding the artistic confusion of discontinuity and inconsequence. But when, in his ambitious bid for national glory, he first dangled this astoundingly novel poem, even that suggestion of a negative order was not there. The incoherence, the want of any kind of order in the progression of thought, and the bewildering disintegration of the narrative medium, were altogether sufficient to create the impression of startling originality. The use of dots, the broken lines, the grammatical inversions, the half-thoughts in accordance with the "mystic ejaculations" which, as *The Vishnu Purana* told him, accompany the yogic meditation, all added to the character of the poem the element of mysticism that was certainly his design. But the design of the afterthought, however deeply deliberated and intelligent, which conferred the numerical division on it, scarcely adds anything to give a pattern or order capable of organizing the heterogeneous material. For the division is neither always of disunited thoughts, nor of orderly stages of developing thought, nor one that prohibits a rearrangement of the numbered units or the reassembling of their contents. Indeed, despite Cowley's claim of an "irreversible order"[611] in it, with a few tell-tale lines held firmly with the fingers, a reader could shake the entire poem like a kaleidoscope, as wildly as he can, without causing much damage to it as a whole. It is even possible that the exercise might do the poem a little good, the pieces, to use Whitman's own phrase, falling into a better place. The only thing this numbering or sectioning has done to the "Song" is to offer slight pauses for breath as in a lengthy oration; it has the effect of paragraphs in an immense essay. But the breaking up into paragraphs was done in the cool calculation of subsequent deliberation, and the scope of reorganization thus limited by the original form in which it had seen the light of print, the best that could be done was to isolate disconnected thoughts from each other wherever the inconsequence was too glaring and the separation looked feasible.

Between the fifty-two sections into which the "Song of Myself" was thus divided, and the eighteen sections, or "Lectures" into which the "Song of Bhagvat" or *Bhagvat-Geeta* is divided, there is of course neither a numerical correspondence, nor, for that matter, a logical correspondence. The great masters at the feet of whom Whitman "sat studying"[612] before he became a master himself, were many; besides, while the *Bhagvat-Geeta* is the revelation of the One Self of Krishna, "Song of Myself" is the revelation of the "Many-in-One," of the multiple selves of the Supreme, the Universal Man, the man of Manhattan, the poet of America, and the philosopher of mankind, out of which Whitman's "Myself" was compounded. But the revelations of the other selves aside, in the sectionalizing or unitizing of the pronouncements of his Supreme Self, revelation as well as instruction, he seems to have availed himself of the *Gita* as a help. Many of these sections of the "Song" correspond in theme to the chapters of the *Gita,* though often it may be simply because they are mere Whitmanizations of Krishna's thought. For instance, the second lecture of the *Gita* is "Of the Nature of the Soul, and Speculative Doctrines," dealing with "immortality," and contrasting the "confined notions" of men who seek "the attainment of worldly riches and enjoyments" with the "true wisdom" of one who has "confidence in the Supreme." The major theme of sections 6 and 7 in "Song of Myself" is immortality of dead men who "are alive and well somewhere," and section 2 has the "confined [houses and rooms] notions" of men who "reckon'd the earth much," and the wisdom that is assured in "the origin of all poems," which suggest Krishna's admonition to Arjun to turn his "mind to things" spiritual.

Chapter six of the *Gita* is "Of the Exercise of the Soul," or Yoga. It describes the yogi who, "united with *Brahm* the Supreme . . . looketh upon all things alike, beholdeth the supreme soul in all things, and all things in the supreme soul." Sections 8 and those that follow it in "Song of Myself," are of this "exercise of the soul" called Yoga, only developed along the lines of the elaborated description he found in the other accounts. The seventh lecture of the *Gita* is "Of the Principles of Nature and the Vital Spirit." Section 3 of the "Song" deals with the two principles of creation and the soul that is "clear and sweet." Lecture 8 is of "Pooroosh," the "Divine and Supreme Being" in whom "is included all nature [and by whom] all things are spread." Sections 13, 14, 15, and 16 of the "Song" are of the invisible "caresser of life," and of all the creatures of the universe that "tend inward to" him. Lecture 9 is "Of the Chief of Secrets and Prince of Science," in which Krishna teaches "the mysterious secret" of "the supreme journey" which "those even who may be of the womb of sin; women; the tribes of Vysya and Soodra: shall go . . . if they take sanctuary with" him.

Section 17 declaring *his* secret that "these are really the thoughts of all men in all ages and lands," Whitman announces in 18 "vivas [even] to those who have failed," and in the next sets his "meal" equally for all, not "a single person slighted or left away."[613]

The following lecture of the *Gita* is "Of the Diversity of the Divine Nature," in which Krishna describes his "divine distinctions . . . without end." Sections 20, 21, and 22 of the "Song" dwell upon the inclusive nature of Whitman's self, in all of which, as we shall see, he develops Krishna's utterances. The eleventh chapter of the *Gita* is of the "Display of the Divine Nature in the Form of the Universe," the vision of Arjun, which sections 33 to 38 in "Song of Myself" closely imitate, the description of "the fall of Alamo" and of the "frigate-fight" in 34, 35, and 36 being probably a concession to the spectacle of the "heroes of the human race," the army assembled on the battlefield of Kurukshetra, rushing on, in Arjun's vision, "towards [the] flaming mouths" of Krishna as "Time," the "destroyer of mankind."

Lecture 12 is "Of Serving the Deity in His Visible and Invisible Forms"; and both forms of devotion being dear to God, Krishna assures his love and regard to all, and declares that he will "presently raise them up from the ocean of this region of mortality." In section 40, Whitman offers to "bestow" "anything" he has, and to "raise" the "descending man," and, in 41, "bringing help for the sick" as well as "for strong upright men," "come[s]" accepting "all idols and images" of human worship. The thirteenth lecture has an "Explanation of the Terms Kshetra and Kshetragna," (*"Prakreetee"* and *"Pooroosh"*), or Body and Soul, and of wisdom, which by conceiving "the *Pooroosh* and the *Prakreetee,"* even if it be from the report of others, helps one to pass beyond the gulf of death. In section 44 Whitman regards that "it is time to explain [himself]," and describes "the forces [that] have been steadily employed to complete" his physical evolution (in Prakriti or Nature), and, in 45, suggesting the "farther and farther" going to the "rendezvous" where "God will . . . wait," finally, in 46, speaks of the "perpetual journey" he tramps.

Lecture 14 is "Of the Three Goon or Qualities," and of the man of wisdom who "hath surmounted the influence of these qualities" and is "absorbed in *Brahm,* the Supreme." Whitman's metaphysics, or what perhaps is a better explanation, his

cleverness, avoids the concept, but section 47 of the "Song" is built
on this lecture by developing its other contents. Krishna reveals in
it: "a most sublime knowledge, superior to others, which having
learnt, all the Moonees have passed from it to superior perfection.
They take sanctuary under this wisdom, and being arrived to that
virtue which is similar to my own, they are not disturbed on the
day of the confusion of all things." The "day of the confusion,"
or of death in the body, becomes Whitman's "that solemn night
(it may be their last)";[614] the "Moonees" are his "athletes," of
whom he is "the teacher"; "tak[ing] sanctuary under this wisdom"
is transformed into: "They and all would resume what I have told
them." The "Moonee," or the wise man, said Krishna, is who
"serveth me alone"; and he is not "disturbed." Whitman makes it
"The driver thinking of me does not mind the jolt of his wagon."
Krishna further said that the wise man is "self-dependent." Whitman converts this into "The boy I love, the same becomes a man
not through derived power, but in his own right." If the Moonees
"arrive to that virtue similar to my [Krishna's] own," Whitman's
disciple "spreads a wider breast than my [Whitman's] own" to
prove "the width of my [Whitman's] own." According to Krishna,
the one that "surmounted the influence of the qualities" is one
"who despiseth not the light of wisdom." The "boy" whom Whitman loves, prefers "those well-tann'd to those that keep out of the
sun." (In the same imitation in section 46, he had asked his "dear
son," or the first edition's "wayfarer," to "habit [himself] to the
dazzle of the light.") And if the wise man "serveth me [Krishna]
alone," "those that know me [Whitman] seek me [Whitman]."

Lecture 15 of the *Bhagvat-Geeta* is a description "Of Purushottama," or the Supreme Being; 16, "Of Good and Evil Destiny";
17, "Of Faith Divided into Three Species"; and 18, the last, "Of
Forsaking the Fruits of Action for Obtaining Eternal Salvation."
Except for Whitman's recapitulation of his own message in section 48, which resembles Krishna's having "made known unto thee
[Arjun] this most mysterious Sastra," it does not seem that the
last four sections of his "Song" have taken any cue for their structural position from the final chapters of the *Gita,* though their
contents, through the usual metamorphosis, have been scattered
among his other sections, as those of lectures 3, 4 and 5, dealing
with "Works," "the Forsaking of Works," and "the Forsaking of

the Fruits of Works," respectively, have been. The first chapter of the *Gita* is of "The Grief of Arjoon," who, standing on the battlefield and called upon to fight and kill, is swayed by compunction and moral confusion, in answer to which Krishna teaches his song; and the different origin of Whitman's "Song," explained already, would naturally have little to borrow from that.

Cursory as this comparison is, it clearly shows that the *Bhagvat-Geeta* had a hand in the fashioning of "Song of Myself." This, as has been indicated, is to a large extent the natural consequence of the fact that Whitman was versifying the contents of the *Gita* page by page, or lecture by lecture, ignoring whatever intractable material there was in it and inserting other material wherever convenient. However, his indebtedness to the *Bhagvat-Geeta* for the structure of his poem is a relatively negligible detail compared to the other things he forces out of the book. One of them is the concept of the "Answerer," for, although the narrator of *The Vishnu Purana* was an answerer of questions, the impact on his fancy of the dialogue of the *Gita* in which Arjun is all questions (saying to Krishna: "I am thy disciple, wherefore instruct me in my duty, who am under thy tuition"[615]) and Krishna is all answers, cannot be overlooked. Another is the metaphor of this world as "a road for traveling souls" repeatedly used in the teaching of Krishna, as the following, culled from several pages, will show:

Stand firm in the path of truth. (p.40)

Wise men, who have abandoned all thought of the fruit which is produced from their actions, are freed from the chains of birth, and go to the regions of eternal happiness. (p.40)

The man who . . . walketh without inordinate desires . . . goeth not astray. (p.43)

The journey of thy mortal frame may not succeed from inaction. (p.45)

Both I and thou have passed many births. (p.51)

I assist those men who in all things walk in my path. (p.52)

Those whose understandings are in him [the Almighty] . . . go from whence they shall never return. (p.59)

The peaceful soul . . . who would keep in the path of one who followeth God, should . . . depend on me alone. (pp.63–64)

Doth not the fool who is found not standing in the path of *Brahm* . . . come to nothing? (pp.66–67)

The *Yogee* who . . . is . . . after many births, made perfect, at length goeth to the supreme abode. (p.67)

The wise man proceedeth not unto me until after many births. (p.71)

The devout souls who know me to be [Brahm] . . . know me also in the time of their departure. (p.72)

At the end of time, he, who . . . departeth thinking only of me, without doubt goeth unto me. (p.73)

I will now summarily make thee acquainted with that path which the doctors of the *Veds* call never-failing; which the men of subdued minds and conquered passions enter; and which, desirous of knowing, they live the lives of *Brahma-charees,* or godly pilgrims. (p.74)

He [of devotion, shall] without doubt go the journey of supreme happiness. (pp.74–75)

Know, O *Arjoon,* that all the regions between this and the abode of *Brahm* afford but a transient residence; but he who findeth me, returneth not again to mortal birth. (p.75)

He who walketh in the former path [of light] returneth not; whilst he who walketh in the latter [of darkness] cometh back upon the earth. A *Yogee,* who is acquainted with these two paths of action, will never be perplexed. (p.76)

I am the journey of the good. (p.80)

Those . . . shall go the supreme journey, if they take sanctuary with me. (p.82)

Those whose minds are attached to my invisible nature have the greater labour to encounter; because an invisible path is difficult to be found by corporeal beings. (p.98)

He who beholdeth the Supreme Being alike in all things . . . goeth the journey of immortality. (p.105)

When the body is dissolved whilst the *Satwa-Goon* prevaileth, the soul proceedeth to the regions of those immaculate beings who are acquainted with the Most High. (p.108)

[Those of evil destiny] being doomed to the wombs of *Asoors* from birth to birth . . . go into the most infernal regions [to which] there are . . . three passages. (p.117)

[A wise man] being freed from these gates of sin . . . goeth the journey of the Most High. (p.118)

The sea as a symbol of "mortal life" is frequently used too: "I presently raise them up from the ocean of this region of mortality, whose minds are thus attached to me." And "wisdom" is regarded as a ship in which to sail upon the ocean of life: "Thou shalt be able to cross the gulf of sin with the bark of wisdom."[616]

Whitman's use of the *Bhagvat-Geeta* seems to make one of the most amazing stories in literary history, because almost every utterance in the "Song of Bhagvat" has been taken up by him and reshaped into the fancy of his poetry. The major processes through which he has rendered the contents of the *Gita* fit for his song are those of verbal alteration, fanciful development, or a philosophically reckless metamorphosis, as the following analysis shows.

The first chapter of the *Gita* being only an account of the grief of Arjun, we may ignore it. The actual "Song of Krishna" commences with his upbraiding Arjun, whose eyes were "overflowing with a flood of tears," in the following words: "Whence, O *Arjoon,* cometh unto thee . . . this folly and unmanly weakness?

... Yield not thus to unmanliness. ... Abandon this despicable weakness ... and stand up."[617] Whitman's 1847 manuscript workings on the subject of "strength," offering, with the "stores of plenty" he has, to "infuse" with "grit" the man "starved of masculine lustiness"—a passage later put into section 40 of "Song of Myself"—looks like the free exercise of his fancy on the admonition of Krishna.

Declaring as unwise Arjun's grief for the death his fighting would cause, Krishna begins his teaching with these words: "I myself never *was not,* nor thou, nor all the princes of the earth; nor shall we ever hereafter cease *to be.* As the soul in this mortal frame findeth infancy, youth, and old age; so in some future frame, will it find the like." After the "mystic" vision of section 5 in "Song of Myself,"[618] Whitman employs the grass imagery in section 6 to describe that "there is really no death," and, in the next, declares: "I pass death with the dying and birth with the new-wash'd babe." And even as Krishna said in the same breath that "this spirit," "ancient, constant, and eternal," is "never to be destroyed in this its mortal frame which it inhabiteth," Whitman in the same line says: "I am not contain'd between my hat and boots." "Both I and thou have passed many births. Mine are known unto me; but thou knowest not thine," said Krishna (p.51). In the same section, Whitman announces: "I am the mate and companion of people, all just as immortal and fathomless as myself,/ (They do not know how immortal, but I know.)" While the soul is constant, "the sensibilities of the faculties giveth heat and cold, pleasure and pain; which come and go, and are transient and inconstant," said Krishna. Combining this with the Sankhya thought of the "Not the Me myself," Whitman says in section 4: "The sickness ... depressions or exaltations. ... They come to me days and nights and go from me again." Krishna follows with the description of the soul which "the weapon divideth" not, and, while those phrases, as we saw earlier, go to another poem, Whitman has a similar passage on the real "I am" that "apart from the pulling and hauling stands."

Says Krishna next: "Death is certain to all things which are subject to birth and regeneration to all things which are mortal; wherefore it doth not behove thee to grieve about that which is inevitable." Apart from his other uses of these words to echo their note of assurance, Whitman even attempted a tentative line on the grimmer first clause, and later shaped it into a poem called "To One Shortly to Die." Experimentally he wrote thus:

> I must not deceive you—you are to die,
> I am melancholy and stern, but I love you—there is no escape for you,
> I do not know your destination, but I know it is real and perfect.[619]

Even his ignorance of the "destination" of the dying man is inspired by the next sentence in the *Gita:* "The former state of beings is unknown; the middle state is evident, and their future state is not to be discovered."

"Make pleasure and pain, gain and loss, victory and defeat, the same, and then prepare for battle," advises Krishna. Whitman seems to have obeyed him with greater alacrity than Arjun, for he shouts:

> I play not marches for accepted victors only, I play marches for conquer'd and slain persons.
> Have you heard that it was good to gain the day?
> I also say it is good to fall, battles are lost in the same spirit in which they are won. (Sec. 18)

Interestingly enough, when thus Whitman comes to cry "Vivas to those who have fail'd!" he comes "with music strong," with his "cornets" and his "drums"; but Krishna and Arjun only "sounded their shells,"[620] or war-horns.

In his disparagement of the "men of confined notions," Krishna speaks of "the controversies of the *Veds"* and warns Arjun to be "free from" them and to "stand firm in the path of truth," because "the knowing divine findeth as many uses in the whole *Veds* collectively, as in a reservoir full flowing with water." From attachment "to riches and enjoyment," Arjun is asked to turn his mind "to things which are spiritual." In his own disparagement of those that "reckon'd a thousand acres [and] the earth much," Whitman copies Krishna's reference to the *Vedas,* and says:

> Have you practis'd so long to learn to read?

Have you felt so proud to get at the meaning of poems?
    (Sec. 2)

And then, like Krishna who enjoined Arjun next to "seek an
asylum then in wisdom alone," the wisdom he was teaching, Whitman asks his readers:

Stop this day and night with me and you shall possess the
    origin of all poems. (Sec. 2)

Apparently part of the wisdom he could teach had to be taught in
the night.

"Men who are endued with true wisdom," according to Krishna,
"are unmindful of good and evil in this world." Whitman proudly
announces: "I am not the poet of goodness only, I do not decline
to be the poet of wickedness also" (Sec. 22) ; he does not "blurt"
about "virtue" and "vice"; he "stand[s] indifferent." Describing
the character of a "wise man," the *Gita* said: "A man is said to be
confined in wisdom, when he . . . of himself is happy, and contented
in himself," and dwelt upon his other virtues—of patience "in
adversity," contentment "in prosperity," freedom from "anxiety,
fear, and anger," and the equanimity with which he "in all things
is without affection; and, having received good or evil, neither
rejoiceth at the one, nor is cast down by the other." The point of
Whitman's use of similar accounts found elsewhere has been discussed, but in the poem he echoes the passage in section 20:

I exist as I am, that is enough,
If no other in the world be aware I sit content,
And if each and all be aware I sit content.

To such a man, further says Krishna, "wisdom floweth . . .
from all sides." When he offers his own wisdom, "the good of the
earth and sun," Whitman says: "You shall listen to all sides and
filter them from your self" (Sec. 2). "Make the event equal,
whether it terminate in good or evil; for such an equality is called
Yog," teaches Krishna; and such an equality is also the refrain of
Whitman's chants. Then follows a very interesting passage in the
"Song of Bhagvat":

The tumultuous senses hurry away, by force, the heart even of the wise man who striveth to restrain them. The inspired man, trusting in me, may quell them and be happy. The man who hath his passions in subjection, is possessed of true wisdom. . . .

The man who attendeth to the inclinations of the senses, in them hath a concern; from this concern is created passion, from passion anger, from anger is produced folly, from folly a deprivation of the memory, from the loss of memory the loss of reason, and from the loss of reason the loss of all! . . . The heart, which followeth the dictates of the moving passions, carrieth away his reason, as the storm the bark in the raging ocean. . . .

The man whose passions enter his heart as waters run into the unswelling passive ocean, obtaineth happiness; not he who lusteth in his lusts.

A note explaining the term "folly" in the passage said: "*Moha,* which signifies an embarrassment of the faculties." Now, if the necessary allowances are made for the pointedly sexual element in it, and for the infinite stages of reconstruction, verbal alteration, intensification, and the like, which finally fashioned it into shape, it should not be difficult to see that section 28 of "Song of Myself" is a splendid exercise of fancy on the passage quoted above, setting forth the condition of a man betrayed by his "tumultuous senses." For almost the same words of the *Gita* and the same description of the stages of confusion can be perceived in Whitman's account. "Flames and ether" make "a rush for [his] veins," with the "force" of the original; the "prurient provokers," the "tumultuous senses" of the *Gita,* stiffen his "limbs," and strain "the udder of [his] heart," heart of a "wise man" though it is, "who striveth to restrain them," because, the senses, "behaving licentious toward" him, are "depriving [him] of [his] best as for a purpose." From this "concern," his "touch," passion is created in his "flesh and blood," and this passion ends in "confusion" and has "no regard for [his] draining strength or [his] anger." Ultimately there is the "loss of memory" and the "loss of reason": for he "talk[s] wildly" and has "lost [his] wits"; and then follows even "the loss of all": for he is "given up by traitors," and finds the "villain touch" "too much for [him]." There is "folly" or "embarrassment" of faculties," too, in the "deluding" to which his "confusion" is subjected. The "enjoyment" of "worldly lusts" was a little earlier described by Krishna as "transient"; even that thought finds a place in Whitman, because the "touch" fetches "the rest of the herd" of senses "to enjoy them a while." The image of the "bark" "carried away" in the "ocean" by the "storm" is also there, shyly suggested in the "headland" to which he is "carried" by the "traitors."

In the previous section, Whitman uses the imagery of a "quahaug in its callous shell," which "were enough" "if nothing lay more develop'd." But of his own divine form, he says:

> Mine is no callous shell,
> I have instant conductors all over me whether I pass or stop,
> They seize every object and lead it harmlessly through me.

For all the mystic meaning readable in them, the lines appear to have sprouted from these words of Krishna: "His wisdom is confirmed, when, like the tortoise, he can draw in all his members, and restrain them from their wonted purposes." Whitman of course has no truck with such restraint; but suggestively enough, these words of Krishna lead to the account of what the "tumultuous senses" do to "the heart" of a "wise man."

In the same account is it said that the wise man "walketh in that night when all things go to rest." We have already observed what Whitman imaginatively made of this. Being "self-delighted" is another of the virtues of Krishna's "wise man." Whitman says, "I dote on myself, there is that lot of me and all so luscious" (Sec. 24).

Declaring to Arjun how he alone knows having "passed many births" while Arjun does not, Krishna, "the lord of all created beings," announces: "As often as there is a decline of virtue, and an insurrection of vice and injustice, in the world, I make myself evident; and thus I appear, from age to age, for the preservation of the just, the destruction of the wicked, and the establishment of virtue." Even so declaring, in section 7, that he alone knows "how immortal" people are, while "they do not know," Whitman, in the next section, presents a description of "the little one [that] sleeps in its cradle," "the suicide [that] sprawls on the bloody floor of the bedroom," and all the sights and sounds of the world, saying at the end, in the first version, "I come again and again."

Obviously he found Krishna's role as the destroyer of the wicked
a trifle intractable for his impersonation; he even changed the last
words into "I come and depart" in the final version, probably
realizing that to "come again and again" only to "mind" the
"show" would be quite an awkward act. But if Krishna appears
"from age to age" "for the preservation of the just," he could at
least express his willingness to be where "the dried grass of the
harvest-time loads the slow-drawn wagon," and "help" (Sec. 9).
For Krishna also said at the same time: "I assist those men who in
all things walk in my path, even as they serve me." Similarly
modifying another utterance of Krishna: "He . . . who . . .
acknowledgeth my divine birth and actions to be even so . . .
entereth into me. Many who . . . filled with my spirit, depended
upon me . . . have entered into me," he describes an act of his
"absorbing" others, instead of their "entering" into him:

> In me the caresser of life wherever moving . . . . . .
> . . . . not a person or object
>   missing,
> Absorbing all to myself and for this song. (Sec. 13)

Asserting the need for faith, Krishna declares: "He who hath
faith findeth wisdom . . . and enjoyeth superior happiness; whilst
the ignorant, and the man without faith, whose spirit is full of
doubt, is lost. Neither this world, nor that which is above, nor
happiness, can be enjoyed by the man of a doubting mind. . . .
Wherefore . . . resolve to cut asunder this doubt, offspring of ignorance . . . with the edge of the wisdom of thy own soul." In
section 43, announcing his faith as "the greatest of faiths," Whitman plays upon "doubt" and "doubting minds" too:

> Down-hearted doubters dull and excluded,
> Frivolous, sullen, moping, angry, affected, dishearten'd
>   atheistical,
> I know every one of you, I know the sea of torment, doubt,
>   despair and unbelief.

"Wisdom [which 'he who is perfected by practice, in due time
findeth . . . in his own soul,'] shineth forth," says Krishna, "with
the glory of the sun." Whitman describes this finding in section 25:

We also ascend dazzling and tremendous as the sun,
We found our own O my soul in the calm and cool of the
daybreak.

In his account of the Yoga exercise, Krishna refers to "the
sacred grass" on which the yogi "sitteth." Whitman invites his
soul to "loafe with [him] on the grass" and it is on the grass that
he heard "the hum of [the soul's] valvèd voice" (Sec. 5). Ignoring many other utterances of Krishna similar to those we have
come upon elsewhere, we hear him say: "The man, O Arjoon,
who, from what passeth in his own breast, whether it be pain or
pleasure, beholdeth the same in others, is esteemed a supreme
Yogee." Whitman has that sympathy: "I do not ask the wounded
person how he feels, I myself become the wounded person" (Sec.
33).

From the seventh lecture onwards the burden of Krishna's Song
is a detailed description of the Supreme, Cosmic, Universal Spirit
that he is. He begins this revelation with these words: "Hear, O
Arjoon ... thou wilt, at once, and without doubt, become acquainted
with me. I will instruct thee in this wisdom and learning without
reserve; which having learnt, there is not in this life any other
that is taught worthy to be known." In the same tone and authority, Whitman offers "the origin of all poems" (Sec. 2), and says:

Long enough have you dream'd contemptible dreams,
Now I wash the gum from your eyes. (Sec. 46)

"There is not anything greater than I," says Krishna. "Nothing,
not God, is greater to one than one's self is," responds Whitman
(Sec. 48). "All things hang on me, even as precious gems upon a
string," says the Singer of the *Gita.* The simile goes into another
poem, "Crossing Brooklyn Ferry":

The similitudes of the past and those of the future,
The glories strung like beads on my smallest sights and hearings. (Sec. 2)

The self-delineation of Krishna that follows in this and the
next lecture has been reproduced for the most part in E. B. Green's

article surveyed before. Although, for obvious reasons, Whitman could not imitate Krishna in all his utterances, a comparison between them and the contents of his poem will show how much the nature of the Cosmic being ascribed to the "I" of the "Song" borrows from the "I" of the *Gita*. Some of the more conspicuous imitations are presented here.

"I am not visible to all, because I am concealed by the supernatural power in me," says Krishna; and "I am moisture in the water." It looks likely that this suggested the swimmers' account in section 11, where Whitman becomes the "unseen hand" that "pass'd over their bodies." "I am sound in the firmament," declares Krishna. "With the twirl of my tongue I encompass worlds and volumes of worlds," cries Whitman (Sec. 25). "This my divine and supernatural power, endued with these principles and properties, is hard to overcome," says Krishna. "I . . . am round, tenacious, acquisitive, tireless, and cannot be shaken away," says Whitman (Sec. 7). Krishna announces: "I am extremely dear to the wise man, and he is dear to me. . . . The devout souls who know me to be [Brahm] . . . know me also in the time of their departure. . . . At the end of time, he, who departeth thinking only of me, without doubt goeth unto me. . . . The man who shall in the last hour call up [the Almighty] goeth unto that divine Supreme Being. . . . He who thinketh constantly of me . . . I will at all times be easily found by [him]. . . . He who findeth me, returneth not again to mortal birth . . . on the approach of night, [when things] are dissolved away." For all the caution Whitman took in modifying this thought for his use, in order to avoid betraying himself, the following lines of section 47 of the "Song" fail to hide the source:

> The soldier camp'd or upon the march is mine,
> On the night ere the pending battle many seek me, and I do
>   not fail them,
> On that solemn night (it may be their last) those that know
>   me seek me.

The soldier is his; so is "the young mechanic . . . closest to" him; and so are "the woodman," "the farm-boy," the "fishermen and seamen." Whitman "love[s] them" all. That is the liberty of poetic imagination. But Krishna was a little stricter: he said, "He my servant is dear unto me, who is free from enmity. . . . He also is beloved of whom mankind are not afraid. . . . He my servant is dear unto me who is unexpecting, just and pure. . . . He also is worthy of my love, who neither rejoiceth nor findeth fault.[621] Whitman could not insist upon special qualifications for his "beloved" ones without defeating his own cleverness in keeping "the secret . . . close."[622]

The theme of Lecture eight is the "never-failing" "path" "which the men of subdued minds and conquered passions enter; and which, desirous of knowing, they live the lives of *Brahmacharees,* or godly pilgrims." The contributions of this chapter appear principally to go into "Song of the Open Road," transformed with Whitman's usual verbal dexterity. The phrase "godly pilgrims" easily gives him his "traveling souls." Since earthly life is "the finite mansion of pain and sorrow," because of which wise men seek Krishna to "go the journey," Whitman would be "done with indoor complaints" (Sec. 1) and "think [that] heroic deeds were all conceiv'd in the open air" (Sec. 4). His "open road" where he travels "strong and content," is, after all, the *Gita's* "journey of supreme happiness"; therefore, he "think[s] whoever [he] see[s on the road] must be happy" (Sec. 4). Krishna says that "all regions between this [earth] and the abode of *Brahm* afford but a transient residence." A little later on he explained further: "The followers of the three *Veds* . . . petition me for heaven. These obtain the regions of *Eendra,* the prince of celestial beings, in which heaven they feast upon celestial food and divine enjoyments; and when they have partaken of that spacious heaven for a while, in proportion to their virtues, they sink back into this mortal life, as soon as their stock of virtue is expended."[623] In section 9 Whitman warns:

However sweet these laid-up stores, however convenient this
   dwelling we cannot remain here,
. . . .
However welcome the hospitality that surrounds us we are
   permitted to receive it but a while.

Incidentally, since the passage partly echoes the doctrine of Karma, the word "laid-up" in it comes from Ward's account of the concept in *A View:* "The Hindoos believe . . . that millions and millions of actions expiated or unenjoyed are laid up for and against every individual, and that the fruits of only a few actions are enjoyed or endured in one birth."[624]

The joys of those "regions above" are temporary, just as those are of the earth. Yet there are men "short-sighted" enough to ask for such "finite" rewards, forgetting that the "journey of supreme happiness" ends only in Him "who is called the Supreme Abode." Says Krishna: "Those whose understandings are drawn away by this and that pursuit, go unto other *Devatas.* They depend upon this and that rule of conduct, are governed by their own principles. . . . Those who worship the *Devatas* go unto them, and those who worship me alone go unto me." Beneath the veil of symbolism, Whitman presents very much the same thought, in section 2:

> I do not want the constellations any nearer,
> I know they are very well where they are,
> I know they suffice for those who belong to them.

The *Devatas,* and their gift to their worshipers, a temporary stay in the regions above, were sufficient for those "governed by their principles." (For Whitman, "the earth, that is sufficient.") The "principles" spoken of here, are, as the translator's note says, "the three ruling qualities already explained" by Krishna, namely, Satwa, Raja, and Tama, making for goodness, passion, and dullness in human nature, and virtue or wickedness in a man's conduct. "The whole of this world being bewildered by the influence of these three-fold qualities," Whitman seems to remind himself of his own untroubled acceptance of them in the immediately next lines, which he puts in parentheses:

> (Still here I carry my old delicious burdens,
> I carry them, men and women, I carry them with me wherever
>   I go,
> I swear it is impossible for me to get rid of them,
> I am fill'd with them; and I will fill them in return.)

The "godly pilgrim," according to Krishna, is to be of "mind and understanding placed in [Krishna] alone"; "intent upon . . .

devotion"; "all the doors of his faculties" "closed up"; "his mind" "locked up" "in his own breast"; "his spirit" "fixed"; "his mind undiverted by another object." Whitman goes on the "open road" even so:

> Gently, but with undeniable will, divesting myself of the holds
>   that would hold me. (Sec. 5)

In section 13, he describes his journey thus:

> Allons! to that which is endless as it was beginningless,
> To undergo much, tramps of days, rests of nights,
> To merge all in the travel they tend to, and the days and
>   nights they tend to,
> Again to merge them in the start of superior journeys.

The *Bhagvat-Geeta* said:

> Those who are acquainted with day and night, know that the day of *Brahma* is as a thousand revolutions of the *Yoogs,* and that his night extendeth for a thousand more. On the coming of that day, all things proceed from invisibility to visibility; so, on the approach of night, they are dissolved away in that which is called *invisible.* The universe, even, having existed, is again dissolved; and now again, on the approach of day, by divine necessity, it is reproduced.

The invisible and eternal "is even he who is called the Supreme Abode," which the "godly pilgrims" "having once obtained, they never more return to earth," says the *Gita.* Whitman modestly announces: "But I know that they go toward the best—toward something great" (Sec. 13). "The fruits of this [wisdom] surpasseth all the rewards of virtue pointed out in the *Veds,"* says Krishna. Declares Whitman:

> Listen! I will be honest with you,
> I do not offer the old smooth prizes, but offer rough new
>   prizes. (Sec. 11)

And the "greater struggle necessary" on his road, for which any one going with him "must go well arm'd," might be an involuntary concession to the *Gita's* insistence on "conquered passions."

To proceed with Krishna's self-revelation of the next chapter and thus to return to Whitman's "Song of Myself": Krishna says, "All things are dependent upon me, and I am not dependent on them." Apparently, "I am a free companion," was all that Whitman could make of it (Sec. 33). "I bear the burthen of the devotion of those who are thus constantly engaged in my service," says Krishna. Whitman offers: "If you tire, give me both burdens, and rest the chuff of your hand on my hip" (Sec. 46). "I am he who partaketh of all worship, and I am their reward," says Krishna. Whitman proclaims:

> Behold, I do not give lectures or a little charity,
> When I give I give myself. (Sec. 40)

Krishna "accept[s] and enjoy[s] the holy offerings of the humble soul, who in his worship presenteth leaves and flowers, and fruit and water." Whitman "lean[s]" to "cotton-field drudge or cleaner of privies," and "swear[s]" that he "will never deny him" (Sec. 40). Krishna is "the same to mankind: there is not one who is worthy of [his] love or hatred." Whitman "make[s] appointments with all" (Sec. 19). "If one, whose ways are ever so evil, serve me alone, he is as respectable as the just man," says Krishna. Whitman's "meal" is "equally set" for "the wicked just the same as the righteous" (Sec. 19). "Remember, O son of *Koontee,* that my servant doth not perish," assures Krishna. Whitman says, "The weakest and shallowest is deathless with me" (Sec. 42).

"Hear again, O valiant youth, my supreme words": so begins the *Gita*'s tenth lecture. Section 42 of Whitman's "Song" commences thus:

> A call in the midst of the crowd,
> My own voice, orotund sweeping and final.

And it hastens to assure: "Not words of routine this song of mine." "I am the soul which standeth in the bodies of all beings," says

Krishna, and continues to name "the chief of [his] divine distinctions" in the same manner. In section 33 of the "Song," after cataloguing the many things he does, Whitman lists some of *his* distinctions in the manner of Krishna, in the same phrase "I am."

In disclosing his "divine distinctions," Krishna, "the incarnation of the Deity," names himself with his earthly name: "Of the race of *Vreeshnee* I am the son of Vasudev." The "I" of the "Song" also makes a similar disclosure: "Walt Whitman, a kosmos, of Manhattan the son" (Sec. 24). "I am also never-failing time: the preserver. . . . I am all-grasping death; and I am the resurrection of those who are about to be," says Krishna. Whitman says:

Distant and dead resuscitate,
They show as the dial or move as the hands of me, I am the
    clock myself. (Sec. 33)

"Amongst the *bards,* I am the prophet *Oosana,*" says Krishna. Whitman announces:

Through me many long dumb voices,
. . . .
Voices of cycles of preparation and accretion,
And of the threads that connect the stars. . . . .
. . . . . . [are] clarified and transfigur'd. (Sec. 24)

"I am the beginning, the middle, and the end. . . . I . . . am the seed of all things in nature," says Krishna. Whitman declares:

Through me the afflatus surging and surging, through me the
    current and index. (Sec. 24)

Speaking of the worship offered to him Krishna says the following:

Men of great minds . . . serve me with their hearts. . . . Men
of rigid and laborious lives come before me humbly bowing down,
for ever glorifying my name; and they are constantly employed
in my service; but others serve me, worshipping me, whose face
is turned on all sides, with the worship of wisdom, unitedly,
separately, in various shapes. . . .

Those who are endued with spiritual wisdom . . . worship me: their very hearts and minds are in me; they rejoice amongst themselves, and delight in speaking of my name, and teaching one another my doctrine.[625]

Whitman has his worshipers too:

My lovers suffocate me,
Crowding my lips, thick in the pores of my skin,
Jostling me through streets and public halls, coming naked to me at night,
Crying by day *Ahoy!* from the rocks of the river, swinging and chirping over my head,
Calling my name from flower-beds, vines, tangled underbrush,
Lighting on every moment of my life,
Bussing my body with soft balsamic busses,
Noiselessly passing handfuls out of their hearts and giving them to be mine. (Sec. 45)

"Pooroosh" is, according to Krishna, "the great God, the most high spirit, who in this body is the observer, the director, the protector, the partaker."[626] The "body" is Prakriti, or the material universe. Whitman's "Song" develops his self-celebration in these directions: in section 8 and 10, he plays the "observer," "peeringly view[ing]" the "show," and seeing "the marriage of the trapper"; the "protector" in section 40, filling "every room of the house . . . with an arm'd force"; and the "partaker," in section 33, where he "take[s] part" in "the cries, curses, roar, the plaudits," and so on.

This imitation of the utterances of Krishna naturally involves an imitation of his language too; and thus one of the more significant gifts of the *Bhagvat-Geeta* to Whitman is the paradoxical style in which he presents his ideas in pairs of opposites. "Song of Myself," observes V. K. Chari, "makes the largest use of the paradoxical expression; there are about thirty seven paradoxical pairs in it on a rough count."[627] Whitman, however, did not invent it; he learned it from Krishna, who says: "I am the father and the mother of the world. . . . I am generation and dissolution. . . . I am sunshine, and I am rain; I now draw in, and now let forth. I am death and immortality: I am entity and non-entity,"[628]

and so on. The "poet" of Manhattan cannot say those things;
but he says these things:

> I am of old and young, of the foolish as much as of the wise,
> Regardless of others, ever regardful of others,
> Maternal as well as paternal, a child as well as a man,
> Stuff'd with the stuff that is coarse and stuff'd with the stuff
>   that is fine,
> One of the Nation of many nations, the smallest the same and
>   the largest the same. . . . (Sec. 16)

> I am the poet of the Body and I am the poet of the Soul,
> The pleasures of heaven are with me and the pains of hell are
>   with me. . . .
> I am the poet of the woman the same as the man. . . .
>   (Sec. 21)

> Partaker of influx and efflux I, extoller of hate and concilia-
>   tion. . . .
> I am not the poet of goodness only, I do not decline to be
>   the poet of wickedness also.
> . . . .
> Evil propels me and reform of evil propels me. . . . .
> . . . .
> I find one side a balance and the antipodal side a balance,
> Soft doctrine as steady help as stable doctrine. (Sec. 22)

The rest of the Song of Krishna seems mostly to have gone into
the other poems of Whitman. But before we continue with it,
a brief glance will be given to a few details from the part so far
surveyed which have similarly entered into his other pages.

"Resolve to fight. . . . Arise and be determined for the battle. . . .
Prepare for the battle"[629] is the call of Krishna. Whitman's "call
is the call of battle" in "Song of the Open Road," section 14.
Speaking of the nature of the soul, Krishna says: "Some regard
the soul as a wonder, whilst some speak, and others hear it with
astonishment; but no one knoweth it, although he may have heard
it described."[630] The following record of a musing of Whitman in
the notebook of his gestation years appears to be a working on it:

> Tongue of a million voices, tell us more? Come, we listen,
> with itchings of desire, to hear your tale of the soul—

Throb and wait, and lay our ears to the wall as we may, we throb and wait for the god in vain—I am vast—he seems to console us with a whispering undertone in lack of an answer—and my work is wherever the universe—but the Soul of man! the Soul of Man! To that, we do the office of the servants who wake their master at the dawn.[631]

"The man who is incapable of thinking, hath no rest," says Krishna. "What happiness can he enjoy who hath no rest?" For "wisdom or the power of contemplation" is what gives "happiness supreme."[632] In one of his fragments, Whitman writes:

Remember how many pass their whole lives and hardly once
    think and never learned themselves to think,

. . . .

As to you, if you have not yet learned to think, enter upon it
    now,
Think at once with directness, breadth, aim, conscientiousness,
You will find a strange pleasure from the start and grow
    rapidly each successive week.[633]

"Those who dress their meat but for themselves, eat the bread of sin," warns Krishna.[634] Whitman's notebook meditation on the unshared eating of meat, examined earlier, may owe something to this too. Elsewhere, in a tentative piece, he writes:

Have you heard the gurgle of gluttons perfectly willing to
    stuff themselves
While they laugh at the good fun of the starvation of others.[635]

Krishna teaches:

Know that it is the enemy lust, or passion, offspring of the carnal principle . . . by which this world is covered. . . . The understanding of the wise man is obscured by this inveterate foe, in the shape of desire, who rageth like fire. . . . Thou shouldst, therefore, first subdue thy passions, and get the better of this sinful destroyer of wisdom and knowledge. . . . When thou has resolved . . . and fixed thyself by thyself, determine to abandon the enemy.[636]

In a poem called "Ah Poverties, Wincings, and Sulky Retreats," with the addition of a few more "foes that in conflict have overcome" him, Whitman speaks of the "tussle with passions and appetites" and "broken resolutions," assuring himself that his

> . . . . real self has yet to come forth,
> It shall yet march forth o'ermastering, till all lies beneath me,
> It shall yet stand up the soldier of ultimate victory.

The human body is described by Krishna as "the nine-gate city" of the soul's "abode."[637] In "Song of the Open Road," Whitman says, in a phrase improved from his early prose line of the 1847 notebook:[638]

> The efflux of the soul comes from within through embower'd gates. . . . (Sec. 7)

"I am . . . the lord of all worlds, the friend of all nature," says Krishna.[639] In "The Sleepers," Whitman says:

> . . . . I see nimble ghosts whichever way I look,
> Cache and cache again deep in the ground and sea, and where it is neither ground nor sea.
>
> Well do they do their jobs those journeymen divine,
> . . . .
>
> I reckon I am their boss and they make me a pet besides. (Sec. 1)

Describing himself, Krishna says: "The ignorant, being unacquainted with my supreme nature, which is superior to all things, and exempt from decay, believe me, who am invisible, to exist in the visible form under which they see me."[640] It is possible that these words inspired Whitman's "Are You the Person Drawn Toward Me?" where he announces: "I am truly far different from what you suppose;" and also are behind the following lines he wrote in a fragment:

To friends.
Did you think then you knew me?
Did you think that talking and the laughter of me, represented
    me?[641]

"Place then thy heart on me. . . . Fix thy mind on me. . . .
Follow me," asks Krishna.[642] "For your life adhere to me," pro-
claims Whitman in "Starting from Paumanok," section 15. "I am
Time, the destroyer. . . ." says Krishna.[643] As the first side of the
"Square Deific," Whitman declares:

........................I am Time, old, modern as any,
Unpersuadable, relentless. . . .

Being the Supreme Spirit, Krishna describes himself thus: "The
great *Brahm* is my womb. In it I place my faetus; and from it is
the production of all nature. The great *Brahm* is the womb of
all those various forms which are conceived in every natural
womb, and I am the father who soweth the seed."[644] Whitman
appears to have struck a rich vein in this mine, for this metaphysical notion is obviously what he converts into his sexual lyricism:

On women fit for conception I start bigger and nimbler babes,
(This day I am jetting the stuff of far more arrogant re-
    publics.)[645]

And the role of the father he plays in the section of "Children of
Adam," where he would "pour the stuff to start sons and daughters
fit for these states"[646] (having "sworn" "the oath of procreation"), "toss[ing] it carelessly to fall where it may,"[647] is a liberal
imitation of Krishna who "soweth the seed" into the womb of all
nature.

To return now to the remaining chapters of the *Bhagvat-Geeta*:
Krishna opens Lecture 15 with a description of "Poorooshottama,"
or the Supreme Soul, which "incorruptible being is likened unto
the tree *Aswattha,* whose root is above and whose branches are below, and whose leaves are the *Veds.*" The many instances so far

seen of Whitman's fanciful treatment of the material of his reading, support the probability that the thought of this description may
have suggested the poem about the "live-oak growing" in "Louisiana," which "with its look, rude, unbending, lusty, made [him]
think of [himself]."[648] The image of the *Veds,* books of divine
knowledge, as the "leaves" of the Tree of God, he freely uses all
over his songs, calling his poems his "leaves." "Here the frailest
leaves of me and yet of my strongest lasting."[649] Even the "live-
oak" of "Louisiana" "could utter joyous leaves." And Whitman
cuts "a twig" of that "live-oak" "with a certain number of leaves
upon it," and brings "it away." Not supposing that he was reporting an actual event, one wonders if, in poetic fantasy, whatever
the new meanings he gave to it as a symbol, he was only echoing
Krishna, who said: "When a man hath cut down this *Aswattha,*
whose root is so firmly fixed, with the strong ax of disinterest,
from that time [eternal absorption is to be sought]." The "lesser
shoots" of the tree are described by Krishna as "the objects of the
organs of sense"; and it is an interesting speculation if in cutting
"a twig with a certain number of leaves upon it," Whitman is
reducing his "own dear friends," that the twig reminds him of, to
"objects of the organs of sense." For, after all, "it remains to [him]
a curious token, it makes [him] think of manly love."

Lecture 16 of the *Gita* explains "the two kinds of destiny prevailing in the world" and the "qualities" with which men "born"
with "divine" or good, and men with "evil," destiny, are "endued."
Whitman patently does not agree with Krishna's definition of
goodness and wickedness, but, all the same, he borrows the law
under which men are born, which incidentally is the result of the
"principles" of their nature. So he says in section 8 of "To Think
of Time":

Of and in all these things,
I have dream'd that we are not to be changed so much, nor the
    law of us changed,
I have dream'd that heroes and good-doers shall be under the
    present and past law,
And that murderers, drunkards, liars, shall be under the pres-
    ent and past law,
For I have dream'd that the law they are under now is enough.

And in his account of the evil set, he even takes a few "qualities" from the original: "Those who are born under the influence of the evil destiny . . . are born of dreadful and inhuman deeds . . . trust to their carnal appetites . . . [and are] overwhelmed with madness and intoxication. . . . Nor is . . . veracity . . . to be found in them." The "shallow people" of his previous line may have been suggested by Krishna's "men of little understandings"; and "ignorant and wicked," by the "ignorance" and "hypocrisy" that, according to Krishna, the men of "evil destiny" are "distinguished by."

For all his disagreement as a "teacher" with Krishna on certain qualities of evil, when as a "man" he talks of himself, as in section 6 of "Crossing Brooklyn Ferry," Whitman seems to concur with him:

> Nor is it you alone who know what it is to be evil,
> I am he who knew what it is to be evil,
> I too knitted the old knot of contrariety,
> Blabb'd, blush'd, resented, lied, stole, grudg'd.
> Had guile, anger, lust, hot wishes I dared not speak,
> Was wayward, vain, greedy, shallow, sly, cowardly, malignant,
> The wolf, the snake, the hog, not wanting in me,
> The cheating look, the frivolous word, the adulterous wish, not wanting,
> Refusals, hates, postponements, meanness, laziness, none of these wanting.

It is obvious that although a considerable part of this poetic confession is also literal truth, Whitman could scarcely claim the entire accomplishment. Nor is it the description of the typical man, representing the evil in all mankind, as critics are naturally persuaded to accept; it simply is a "piece" that grew out of his reading, and was shaped by his fancy to fall into "place" in some "envelope." In other words, he "mused" on the following description by Krishna of "what is the nature of evil":

> Those . . . of the evil destiny are distinguished by hypocrisy, pride, presumption, anger, harshness of speech, and ignorance. . . . They . . . know not what it is to proceed in virtue, or recede

from vice; nor is purity, veracity, or the practice of morality to be found in them. . . . They trust to their carnal appetites . . . are hypocrites. . . . They adopt false doctrines . . . abide by their inconceivable opinions. . . . Fast bound by the hundred cords of hope, and placing all their trust in lust and anger, they seek by injustice the accumulation of wealth, for the gratification of their inordinate desires. . . . Being self-conceited, stubborn . . . placing all their trust in pride, power, ostentation, lust, and anger, . . . they hate me in themselves and others.

Whitman, we may note, charges himself, in the same breath, with "little understanding" and "inconceivable notions": "My great thoughts as I supposed them, were they not in reality meagre?" And the "knot of contrariety," which Miller regards as "Satan's knot,"[650] could as well be an echo of an earlier line in a similar description, in which Krishna says: "Those who are free from pride and ignorance . . . have their minds constantly employed in . . . restraining the inordinate desires, and are freed from contrary desires, whose consequences bring both pleasure and pain, are no longer confounded in their minds" (pp. 111–112).

Speaking of those evil men, Krishna says: "I cast down upon the earth those furious abject wretches, those evil beings who thus despise me, into the wombs of evil spirits and unclean beasts. Being doomed to the wombs of *Asoors* from birth to birth, at length not finding me, they go into the most infernal regions." Even this divine wrath has been matter for Whitman's poetic exercises, as in the fragment, noticed earlier, where he utters his maledictions on "those who have injured [him] so much." Some of the expressions of his anger resemble Krishna's:

Damn him! how he does defy me,
. . . .
I will not listen—I will not spare—I am justified of myself:
For a hundred years I will pursue those who have injured me
    so much.[651]

Much as we have seen of how Whitman adapts the contents of the "Song of Bhagvat" to the fancies of "Song of Myself," we shall yet notice two more instances. Krishna says to Arjun: "Attend now to these my supreme and most mysterious words, which I will now for thy good reveal unto thee, because thou art dearly beloved of me. . . . This is never to be revealed by thee to any one who . . . is not my servant."[652] Whitman says:

> This hour I tell things in confidence,
> I might not tell everybody, but I will tell you. (Sec. 19)

And like Krishna, again, who asked Arjun to "cut asunder the bonds of doubt," assuring him that when, in true knowledge, a man "findeth my [Krishna's Divine] nature" his soul is "delivered from birth and death, old-age and pain, and drinketh of the water of immortality,"[653] Whitman assures "any one dying," thus:

> Sleep—I . . . keep guard all night,
> Not doubt, not disease shall dare to lay finger upon you,
> I have embraced you, and henceforth possess you to myself,
> And when you rise in the morning you will find what I tell
>   you is so. (Sec. 40)

The "beloved" of Krishna, we may observe, are "delivered" from "death"; Whitman's "lovers of me [are] bafflers of graves." (Sec. 40)

At the end of all his teaching, Krishna asks: "Hath what I have been speaking, O *Arjoon,* been heard with thy mind fixed to one point? Is the distraction of thought, which arose from thy ignorance, removed?" In an experimental fragment Whitman asks too:

> Have I refreshed and elevated you?
> . . . . Have you
>   received from me new and valuable hints about your em-
>   ployment?
> Have you gone aside after listening to me and created for
>   yourself?
> Have I proved myself strong by provoking strength out of
>   you?[654]

One of the arguments upon which Allen is persuaded to attribute Whitman's concept of "Prudence"—which, as we have seen, is merely another name for the Hindu Law of "Karma"—to an independent thought of his own, is his apparent insistence on "perpetual . . . promotions," while, as Allen feels, the Hindu doctrine does not postulate a "perpetual" promotion,[655] sin often causing a delay or retrogression. But this little detail does not make Whitman's thought original, at least because in the translator's "Notes" to the *Bhagvat-Geeta* he read that "by repeated regenerations, all their [men's] sins are done away, and they attain such a degree of perfection as will entitle them to what is called *Mooktee,* eternal salvation, by which is understood a release from future transmigrations, and an absorption in the nature of the Godhead, who is called *Brahm.*"[656]

The contribution of the "Notes" to Whitman's thought is considerable too. For instance, among these explanations of terms and concepts, there is, narrated in full, "the story of churning the ocean," an ancient Hindu legend, included because it "is of such a curious nature, and, in some parts, bears such a wonderful affinity to Milton's description of the war in heaven, that the Translator thinks it will afford the reader an agreeable contrast to the subject of this work [*Bhagvat-Geeta*]."[657] Since the account of the "old-time sea-fight" that Whitman inserts in the obviously philosophical "Song of Myself" is not governed by any kind of artistic necessity, it is possible that, just as many "dumb, beautiful ministers," "great or small," were made to "furnish [their] points toward the soul"[658] he assumed for celebration in the poem, even so this narration of "An Episode from the Mahabharata" to form an "agreeable contrast to the subject" of the *Gita* (a work which so fruitfully supplied him with "materials" for the "identity" of the "Song"), provided the impetus for the description of a battle in it. Of course, he has not taken the battle itself from this account; he has taken it from what would be closer to the American "point of view," the "Life and Character of the Chevalier John Paul Jones etc.," by John Henry Sherbourne.[659] Yet another poem of his took its birth in this.

When, according to the legend, the "Soors and the Asoors" churned the ocean for the "water of immortality," with the mountain "Mandar" for a churn, "thousands of the various productions of the waters were torn to pieces by the mountain, and confounded with the briny flood; and every specific being of the deep, and all the inhabitants of the great abyss which is below the earth, were annihilated; whilst, from the violent agitation of the mountain, the

forest trees were dashed against each other. . . . And now a heterogeneous stream of the concocted juices of various trees and
plants ran down into the briny flood." For all the philosophical
heights to which Whitman's powerful fancy raises the 1860 poem,
"The World Below the Brine," cosmically linking the denizens of
that sphere to "beings like us who walk this" and to those "who
walk other spheres," it is basically a catalogue of the "inhabitants
of the great abyss which is below the earth."

The paradoxical style of Whitman as a poet does not seem to
be the only technical lesson he learned from the *Bhagvat-Geeta,*
for another stylistic device of his, namely, of crowding many nomi-
natives together with a verb that often comes, if it comes at all,
at the end of a long list of cumulatively organized images, appears
to have been taught at the same source. Explaining one of Krishna's
utterances a note says: *"Dwandwa*—a term in grammar, used
where many nouns are put together without a copulative, and the
case subjoined to the last only, which is a mode of composition
much admired by the Poets." Another note explains that "the Poets
of India, like the Bards of Britain, were revered as Saints and
Prophets";[660] and in Whitman's combining "prophetical screams"
with poetic "songs," this description might have had something to
do.

That, in a glance which ignores many details, is the part played
by the *Bhagvat-Geeta* in Whitman's poetry, a part he did his best
to conceal both by the cleverness of his artistic transformation and
the confusion of a downright denial. It is no wonder that those
critics and readers of *Leaves of Grass* who read the *Gita,* from
Emerson to Mercer, found parallels between them. What *is* a
wonder is the patience with which he worked the words and suggestions of the book into a shape and meaning all his own, though
most of the time ending up in plain corruption.

Any reference to J. Cockburn Thomson's 1855 translation of
The Bhagavad-Gita, a copy of which Whitman came to possess
and, in all likelihood, unwilling to possess, soon gave away, is
rendered superfluous by the fact that he had read and squeezed
out of the Song of Krishna whatever it could yield for his poetic
venture, years before Thomas Dixon of Sunderland, according to

the evidence we have, gave it to him in "Dec. 1875." Yet, while perhaps the more thorough rendering of the text it presented held no special allurement for him to read Krishna again, either for curiosity or for inspiration to his exercises in verse, he seems to have read its "copious notes" and the very elaborate and systematic "introduction on Sanskrit Philosophy and other matters," which further distinguish it from Wilkins's and Schlegel's translations, as his marginal notations on "Vyasa" and the "Sutas," and the "notes" on the Epics of India, made from the book, indicate. Not that there was anything new for him to learn from the scholarly introduction whose several sections dwelt "On the Origin of Philosophical Ideas in India," "On the Schools of Indian Philosophy," specially "The Sankhya System," "The Yoga, of Patanjali," and "The Philosophy of the Bhagavad-Gita," ending with "Remarks on the Bhagavad-Gita" itself. He had already gathered all that and more from the very "fountain-heads," Colebrooke and others, from whom Thomson himself had drawn his information.

Still, in an idle hour's casual glance, he read the text too; and the long habit, so deeply formed, of gathering attractive words and thoughts from his reading to shape into the lines of his own prophetic message could not be easily shed. So, even as he had versified the utterances of Wilkins's Krishna and played the Deity in the 1855 "Song of Myself," now he versified Thomson's Krishna who said: "For I indeed am the representative of the Supreme Spirit,"[661] and reduced his stature in the 1889 poem, "A Voice of Death," to declare: "I too [am] a minister of Deity."

Though, in spite of the caution this study persuades us to exercise in accepting statements and records of Whitman about himself and his prophetic activity, there is no reason for, nor any useful service in, questioning the authenticity of the date of his coming into possession of Thomson's *Gita*, it still looks as if he had read even this translation much earlier than 1875, if that is truly the time he got Dixon's gift. For the 1860 poem, "O Living Always, Always Dying," though its thought was in any other page of Hindu writings he read before 1855, has a title suspiciously resembling a footnote in Thomson's translation explaining a saying of Krishna that was rendered differently by Wilkins:

Lit., 'Constantly born and constantly dying;' that is, born and dying with every new body which it enters.[662]

And, in his introduction, Thomson describes Krishna as "the eighth and most important of the incarnations of Vishnu—who in his character of Preserver of mankind was supposed to descend to earth in certain earthly forms (*avatáras*) for the purpose of protecting or extending his religion—Krishna was himself raised to an equality with Vishnu, and identified with the Supreme One."[663] Whitman's raising himself to an equality with the Supreme One, had been, so to speak, accomplished without Thomson's aid, but the possibility of these words being behind the following lines of his 1860 "So Long" is there:

I feel like one who has done work for the day to retire awhile,
I receive now again of my many translations, from my avatars
   ascending, while others doubtless await me.[664]

14

THE VOICE OF SAINTS
AND A CITY OF ORGIES

RAJAH RAMMOHUN ROY'S "TRANSLATIONS OF SEVERAL PRINCIPAL Books, Passages, and Texts of the Veds, and of some Controversial Works on Brahmanical Theology,"[665] was another medium through which the ancient Sanskrit scriptures were made accessible to early nineteenth-century America. The Astor collection of Oriental literature had this book in the 1850's, when Whitman used to spend his time in "a long study . . . in some prominent New York Library."[666] While over half its contents are articles of a controversial nature, discussing certain corrupt practices and superstitions that had degenerated the Hindu society of those days, the arguments are always supported by copious extracts from the foundations of Hindu philosophical thought, the scriptures themselves. But the first half contains direct renderings into English of the best part of Hindu philosophy: translations of "An Abridgement of the Vedant, or Resolution of the Veds," "The Moonduk-Oopunishad of the Uthurv-ved," "The Cena-Upanishad, one of the Chapters of the Sáma-Veda," "The Kuth-Oopunishad of the Ujoor-Ved," "The Ishopanishad, one of the Chapters of the Yajur Veda," all "according to the Gloss of the Celebrated Shunkará-charya," and a "Translation . . . of a Sungskrit Tract, inculcating the Divine Worship," or, the famous "Gayatri," the mystic prayer of the Brahmin sages.

Colebrooke and the other Oriental scholars, as we have observed, had their accounts, with even a few extracts, of the Upanishadic passages. But a complete text of the four major *Upanishads* was offered by Roy's book alone to Whitman's plans for studying at the feet of the great masters,[667] and, as such, the part played by it in the "wisdom" with which he made his "leaves" for America cannot be disregarded, though he had known much of its contents before reading it. To emphasize that the close similarity noticed by critics such as Carpenter between Whitman's "subtle and profound" utterances and the passages in Upanishads is not accidental, some conspicuous illustrations of the way in which he "seems to *liberate* the good tidings and give it democratic scope and worldwide application unknown in the elder prophets"[668] are presented here.

In his "Translation of an Abridgement of the Vedant," Roy observes: "Byas, also . . . found the accurate and positive knowledge of the Supreme Being is not within the boundary of comprehension; i.e., that *what,* and *how,* the Supreme Being is, cannot be definitely ascertained. He has therefore, in the second text, explained the Supreme Being by his effects and works, without attempting to define his essence; in like manner as we, not knowing the real nature of the sun, explain him to be the cause of the succession of days and epochs."[669] Elsewhere it is said again: "His substance does not come within the reach of vision; no one can apprehend him through the senses . . . ," and, "Neither through speech, nor through intellectual power, nor yet through vision, can man acquire a knowledge of God.[670] One of the early exercises of Whitman's poetic endeavour along new lines, produced the following fragment, preserved in *Notes and Fragments:*

> There is no word in any tongue,
> No array, no form of symbol,
> To tell his infatuation
> Who would define the scope and purpose of God.
>
> Mostly this we have of God: we have man.
> Lo the sun;
> Its glory floods the moon. . . .[671]

One can see that these lines are a tentative recomposition of the words and thought of the above passages. Not that Roy alone taught him the incomprehensibility of God; but Whitman was not learning anything when he read the "great masters"; he was merely making poems out of what they said. So he takes even the analogy of the sun, and with his characteristic fancy builds a slightly different thought, as he does with the main idea itself, by transferring the inadequacy of "array" and "symbol" to the man "who would define," who is himself developed out of the notion of "effects" by which Byas, or Vyasa, explained the Supreme Being. The fragment is also an interesting illustration of how the effect of a mystic imagination can be produced by verbal sleight.

From the same abridgement of the Vedanta, Whitman also gathered that "the 'pure Light of all lights' is the Lord of all creatures," that "every one, on having lost all self-consideration in consequence of being united with divine reflection, may speak as assuming to be the Supreme Being," and that "it is therefore optional . . . with every individual, to consider himself as God, under this state of self-forgetfulness and unity with the Divine reflection, as the Ved says, 'You are that true Being' (when you lose all self-consideration), and 'O God I am nothing but you.' "672 Only, Whitman refused to lose "all self-consideration," and, instead of the "self-forgetfulness" recommended, clung to self-consciousness, and, as an unfortunate result, twisted the Vedic line into: "O God You are nothing but me." A similar twist appears to give him his declarations of "the theory of the earth," which he holds up as the ideal for the emulation of man in "A Song of the Rolling Earth" and in "Kosmos." Roy had said: "Also the Ved compares the knowledge respecting the Supreme Being to a knowledge of the earth, and the knowledge respecting the different species existing in the universe to the knowledge of earthen pots, which declaration and comparison prove the unity between the Supreme Being and the universe."673

A footnote in the "Translation of the Moonduk-Opunishud" repeats the familiar road image. "According to Hindoo theologians," it says, "there are two roads that lead to distinct heavens. . . . The former is the path to the habitation of Bruhma." It is also said that "external objects are the roads" for the soul, and that a "man who has intellect as his prudent driver, and a steady mind as his rein, passing over the paths of mortality, arrives at the high glory of the omnipresent God."674

The lovely phrase of Whitman, "the caresser of life," and the lines describing its activity in "Song of Myself," on which critical admiration has so fondly dwelt:

> In me the caresser of life wherever moving, backward as well
>   as forward slueing,
> To niches aside and junior bending, not a person or object
>   missing,
> Absorbing all to myself and for this song (Sec. 13),

appear to have grown out of the following passages in Roy:

> He who knows him ["the Supreme and Immortal"] as re-
> siding in the hearts *of all animate Beings,* disentangles the knot
> of ignorance in this world. . . . God . . . is styled the operator
> in the heart; he is . . . all sustaining; for on him rest all ex-
> istences. . . . The omnipresent spirit, extending over the space
> of the heart, which is the size of a finger, resides within the
> body. . . . That spiritual Being acts *always* and moves in heaven;
> preserves all material existence as depending on him; moves in
> space; resides in fire; walks on the earth; enters like a guest
> into sacrificial vessels; dwells in man, in gods, in sacrifices;
> moves throughout the skies; seems to be born in water, *as fishes
> &c.;* produced on earth, *as vegetables,* on the tops of mountains,
> *as rivers* . . . yet is he truly pure and great. . . . God is but one;
> and . . . is the operating soul in all objects. . . . He overspreads
> all creatures. . . . The Supreme Being . . . resides in the heart,
> his resplendently excellent seat: those *discriminating* men, who
> know him *as the origin of intellect and of self-consciousness,*
> are possessed of the real notion of God. (pp. 33–102).

The voyage imagery that recurs in Whitman's poems may owe
something to Roy, too, in his quotation of these Vedic passages:
"Blessed be ye in crossing over the ocean of dark ignorance to absorption into God"; "God . . . is the conveyor of those who wish to
cross the ocean of ignorance."[675] Roy also has that beautiful Upanishadic passage comparing God and the individual soul to "two
birds," from which Whitman gets "the uncaught bird" of his
"Song of the Universal," which "is hovering, hovering,/High in
the purer, happier air":

> Two birds (*meaning God and the soul*) co-habitant and co-
> essential, reside unitedly in one tree, *which is the body.* One of
> them (*the soul*) consumes the variously tasted fruits of its

actions; but the other (*God*), without partaking of them, witnesses *all events*.[676]

According to "Kuth-Oopunishud," "the soul, although it is immaterial, yet resides closely attached to perishable material objects."[677] Whitman seems to have remembered this beautiful balanced sentence just to make his line:

> I help myself to material and immaterial,
> No guard can shut me off, no law prevent me.[678]

Probably the saddest of the uses to which Whitman in his poetic ambition put the Hindu scriptures is the absurd reduction to the "Calamus" message for which, in his imitation of God, his wild and irresponsible fancy employs the sublime utterances of a spiritual nature. The "Moonduk-Opunishud" said:

> There are two sorts of knowledge; one superior and the other inferior. . . . Now the superior kind . . . is that [which] through absorption into the eternal Supreme Being may be obtained. . . . A wise man . . . forsakes all idea of duality. . . . He then directs all his senses towards God alone . . . and on him exclusively places his love, abstracting at the same time his mind from all worldly objects by constantly applying it to God. . . . A knowledge of God, *the prime object*, is not acquirable from study of the Veds, nor through retentive memory, nor yet by continual hearing of spiritual instruction: but he who seeks to obtain a *knowledge* of God is gifted with it, God rendering himself conspicuous to him.[679]

And, describing how "those fools who, immersed in ignorance, *that is, the foolish practice of rites,* consider themselves to be wise and learned, wander about . . . like blind men when guided by a blind man,"[680] the same passage further sets forth the difficulty of the knowledge of God. The path that leads to it is elsewhere compared to a "passage over the sharp edge of a razor."[681] Many another page in Roy is full of the unworldliness, discrimination, and self-subjection necessary for the acquisition of it. When, playing God for *his* lovers to seek, Whitman shouts out for any one who "would become [his] follower," and "sign himself a candidate for [his] affections,"[682] and declares the "paths untrodden" he is to take:

> In the growth by margins of pond-waters,
> Escaped from the life that exhibits itself,
> From all the standards hitherto publish'd, from the pleasures,
>   profits, conformities . . .[683]

he cruelly illtreats the voices of saints too. He takes the difficult path of the Supreme Being, and makes it "suspicious." If the seeker of God has to sacrifice "worldly objects" and pleasures, Whitman's candidate is told,

> You would have to give up all else, I alone would expect to be
>   your sole and exclusive standard,
> Your novitiate would even then be long and exhausting,
> The whole past theory of your life and all conformity to the
>   lives around you would have to be abandon'd. . . .[684]

In the same travesty, knowledge of him, Whitman, like that of God, which is not in the *"Veds,"* nor with those who hear "spiritual instruction" or practise "rites," is:

> . . . not what I have put into it that I have written this
>   book,
> Nor is it by reading it you will acquire it,
> Nor do those know me best who admire me and vauntingly
>   praise me. . . .[685]

And if the God-seeker, as Yoga said, runs away from the busy world "to a jungle, on the bank of a river of fresh running water to drink and to bathe in,"[686] thus to find a retreat for his meditation and union with God, Whitman enjoins his lovers to come

> . . . by stealth in some wood for trial,
> Or back of a rock in the open air,
> (For in any roof'd room of a house I emerge not, nor in
>   company,
> And in libraries I lie as one dumb, a gawk, or unborn, or
>   dead.)[687]

The borrowed words and idiom, supported by the nobler thoughts he has elsewhere uttered in his poems, may well tend to raise the feeling dwelt upon in these passages from its position "thrusting [him] beneath [his candidate's] clothing"[688] to a more mystic "real reality" "behind the mask" or "show of appearances"[689]— phrases that have become the stock of his poetic vocabulary and whose use for a painfully insober message helps the true meaning to elude the reader— but the language of sages for the transactions of a "city of orgies, walks and joys[690] seems somewhat a literary blasphemy.

The astronomical sense with which, in imagery and emotion, Whitman dazzles his readers may owe a little to Roy's pages also, which explain that the concept of a universal spirit as pervading and vitalizing space and all things in it is, for some, the result of the knowledge that "there are innumerable millions of bodies, properly speaking worlds, in the infinity of space . . . [which] move, mutually preserving their regular intervals between each other, and that they maintain each other by producing effects primary or secondary, as the members of the body support each other." It is even possible that "the *Friendly Society,* established by [Roy] . . . to renew and strengthen their own faith in the purer doctrines [of] the Veds,"[691] suggested Whitman's "institution of the dear love of comrades"[692] and "brotherhood of lovers,"[693] regardless of the difference in the objective.

"The omnipresent spirit," said one of Roy's passages, ". . . is the Lord of past and future events; He alone pervades *the universe* now and ever."[694] Whitman's lines in "Song of Myself" are strikingly similar:

The past and present wilt—I have fill'd them, emptied them,
And proceed to fill my next fold of the future. (Sec. 51)

His other assertion in section 24 of the same poem: "Divine am I inside and out, and I make holy whatever I touch or touch'd from," may owe its thought elsewhere, but its words seem to come from the following extract: "As the sun, though he serves as the eye of all living creatures, yet is not polluted externally *or inter-*

nally by being connected with visible vile objects, so God, the soul
of the universe, although one and omnipresent, is not affected by
the sensations of individual pain."[695] The poem "The Sleepers"
probably received some suggestion from this passage:

> The Being who continues to operate even at that time of sleep,
> when all the senses cease to act, and then creates desirable objects
> of various descriptions, is pure and the greatest of all. . . . As
> fire, although one in essence, . . . appears in various forms and
> shapes, according to its different locations, so God, the soul of the
> universe, though one, appears in various modes, according as he
> connects himself with different material objects, and, *like space,*
> extends over all.[696]

One of the principal objects of the Vedic prayers, in fact the
subject of the mystic "Gayatri," "a Sungskrit Tract, inculcating
the Divine Worship," is the sun, as the symbol of the divine
Spirit. Translations of these prayers to the sun are found in all the
Hindu writings Whitman has read. We have already noticed the
inspiration they have given to the lines in "Song of Myself" that
treat of the sunrise in the sky and the "sun-rise" within Whitman's
soul. Toward the end of his life, when the evening shadows were
lengthening around him, Whitman wrote an apostrophe to the sun,
and called it "Thou Orb Aloft Full-Dazzling." The mysticism of
the early lines is not in this 1881 poem; it is merely a lyric of the
poet's love for the "fructifying heat and light" of the sun "that
impartially infoldest all" and "givest so liberally." Claiming to
"understand" the sun's "perturbations, sudden breaks and shafts
of flame gigantic," from having "know[n] those flames, those perturbations well" within himself, and offering to utter a "special
word" for him, Whitman, the sun's "lover" who has "always"
loved him, yet launches an invocation thus:

> Shed, shed thyself on mine and me, with but a fleeting ray out
>   of thy million millions,
> Strike through these chants.
> Nor only launch thy subtle dazzle and thy strength for these,
> Prepare the later afternoon of me myself—prepare my length-
>   ening shadows,
> Prepare my starry nights.

Though the words of this prayer to the "sun of noon refulgent" were uttered when the cool evening was slowly darkening into the "starry nights," the mood and the notes have a keen resemblance to what he read in the bright morning of his poetic career in the following passages of "the Ishopanishad" in Roy:

15th. "Thou hast, O sun," (*says to the sun a person agitated on the approach of death, . . .*) "thou hast, O Sun, concealed by thy illuminating body the way to the true Being, who rules in thee. Take off that veil for the guidance of me thy true devotee."

16th. "O thou" (continues he), "who nourishest the *world,* moves singly, and who dost regulate the *whole mundane* system—O sun . . . disperse thy rays for my passage, and withdraw thy violent light, so that I may by thy grace behold thy most prosperous aspect."—"*Why should I*" (*says he, again retracting himself on reflecting upon the true divine nature*), "*why should I entreat the Sun, as* I AM WHAT HE IS," that is, "*the Being who rules in the sun rules also in me.*"[697]

And the possible inspiration of the last italicized part to Whitman's earlier lines also cannot be overlooked.

15

SOLAR OR LUNAR?

SUCH, THEN, ARE THE "GROUNDS FOR LEAVES OF GRASS AS A poem" that Whitman found in the Hindu works, having "abandon'd the conventional themes, which do not appear in it," and diligently seeking "the different relative attitude towards God, towards the objective universe, and still more (by reflection, confession, assumption, &c.) the quite changed attitude of the ego, the one chanting and talking, towards himself and towards his fellow-humanity"—"ideas" whose "contrast," when "compared with establish'd poems," should be evident.[698] Such also is the process by which "the great poet absorb[ed] the identity of others and the experience of others . . . and . . . press[ed] them all through the powerful press of himself."[699] For, after all, as he himself said, in a candor as disarming as his other statements, "first class literature does not shine by any luminosity of its own; nor do its poems. . . . The actual living light is always curiously from elsewhere—follows unaccountable sources, and is lunar and relative at the best."[700] The right phrase, incidentally, seems to be "uncountable sources," and the "sizable element of bluff"[701] with which he presented the light of a lamp lit at a neighbor's fire as the "inner light" of a divine illumination, strange. *Leaves of Grass* was neither "a message from the Heavens whispering to [him] in sleep,"[702] nor was it "there, though unformed, all the time, in whatever answers the laboratory of the mind";[703] it was simply the product of earthly ambition, labor and achievement, only with a good deal more than the ordinary degree of "tricks" with which literary business is normally conducted—"tricks" by means of which he kept "the roots of everything in L[eaves] O[f] G[rass] underground—out of sight."[704]

428

But extensive as our survey has been, it still does not cover many other spots of the vast pasture where "the magnificent idler"[705] loafed and gathered the grass to present it as "the scented herbage" of his own "breast."[706] There is, for instance, Alger's *Poetry of the East,* which he so fondly carried with him for years and read from to the soldiers in the hospitals in Washington. A little of what else he did to it for his own purposes has been noticed in these pages, and Kennedy's article in *The Conservator* refers to a few more borrowings from it.[707] But yet his use of the book as a storehouse of material—his usual way of treating books—is by no means limited to these two. A careful study will find some more lines from the specimens of the poetry of the East given in it worked bodily into his later poems, many of his utterances in them colored by the account of the mysticism of the Sufis in its Introduction, and a few of his smaller pieces actually owing their inspiration to its tiny samples. It would, however, be of little profit to pursue the inquiry because, even if the discovery may provide further illustration of Whitman's art of making poems, the book will be found to have added very little to the making of the philosopher the poet made himself to be. For Whitman was the philosopher that he was already in 1855 and his subsequent readings hardly supply anything fundamental in his thought or significant in quality. For the same reason are the other "scholarly books on the East" which he even had the fancy to buy, namely, Whitney's *Oriental and Linguistic Studies,* and J. Muir's *Religious and Moral Sentiments metrically rendered from Sanskrit,*[708] given no special attention in this study.

Of the books that went into the making of the 1855 poems themselves, many have not been noticed, or if noticed, given sufficient regard, such, for example, as the Epics and Dramas of India, and the innumerable transactions and journals of learned societies engaged in Oriental researches that were available in the Astor, Mercantile, and New York Society libraries. Many a patient hour was, beyond doubt, spent by Whitman among these in the eight long years when he secretly cherished his glorious purpose, and many a page in them has yielded its occult content to the mechanism of verbal amplification he operated on it to produce his poems. But since, apart from being a weary task, the investigation would make no valuable addition to our understanding of how one of the masterpieces of world literature came to be written, this study has ignored them all.

PART THREE:

The Leaves

1

THE MAKING OF A MASTERPIECE

"THE RADICAL DEFECT" OF *Leaves of Grass,* ACCORDING TO BLISS
Perry, "is that the raw material of fact is but imperfectly crys-
tallized by the imagination. In passing through the creative imagination of a poet crude fact undergoes a structural change, like iron
transmuted into steel. But often, in *Leaves of Grass,* this change
has failed to take place. Sometimes it is not only imagination, but
even thought is lacking."[1] The reason for this defect is not far to
seek; it lies in the fact that the "raw material" Whitman used for
his poetry was not the iron ore that the chemistry of creative
imagination transmutes into steel, but bits of finished steel
wrenched violently from completed structures and put through a
physical process of bending, cutting, whittling, and even coloring,
into another shape and use. The strongest operations of imagination
hardly succeed in such a task. A ship built out of the dismembered
parts of others, whatever the beautiful paint given to cover it,
will not have the smoothness and the integration of an original
construction. The contradictions and conflicts that mark his teaching, which so self-consciously he explained to be the result of the
"multitudes" he contained, are but the necessary outcome of the
process by which he assembled the parts of his message, not through
an imaginative synthesis of "the thoughts of all men of all ages,"[2]
but through a stringing together of words and ideas found in his
search for pliant and malleable material among what he realized
under the Transcendentalist influence to be "the true source of
noble inspirations,"[3] the "ancient Hindu poems."[4] It is almost a
schoolboy's exercise, whether of laziness or hurry or an indifferent

433

conscience, pieced together from the many printed pages of the school library, that gave him his first edition of *Leaves of Grass*. And very much like the schoolboy whose unreasonable panic of a guilty conscience, forgetting its own cleverness in making detection impossible through the many tricks of using words of one page for the thoughts of another, of mixing up the lines of several books, of rearranging, diluting, extending, and such other devices calculated to create the impression of originality, betrays itself in an excessive assertion of independence and of honesty in dependence, he too pointedly emphasized his originality in his self-reviews and his honesty or "perfect candor" in the Preface. The effort paid off; a great "Master" trustingly accepted it as "the most extraordinary piece of wit and wisdom that America has yet contributed," wondering, however, if this "beginning of a great career" did not have "a long foreground somewhere, for such a start."[5] Not only did the student pass the examination, but came off with flying colors, and, if we could use the expression, was acclaimed a prodigy. "The sunbeam was no illusion."[6] Modesty, provided any of it survives inordinate ambition, could be a severe moral challenge in these circumstances, and it needs a greater courage than youth and ambition are capable of to turn in one's award and shed a remorseful tear. Besides, there was, after all, considerable industry, even original exercise of mind, in the work, enough to soothe an irate conscience if it subsequently woke up. Thus seems to have started the career of Whitman, pride and satisfaction ministering to ambition. The suggestion of "a long foreground" slowly became an unbearable burden on the consciousness of the prodigy, and he had to create enough myths to hide it.

Like the boy astonishing his teachers with the wisdom of an adult, the journalist of Manhattan astonished his American readers with "the large utterance of the early gods"[7] in his poetry. But while others thought, with Wolfe, that it was because he was "inspired by familiarity with the same subjects: the surging sea, the windswept mountains, the star-decked heaven, the forest primeval," Thoreau, who had actually heard the large utterance of the early gods, and knew that a mere familiarity with "the surging sea" or the "forest primeval" could hardly give the godly voice in which Whitman uttered his words, traced it home to "the

Orientals." And like the schoolboy again, Whitman seems to have found that a denial was the only way to save his face.

Having saved his face that way, it became necessary for him to keep it that way. If the voice of a god in the "son" of "Manhattan," "no stander above men and women,"[8] was a trifle unnatural, he would become a god, or, what is equivalent to it, a God-inspired man. The Self he had sung of in the poem and assumed for artistic purposes had now to be assumed in a more real sense, for life. The ignorant enthusiasm of the admirers, on whom the utterances of a brilliant versifier fell like the voice of God, with enough of the mystery of sound added to the mystery of sense to confuse reaction, offered an irresistible persuasion and an equally irresistible compulsion to this act, very much as would the applause and innocent pride of parents and relatives for the boy who brought home the award. And thereafter he played the part he had assumed with all the intelligence he could summon to his aid, and built up a magnificent stage, detail by detail, prop by prop, to do so. He created the necessary mystery about his personal life, parentage, and early life and preparatory years, through all the devices of exaggerated statement or oblique reference, cleverly dropped hints or cleverly concealed facts, and a behavior calculated to suit the character of the man who uttered such biblical wisdom.

In the utterance of that wisdom, there was much to support the faith he created and maintained. The style he had used in the first edition had enough to suggest the quality of mysticism—if that is the way in which God and God's prophets reveal—with its ejaculations, broken thoughts, obscure lines, and with its jumbling of words whose excess and incoherence, its typographical idiosyncrasies whose novelty, and its irregular syntax whose strangeness, were all designed for the effect of a trance or mystic inspiration. All these helped to convert the mystery of the uncomprehended into the mysticism of the incomprehensible. Behind them were, of course, a genuine poetic skill in the use of words, and a strong fancy that supplied what he expected from the "style" of his notion: ". . . powerful words, orations, uttered with copiousness and decision, with all the aid of art, also the natural flowing vocal luxuriance of oratory."[9]

But there is no miracle in the making of *Leaves of Grass,* in any sense of the term in which critics have had to use the word as an explanation of the curious phenomenon of a poet who with "not even much early promise . . . materialize[d] like a shape from the depths."[10] The story of Whitman's sudden emergence—sudden in the sense that we are not given to see the long eight-year preparation of the impressive debut on the stage in 1855—has all the trappings and trimmings of a mysterious event, but it is the mystery of deliberate secrecy, not of the inexplicable something that happens unsought and unplanned by mortal mind. There is neither the abrupt emancipation of a hidden power through the releasing and vitalizing influence of an intense experience.

"Who emancipated him?" Binns had to ask, "May we not suppose it was a passionate and noble woman who opened the gates for him and showed him himself in the divine mirror of her love?"[11] Himself misled partly by the attractiveness of the notion and partly by the myth of the illegitimate children Whitman had fabricated to prove one of his non-existent virtues, Binns with his "dark lady" supposition led others on one of the many wild goose chases that have marked Whitman criticism. The passionate and noble woman with a divine mirror of love slowly changed color at one stage, and was even found to be a real dark lady by Harvey O'Higgins, whose contempt for Whitman's "alias" was satisfied with a "coloured" grandson.[12] Then again, the dark "dark lady" underwent another transformation, this time of a basic kind, in which identity, as all evidence declares, lay the truth about "her"; for it was only a verbal change that had made "a man" whom Whitman had "casually met" in a "populous city" into "a woman."[13] Yet, while discovering the unpleasant "secret" that Whitman's emancipation was not through a "divine" love, for the simple reason that "Whitman played the female role in these relationships"[14] not so divine at all, Cowley again sought the source of the poet's birth in some sexual experience: "The poems suggest that, at some moment during the seven shadowy years, he had his first fully satisfying sexual experience. It may have been as early as his trip to New Orleans in 1848."[15] However, it was neither a "noble woman," nor a dark woman, nor the boys Whitman went seeking in the "city of orgies" for their "frequent and swift flash of eyes offering [him] love,/Offering response to [his] own"[16]— in a word, it was no sexual experience "fully satisfying," divine or profane—that gave him the "shape" with which he "materialize[d]" from "the depths." Nor was it "O heaven! what flash and started endless train of all!"[17] Nor again was it "the meditation, the devout ecstasy, the soaring flight."[18] It was simply a talented, young, ambitious writer stirred by "the call for an original, native poet,"[19] realizing the limitations of his own powers for the honor, discovering the kind of things with which to create the effects of originality and greatness, and practicing hard and mastering the technique with which to transform those things into a shape beyond possible detection. In this design, on the one hand the consummate skill in versification and the patiently worked out mutations, verbal as well as of thought, with their additions, amplifications, and combinations, helped, and on the other hand, the fact that the things he thrust across his "native" counter were foreign enough not to raise dangerous suspicions. Yet in diverse ways he created good faith in his originality—and the genius behind the originality—through a complicated web of dissimulation, falsehood, and pretence, which by its very size and complexity succeeded in hiding the truth.

It is not merely the ingenuous mistrustlessness of human nature that made this extraordinary venture possible; there seem to have been many other factors by themselves capable of creating the psychological condition for the success of such a scheme. Among them must principally be noticed the continued ignorance of the material Whitman so systematically converted into his poetry. While Plato or Aristotle, or the German philosophers, were common knowledge to early nineteenth-century American intellectuals, the source from which he drew his "wit and wisdom" was not known to many beyond the Transcendentalists of Concord. And their suspicion, or whatever outlived the indubitably clever reincorporation in which Whitman presented this wisdom, was allayed by the positive declarations of independence the poet made and the answer with which he met Thoreau's inquiry. Not negligible is the element of national pride that burst out so rapturously in the songs of the Poet of the Land; it had an irresistible appeal and was flattering to the national spirit of many a reader. The maternal pride in the honor the son brought home could hardly be expected to have room for misgiving or suspicion. Besides, there were, "put in [his] poems: *American things, idioms, materials, persons, groups, minerals, vegetables, animals, etc.,*"[20] enough to drive anyone to the passionate satisfaction of O'Connor, who declared that *Leaves of Grass* was really "a work purely and entirely American, autochthonic, sprung from our own soil [with] no savor of Europe nor of the past; nor of any other literature in it."[21]

If the "tricks" on which Whitman built his bardic glory were confined to the first edition of *Leaves of Grass,* it would be almost understandable and excusable weakness on the part of an ambitious young poet, even if he made his poems by a skillful permutation of borrowed material. But the tricks became a habit with him, a habit of elaborating in verse the lines and suggestions of printed books that contained what he did not himself have—philosophical thought. Even the undeniably original theme of the "Calamus" poems, is, as we have seen, expressed in the language of his philosophical sources, mercilessly adapted to a profaner subject. In his paths untrodden and untreadable, he plays Krishna to his Arjunas. Almost to the last chant he sang in his "New Bible" he often made a song out of a printed page. "Eidólons" with its idea and title taken from the *Asiatic Researches* was published in 1871; "To the Man-of-War-Bird" with its borrowings from Alger's *Poetry of the East,*[22] in 1876; and "Thou Orb Aloft Full-Dazzling" with its Brahmanical prayer, in 1881, to give a few instances beyond those examined in our survey. This method of composition, unique to him, appears to have been the necessity of a poet who definitely lacked the creative imagination that gives a local habitation and a name to airy nothings, and who possessed, in a phenomenal degree, the power of embellishing the local habitation and the name that things already have. His seems to be the power of construction, an attractive assembling of things to a shape, rather than of creation, bringing things into existence primarily.

"Mine are not," wrote Whitman himself in a note, "the songs of a storyteller . . . but of an American constructor." Though he meant "constructor" differently, he seems to have achieved "the Great Construction of the New Bible"[23] through assemblage. And often construction is, and appears as, creation: the paper flower can be even more dazzling than the blossom of nature, and can with skill be made to look more like a flower than the flower itself. It is this magic of a poet's skill that Whitman appears to have built in himself through those years during which he silently and secretly worked on what he in retrospective pride called his message. With the skill that so systematically and constantly operated upon the imagination of nobler minds, "great maters," the power necessarily developed in him with which to exercise his imagination similarly.

From this issue some of his later poems, whose philosophical emotion or thought cannot be directly traced to an immediate literary derivation. And, it must be noticed, where in later years the lyric emotion, completely independent of the imitated philosophical thought, breaks forth in passion, doubt, fear, or grief, he strikes a truer note. "When Whitman speaks of the lilacs or the mockingbird his theories and beliefs drop away like a needless pretext," said T. S. Eliot.[24] It is when he drops those "theories and beliefs" that he had picked up and grafted on his poetic operations just in order to be a philosopher-poet, that Whitman's voice is truly poetic, because it is sincere, or, in other words, his own. His fear touches us, his doubts touch us, his sorrow touches us; there is the genuine passion that his heart has felt. But when he assumes the other voice, it is the powerful magic of sounds that charms us; the passion that alone makes lyric poetry is not there, because it is a voice that does not belong to him.

This raises a question of fundamental importance: what is originality in a poet? In the strictest sense of the term, there is no originality in literary creation. "It is from the writings of others that any author must of necessity get most of his ideas." Even if, as Shephard says, "Whitman's method of appropriating another's ideas is his own, unparalleled . . . in the story of literary borrowings,"[25] borrowing is there as the fundamental process of literary activity. That Whitman borrowed not from one, as Shephard thought, but from several people, is one aspect of the question. But his borrowing is not like the occasional use of a neighbor's charity; he seems to have taken care of the best part of his life on the helpless charity of all his neighbors and acquaintances, even of those he casually ran into in the streets. Strange as it may look in the figure, in the reality of artistic activity it might be regarded as natural, considering that, unlike domestic property, literary products belong to no one in particular, and, by virtue of being published, are the common possessions of mankind and therefore a writer has every right to use them. So if, as Cebría Montoliu said, we could also say that Whitman only absorbed "the ideas that were floating in the intellectual atmosphere of his time and swallow[ed] everything, without making distinctions, transforming all into his own substance, even the most contradictory opinions and theories,"[26] there would be nothing more to say. But, unfortunately, Whitman did not *absorb* the ideas, not even *borrow* them; he did something else that stretches the most liberal connotation of the term originality beyond the breaking point. He took the ideas, made verses of them, called them his own, insisted on others' calling them his own, and by extraordinary ways, ways that "put a severe strain on patience,"[27] made it impossible for people not to call them his own. And, like the humorist in the story, he even attempted to alter himself to the cut of the suit he donned.

Literary criticism in the case of Whitman is in the sad predicament of having to plead guilty to what has been called "the personal heresy." This has resulted not from the lyricism of Whitman's poetry, but from his insistently repeated assertions (regardless of how many meanings in which, as his fancy catches him, he uses the word "self"—his own self, "One's-self," "Individuality," "You," "average identity," etc.) of the autobiographical character of *Leaves of Grass*. Taking "A Backward Glance O'er Travel'd Roads" as the considered explanation, we hear him declare that it was "an attempt, from first to last, to put *a Person,* a human being (myself, in the latter half of the nineteenth century, in America) freely, fully and truly on record." We observe that he takes care again to repeat, as if the world would forget his unforgettable repetitions of it, that " 'Leaves of Grass' (I cannot too often reiterate) has mainly been the outcropping of my own emotional and other personal nature."[28] Ignoring the evident falseness of the latter declaration for a while, we may note that *Leaves of Grass* is the attempted record, free, full and true, of *"a Person."* But, as is obvious, it is not a "Life, Adventures and Opinions of Walt Whitman" in verse, presented in several songs. And despite his fond notion that "the Iliad is notably objective but 'Leaves of Grass' are profoundly subjective," and despite the ever-present "style of composition[,] an animated ego-style—'I do not think,' 'I perceive'—or something involving self-esteem, decision, authority,"[29] in them, there are many poems that are objective, and have nothing of the *Person* on record. That is not much of a flaw and we shall ignore it. But the basic flaw lies in the personality of the "Person" he created or constructed, out of the limbs torn from other persons: a kind of creation that made the monster of Frankenstein. For the identity he celebrates in *Leaves of Grass* is neither a purely human being, nor an average individual, nor the typical man, nor the soul, nor the Spirit: it is a medley of all these; a robe pieced together from various dresses, gorgeous but incongruous.

The plan to sing the song of "average identity," contrary to Whitman's vehement declarations, was a matter subsequent to the composition of "Song of Myself," which, again, far from being the "outcropping of [his] own emotional and other personal nature" was merely a skillful imitation of the yogic self-celebration conjoined to the utterances of an early god he discovered in the unknown corners of Hindu philosophy. That by superadding to them the ungodly "outcroppings" of his "own emotional and other personal nature" he accomplished an appropriateness valid enough for his poetic purposes was an unfortunate thing, inasmuch as it gave him an irresistibly dazzling artistic position, an identity for his literary operations, which a more honest or careful writer would surely have avoided for the obvious incompatibility of it. But with breathtaking audacity Whitman accepts it and permanently assumes it, regardless of how irreconcilable is the yogi of Sankhya or the god of the *Gita* with the ambitious poet of America or the son of Manhattan.

The more honest or careful writer, granting that he made Whitman's mistake of ignoring how far apart are the identity of the godly soul and the identity of the mortal man, might have achieved a better harmony, in the only way in which the incongruous ingredients could be reconciled, namely, by assimilating the inferior into the superior, in other words, by eliminating the inferior. Whitman clung to both and tried to make a virtue of the "multitudes" he contained. The cosmic wisdom he offers, had it been offered alone—no matter that it was not his own—would have made a Blake or a Wordsworth or an Emerson of him; the private passion alone, no matter how sad and sickly it was, would have made another Keats or Shelley; the nationalism alone would have made a Kipling, of course without the militant drum. To make a single "Bible" out of all these, insisting: "My poems when complete should be *a unity,* in the same sense that the earth is, or that the human body . . . or that a perfect musical composition is,"[30] was neither philosophically sound nor artistically tenable.

But Whitman made it; and if we accept the net verdict of criticism, he was successful in it. The element of confusion so glaringly present in the gift of this New Moses has of course not escaped the notice of intelligent admiration, but the virtues glitter so brightly, with a light so far beyond that of an earthly lamp, that the darkness of the corners seems trivial and negligible. To a great genius much is forgiven, where the successes are so conspicuous, the failures are not to be scanned. But the unfortunate truth is that the light he dazzles us with is the reflection of a magic mirror held to the sun, and the dark shadows are not from the spots of the resplendent orb, but from the cracks of a mirror made of several pieces of glass.

Yet the magic of the mirror is, beyond doubt, undeniable. As far as a poet is a wordsmith, or, to use Whitman's own term, a "language-shaper";[31] as far as he is a sensitive mind with a power of feeling far beyond the common man; as far as he expresses so well what was never so well expressed; and as far as his art is composition, so far Whitman's greatness is unquestionable. Eighteenth-century England's wit is his; the passionate Elizabethan lyric is his; but the vision that saw the light that never was on land or sea is certainly not his. What he gives us is an astoundingly clever reproduction, in the artificial, of the natural vision that the truer saints and sages have seen. The consummate genius with which he exhibits it almost blinds us to the mechanical apparatus that projects the spectacle before us; yet it is the greatness of photography, not of painting. "In these 'Leaves' everything is literally photographed."[32]

"A master of versification," so Eliot called Whitman.[33] While the observation in an implicit manner denies a superior power that makes a great poet, it is yet in a way an accurate description of Whitman. His is essentially a genius for verse, only this secondary virtue of a poet has such an extraordinary efficiency in him as to create the illusion of the primary one. Years of hard work patiently transforming borrowed thoughts into lines of verse appear to have developed that skill in him to that eminent degree. If, instead of the mechanical versification of the contents of his reading, he had meditated seriously, even if his immediate plan was not to learn but to find matter for his proposed poetry, the philosophic pages he read might have roused profound thought in him, from which the native talent he already possessed could have caught fire. "A good poet's *made* as well as *born*," as he wrote down in his records.[34]

But if he was painfully aware that he was not so born, and yet wanted to be a good poet, it was sad that he did not realize that the making of a poet, though it is through reading and learning, did not lie in constructing poems from an artificial linguistic exercise on the matter in printed books. That linguistic skill, with the accompanying fancy, seems to be all that he cultivated, and he was probably content with it because he found, with Emerson's unsuspecting acclamation, that he had accomplished what he had wanted to. And with the power of developing into lines of verse any stimulating thought he read or heard, and with the mystic touch cultivated alongside, he kept on the poetic exercise in the years to come. For ample supply of material he had gathered sufficient notes in his "storehouses of information," the most vital parts of which he took care to burn before he died lest the inquisitive hands of amazed researchers should discover the secret of his poetic operations.

Few critics have failed to notice how in the evolution of the final *Leaves of Grass* there is a marked decline in the so-called visionary quality of his poetry. Even by the time of the second edition, as Cowley observes, "Whitman was less visionary and more calculating in his methods."[35] "He lost in power as he grew older," said Basil de Selincourt.[36] The reason is quite obvious. With years of patient artistry he had cleverly reproduced the vision of the Hindu sages, and had managed to construct "Song of Myself," "one of the great visionary poems of modern time."[37] In the next two editions he still had some things left to take from the source of the vision, but at some point he emptied what remained of the gold mine, already nearly exhausted in that long song. There was no more "vision" to give. He could thereafter carry on only through "mere inflation," stretching out details into repetitive extensions, elaborating meanings implicitly suggested, and producing tiny reflections of the earlier vision, or, otherwise, falling back upon his own native wisdom, sufficiently trained already in the early exercise, to work on the subjects he had announced in his manifesto, the 1855 Preface.

The visionary quality of the 1855 *Leaves of Grass* owes much to the verbal devices, including the typographical, philological, and prosodic peculiarities that he designedly placed in it. The basic reason for these is of course to lend a mystic character to the poems. It is also possible that he regarded them as a means of diminishing resemblances to their sources. It is even likely that the entire stylistic complex was a compromise with the difficulty of handling the abstruse material in the conventional form. For, if the entire poem "Song of Myself" had an organic origin in one integrated emotional or intellectual activity of native imagination, it would have had an integrated form born with it at the moment of conception, no matter how much subsequent revision went into its composition. But, as we have seen, he built his poem bit by bit, transplanted into his pages from many books. Then there was the scrambling and reconfiguration. These processes through which he composed his verse are not the ones to give a poem any kind of recognizably artistic shape. What lacked a mental organization simply because it did not have its basic origin in the mind demanded too much for the material organization as a work of art. And Whitman, regardless of what the critics say, did not possess the power of a great poet that is called the mastery of his materials. At least in this case, he had, to use a popular phrase, bitten off much more than he could chew. The cleverest solution to the problem, one capable of meeting the challenges, was to make an art of artlessness—the wildness, if it were wild enough, would make the new law of art. Bad grammar, irregular syntax, corrupted words, all came in as the fashion of his art, but there is a part of them sprung from the necessity of his workmanship.

Even as the visionary quality disappears in his later poems, much else disintegrates in the growth of *Leaves of Grass*. The voice in which he had uttered the early confidence and assurance becomes weaker and weaker, and the voice of grief and pain and doubt and fear becomes insistent, because that is his own true voice. Merely versifying the Hindu philosopher, he had declared that Death, the "bitter hug of mortality,"[38] did not alarm him. He could still, if it came to preaching the Messianic wisdom he had learned at the feet of the great masters, keep on philosophically chanting that he was "O living always, always dying,"[39] or claim Christ for a "comrade,"[40] but "yet, yet, [the] downcast hours" will "cling at [his] ankles" like "weights of lead," and he will hear the "mocking voice" say: *"Matter is conquerer—matter, triumphant only, continues onward."*[41] Therefore, forgetting that he had once owned none, not even God, to be superior to himself he decides on "saluting yet the Officer over all."[42]

One of the most interesting details in the complicated system of devices by which Whitman wanted to create the impression of a mystic's revelation in his poems, is the almost artless use of the word "mystic" itself, a word that naturally started another of those vain hunts after truth. There is as much of the "mystic" about Whitman as there is of the "secret"[43] that he wrote of to set humble imagination agog with puzzled awe. "I am a look— mystic—in a trance—exaltation," he wrote in a fragment.[44] He also wrote in the same passage: "Something wild and untamed— half savage," and described "the trickling sap that flows from the end of the manly maple." He had mastered the trick of an expression whose incoherence and vagueness resembled the "strange wild way" of the "Hebraic spirit of prophecy,"[45] and used it plentifully on the flights of a doubtlessly superb picture-making fancy, enough to pass his claim at first sight that "the interior and foundation quality of the man [himself] is Hebraic, Biblical, mystic."[46]

The words of the fragment above are too much to be the record of a mystic's self-description. A mystic who *is* "in a trance" can hardly write that he is a "mystic—in a trance," and the "trickling sap that flows from the end of the manly maple" would hardly be the thing he would realize in his "exaltation." The power that described the "hairy wild-bee"[47] of the human anatomy as the "manly maple" from the end of which flows the "trickling sap," is not the imagination of a mystic who has been led "to the ecstatic contemplation of the naught."[48] It has but the skill of beautiful metaphors, exquisite images, oblique idiom, rich vocabulary, and so on, to communicate a passionate sensibility that can run into sufficient emotional excesses for purposes of lyric activity. In the transformation into the lyric utterances of his poetic form, the essentially profound thought upon which as a versifier he was operating with this skill could scarcely fail to create the effect of the mystic emotion, particularly when he designed such an impression deliberately.

The mysticism of technique can be as powerful in its results as the mysticism of imagination. The "Calamus" and the "Adamic" songs, and even the other poems that deal with a manifestly less prophetic subject matter, the unborrowed passions of the true Whitman, "of Manhattan the son," do yet have a mystic quality, simply because he had trained his poetic skill through the early exercises on prophetic matter in the habit of veiled expression and metaphorical intensity. The use of a philosophic idiom, reared upon the sublime thoughts he had so intricately played with, becoming a habit, he applies it to whatever inspires him—to a poem, to a passage in prose, or to a fragmentary record. And the incongruity itself often forms the basis of the mystic impression he creates. The mysticism that there is in him is the mysticism of manner, not of matter. What is merely the mysticism of frenzy seems like the frenzy of mysticism. It would have been some consolation to this disillusioned research into the meanings of Whitman's poems to agree with Allen when he distinguishes between original or genuine mysticism and derived or literary mysticism and inclines to regard Whitman's as of the latter type,[49] but it appears from the knowledge of Whitman's method of making verses this study has led us to, that we shall have to stretch the signification of the term "derived" far beyond the limit within which Allen applied it.

For literary mysticism is not an imitation in words of the thoughts of a mystic's experience. It is an act of imagination paralleling that of a true mystic, because at a point imagination reaches a similar height of comprehension and experiences the truths of life, or discovers them. It is the act of an imagination inspired by the study of mystics' experiences. It is not an act of versification of the record of a mystic's thoughts, however brilliantly and convincingly the versification is made. That, for all this artificial imitation, Whitman undeniably surrounds the reader with the half-lit and mysterious, invisible but not insensible, world of mysticism, and that even a stubborn reader feels the consciousness of a mystic mind behind the lines of his poetry, are only tributes to his poetic skill. He can create an illusion that forces a suspension of disbelief, whether one is willing or not, and that is, no doubt, as much the glory of art as anything else. But that seems to be all.

The way in which Whitman created his poems, the manner in which he offered them, and the light in which he presented himself as their author all succeeded in their objective—an aura of mystery, in which alone he felt that he and his work, as the great poet of a great nation and the great message of a great philosopher, would be accepted by the world. His lineage, his background, his early life had none of the promise. The miracle of a sudden transformation might do for the reader, but to the man who knew the truth of there being no sudden transformation like that of a "butcher's boy" into the greatest poet of all in his own story, there was the need for something more. So he carefully gilded the lily of his early life. All great poets have an inner call; so he said he wrote his first *Leaves* "under great pressure,—pressure from within." He had felt that he *"must* do it."[50] A great poet owes much to heredity, so he created an idealized picture of his parents. A poet who voices his nation must know all the land, so he pretended that he had traveled all over America. A poet who speaks a transcendental wisdom must speak in a transcendental voice, so he carefully reproduced the details of mystic speech. A great Messiah, obviously God-inspired, must have secret depths to his being and life, so he created a "secret" and fondly alluded to it. Having none in reality, he took care not to divulge it.[51]

Each one of these acts has misdirected criticism. Each one has built its own version of Whitman, and its own way of understanding his poetry. Each one has raised its own meaning and explanation. Each one has created a myth of its own. Some of the shallow myths in course of time broke under the weight criticism had to raise on them; some disintegrated simply at second sight. But there are many among them that have endured just because their roots went so deep and became so entangled in the earth that the complicated task of plucking them out even to see them was physically impossible.

It was an immense pyramid that Whitman built for himself, the size of which alone was sufficient for the safety of the resting-place. And time has offered an equal safety to whoever rests there. If the mummy dug up now proves to be an ambitious court-jester[52] who played an incredible trick long ago, there is sentiment enough to let the bones lie. For, after all, the pyramid is the work of art, and the world has little interest in the Pharaoh that lies in the coffin.

APPENDIX I, a

Abstract of Whelpley's Article on *The Institutes of Menu*

[Menu's] Laws were promulgated as early as the thirteenth
century B.C. . . . Sacred are they. . . . The body of the law is
named, in Sanscrit, dherma-shastra; *dherma,* like the Latin *term,*
meaning law, or unit; and *shastra,* any inspired work. . . . The
divine sages, wishing to learn of Menu the origin of law and of
the world, approached him . . . [who], in compliance, began with
a history of creation. . . . Creation . . . was a work of Brahma,
who is the principal person of the three that emanated from
Brehm, the Vast, ineffable, One. . . . [His] first thought . . .
was, to produce the world like an egg, in the ocean of Being.
*But he was in the egg, and resolved himself therein; producing
the male and female principle.* . . . By other efforts of thought,
Brahma originated the forms of things, in succession, ending with
Man.

Matter is of a feminine, *form* of a masculine, nature: their
conjunction gives origin to Maia, or Nature; who is Delusion
(appearance). . . . (pp. 510–11)

In a footnote explaining the "divine Spirit" that is within human
beings, Whelpley summarizes three verses or stanzas of Menu as
follows:

Man, according to Menu, has a three-fold life; the organic soul
of the body, which is transmigratory; the passion, intelligence
and affection; and that Divine Spirit, which is the source of
Justice, and one with God. (p. 511)

Quoting Colebrooke from the *Asiatic Researches,* Whelpley, in
his analysis of Menu's third chapter, describes how "in the ancient
poetry of India, Woman is named the giver of heaven . . ." (p.
513), and, in a brief note on the Hindu practice of *"Yoga* meaning beatitude, or absorption into the divine Essence," alludes to

the description of a yogi given in "the Sacontala of Colidos" (p. 515). And later on, discussing Menu's theory of punishment, he quotes his "admonition": " 'The soul itself is its own witness; offend not thy conscious soul: The sinful have said in their hearts, "none see us;" Yes, the gods distinctly see them, and so does the spirit within their breasts.' The judge must admonish the witness thus: 'O, friend to virtue, that supreme Spirit, which thou believest to be one and the same with thyself, resides in thy bosom perpetually, and is an all knowing inspector of thy goodness, and of thy wickedness.' " A footnote explains the term supreme Spirit as "Not the soul, nor the life subject to transmigration, but the infusion or emanation of Brehm, the *One.*" (p. 517)

If Whitman wanted further books to read, another footnote recommends the "Ramayana of Valmecki (trans. by Carey and Marshman)," from which a quotation has been made about the "three worlds" of Indian cosmology. (p. 519)

> The twelfth and last chapter of these Institutes contains the whole doctrine of transmigration, and of the final absorption of the soul.
>
> Actions, says Menu, bear fruit according to their spirit, whether good or evil; and from the actions of men proceed their various transmigrations. Bad thoughts are held equivalent to bad actions. "For sinful acts of the body, a man shall assume a vegetable or a mineral form," &c. Sins of the mind are punished in other degrees.
>
> Three souls inspire every human being:—"the vital spirit, which gives motion to the body, and an internal spirit, named *Mahat,* or the Great Soul, [the Anima Mundi, Intellect, and Passion]." "These two, the vital spirit and the reasonable soul, are closely connected with the Supreme Spirit, or Divine Soul, which pervades all beings, high or low." "From the substance of that Supreme Spirit, are diffused, like sparks of fire, innumerable vital spirits (souls subject to transmigration, *species*) which perpetually give motion to creatures."

After a brief account of transmigration, Whelpley continues:

> Finally a pure mortal, or a demi-god, may aspire to be united with Brahma, or with his immediate emanation; but at the end of time, Brahma and the gods, are to become one with Brehm, the vast One. . . .

The book concludes with an enunication of the esoterical doctrine of the Brahmins. . . . "All nature" [both visible and invisible] must be considered "as existing in the divine spirit; for when he (the priest) contemplates all [the boundless] nature as existing in the divine spirit, he cannot give his heart to iniquity." "The divine spirit alone is the [whole] assemblage of gods [all worlds are seated in the divine spirit], and [the divine spirit, no doubt] produces the connected series of acts performed by embodied souls." "He (the Brahmin) may contemplate the subtile ether in the cavities of his body (animal spirits), the air in his muscular motion and sensitive nerves; the supreme solar and igneous light in his digestive heat and his visual organs; in his corporeal fluids, water; in his flesh, earth; in his heart, the moon; in his auditory nerves, (the genii or) guardians of eight regions of the world; . . . in his progressive motion, Vishnu; [in his muscular force, Hara; in his organs of speech, Agni; in excretion, Mitra; and procreation, Brahma]."

"But he must consider the supreme omnipresent Intelligence as the sovereign lord of them all [a spirit which can only be conceived by a mind slumbering; but which he may imagine more subtile than the finest conceivable essence, and more bright than the purest gold]." Then follows a passage, which is doubtless the key of all heathen mystery. "Him, some adore, as transcendently present in elementary fire; others in Menu, lord of creatures; . . . Some, as more distinctly present in Indra; . . . others in pure air; others as the most high eternal Spirit." "It is he, who pervading all beings in five elemental forms—(earth, water, air, fire, and ether),—causes them, by the gradations of birth, growth, and dissolution to revolve in this world like the wheels of a car," (passing the round of transmigration, becoming absorbed, and again projected into the world). "Thus, the man, who perceives in his own soul that Supreme Soul, which is present in all creatures, acquires equanimity toward them all, and shall be absorbed at last into the highest essence, even that of 'the Vast One' himself." . . . Thus ends the law of Menu. (pp. 519–21)

In some of the quotations reproduced, Whelpley, in a hurry or from memory, misquotes or quotes with omission. I have therefore supplied the missing words from the original text to make the meaning clearer, taking care to supply them only from the extracts that the *Dial* magazine printed in its January 1843 issue. As regards that, besides the "Leaves" on "Heetopades" that are torn from the *Dial,* there are other indications of Whitman's having read the *Dial,* and the January 1843 issue of it, as will be seen in our study.

Appendix I, b
Abstract of *The Whig Review's Festus*

Festus makes

original disclosures, one would think he had been specially authorized to complete the Revelation begun by the prophets and evangelists of old. Probably he draws from the same source with them [p. 48]. "He spake inspired; night and day thought came unhelped, unsought, like blood to his heart; God was with him; and bade old Time unclasp his heart to the youth, and teach the book of ages." And yet "the course of study he went through was of the soul-rack [p. 49]." ". . . he knew himself a bard ordained,/More than inspired, inspirited of God [p. 49]." "He wrote the book, not in contempt of rule,/And not in hate, but in the self-made rule/That there was none to him, but to himself/He was his sole rule, and had right to be [p. 49]." The poem . . . is a sort of abstract, and fifth essence of human life, or, in the author's words, "a sketch of world-life [p. 49]." "All along it is the heart of man/Emblemed, created and creative mind [p. 50]." The following is . . . the author's account of himself: "All things talked thoughts into him. The sea went mad,/And the wind whined as 'twere in pain, to show/Each one his meaning; and the aweful sun/Thundered his thoughts into him, and at night/The stars would whisper theirs, the moon sigh hers [p. 127]." "Thus saith the bard to his work: *I am/Thy god, and bid thee live, as my God me:*/I live or die with thee, soul of my soul [p. 128], [and declares] oh! everything/To me seems good, and lovely, and immortal;/The whole is beautiful; and I can see/Nought wrong in man or nature [p. 126]." The author claims to be, and claims the right to be, a law unto himself. By this he probably means, that his work is organic [p. 57]. Assuredy "Festus" has a right to be tried by its own innate laws, *provided it has any* [p. 57]. By the dramatic form of his work, the author of course promised a development of character, an embodiment of life. In the preface, moreover, he promised that the hero should represent mankind—should be an impersonation of humanity itself, especially of youth. Here we expected to find what is most permanent and universal in human nature, gathered up into a form of individual life . . . a concentration of humanity in whom we could all see more or less of ourselves, and of what is most inward and essential in ourselves [p. 57]. The book is . . . an eclecticism of . . . Calvinism, Fatalism, Universalism, Swedenborgianism, Pantheism [p. 137]. Festus, is "an ominist and believer in all religions." And he believes in them all, not merely as essays or approximations towards "the absolutely true religion," but as fragments thereof, yet to be reunited into their original whole; and he probably designed his work as an effort towards this reunion. In justice to him, however, we ought to state, that he regards Christianity as, on the whole, the largest and best of those fragments. . . . "All are relatively true and false/As evidences and earnest of the heart/ To those who practice or have faith in them [p. 137]." As might be expected, therefore, the book is a tissue of theological contradictions . . . under [which] runs a tolerably uniform spirit which may be best defined, perhaps, as subjective transcendentalism [p. 138], [according to which] every man is to be, or to make a truth, a law, a religion, a God, a Saviour, a heaven, for himself [p. 139].

Appendix I, c
Laws of Menu in E. B. Green's Article

This universe existed only in the first Divine idea, yet unexpanded, as if involved in darkness, imperceptible, undefinable, undiscoverable by reason, and undiscovered by revelation, as if it were wholly immersed in sleep.

He, having willed to produce various beings from his own divine substance, first with a thought, created the waters, and placed them in a productive seed.

The seed became an egg, bright as gold, blazing like the luminary with a thousand beams; and in that egg he was born himself, in the form of BRAHMA, the great forefather of all spirits.

The waters were called *nara,* because they were the production of NARA, or the Spirit of God; and since they were his first *ayana,* or place of motion, he thence is named NARA-YANA, or moving on the waters.

From THAT WHICH IS, the first cause, not the object of

sense, existing everywhere in substance, not existing to our perception, without beginning or end, was produced the divine male, famed in all worlds under the appellation of BRAHMA.

He whose powers are incomprehensible, having thus created both me and this universe, was again absorbed in the Supreme Spirit, changing the time of energy for the time of repose.

When that Power awakes, (for though slumber be not predicable of the sole eternal Mind, infinitely wise, and infinitely benevolent, yet is is predicated of BRAHMA, figuratively, as a general property of life,) then has this world its full expansion; but when he slumbers with a tranquil spirit, then the whole system fades away:

For while he reposes, as it were, in calm sleep, embodied spirits, endued with principles of action, depart from their several acts, and the mind itself becomes inert.

And when they are once absorbed in that supereme essence, then the divine soul of all beings withdraws its energy, and placidly slumbers.

Then, too, this vital soul of created bodies, with all the organs of sense and of action, remains long immersed in the first idea, or in darkness, and performs not its natural functions, but migrates from its corporeal frame......

Thus the immutable Power, by waking and reposing alternately, revivifies and destroys, in eternal succession, this whole assemblage of locomotive and immovable creatures. [p. 273]

Appendix I, d
Abstract of Whelpley's "Middle-Asiatic Theology"

Kapila, another religious mendicant, founded the SANCHYA system, which is still studied. It derives all things from two principles, the male and female, according to the Vedas, and the book of Menu. Nature, in this system, is the female, Form (or Spirit,) is the male; but these terms are figuratively, and not literally taken, though the Hindoo poets use them in a literal sense. The *spirit,* according to Kapila, is distinct from the *body,* and from every other spirit. A spirit in a body is subject to sorrow, because whatever has body must suffer change and pain. [pp. 72–73]

But the Enthusiasm of the Buddhists holds no society with the believing Imagination. Trusting that the world exists of itself, and that it sprang, not out of Being, but out of Nothing, it regards all good and evil as only relative. [p. 73]

The Yoga system, founded by Patanjala, a hermit and ascetic, bases all happiness in self-denial and contemplation. [p. 73]

Of the two members of the philosophical system, the most remarkable is the idealism (or transcendentalism) of Gautama. . . . The Idealist affirms that there are two modes of thought;— *first,* the mode of induction used by the chemists and physiologists, who confine their thoughts to experience, reasoning upon the evidence of sense and sensation;—*second,* that of the Idealists, who begin with the consciousness of existence, and from that point build out a system of thought which shall explain the universe. [p. 73]

If there was a beginning, the world sprang out of nothing, and must end in nothing. Such is the god of Buddhism—the god of understanding—NOTHING, *the Scientific "Absolute."* Operations of mind are consequently a motion of gross matter; and the soul itself is no more than a condition of the body. . . . To a Buddhist . . . if all things move according to nature and necessity only, every act must be followed by its just result, according to its nature. [p. 74]

The Supreme [say the Vedanta books] may exist in what form or shape he pleases, as fire or water, or any material appearance. [p. 75]

The perfection of transcendental knowledge is gained by such contemplation as separates the transient from the eternal. . . . This Eternal is not "time without end," but a state of pure *being in which time, space and substance are embraced under one thought.* [Footnote pp. 75–76]

The world is said to be without life, but inspired and moved by Divinity. *"Divinity* is therefore one with Life." . . . It makes God to be a Power, imagined as though moving and flowing through the world. . . . The ancient Vedanta doctrine looks upon God as not only the maker but the sustainer of the world. . . . He is the Vast One, without form, the Source of all the worlds and deities,—he has neither time nor place, nor light nor darkness, nor life nor death, but is the Cause of all.—. . . In our thoughts, says the author of Vedanta Sara, it is only *pride* which makes us speak of *I, thou,* and *he;* for all, indeed, are one, in the Soul of the World: This pride is named avidya, and signifies self-love, being given for the conduct of affairs in this life; but divine knowledge overcomes it. [pp. 76–77]

Avidya, in short, is identical with Mahat, the Mundane Soul. Life, says the Hindoo mystic, is a conflict between avidya and that divine spirit, which distinguishes man above brutes. If the human soul fails of this Divine Spirit, it must fall, at death, into the bodies of animals, or into the hell of torment. [p. 77]

That which has a beginning must have an end;—the created or animal soul, therefore, shall not always exist, but (together with the mahat or intellectual soul) shall be reabsorbed or re-assumed by the creator. [p. 78]

The sublime ideas of Menu and the ancient Vedas suffered a pantheistic misconstruction. The created spirit of life began to be mistaken for the Eternal, unrevealed source. [p. 79]

Contemplating the world as an inexplicable mystery, the Hindoo pantheist attributes everything to the immediate agency of a god. Death and destruction is the work of Siva or of Cal, (time;) life is the presence of Vishnu, and the creation the work of Brahma. Every deity is paired with an Energy, or female principle. . . . Every female deity has the title of *Matri,* or mother, being the mother of inferior gods, who represent physical or physiological principles. [p. 79]

APPENDIX II, a

Ward's Account of the Tantric Sects

The proselytes to this sect are chiefly brahmins, and are called vamacharees. . . . The rules of this sect are to be found more or less in most of the Tantras. . . . When a Hindoo wishes to enter into this sect, he sends for a person who has already been initiated, and . . . begs him to become his religious guide. The teacher then places this disciple near him for three days, and instructs him in the ceremonies of the sect . . . after which he makes a declaration, that he has from that period renounced all the ceremonies of the old religion, and is delivered from their yoke; and as a token of joy celebrates what is called a vriddhi shraddha. . . . What follows is to be done in darkness. . . . Each of the vamacharees is to place by his side one of the females. . . . *The teacher now informs his disciple, that from henceforward he is not to indulge in shame, nor dislike to anything, nor prefer one plan to another, nor regard ceremonial cleanliness or uncleanliness, nor cast; and that though he may freely enjoy all the pleasures of sense, the mind must be fixed on his guardian deity, that is, he is neither to be an epicure nor an ascetic, but to blend both in his character, and to make the pleasures of sense, that is, wine and women, the medium of absorption into Brahma; since women are the representatives of the wife of Cupid, and wine prevents the sense from going astray.* . . . The vessels from which the company are to drink . . . may be formed of . . . the cocoanut, or a human skull: but the latter is to be preferred. The spiritual guide then gives as much as a wine glass of spirits to each female, as the representative of the divine energy, and the men drink what they leave. At this time the spiritual guide declares, that in the Satya yuga the people were directed in their religious duties by the vedas [etc.] . . . and, in the Kaliyuga, the tantras are the only proper guides to duty. . . . The disciple next worships each male and female separately, applying to them the

457

names of Bhairava and Bhairavi, titles given to Shiva and Durga.
. . . During his initiation he is not to drink so as to appear in-
toxicated . . . but having habituated . . . he may take more, till
he falls in a state of intoxication; still however so as to rise
again after a short interval, after which he may continue drinking the nectar, till he falls down completely overcome, and
remains in this state of joy, thinking upon his guardian deity.
He is now known as avadhoota. . . . He is to drink spirits with
all of the same profession; to sleep constantly in a house of ill-
fame. . . . These vamacharees adore the sex, and carefully avoid
offending a woman. . . . They also practise the most debasing
rites . . . while naked and in the presence of a naked female.—
*It might seem impossible to trace ceremonies gross as these to
any principle except that of moral depravity; but . . . the reader
is aware that the regular Hindoo theologians attribute all the
vices to the passions, and consider that their subjugation, or
annihilation, is essential to final beatitude; they therefore aim at
the accomplishment of their object by means of severe bodily
austerities. The vamacharees profess to seek the same object, not
by avoiding temptation, and starving the body, but by blunting
the edge of the passions with excessive indulgence.* (Italics
added) They profess to triumph over the regular Hindoos, reminding them that *their* ascetics are safe only in forests, and
while keeping a perpetual fast, but that *they* subdue their passions in the very presence of temptation. (pp. xxxviii–xli)

Elsewhere in the book, in an account of the "Worship of Human
Beings": of "the religious guides" by their disciples, their husbands
by the brahmin wives, and of the "daughters of the brahmins, till
they are eight years old . . . as forms of the goddess Bhagavati,"
Ward again refers to the Tantric sect and their "most extraordinary and shocking mode of worship":

The person who wishes to perform this ceremony must first,
in the night, choose a woman as the object of worship. If the
person be a dakshinacharee he must take his own wife, and if a
vamacharee, the daughter of a dancer, [etc.] and place her on
a seat, or mat; and then . . . succeeds the worship of the guardian
deity; after this that of the female—who sits naked.—

*Here things too abominable to enter the ears of man, and im-
possible to be revealed to a christian public,* are contained in

the direction of the shastra . . . The benefits promised to the worshippers are riches, absorption in Brahma, etc. (pp. 192–93).

A similar description occurs on a later page, in which the priest, after the usual ceremonies, "worships the goddess, the guardian deity of the person to be initiated . . . and worships the men and women who are present. . . . (p. 195)

Appendix II, b
Ward's Account of Hindu Philosophy

[On] the nature of the *Divine existence* . . . Kapila says, "The most excellent spirit is known only to himself. The nature and existence of God are inscrutable. . . . We know nothing of God but by inference." . . . "I am all that hath been, is, and shall be; and my veil no mortal hath ever yet uncovered' (Inscription upon the Egyptian temple at Sais). . . . Kapila . . . says "The universe is the work of nature as possessed of the three qualities: nature is capable of the work of creation, for behold the spider producing the web from its bowels. . . ." . . ."[The vedas] . . . declare that matter possesses motion (agitation)" . . . "Nature or chaos is the mother of the universe." . . . This [a Greek thought] agrees with the opinions of the Hindoo atheists, "that the body was to be identified with spirit." . . . Gautama very pointedly combats this idea of the world proceeding from nature: "If it be said, that nature is to be identified with things themselves, then you make the cause and the effect the same; or if you mean that nature is something separate from things, then what have you obtained, for this which you call nature must be competent to the work of creation, &c., and this is what we call God." . . .
Relative to the *Divine Nature* . . . the Vedantis speak of God . . . as a being perfectly abstracted. . . . "He is the soul of all creatures" (Veda-Vyasa). . . . Some philosophers taught, that although God pervaded all things, he remained untouched by visible objects: "Spirit has no intercourse with visible objects: the intercourse is that of intellect" (Patanjali). "Whether clothed or unclothed, since I resemble the purity of a mirror, of ether, and of simple knowledge, I (spirit) am the same. . . . Spirit is distinct both from matter and from the works formed of matter, for spirit is immutable. . . . The vital spirit through its vicinity to the world as sovereign, influences inanimate things

as the load-stone the neddle" (Kapila). . . . In the Vedanta
school . . . God was matter as well as life: "Brahma is the
cause of things as well as the things themselves. . . ." . . . Seneca
says, "What is God? He is all that you see; and all that you do
not see. . . ." The whole material universe is as it were the
clothing or body of the deity, while the vital part is the soul.
God in this state is called the virata-purusha. . . . A number of
the Hindoo philosophers declared that God was visible. One
says, "God is to be seen by the yogi." "The visible form of God
is light." . . . By other sages the Great Spirit and the spirit in
man are identified as one: . . . "Brahma and individuated spirit
are one." . . . "If a person well understands spirit, he (knows
himself to be) that spirit." "This is the voice of the veda and
the smritees, Spirit know thyself." . . . The opinions of all these
sages respecting God may be thus summed up:—Kapila admits
a deity, but declares that he is wholly separate from all terrene
affairs; and is in fact "the unknown God;" that the soul in
a state of liberation is God; that nature is the source of everything.—Patanjali maintains exactly the same opinions.—Jaimini
acknowledges a God distinct from the soul . . .—Veda-Vyasa
speaks of God as sometimes perfectly abstracted, and, according
to the Egyptian idea, "remaining in the solitude of his own
unity;" and at other times as uniting to himself matter, in which
union he is considered as the animal soul. . . Gautama and Kapila
speak of God as distinct from the soul; as an almighty Being,
creating the universe by his command, using atoms. They consider the soul as separate from the Great Spirit, and as absorbed
in it at the period of liberation.—The Satwatas and the Pouranics
speak of God as essentially clothed with body: the former taught,
that God, in the energy of joy, gave birth to the world proceeding
from himself. . . .

On the subject of *creation* . . . by several philosophers matter
itself was considered as capable of the work of creation.
. . . Kanada . . . says, "In creation two atoms begin to be agitated,
till at length they become separated from their former union,
and then unite, by which a new substance is formed, which
possesses the qualities of the things from which it arose." . . .
[Some others] believed that God united himself to matter, and
thus formed the world. . . . These philosophers speak of the
power or force which causes the procession and continued
progress of things as residing in . . . illusion. . . . Thus Veda-
Vyasa: "The mass of illusion forms the inconceivable and unspeakable energy of God, which is the cause of all things. In

creation, God united to himself shakti, or energy, in which reside the three qualities." [Then follows the thought of the male and female principles in creation, noticed earlier.] . . . Gautama taught the doctrine of an archetype or pattern from which all things were created. . . . Kapila also says, "from the elements water, fire, air and space, and the primary atoms, combined, a pattern or archetype is formed, from which the visible universe springs." . . . Some philosophers taught that the world was eternal. Hence, says Kapila, "This universe is the eternal tree Brahma, which sprang from an imperceptible seed (matter)." . . . There were others who taught that matter, atoms, and the primary elements, were eternal. . . . Kanada says, "Atoms are uncreated, and are of four kinds, from which arose earth, water, light and air." . . . Gautama says, "From God, as a body of light, the primary atoms issued." . . . Yet there were some philosophers whose conceptions of God as the creator were more correct: Patanjali says, "The universe arose from the will or the command of God, who infused into the system a power of perpetual progression." . . .

. . . Respecting the *world* itself . . . Vyaghrakarna says, "The world is false though God is united to it." . . . Kapila speaks more rationally when he says, "The world resembles a lodging-house; there is no union between it and the occupier:" and Kanada thus corrects the folly of these ascetics: "Visible objects are not to be despised, seeing the most important future effects arise out of them."
As far as these philosophers were yogis, or advocates for the system of absorption, they necessarily felt but little reverence for *the gods,* since they considered absorption, to which the gods themselves had not attained, as a felicity greater than all their heaven could supply. . . . The Hindu philosophers never directed their disciples to worship Brahma, the one God, except by the forms denominated yoga, and in which we find little that can be called worship. . . . When these ascetics condescend to notice the gods, they speak of Brahma just as Hesiod and others speak of Jupiter, that he is "the father of the gods, and that to him the creation of all things is to be attributed." They also give Brahma two associates, Vishnu and Shiva, and in the hands of this triumvirate place the work of general creation, preservation and destruction. . . . It is inculcated in every part of the Hindoo writings that the gods were created. . . . What work is there assigned to the other gods? Most of the gods, who are not the varied forms of these three, preside over some particular

part of creation or of terene affairs. . . .

Respecting the state of man in this world the Hindoo philosophers appear to have taught, that all men are born under the influence of the merit or demerit of actions performed in some prior state; that the preponderance of merit or demerit in these actions regulate the quantity of each of the three qualities (gunas) in each individual, viz. of the quality leading to truth and consequent emancipation, of that to activity, and of that to darkness, respectively termed the satwa, raja and tama gunas; which qualities have an overwhelming influence on the actions and effects of the present birth. . . . According to this system . . . "Men are born subject to time, place, merit and demerit." "God formed creatures according to the eternal destiny connected with their meritorious or evil conduct." . . . "Some say, that the very body, the senses, and the faculties also, are the fruits of actions." "Works of merit or demerit in one birth, naturally give rise to virtue or vice in the next." . . . Seneca says, "Divine and human affairs are alike borne along in an irresistible current; cause depends upon cause; effects arise in a long succession."

Respecting the human *body,* the opinions of three distinguished philosophers may suffice: Kanada says, "The body is composed of one element, earth: water, light, air, and ether are only assistants." . . . Kapila . . . delivers this opinion: "In the midst of that universe surrounding egg . . . by the will of the self-existent was produced the sthoola-sharira (from sthoola, gross, and sharira, body). . . . Causing the rare subtle parts of his own linga-sharira to fall as clothing upon the souls proceeding from himself, God created all animals." . . . Vashishta says, "From the quality leading to truth in space, arose the power of hearing; from the same in air, arose feeling; in fire, sight; in water, taste; in matter, smell. From the quality leading to activity united to space, arose speech; from the same in air, arose the power of the hands; in light, that of the feet; in water, that of production; and in earth, that of expulsion; and from this quality in the whole of the five elements, arose the power of the five breaths, or air received into or emitted from the body. The five senses, the five organs of action, the five breaths, with the mind and the understanding, form the embryo body: a particular combination of these forms the body in its perfect state." . . .

The *soul* was considered by all these philosophers as God. . . .

These philosophers further taught that mana, the *mind,* and buddhi, the *understanding,* were assistants to the soul, and not faculties of the spirit. They considered all living creatures as possessed of souls; the soul of a beast being the same as that in rational creatures, that in beasts being only more confined than that in man. "All life in Brahma." . . . The Hindoo sages distinguished, however, between the soul and animal life, the latter of which they spoke of as being mere vital breath. . . .

Having thus brought man on the stage of action, the Hindoo sages point out three modes of *religion,* the lowest of which relates to the popular ceremonies, and the fruit of which will be a religious mind, and a portion of merit and happiness. . . . The next mode is that of devotion, the blessings promised to which are comprised in a dwelling near God in a future state. But that which these sages most exalted was the pursuit of divine wisdom, either in connection with ceremonies or without them, by discrimination, subjection of the passions, and abstraction of mind. The fruit promised to this abstraction is liberation or absorption. On these subjects we have the following opinions: "Future happiness is to be obtained by devotion. . . ." "Those ceremonies by which the knowledge of the divine nature is obtained, and by which all evil is for ever removed, we call religion." "Perform the appointed ceremonies for subduing the passions; listen to discourses on the divine nature, fix the mind unwaveringly on God, purify the body by incantations and other ceremonies, and persuade thyself that thou and the deity are one." . . . Shankaracharya . . . opposed to all works . . . says, "Works are wholly excluded, and knowledge alone, realizing everything as Brahma, procures liberation."—In direct opposition to this, Garga says, "The man who is animated by an ardent devotion, whatever opinions he embraces, will obtain final emancipation." Narada suggests another way to beatitude: "Reliance on a religious guide, singing the praises of God, and abstraction, lead to future blessedness." . . . The ancient system . . . strongly recommended abstraction. . . . Wisdom, or rather discrimination was considered as the most effective agent, united to bodily austerities. . . . This discrimination was to be connected with yoga [a brief description of which follows].

On the subject of *death* . . . Shuna-Shepha says, "Material things undergo no real change; birth and death are only appearances." . . .

Of *transmigration* these philosophers thus speak: "The impress of actions (the mark of merit or demerit left on the mind by actions) is to be attributed to illusion. Actions performed under the influence of illusion are followed by eight millions of births." "He who at death loses the human form, loses the impressions received in the human state; but when he is born again as a man, the impressions of humanity are revived." . . . "The five sources of misery, that is, ignorance, selfishness, passion, hatred, and fear, which spring from the actions of former births, at the moment of a person's birth become assistants to actions. . . . Men who are moved by attachment, envy, or fear, become that upon which the mind is stedfastly fixed." . . .

Liberation, or absorption, was thus treated of by the Hindoo sages: "Emancipation consists in the extinction of all sorrow." "Future happiness consists in being absorbed in that God who is a sea of joy." . . . "The vedanta teaches, that discriminating wisdom produces absorption into Brahma; the Sankhya says, absorption into life." "Emancipation is to be obtained by perfect abstraction of mind." . . . Jamadagni . . . however, rejects the idea of the extinction of all identity of existence in a future state: "The idea of losing a distinct existence by absorption, as a drop is lost in the ocean, is abhorrent: it is pleasant to feed on sweetmeats, but no one wishes to be the sweetmeat itself."

The Hindoo sages were not all agreed respecting the *dissolution* of the *universe.* . . . Kapila says, "That in which the world will be absorbed is called by some crude matter, by others illusion, and by others atoms." . . . Jaimini, on the other hand, maintains, that "The doctrine of the total dissolution of the universe is not just. . . . The world had no beginning, and will have no end: as long as there are works, there must be birth, and a world like the present as a theatre on which they may be performed, and the effects passed through." . . . Others taught, that some parts of the universe, or of the order of things, were eternal.

NOTES

Part I

1. G. W. Allen, ed., "Walt Whitman's Philosophy," *Walt Whitman Abroad,* (Syracuse, N. Y.: Syracuse University Press, 1955), p. 215.
2. Frank E. Sanborn, "Reminiscent of Whitman," *The Conservator,* May 1897.
3. Thoreau's letter to Harrison Blake, December 6–7, 1856, in *Familiar Letters,* ed. F. E. Sanborn (Boston and New York: Houghton, Mifflin & Co., 1894), p. 347.
4. G. W. Allen, *The Solitary Singer* (New York: Macmillan & Co., 1955), p. 141.
5. "A Backward Glance O'er Travel'd Roads," *The Complete Writings of Walt Whitman,* ed. Bucke, Harned & Traubel (New York: G. P. Putnam's Sons, 1902), 3: 55.
6. See G. W. Allen, *Walt Whitman Handbook* (Chicago: Packard and Co., 1946), pp. 10–13.
7. W. S. Kennedy's phrase in *The Flight of a Book for the World* (West Yarmouth, Mass.: The Stonecroft Press, 1926), pp. 26–27.
8. Allen, *Walt Whitman Handbook,* p. 458.
9. Thoreau's letter to Walt Whitman, December 12, 1856, in *Letters (of H. D. Thoreau),* ed. R. W. Emerson (Boston and New York: Houghton, Mifflin & Co., 1891), p. 150.
10. "Hamilton Mabie on Whitman," *The Conservator,* December 1903.
11. Allen, *Walt Whitman Handbook,* p. 458.
12. *Ibid.*
13. Sister Mary Eleanor, "Hedge and Whitman," *MLN,* June 1946, and Miss O. W. Parsons, "Whitman the Non-Hegelian," *PMLA* December 1943. Also see *Walt Whitman Handbook,* p. 456.
14. Leon Howard, "For a Critique of Whitman's Transcendentalism," *MLN,* 1932, 47: 79–85.
15. V. K. Chari, *Walt Whitman in the Light of Vedantic Mysticism* (Lincoln: Nebraska University Press, 1964).
16. O. L. Triggs, *The Complete Writings,* 10: 104.
17. R. M. Bucke, "Memories of Walt Whitman," *Walt Whitman Fellowship Papers,* Philadelphia, 1894.
18. Emerson's famous letter to Walt Whitman, Malcolm Cowley, ed., *The First (1855) Edition of Leaves of Grass* (New York: The Viking Press, 1959), p. ix.
19. *Ibid.*

20. Harvey O'Higgins, "Alias Walt Whitman," *Harper's Magazine,* May 1929.

21. "Memories of Walt Whitman."

22. "Walt Whitman and the Cosmic Sense," *In Re Walt Whitman,* ed. Traubel, Bucke & Harned (Philadelphia: David McKay, 1893), p. 338.

23. *The Evolution of Walt Whitman* (Harvard University Press, 1960), 1: 50.

24. *Notes and Fragments,* ed. R. M. Bucke (Ontario: A. Talbot & Co., 1899), p. 49, no. 170.

25. No. 87 on p. 276 of *The Complete Writings,* 3, and no. 116 on p. 37 of *Notes and Fragments.*

26. Ll. 611–617, 1855 edition.

27. *Notes and Fragments,* p. 40.

28. *Catha-Upanishad,* from H. T. Colebrooke, "Essay on the Philosophy of the Hindus," Part 5, *Transactions of the Royal Asiatic Society* (London, 1827–1835), 2: 16. Whitman's reading of this and the next line will be shown later (Part 2, chaps. 4 and 14).

29. From the "Translation of the Kuth-Oopanishud," Raja Rammohun Roy's *Translation of the Principal Books, Passages and Texts of the Veds* (London: Parbury, Allen & Co. 1832), 2nd ed., p. 73.

30. *The First (1855) Edition of Leaves of Grass,* introduction, p. xii.

31. Bliss Perry's phrase: *Walt Whitman* (New York: Houghton Mifflin & Co., 1906), 2nd ed., p. 286.

32. *Walt Whitman* (Philadelphia: David McKay, 1883), p. 61. Though the connotations of "saving" and "regeneration" are different, the point is his denial of "any particular religious experience."

33. Henry B. Binns, *A Life of Walt Whitman* (London: Methuen & Co., 1905).

34. Leon Bazalgette, *Walt Whitman: the Man and his Work,* tr. Ellen Fitzgerald (Garden City: Doubleday, 1920).

35. Basil De Selincourt, *Walt Whitman: A Critical Study* (London: Martin Secker, 1914).

36. Emory Holloway, *Walt Whitman: An Interpretation in Narrative* (New York: Knopf, 1926).

37. Whitman's own note: *The Uncollected Poetry and Prose of Walt Whitman,* ed. Emory Holloway (Garden City: Doubleday, Page and Co., 1921), 2: 88.

38. *Ibid.,* p. 102, n.

39. *In Re Walt Whitman,* p. 35.

40. (New York: E. P. Dutton, 1923).

41. *In Re Walt Whitman,* p. 35.

42. *Ibid.,* p. 39.

43. Edward Hungerford, "Walt Whitman and His Chart of Bumps," *American Literature,* Jan. 1931, pp. 350–384. The theory is accepted by Mark Van Doren in "Walt Whitman, Stranger," *American Mercury* 35 (July 1935), 277–85.

44. Asselineau's phrase. *The Evolution of Walt Whitman,* 1: 50.
45. Haniel Long, *Walt Whitman and the Springs of Courage* (Santa Fe Writers' Editions, 1938).
46. *Walt Whitman* (Paris, 1929). I am indebted to Allen, *Handbook,* pp. 61–62, for the summary.
47. *Reminiscences of Walt Whitman* (London: Alexander Gardner, 1896), p. 78.
48. Introduction to the *First (1855) Edition of Leaves of Grass* (New York: The Viking Press, 1959), p. xxvi.
49. "For a Critique of Whitman's Transcendentalism."
50. *Walt Whitman's Pose* (New York: Harcourt, Brace & Co., 1936), p. 62.
51. Fred Manning Smith, "Whitman's Poet-Prophet and Carlyle's Hero," *PMLA,* 55 (1940): 1146–64, and "Whitman's debt to Carlyle's Sartor Resartus," *MLQ,* 3 (March 1942): 51–65.
52. Introduction to The *First (1855) Edition of Leaves of Grass,* p. xxvi.
53. David Goodale, "Some of Whitman's Borrowings," *American Literature* 13 (May 1938): 202–18.
54. *Pictures,* An Unpublished Poem by Walt Whitman, ed. Emory Holloway (New York: The June House, 1927).
55. Goodale, "Some of Whitman's Borrowings."
56. *Walt Whitman's Pose.*
57. *The Pall Mall Gazette* (Feb. 16, 1866).
58. "Walt Whitman," *The Fortnightly Review* 6 (1866): 538–48. Conway was not quite ignorant of Oriental literature either; he later published an anthology of Oriental verses.
59. Allen, *Handbook,* p. 459.
60. *The Fortnightly Review* 6.
61. Emile Legouis and Louis Cazamian, *A History of English Literature,* rev. ed. (London: J. M. Dent and Sons, Ltd, 1947), p. 1323.
62. *Days with Walt Whitman* (New York: Macmillan & Co., 1906), pp. 76–78.
63. *Ibid.,* pp. 94–102.
64. *Ibid.,* p. 23.
65. "Walt Whitman: The Camden Sage," *Modern Poet Prophets* (Cincinnati: The Robert Clarke Co., 1897), p. 259.
66. *Ibid.,* p. 254.
67. *Reminiscences of Walt Whitman,* p. 137.
68. *Ibid.,* p. 170.
69. *Ibid.,* p. 172.
70. *In Re Walt Whitman,* p. 161.
71. *Ibid.,* p. 223.
72. *Walt Whitman Fellowship Papers,* IV year, Philadelphia, 1897.
73. *Canada Monthly,* 10 (011): 438–43.
74. "Walt Whitman, Christian Science, and the Vedanta," *The Conservator,* February 1905, pp. 182–85.
75. *Prophets of New India* (Almora, 1944), p. 69.

76. *Parallel of Ideas in "Leaves of Grass" and the "Bhagavad-Gita"* (Ph.D. diss., University of California, 1933). I am grateful to the Library of the University of California for its loan to me.
77. Introduction to the First (*1855*) *Edition of Leaves of Grass,* pp. xi, xii.
78. Harned Collection, Item 218, Sheet 1956, Library of Congress, Washington, D.C.
79. *Walt Whitman Reconsidered* (New York: William Sloane Associates Inc., 1955), p. 89.
80. *Walt Whitman* (Boston: Houghton, Mifflin & Co., 1906), pp. 276–277.
81. *Walt Whitman: An Interpretation in Narrative,* p. 156.
82. *Parallel of Ideas,* p. 25.
83. *The Life of Swami Vivekananda,* by his Eastern and Western Disciples, 2nd ed. (Calcutta: Gowranga Press, 1915), 3: 199.
84. "Whitman's Relation to Morals," *The Conservator,* April 1896. Also introduction to his *Walt Whitman: A Study* (Boston: Houghton, Mifflin & Co., 1896).
85. *Walt Whitman Handbook,* p. 474.
86. Bucke, "Notes on the Text of Leaves of Grass," *The Conservator,* June 1896.
87. Whitman's own words, *Notes and Fragments,* p. 72.
88. *Ibid.,* p. 58. It is curious (probably deliberate) that he does not mention India.
89. *Ibid.,* p. 7.
90. From Whitman's own eulogistic review of his poems, *The United States Review,* Sept. 1855, 5: 206.
91. J. A. Symmonds's phrase, *A Study of Walt Whitman* (London: John C. Nimmo, 1893), p. 7.
92. From another of Whitman's self-reviews, *The Brooklyn Daily Times,* 29 Sept., 1855.
93. Bucke, *Walt Whitman* (Philadelphia: David McKay, 1883), p. 21; "An 'official portrait,' edited and partly written by Whitman himself," Allen, *Handbook,* p. 97.
94. *The Complete Writings,* 9:12. From one of his self-reviews.
95. The line quoted by Carpenter: "These are really the thoughts of men of all ages" etc., "Song of Myself," sec. 17.
96. H. L. Traubel, *With Walt Whitman in Camden* (New York: D. Appleton & Co., 1908), 2: 472.
97. Whitman's letter to Kennedy: *Reminiscences of Walt Whitman,* p. 76.
98. *Ibid.,* p. 82.
99. "Notes and Fragments," The *Complete Writings,* 9: 172.
100. In a Camden Newspaper: Newton Arvin, *Walt Whitman* (New York: Macmillan & Co., 1938), p. 194.
101. C. J. Furness, "Walt Whitman's Estimate of Shakespeare," *Harvard Studies and Notes in Philosophy and Literature,* Harvard University, 1932, 14: 1.

102. Bucke, "Memories of Walt Whitman."

103. *Ibid.* I cannot help noticing how this explanation contradicts his own "revelation" theory of Whitman's having got his "cosmic" wisdom in a "vision" that "comes, when at all, suddenly" like that of "Buddha or St. Paul or Mohammed"; in "June 1853." *In Re,* p. 338.

104. Bucke, *Walt Whitman,* p. 21.

105. Bucke's words, "The Man Walt Whitman," *In Re,* p. 62.

106. Bliss Perry's words, *Walt Whitman,* p. 47.

107. Bucke, *In Re,* p. 63.

108. M. D. Conway, *Emerson At Home and Abroad* (London: Trubner & Co., 1883), p. 126. Whitman's reading of the reviews will be noticed later in our study (Part 1, chap. 8).

109. *The Uncollected Poetry and Prose of Walt Whitman,* ed. Emory Holloway, 2: 75.

110. Bliss Perry, *Walt Whitman,* p. 68.

111. *Ibid.,* p. 73.

112. *The Flight of a Book for the World,* p. 11.

113. *The Conservator,* February 1907, and August 1897, "On the Trail of the Good Gray Poet," and "Identities of Thought and Phrase in Emerson and Whitman," respectively.

114. *The Uncollected Poetry and Prose,* 2.

115. *Walt Whitman's Workshop* (New York: Russel & Russel Inc., 1928), reissued 1964.

116. Bucke, *Walt Whitman,* p. 135.

117. Esther Shephard, *Walt Whitman's Pose,* p. 271.

118. *Notes and Fragments,* part III. (Part II as arranged in *The Complete Writings,* 9.)

119. *Walt Whitman,* p. 21.

120. *In Re Walt Whitman,* p. 39.

121. Bucke, *Walt Whitman,* p. 33.

122. *Notes and Fragments,* part VI. (Part V as arranged in *The Complete Writings,* 9.)

123. Bucke, *Walt Whitman,* p. 21.

124. Bliss Perry, *Walt Whitman,* p. 291.

125. *Walt Whitman* (New York: Macmillan & Co., 1938).

126. Malcolm Cowley, "Walt Whitman the Philosopher," *The New Republic,* Sept. 29, 1947.

127. Bucke's phrase in "Walt Whitman the Man," *In Re.*

128. *Walt Whitman,* p. 190.

129. Bucke, *Walt Whitman,* p. 52.

130. *Notes and Fragments,* Part VI (V as arranged in *The Complete Writings,* 9.)

131. *Walt Whitman,* p. 37.

132. Bliss Perry, *Walt Whitman,* p. 37.

133. *The Uncollected Poetry and Prose,* 1: 126–127.

134. *Notes and Fragments,* p. 70.

135. *"Leaves of Grass* and the American Paradox," *Whitman: A Col-*

lection of Critical Essays, ed. R. H. Pearce (Englewood Cliffs, N. J.: Prentice Hall, 1962), pp. 28–29. Kinnaird's footnote notices the "exception of 'Europe' and 'A Boston Ballad.' "

136. "Essay on Poetry," quoted from Conway's *Emerson at Home and Abroad,* p. 129.

137. G. W. Allen, *The Solitary Singer* (New York: Macmillan & Co., 1955), p. 172.

138. L. Daniel Morse, "Dr. Daniel G. Brinton on Walt Whitman," *The Conservator,* November 1899.

139. *Modern Philology,* November 1953, 51: 102.

140. Kennedy, *Walt Whitman,* p. 24. Barnet Phillips also reports it, slightly differently, in "Walt Whitman's Way," *Harper's Weekly,* 2 April, 1892.

141. Furness, *Walt Whitman's Workshop,* pp. 19–20.

142. Section 2, final edition.

143. July 23, 1878: *The Complete Writings,* 4: 213–214.

144. *Ibid.,* 9: 96. The word is found again in note 18.

145. W. R. Alger (Boston: Whittemore, Niles and Hall, 1856).

146. Roger Asselineau, *The Evolution of Walt Whitman,* 2: 302, n. 302.

147. *The First (1855) Edition of Leaves of Grass,* p. xii.

148. Asselineau, The *Evolution of Walt Whitman,* 2: 303.

149. The *Uncollected Poetry and Prose,* 1: 27.

150. *The Poetry of the East,* p. 45.

151. *The Complete Writings,* 4: 163.

152. W. S. Kennedy, "Notes on the Text of 'Leaves of Grass,' " *The Conservator,* February 1898. Kennedy traces many more such parallels with Alger's book in the same article.

153. Alger's own words: *The Poetry of the East,* p. 30.

154. No. 338; Bucke's list, *Notes and Fragments,* part VI (Part V as arranged in *The Complete Writings,* 9.)

155. *The Conservator,* August 1896.

156. Manuscript Notebook 2, The *Uncollected Poetry and Prose,* 2: 79–80.

157. Sec. 1.

158. Sections 44 and 45 of the final edition. Here, lines from 1163 to 1196 of the 1855 edition.

159. "A Backward Glance O'er Travel'd Roads," *The Complete Writings,* 3: 44.

160. "Song of Myself," sec. 45.

161. Malcolm Cowley, introduction to the *First (1855) Edition of Leaves of Grass,* p. xxvi.

162. "The Base of All Metaphysics," "Calamus" section, *Leaves of Grass.*

163. "When I Read the Book," "Inscriptions" section, *Leaves of Grass.*

164. *Notes and Fragments.* The notes on Goethe are made from Carlyle's notes; those on the German Metaphysicians from Hedge's "Prose Writers of Germany"; and those on Cervantes, entirely biographical, begin with a passage collected, as Bucke notes, "not known from where" (p. 83).

165. *Ibid.*, part III. (II in *The Complete Writings*, 9.)
166. *Ibid.*
167. *Ibid.*, p. 181.
168. *The Conservator*, August 1897. The second of the quotations is the title of his article.
169. *The First (1855) Edition of Leaves of Grass*, p. xxvi.
170. Note on item 65 of the Swartz Collection Sales Catalogue of Whitman material.
171. Vol. 4 (or Vol. 1 of *The Complete Prose Works*) onwards.
172. *Ibid.*, pp. 213–214.
173. *Ibid.*, p. 212.
174. *Ibid.*, p. 318.
175. *Ibid.*, p. 320.
176. That Whitman read these will be shown later on (Part 2, chaps. 6 and 14).
177. *The Complete Writings*, 4: 321.
178. *Ibid.*, 5: 13.
179. *Ibid.*, "Democratic Vistas," p. 56, and n.
180. *Ibid.*, p. 95.
181. *Ibid.*, p. 118.
182. *Ibid.*, p. 136, n.
183. *Ibid.*, "Poetry Today in America," p. 224.
184. *Ibid.*, pp. 276–277. Neither the condemnation of Shakespeare nor the praise of the Indian epics is to be taken seriously, because elsewhere he speaks of the feudalism of India. See n. 62, "Notes and Fragments," *The Complete Writings*, 9: 103–104.
185. *Ibid.*, p. 278.
186. *Ibid.*, p. 292.
187. *Ibid.*, "Little or Nothing New After All," p. 296.
188. *Ibid.*, "November Boughs," 6: 102.
189. *Ibid.*, p. 104.
190. *Ibid.*, pp. 106–107.
191. *"Indian Idylls from the Sanskrit of the Mahabharata"* (Boston: Robert Brothers, 1883).
192. *The Complete Writings*, 6: 183.
193. *The Uncollected Poetry and Prose of Walt Whitman*, 1: p. 40.
194. Bucke's phrase. Introduction to *Notes and Fragments*.
195. *Notes and Fragments*, p. 57. (Parts as arranged in *The Complete Writings*, 9.)
196. *The Complete Writings*, 9: 53–54.
197. *Ibid.*, p. 79.
198. *Ibid.*, p. 96.
199. *Ibid.*, p. 99.
200. *Ibid.*, p. 102.
201. The phrase is from the Duke University Catalogue of Whitman material, Trent Collection, p. 37.
202. "Notes and Fragments," *The Complete Writings*, 9: 103–104.

203. *Ibid.,* p. 105.
204. *Ibid.,* p. 149.
205. *Ibid.,* pp. 168–169.
206. *Ibid.,* pp. 172–173.
207. *Ibid.,* p. 186.
208. *Ibid.,* p. 210.
209. *Ibid.,* pp. 211–213.
210. In "Some of Whitman's Borrowings."
211. *The Complete Writings,* part III of "Notes and Fragments" continued, 10: 8.
212. *Ibid.,* 9: 214.
213. *Ibid.,* p. 216.
214. *Ibid.,* p. 217.
215. *Ibid.,* p. 229, editorial n.
216. *Ibid.,* p. 229.
217. *The Westminster Review,* October 1848, 50: 17–32.
218. The implications of the whole argument are analyzed in Part 2, chap. 13.
219. *The Complete Writings,* 10: 9.
220. *Ibid.,* p. 14.
221. Entry no. 231: "Original Walt Whitman manuscripts."
222. Berg Collection, New York Public Library, No. 223800B, pp. 3–4 and 6.
223. The book and the pinned notes are in Mr. Feinberg's collection. I am grateful to Mr. Feinberg for permission to examine them.
224. *The Complete Writings,* 10: 51.
225. Harned Collection, item no. 73.
226. *The Complete Writings,* 10: 50. The source will be mentioned later (n. 263).
227. *Walt Whitman's Workshop,* p. 201.
228. *The Conservator,* February 1898.
229. *The Evolution of Walt Whitman,* 2: 302, n. 302.
230. *Letters (of H. D. Thoreau),* ed. R. W. Emerson, p. 150.
231. *Ibid.,* p. 153. I have not been able to lay hands on Whitman's own letter, to which this is a reply, but its contents can easily be inferred from this.
232. "Some Personal and Old Age Jottings," *The Complete Prose Works of Walt Whitman* (Boston: Small and Maynard Co., 1907), p. 521.
233. Mr. Feinberg told me he acquired it from Mrs. Traubel.
234. In the discussion of *Gita,* on a later page (Part 2, chap. 13, n. 581).
235. "Notes and Fragments," *The Complete Writings,* 10, part V.
236. *Pictures.*
237. *Ibid.,* introduction.
238. *Notes and Fragments,* p. 10.
239. "Indian Epic Poetry," *The Westminster Review,* October 1848.
240. "Some of Whitman's Borrowings."

241. "Indian Epic Poetry."
242. *The Complete Writings,* 1: xxix.
243. The words "favorite and pupil" are repeated in Wilkins' preface too. The *Bhagvat-Geeta* will be discussed later (Part 2, chaps. 13 and 14).
244. *I Sit and Look Out,* ed. Holloway, Vernolian and Schwarz (New York: Columbia University Press, 1932), p. 64.
245. *Walt Whitman's Pose,* p. 341.
246. *Faint Clews and Indirections,* ed. Clarence Gohdes & Rollo G. Silver (Durham, N. C.: Duke University Press, 1949), p. 28. Also Trent Catalogue, Duke University Press, item no. 31, p. 25.
247. *Walt Whitman,* p. 281.
248. *Walt Whitman's Pose,* p. 251.
249. *Notes and Fragments,* no. 309, p. 203.
250. *Ibid.,* no. 314, p. 203.
251. *The Evolution of Walt Whitman,* 2: 302, n. 302.
252. The extracts are all from the *Dial's* pages.
253. *The Uncollected Poetry and Prose,* 2: 66.
254. "Sundown Papers" no. 7, and an 1846 article in "The Brooklyn Daily Eagle": *The Uncollected Poetry and Prose,* 1: 37–39 and 123.
255. *Ibid.,* 1: 68.
256. "To a Common Prostitute."
257. Chandala was a person of the lowest social order in the ancient Hindu society.
258. Cf. Whitman's insistence on health.
259. With this and the one that follows may be compared Whitman's: "The prudence of the greatest poet knows that the young man who composedly perilled his life and lost it has done exceedingly well for himself," in Preface to the 1855 Edition of *Leaves of Grass,* Cowley's edition, p. 21.
260. "Whitman," *The Conservator,* May 1905.
261. *Days with Walt Whitman,* p. 43.
262. *Notes and Fragments,* p. 78. (Part II as in *The Complete Writings,* 9.) This and the next one have already been quoted earlier in this book. But the repetition was thought necessary to make the point clear.
263. *The Complete Writings,* 10: 50.
264. *The Uncollected Poetry and Prose,* 2: 85.
265. *Notes and Fragments,* p. 31.
266. H. D. Thoreau, *A Week On the Concord and Merrimac Rivers* (Boston: Houghton, Mifflin & Co.), 2nd ed., 1891, pp. 159–160; first published 1849. Whitman has written on the flyleaf of his copy: "Thoreau called upon me in Brooklyn 1856 and upon my giving him L. of G. first edition–gave me this volume–We had a two hours talk & walk–I liked him well–I think he told me he was busy at a surveying job down on Staten Island. He was full of animation–

seemed in good health—looked very well." The book, an 1849 edition, is now in Mr. Feinberg's collection, to whom I am indebted for the quotation.

267. Sir William Jones, preface to the "Institutes of Menu," *Works,* 3: 54. The book will be noticed later (Part 2, chap. 5).
268. *Walt Whitman's Workshop,* p. 49. Cf. the verse of "Heetopades" quoted: "The difference between the body and the qualities is infinite; the body is a thing to be destroyed in a moment, whilst the qualities endure to the end of creation."
269. W. S. Kennedy, in *The Flight of a Book for the World,* regards the "I" as the distinct total of the Soul and the Body, while C. J. Furness, in *Walt Whitman's Workshop,* considers the "I" to stand for the poetic genius. But Whitman has played the Supreme Soul more often.
270. "Song of Myself," sec. 24.
271. Introduction to *The First (1855) Edition of Leaves of Grass.* p. x.
272. The Reverend W. Ward, *A View of the Hindoos,* 1: 382. Further discussion in Part 2, chaps. 7, 8, and 9.
273. *The Uncollected Poetry and Prose,* 2: 75.
274. "Song of Myself," sec. 42.
275. *Ibid.,* ll. 32–35, first edition.
276. *The Uncollected Poetry and Prose,* 2: 83 and 66. The "Orphic Saying" is no. X, called "Apotheosis."
277. This and the next are from the January 1841 *Dial.*
278. Section 4.
279. *Notes and Fragments,* no. 86, p. 109.
280. *Ibid.,* no. 83, p. 108.
281. *Notes and Fragments,* pp. 161 and 179.
282. *The Uncollected Poetry and Prose,* 2: 66.
283. The lines are entitled "Concerning Ourselves" in "First Principles."
284. Item no. 416 in Bucke's list, *Notes and Fragments.*
285. *Ibid.,* no. 150, p. 126.
286. "Chanting the Square Deific: A study in Whitman's Religion," *American Literature,* May 1937, Vol. 9.
287. "Inscription at the entrance of L. O. G," *Walt Whitman's Workshop,* p. 174.
288. "So Long."
289. "A Backward Glance."
290. "To Him That Was Crucified."
291. "Song of Myself," sec. 5.
292. *Notes and Fragments,* no. 76, p. 29.
293. *Walt Whitman's Workshop,* p. 131.
294. *The Uncollected Poetry and Prose,* 2: 68.
295. *Ibid.,* p. 64. The suggestion of this argument is not that the sentiment was inspired by "Festus," because, as will be shown later, it has a more serious inspiration.
296. See Appendix I, b. The extracts from page 126 onwards are from the second part of the review in the February 1847 number.

297. *The Solitary Singer,* p. 159.

298. "Whitman and the Cosmic Sense," *In Re Walt Whitman,* p. 341.

299. James E. Miller Jr., *A Critical Guide to "Leaves of Grass"* (University of Chicago, 1957), p. 10.

300. *The Uncollected Poetry and Prose,* 2: 72–73.

301. Edward Carpenter, *Days With Walt Whitman,* p. 43. Whitman elsewhere has said that the meaning of his poems eludes him too.

302. "To Think of Time," sec. 6.

303. Preface to the 1855 *Leaves of Grass,* Cowley's edition, p. 19.

304. *Notes and Fragments* (or, *The Complete Writings,* 9: 102 and 105).

305. *The Complete Writings,* 9: 229.

306. *Days With Walt Whitman,* p. 23.

307. Preface to the 1855 *Leaves of Grass,* Cowley's edition, p. 7.

308. *Ibid.,* opening line of the Preface, p. 1.

309. "Passage to India."

310. "Manuscript of *Passage to India*", *Workshop,* p. 213.

311. "Prayer of Columbus."

312. *Notes and Fragments,* notes 60 and 61, p. 144.

Part II

1. *Notes and Fragments,* no. 60, p. 168. The description of the paper is Bucke's in a footnote.

2. *Ibid.,* no. 12, p. 56.

3. *Ibid.,* no. 9, p. 78.

4. *Ibid.,* no. 16, p. 57.

5. *Ibid.,* no. 14, p. 57.

6. *Ibid.,* no. 82, p. 171.

7. Collected in *Walt Whitman's Workshop,* pp. 39–53.

8. *Notes and Fragments,* no. 4, pp. 152–154.

9. *The Uncollected Poetry and Prose,* 2.

10. *Notes and Fragments,* no. 176, pp. 140–141.

11. *Ibid.,* no. 190, pp. 143–145. No. 176 appears as part of this long fragment.

12. *Ibid.,* from the same note.

13. *Ibid.,* no. 38, p. 64.

14. "Song of Myself."

15. From the foreword to *Rivulets of Prose,* ed. Carolyn Wells and A. E. Goldsmith (New York: Greenberg, 1928), p. xvii.

16. J. A. Symmonds, *A Study of Walt Whitman* (London: John C. Nimmo, 1893), p. 12.

17. Manuscript Notebook no. 1, *The Uncollected Poetry and Prose,* 2: 63–76. The quotations that follow are from the same pages.

18. H. B. Binns, *A Life of Walt Whitman,* p. 55.

19. R. M. Bucke, *Walt Whitman,* p. 21.

20. Bliss Perry, *Walt Whitman,* p. 73.

21. R. M. Bucke, *Walt Whitman,* p. 135. Whitman's words quoted.

22. *Ibid.,* p. 24.
23. Whitman's words. "A Backward Glance," *The Complete Writings,* 3 : 44.
24. Except "Europe" and "A Boston Ballad."
25. Emerson's congratulatory letter to Whitman.
26. Whitman's words.
27. G. W. Allen, *Walt Whitman Handbook,* pp. 62–63.
28. *Notes and Fragments,* no. 163, pp. 128–129.
29. *Ibid.,* n.
30. Whitman's letter to Kennedy, *Reminiscences of Walt Whitman,* p. 76.
31. Because the article Whitman refers to is of May 1847, Bucke must have had exceptionally strong evidence from the "paper" and the "writing" to ascribe it to the early fifties.
32. Frederick Ives Carpenter, *Emerson and Asia* (Cambridge: Harvard University Press, 1930).
33. "The Over-Soul," *The Complete Works of R. W. Emerson* (Boston: Houghton Mifflin & Co., Centenary Edition), 2: 288.
34. Whitman's own description: *Notes and Fragments,* p. 170.
35. See Frederick Saunders, *New York in a Nutshell, or Visitor's Handbook to the City of New York* (1853) ; W. J. Rhees, *Manual of Public Libraries in U.S.A.* (Philadelphia, 1859) ; and Charles C. Jewett, *Notices of Public Libraries in U.S.A.* (Washington, D.C., 1851).
36. Only the principal books of this list and the others following, or those that will be cited in our study, are traced to their pages in the catalogues.
37. Pp. 205–214 of the catalogue.
38. I am indebted to the librarians of the libraries concerned for the information.
39. "British Literature."
40. His own words quoted earlier.
41. "Song of Myself," Sec. 3.
42. *Walt Whitman's Workshop,* p. 49. Some of Whitman's thoughts are repeatedly noticed because of the multiplicity of their origin.
43. Lt. Francis Wilford, "On Egypt and Nile," etc., 3: 358–59. The quotations from the *Researches* in this study are from the London edition.
44. Sir Wm. Jones, "On the Gods," etc., 1: 253.
45. J. D. Paterson, "On the Origin of Hindu Religion," 8: 52–53.
46. H. H. Wilson's footnote, *The Vishnu Purana,* p. 10.
47. The Reverend W. Ward, *A View,* 1: introduction, p. xxxi. The spelling of names is changed to the modern practice. The quotations from *A View* in this study are from the second edition (Serampore, 1818–20).
48. Cf. Whitman:

> "Or Time and Space,
> Or shape of Earth divine and wondrous,
> Or some fair shape I viewing, worship,

Or lustrous orb of sun or star by night,
Be ye my Gods." ("Gods.")

49. "On Egypt and Nile," etc., *Researches,* 3: 359–60.
50. *Ibid.,* p. 361.
51. *The Uncollected Poetry and Prose,* 2: 66.
52. "On Egypt," etc., *Researches,* 3: 372–73.
53. *A Critical Guide to 'Leaves of Grass,'* p. 190.
54. *Ibid.,* p. 191.
55. *The Flight of a Book for the World,* sec. II, pp. 180–81. Kennedy's elucidation may be compared with the last of the extracts from Wilford's article preceding this discussion.
56. *The Unseen Universe, or Physical Speculation as a Future State,* B. Stewart and P. G. Tait, 6th ed. (London: Macmillan & Co., 1876) ; quotations pp. 243 and 248.
57. "On Egypt," etc., *Researches,* 3: 359.
58. *Walt Whitman's Pose,* p. 215.
59. *Walt Whitman,* pp. 155–56.
60. *With Walt Whitman in Camden,* Vol. I, p. 186.
61. *The Evolution of Walt Whitman,* Vol. I, pp. 64–65.
62. *Ibid.,* p. 180, n.
63. C. J. Furness, *Leaves of Grass by Walt Whitman,* Reproduced from the Facsimile First Edition (Columbia University Press, 1939), pp. ix–xi.
64. *The Solitary Singer,* p. 563.
65. *American Notes and Queries,* February 1947, 6: 167–68.
66. Sculley Bradley and J. A. Stevenson, *Walt Whitman's Backward Glances,* (Philadelphia: University of Pennsylvania, 1947), pp. 31 and 22.
67. H. L. Traubel, *With Walt Whitman in Camden,* 1: 10–11.
68. Advertisement to "A strong Bird on Pinions Free," separate volume, 1872. Also *Walt Whitman's Workshop,* p. 187.
69. *Notes and Fragments,* no. 72, p. 170.
70. *The Complete Prose,* p. 268.
71. *The Uncollected Poetry and Prose,* 2: 64.
72. *Ibid.,* p. 70.
73. *Notes and Fragments,* no. 60, p. 168.
74. *The Evolution of Walt Whitman,* 1: 286. Carlyle's line is from Every Man's Library edition, p. 247.
75. *The Uncollected Poetry and Prose,* 2: 90.
76. Essay No. II, *Researches,* 7: 236 and 235.
77. Essay No. III, *Researches,* 7: 290 and 302.
78. *Works,* 1: 139–40.
79. *Ibid.,* 4: 243–44.
80. *Researches,* 3: 255. "Notes on the Meaning of Words."
81. Last two lines of "Our Old Feuillage."
82. *Researches,* 5: 363 and 365.
83. *Ibid.,* 1: 345.

84. *Ibid.*, 8 : 402.
85. *Ibid.*, 5 : 349.
86. Lines of the 1855 edition; Cowley's edition, p. 77. Whitman removed the phrase "the vapor from nostrils of death" in the final version.
87. *A Critical Guide to Leaves of Grass*, p. 29.
88. Colbrooke, "On the Vedas, or Sacred Writings of the Hindus," *Researches*, 7.
89. *Notes and Fragments*, no. 175, p. 49.
90. Colebrooke, "On the Vedas," etc., *Researches*, 7.
91. "A Woman Waits for Me," 1856. We may kindly overlook the ironical significance the last line wears in the light of our knowledge of Whitman's personal sex life, but possibly this is one of the true illustrations of Jean Catel's "compensation" theory.
92. "Spontaneous Me," 1856.
93. Section 13.
94. *Ibid.*
95. "Song of Myself," ll. 1274–75 first edition, section 48 of the final version.
96. *Ibid.*, section 48.
97. Section 2.
98. "First drafts and Rejected Lines", *Notes and Fragments*, no. 127, p. 39.
99. Colebrooke, "On the Vedas, etc.," *Researches*, 7.
100. *Ibid.*
101. "On the Mystical Poetry of the East," *Researches*, 3 : 170–71.
102. The Essays were collected into *Works*, Vol. I (London, 1837), and *Essays on the Religion and the Philosophy of the Hindus*, (London: Williams and Norgate, 1858). The quotations from the *Transactions* in this study are from their London edition.
103. *The First (1855) Edition of Leaves of Grass*, p. 84.
104. *Ibid.* The next quotations are from the same section.
105. *A Critical Guide to 'Leaves of Grass,'* p. 31.
106. *Ibid.*, p. 32. Miller does not actually insist on a real mystical experience in Whitman, but regards *Song of Myself* as an imaginative recreation of such an experience.
107. *Transactions*, 1 : 578.
108. *Ibid.*, 2 : 25, 30–31, and 32–33.
109. *Ibid.* ("Recapitulation"), p. 38.
110. *Ibid.*, p. 15.
111. Allen, *The Solitary Singer*, p. 443.
112. Kennedy, *The Flight of a Book*, p. 201.
113. Allen, *The Solitary Singer*, p. 443.
114. Colebrooke, *Transactions*, 1 : 553.
115. *Ibid.*, 2 : 9, n.
116. *Ibid.*, 1 : 95.
117. *Ibid.*, 1 : 32.
118. *Notes and Fragments*, no. 65, p. 27.
119. Allen, *The Solitary Singer*, p. 166.

120. Miller, *A Critical Guide,* p. 130.

121. *Transactions,* 1: 566.

122. *Ibid.,* 2: 37–38.

123. *Ibid.,* 2: 38.

124. This and the following extracts are from the 1855 edition.

125. *Transactions,* 2: 11.

126. *Ibid.,* 1: 31–32.

127. *Sankhya Karika* (of the Astor Catalogue), pp. 123 and 128. This book will be noticed later (chap. 10).

128. *Notes and Fragments,* nos. 168–69, pp. 48–49.

129. "Death of Thomas Carlyle", *The Complete Prose,* p. 163.

130. "A Song of Joys." Cf. the phrase, "excrementitious body" with the "perishable body composed of flesh, bones and excrement" in Vishnu sharma quoted earlier.

131. "Eidólons."

132. *Notes and Fragments,* no. 24, p. 14.

133. Colebrooke, *Transactions,* 1: 30–31.

134. Ward, *A View,* 1: 369. Whitman's reading of it will be noticed later (chaps. 7, 8, and 9).

135. Colebrooke, *Transactions,* 1: 100.

136. *Notes and Fragments,* no. 28, p. 60.

137. Colebrooke, *Transactions,* 1: 30.

138. *Notes and Fragments,* no. 37, p. 18.

139. Colebrooke, *Transactions,* 1: 35. Cf. Whitman's "opposite equals advance" ("Song of Myself," sec. 3).

140. Preface to the 1855 edition of *Leaves of Grass,* p. 19 of Cowley's edition.

141. *Notes and Fragments,* no. 150, p. 45.

142. Colebrooke, *Transactions,* 1: 40.

143. *Ibid.,* p. 41.

144. *Notes and Fragments,* no. 59, p. 26.

145. Colebrooke, *Transactions,* 1: 40–41.

146. Preface to the 1855 *Leaves of Grass,* p. 19 of Cowley's edition.

147. Colebrooke, *Transactions,* 1: 42.

148. *Ibid.,* p. 97.

149. *Notes and Fragments,* no. 65, p. 27. And, "How can there be immortality except through mortality?" asks Whitman, in note 119, p. 38.

150. *Transactions,* 1: 97–98.

151. *Ibid.,* 1: 110–111.

152. *Walt Whitman,* pp. 276–77.

153. *Transactions,* 1: 440.

154. Sections 22 and 2.

155. "A Sun-Bath—Nakedness", *The Complete Prose,* pp. 97–98.

156. *Transactions,* 1: 551.

157. "Song of Myself," sec. 2, first edition.

158. *Transactions,* 1: 551.

159. "As procreation, so the Soul," *Notes and Fragments,* no. 61, p. 27.

160. *Transactions,* 1: 554.
161. *Ibid.,* pp. 557–558.
162. *Reminiscences of Walt Whitman,* p. 139.
163. Colebrooke, "On the Philosophy of the Hindus," *Transactions,* 1: 558–60.
164. "A Song for Occupations."
165. "To Think of Time", sec. 7, first edition, Cowley's, p. 102.
166. Colebrooke, *Transactions,* 1: 99.
167. *The Uncollected Poetry and Prose,* p. 69.
168. Colebrooke, *Transactions,* 1: 564.
169. "Song of Myself," sec. 44.
170. Colebrooke, *Transactions,* 1: 561–562.
171. "Song of Myself", sec. 50, first edition.
172. Colebrooke, *Transactions,* 1: 565–66.
173. *Ibid.,* pp. 567–568.
174. *Notes and Fragments,* no. 65, p. 27.
175. "Song of Myself," sec. 48.
176. *Transactions,* 1: 568.
177. 'On the Philosophy of the Hindus,' *Transactions,* 2: 1–39.
178. *The Uncollected Poetry and Prose,* p. 79.
179. "The Mystic Trumpeter," sec. 8.
180. "Song of the Open Road," sec. 8.
181. First edition.
182. "The germ idea of Whitman's 'noiseless patient spider' poem," *The Conservator,* Jan. 1904. The metaphor of the spider to describe creation is commonly used in all Hindu writings, and is repeatedly found in the books we are noticing. For instance, E. B. Green's article quoted the Vedic passage with the figure, which occurs again in the next few pages.
183. *Walt Whitman's Workshop,* p. 173.
184. First edition, sec. 4.
185. *The Uncollected Poetry and Prose,* 2: 64.
186. "Song of Myself," sec. 20.
187. *Ibid.,* sec. 16.
188. *The Uncollected Poetry and Prose,* 2: 86. The thought is left incomplete.
189. "Thoughts," 1860, sec. 1.
190. "A Song of Joys."
191. *Whitman as Man, Poet and Legend* (Southern Illinois University Press, 1961), p. 82.
192. *Walt Whitman,* pp. 276–77.
193. "A Song of the Open Road," sec. 13.
194. "Sail Out for Good, Eidólon Yacht."
195. *Days with Walt Whitman,* p. 38.
196. Clara Barrus, *Whitman and Burroughs: Comrades* (Boston and New York: Houghton, Mifflin Company, 1931), pp. 17 and 15 respectively.
197. *Walt Whitman,* p. 221.

198. *Ibid.*
199. *Walt Whitman Abroad,* p. 248.
200. Whitman's use of the idea will be noticed in the coming pages (ch. 9).
201. 3: 412–36.
202. 6: 421–22 (London edition, 1799).
203. "Crossing Brooklyn Ferry," sec. 2.
204. "A Song for Occupations," sec. 5.
205. *Walt Whitman's Workshop,* p. 173.
206. *The Uncollected Poetry and Prose,* 2: 64.
207. *Whitman and Burroughs,* p. 17.
208. *Walt Whitman,* p. 221.
209. "Song of Myself," sec. 19.
210. "Whitman" in *Whitman: A Collection of Critical Essays,* or in *Selected Essays* (Penguin Edition, 1950).
211. "To a Common Prostitute."
212. "Faces," 1855 edition, sec. 4.
213. *Works,* 6: 424–25.
214. "Song of Myself," sec. 5, 1855 edition.
215. Quoted by Kennedy in *Reminiscences of Walt Whitman,* p. 33.
216. "Song of the Answerer," 1855 edition.
217. "Song of Myself," sec. 20, 1855 edition.
218. 6: 429.
219. L. D. Morse, "Dr. Daniel Brinton on Walt Whitman," *The Conservator,* November 1899.
220. "Chanting the Square Deific," *American Literature* 9, May 1937.
221. *The Vishnu Purana* (London: John Murray, 1840), pp. 9, 32, and 154–155.
222. *Ibid.,* p. 7.
223. J. T. Trowbridge, *My Own Story* (Boston: Houghton Mifflin & Co., 1903), pp. 393–94.
224. *American Literature* 9: 191 and 195.
225. *The Vishnu Purana,* Book V, Chap. II, pp. 500–501.
226. *Works,* 6: 318.
227. *Ibid.,* pp. 333–35.
228. *Ibid.,* 367–68.
229. *Walt Whitman's Workshop,* p. 49.
230. *Works,* 6: 368.
231. *A View,* 2: xiii–xiv.
232. *Works,* 6: 382.
233. 1855 edition.
234. *Works,* 3: 72–73.
235. *Ibid.,* 67–69.
236. Sec. 32.
237. Walker Kennedy called the passage "mere verbal jugglery." See *The Conservator,* February 1895, "Reply to a Criticism," by Francis Howard Williams.
238. 1: 399–400. (2nd edition, Serampore.)

239. *Ibid.,* p. 431. The term "personal identity" is in the text.
240. *Notes and Fragments,* p. 56.
241. "Song of Myself," sec. 21, and *Notes and Fragments,* p. 18.
242. *A View,* 1: 437. In all quotations from Ward, the spelling of names is modernized in keeping with the present practice.
243. 1855 edition.
244. *The Complete Prose,* p. 243.
245. *A View,* 1: 445.
246. *A View,* 2: xxxvii.
247. *Ibid.,* p. xxii.
248. *Ibid.,* p. 295.
249. *Ibid.,* p. 361.
250. *A View,* 2: i–iii.
251. *Walt Whitman's Workshop,* p. 173.
252. *The Uncollected Poetry and Prose,* 2: 64.
253. "Song of Myself," sec. 46.
254. *Ibid.,* sec. 45, 1855 edition.
255. *Notes and Fragments,* p. 45.
256. *A View,* 2: iv–vi.
257. *Walt Whitman's Workshop,* p. 46.
258. "To Think of Time," sec. 6.
259. "Song of Myself", sec. 22, 1855 edition.
260. "Song of Myself", sec. 44.
261. *A View,* 2: iv.
262. *Notes and Fragments,* p. 53.
263. "The Sleepers", sec. 7, 1855 edition.
264. "To Think of Time", sec. 8.
265. *Walt Whitman's Workshop,* p. 43.
266. *Transactions,* 2: 238–39.
267. *Walt Whitman,* p. 294.
268. *A View,* 2: xvi–xvii.
269. *Ibid.,* p. xiv.
270. "Starting from Paumanok", sec. 10.
271. Sec. 3. Ward's "invisible existences," it may be observed, becomes Whitman's "unseen existences."
272. *A View,* 2: lxviii.
273. *Ibid.,* p. lxix.
274. *The Uncollected Poetry and Prose,* 2: 73.
275. "Rejected Fragments," etc., *Notes and Fragments,* no. 42, p. 20.
276. *The Uncollected Poetry and Prose,* 2: 70 and 74.
277. *Notes and Fragments,* no. 40, p. 19.
278. *A View,* 1: 300–301 and 309–310.
279. *A View,* 2: lxix.
280. *The Uncollected Poetry and Prose,* 2: 72.
281. *Notes and Fragments,* no. 123, p. 38.
282. *Ibid.,* no. 136, p. 41; no. 135, p. 40; and no. 134, p. 40.
283. *Ibid.,* no. 76, p. 274 of *The Complete Writings,* 3.

284. *The Uncollected Poetry and Prose,* 2: 71–72.

285. *Notes and Fragments,* no. 175, p. 49.

286. "A Woman Waits for Me."

287. *A View,* 1: xxiii.

288. *Ibid.,* p. xxiii.

289. *A View,* 1: xlviii.

290. *Ibid.,* p. 218.

291. *Ibid.,* p. 261.

292. "Identities," *The Conservator,* August 1897.

293. *A View,* 1: xlii.

294. 1855 edition.

295. *A Critical Guide,* p. 20.

296. *A View,* 1: 303.

297. Sec. 7, 1855 edition.

298. *A View,* 1: 305–306.

299. *Ibid.,* pp. 314 and 317.

300. *Essays on the Religion and the Philosophy of the Hindus,* p. 147. The treatise referred to is the *Sankhya Karika* of the Astor Library List.

301. *A View,* 1: 319–55.

302. Poem of the same title, 1871.

303. Sec. 24, 1855 edition.

304. "Passage to India," sec. 8.

305. "Starting from Paumanok," sec. 5.

306. *The Uncollected Poetry and Prose,* 2: 81.

307. Words in which the visionary experience is described to have befallen the poet: "Song of Myself," sec. 5.

308. "Song of Myself," sec. 4, 1855 edition.

309. "Me Imperturbe."

310. "That Shadow My Likeness." Also p. 91 of *The Uncollected Poetry and Prose,* 2.

311. "Song of Myself," sec. 33. The next quotation is from the same.

312. *Ibid.,* sec. 21.

313. *A View,* 1: 337, 338, and 344 respectively.

314. "Song of Myself," section 22. The word "witness" was found in Colebrooke's account, as originally used in *Sankhya Karika.*

315. "Song of Myself", sec. 8.

316. *Walt Whitman in the Light of Vedantic Mysticism,* p. 106.

317. "Song of the Answerer," sec. 2.

318. *Walt Whitman in the Light of Vedantic Mysticism,* p. 75.

319. *A View,* 1: 342–343.

320. "Song of Myself," sec. 48.

321. "Laws for Creations."

322. *The Uncollected Poetry and Prose,* 2: 64, 68, and 83 respectively.

323. "Song of Myself," sec. 24.

324. Esther Shephard's phrase: *Walt Whitman's Pose,* p. 117. Fowler's phrenological chart of Whitman is in the same on p. 43.

325. *Notes and Fragments,* p. 82.

326. *Walt Whitman's pose,* p. 43.

327. *A View*, 1: 346 and 351.
328. *Ibid.*, p. 354.
329. "Song of Myself," sec. 20.
330. Introduction to V. K. Chari's, *Walt Whitman in the Light of Vedantic Mysticism.*
331. R. M. Bucke, *In Re. Walt Whitman*, p. 341.
332. "Song of Myself," sec. 46.
333. *The Solitary Singer*, p. 138.
334. Malcolm Cowley, "Walt Whitman the Poet," *The New Republic*, October 20, 1947.
335. O. L. Triggs, *The Complete Writings*, 10: 104.
336. Unless otherwise indicated, the lines quoted from Whitman are from "Song of Myself," 1855 edition.
337. *The Uncollected Poetry and Prose*, 2: 70.
338. *A View*, 1: 346.
339. *Ibid.*, p. 349.
340. *Notes and Fragments*, p. 37.
341. *A View*, 1: 348
342. *Ibid.*, p. 338.
343. *Ibid.*, p. 348.
344. *Ibid.*, p. 354.
345. *Ibid.*, p. 351.
346. *Ibid.*, p. 350.
347. *Ibid.*, p. 340.
348. *Asiatic Researches*, 5: 353.
349. *The Continuity of American Poetry* (Princeton: Princeton University Press, 1961), pp. 69–83.
350. *A Critical Guide to Leaves of Grass*, introduction.
351. *Ibid.*, introduction.
352. *Ibid.*, pp. 6–7.
353. *Ibid.*, p. 4.
354. *Ibid.*, p. 8.
355. *The First (1855) Edition of Leaves of Grass*, pp. xxvi–xxvii.
356. *A View*, 1: 377–94.
357. *A Critical Guide to Leaves of Grass*, p. 8.
358. *Ibid.*, p. 9.
359. *A View*, 1: 379.
360. *A Critical Guide to Leaves of Grass*, p. 9.
361. The second section of "Song of Myself" goes beyond the "senses" to "the play of shine and shade on the trees," etc.
362. Whitman speaks of his "respiration and inspiration," and of "the passing of . . . air through [his] lungs." "Song of Myself," sec. 2.
363. The last words are from the final version of the passage.
364. *The Complete Writings*, 3: 112.
365. "A Song of Joys."
366. Preface of the 1855 *Leaves of Grass;* Cowley's edition, p. 11.
367. "Carlyle from the American Points of View" *The Complete Prose*, p. 167.

368. *Notes and Fragments*, p. 73.
369. *A Critical Guide to Leaves of Grass*, p. 10.
370. "Song of Myself," sec. 20.
371. "Crossing Brooklyn Ferry," sec. 9.
372. "Song of Prudence."
373. "Starting from Paumanok," sec. 7.
374. *Notes and Fragments*, pp. 45 and 27.
375. James E. Miller Jr., *A Critical Guide to Leaves of Grass*, p. 4.
376. "A Backward Glance O'er Travel'd Roads" in the version of January 5, 1884 *Critic; Walt Whitman's Backward Glances*, pp. 19–20.
377. *A Critical Guide to Leaves of Grass*, p. 4.
378. *Ibid.*, p. 4.
379. "Salut au Monde!"
380. Poem of the same name.
381. "Prayer of Columbus."
382. "Passage to India," sec. 8.
383. His own words. "Song of Myself," sec. 33.
384. "Song of Myself," sec. 16.
385. *Ibid.*, sec. 44.
386. *Ibid.*, sec. 24.
387. *Ibid.*, sec. 24.
388. *Ibid.*, sec. 34, final version.
389. H. B. Binns, *Walt Whitman*, p. 166.
390. Pages 20–21, and the explanatory note.
391. *Notes and Fragments*, p. 79.
392. *Walt Whitman's Workshop*, p. 189.
393. *Ibid.*, p. 189.
394. *Ibid.*, pp. 190–191.
395. *A View*, 1: 322.
396. *The Complete Prose*, p. 292.
397. *Notes and Fragments*, p. 40.
398. *The Complete Prose*, pp. 226–27.
399. *Ibid.*, p. 246.
400. *Ibid.*, p. 502.
401. *Walt Whitman's Workshop*, p. 190.
402. *Notes and Fragments*, no. 21, p. 58.
403. *Ibid.*, no. 63, p. 71.
404. "Are You the New Person Drawn Toward Me?"
405. *Notes and Fragments*, no. 175, p. 132.
406. *Ibid.*, p. 140 (from the same discussion).
407. *A View*, 1: 365–67.
408. *Ibid.*, pp. 349, 350 and 340.
409. *Notes and Fragments*, no. 46, p. 21.
410. *A View*, 1: 399 and 412–13.
411. *Ibid.*, pp. 399–400, 411–12, 415, and 417.
412. *Notes and Fragments*, no. 47, p. 22.
413. *A View*, 1: 414.

414. "Song of the Answerer," sec. 1.
415. *A View,* 1: 421.
416. *Ibid.,* p. 423.
417. *Ibid.,* pp. 441–42.
418. *Ibid.,* p. 443.
419. *Ibid.,* p. 435.
420. "To Think of Time," sec. 7.
421. "Starting from Paumanok," sec. 13.
422. *Notes and Fragments,* no. 65, p. 27.
423. *Walt Whitman's Workshop,* pp. 132–173.
424. Sec. 12.
425. *Sankhya Karika* (Oxford: Oriental Translation Fund Publications, 1837, Astor Library List), verses 56–61, pp. 166–73.
426. Whitman's "Spontaneous Me," describing the "Spontaneous me, Nature," appears to have been born in this and the comment of the first of the verses quoted above.
427. *Sankhya Karika,* verse 21, pp. 76–78.
428. *Ibid.,* p. 77.
429. *Ibid.,* pp. 31–32.
430. *Ibid.,* pp. 69–70.
431. *Ibid.,* verse 19, p. 72.
432. *The Vishnu Purana* (London: John Murray, 1840), introduction, p. v.
433. *Ibid.,* p. lxxv.
434. *Ibid.,* 4: 487–89. The next one is part of the same passage.
435. *The Uncollected Poetry and Prose,* 2: 67–68.
436. Sec. 5, final version.
437. *The Solitary Singer,* p. 155.
438. "As They Draw to a Close."
439. *The Complete Prose,* p. 237.
440. *The Vishnu Purana,* p. lx.
441. *Ibid.,* p. 143.
442. W. S. Kennedy, *Reminiscences of Walt Whitman,* p. 139.
443. *The First (1855) Edition of Leaves of Grass,* pp. xiv, xxi, and xxiii.
444. *In Re Walt Whitman,* pp. 161 and 165–66.
445. *The Vishnu Purana,* p. 131.
446. *Ibid.,* pp. 155–56. The footnote following is on p. 156.
447. "A Song of the Open Road," sec. 6.
448. "Song of Myself," sec. 30.
449. *Notes and Fragments,* pp. 73 and 71.
450. "Carlyle from the American Points of View," *The Complete Prose,* p. 167.
451. *Notes and Fragments,* p. 120.
452. *The Vishnu Purana,* p. 157.
453. *Ibid.,* p. 4.
454. "A Song of the Rolling Earth," sec. 2.
455. *The Vishnu Purana,* p. 39.
456. *Ibid.,* p. 136, footnote.
457. *Ibid.,* p. 157.
458. *Ibid.,* p. 135.

459. *Ibid.*, p. 137. The various names are of God.
460. "Song of Myself," sec. 48.
461. *Ibid.*, sec. 23; also "Song of the Universal" where he says: "Yet again, lo! the soul, above all science."
462. *The Vishnu Purana*, pp. 137–39. The next one is from the same passage.
463. "Song of Myself," sec. 23, final version.
464. *The Vishnu Purana*, pp. 130–33.
465. "Song of the Answerer," final version.
466. *The Vishnu Purana*, p. 139.
467. "Song of the Open Road," sec. 11.
468. *The Vishnu Purana*, pp. 139–140.
469. "Crossing Brooklyn Ferry," sec. 2.
470. *The Vishnu Purana*, p. 163. The words in brackets are a footnote.
471. "Song of the Open Road," sec. 14.
472. *The Vishnu Purana*, p. 650.
473. *Ibid.*, pp. 226, 227, 228, and 624.
474. "Song of the Open Road," sec. 11.
475. *The Vishnu Purana*, p. 296.
476. *Ibid.*, p. 338.
477. G. W. Allen, *The Solitary Singer*, pp. 124 and 125.
478. Jones's *Works*, 3: 73 and 461; also the *Whig Review* article of E. B. Green.
479. *The Vishnu Purana*, pp. 9–10 and 12.
480. *Ibid.*, p. lix.
481. *Ibid.*, p. 19.
482. *Notes and Fragments*, item 336 of the list.
483. *The Uncollected Poetry and Prose*, 2: 86.
484. *The Vishnu Purana*, chap. 7, Book II, pp. 212–14.
485. "Song of Myself," sec. 33, final version.
486. P. 213.
487. Pp. 27–33. The quotation is from p. 32.
488. Pp. 214–15.
489. "Me Imperturbe."
490. *The Vishnu Purana*, pp. 215–16.
491. "Apparitions."
492. "And Yet Not You Alone."
493. *The Vishnu Purana*, pp. 241–42.
494. *Ibid.*, 247–48.
495. *Ibid.*, 249–50. The next one is from the same.
496. *Ibid.*, p. 248.
497. "Song of Myself," sec. 32.
498. *The Vishnu Purana*, pp. 251–53.
499. *The Complete Prose*, p. 262.
500. "Song of the Exposition," sec. 7.
501. "Song of the Open Road," sec. 10.
502. *The First (1855) Edition of Leaves of Grass*, p. 14.
503. *The Vishnu Purana*, pp. 255–56.
504. *Ibid.*, p. 414.

505. *Ibid.*, pp. 641–42, and n.
506. *Ibid.*, p. 643.
507. "Rejected Poems," *The Complete Writings*, 3: 302.
508. *The Complete Prose*, p. 231.
509. *The Vishnu Purana*, pp. 651–52.
510. *Ibid.*, pp. 651, 652 and 653. The following is from pp. 657–658.
511. "A Promise to California."
512. "In Paths Untrodden."
513. The title of Haniel Lang's book on Whitman.
514. "Whitman played the female role in these relationships." Malcolm Cowley, "Walt Whitman: The Secret," *The New Republic*, April 8, 1946.
515. *The Vishnu Purana*, pp. 655–56.
516. *Ibid.*, pp. 166–203. The quotations are from pp. 166, 203, and 173.
517. *Ibid.*, pp. 167–72.
518. *Ibid.*, pp. 174 and 179.
519. *Ibid.*, p. 199.
520. *Ibid.*, p. lxi.
521. *Ibid.*, p. 216.
522. G. W. Allen, *The Solitary Singer*, p. 183.
523. *Ibid.*
524. *The Vishnu Purana*, pp. 167–72. The next one is from the same.
525. "Song of the Answerer."
526. *The Vishnu Purana*, pp. 3–4.
527. *Ibid.*, p. 660.
528. *Ibid.*, p. x.
529. *Notes and Fragments*, p. 52.
530. "Now Precedent Songs, Farewell."
531. "Starting from Paumanok," sections 4 and 5.
532. *The Vishnu Purana*, pp. 3 and 6.
533. "The Return of the Heroes," sections 2 and 3.
534. "Thou Mother with Thy Equal Brood," sections 5 and 6.
535. *The Vishnu Purana*, pp. 174–78.
536. The 1872 Preface, *The Complete Prose*, p. 272.
537. "Song of the Open Road," sec. 11.
538. *The Vishnu Purana*, pp. 245–46.
539. "Song of the Open Road," sec. 14.
540. *Ibid.*, sec. 10.
541. *Ibid.*, sec. 2.
542. *Ibid.*
543. "Song of Myself," sec. 51.
544. *The Vishnu Purana*, p. 178. n.
545. Secs. 21 and 22.
546. *The Bhagvat-Geeta*, p. 43. Whitman's reading of it will be discussed later.
547. *The Vishnu Purana*, pp. 59–61.
548. *Notes and Fragments*, p. 126.
549. *The Vishnu Purana*, pp. 294, 295, and 305.
550. *Ibid.*, pp. 306 and 305.

551. Sec. 40.
552. *The Vishnu Purana*, pp. 305–306.
553. *Ibid.*, p. 305, n.
554. *The Uncollected Poetry and Prose*, 2: 80.
555. P. 46. Later woven into the 1865 poem "Thick-Sprinkled Bunting."
556. *The Vishnu Purana*, Book I, chaps. xi and xii.
557. *Ibid.*, p. 230.
558. *The Complete Prose*, p. 277.
559. *Ibid.*, p. 277.
560. *Walt Whitman's Workshop*, p. 132.
561. *The Vishnu Purana*, pp. 290–96.
562. *The Complete Prose*, pp. 269–71.
563. *The Complete Writings*, 3:44.
564. *Reminiscences of Walt Whitman*, p. 100.
565. Whitman's words: *The Complete Prose*, p. 277.
566. Parasara narrated the *Purana* at the instance of his teacher, and Whitman in "Eidolons" "met a seer" who asked him to "put in [his] chants."
567. George Hendrick, introduction, *The Bhagvat-Geeta*, 1785, Translated with notes by Charles Wilkins (A facsimile reproduction with an introduction by George Hendrick, Gainsville, Florida: Scholars' Facsimiles and Reprints, 1959), p. xi.
568. *Ibid.*, p. xi.
569. *Ibid.*, p. x.
570. *Ibid.*, p. xi.
571. *Ibid.*
572. *A Week on the Concord and Merrimac Rivers*, p. 145.
573. *Ibid.*, pp. 151 and 153.
574. *Days with Walt Whitman*, p. 43.
575. "Song of the Exposition," sec. 1.
576. "A Broadway Pageant," sec. 2.
577. *A Week*, p. 153.
578. *Notes and Fragments*, p. 57.
579. *Ibid.*, p. 168.
580. Introduction to the facsimile edition of *The Bhagvat-Geeta*, pp. xi and x.
581. "Detroit Library Catalogue," p. 124. The copy is in the Feinberg Collection. But despite the descriptive note in the Catalogue about the "marginal notations by Walt Whitman throughout," the only words, apart from the "notes on 'Mahabharata' and 'Ramayana' pinned to p. xxxv of Introduction," are: "The Hindu *Sutas*, i.e. charioteers & poets," on one side of page xxxii, and on the bottom of page cxxxiii, the description of Vyasa quoted earlier in this book. Mr. Feinberg told me that that was the copy he got from Anne Montgomerie Traubel, to whom, it appears, Whitman gave his "presentation" copy. As does the note in the Catalogue, Elsa Baker, in her article "What Whitman learned from the East" (Canada Monthly, 10 (011) 438–443), says that Whitman's copy of the *Gita* has marginal notes. Mercer, in "Parallel of Ideas between *Bhaga-*

vadgita and *Leaves of Grass"* (Ph.D. diss., University of California, 1933, p. 32), says, quoting from Mrs. Traubel's letter to her of 6 February 1931, that the copy in Mrs. Traubel's possession does not have the notes. There seems to be some mystery about this too. Did Whitman have another copy?

582. "How Solemn as They One by One."
583. "Song of the Exposition," sec. 1. and Emerson's description of *Leaves of Grass* (sec. p. 1 of our study).
584. *The Bhagvat-Geeta*, pp. 36–37.
585. *The Vishnu Purana*, pp. 136–37.
586. "Rejected Poems," *The Complete Writings*, 3: 292–95.
587. *The Bhagvat-Geeta*, pp. 89–97.
588. With this passage may be compared Whitman's announcements in "Starting from Paumanok": "See revolving globe. . . See, vast trackless spaces. . . . See, steamers . . . pastures . . . cities . . ." etc., (Secs. 2 and 18), and in *Notes and Fragments* (p. 12),

> We effuse spirituality and immortality,
> We put a second brain to the brain,
> We put second eyes to the eyes and second ears to the ears

and the line: ". . . It is because the universe is in myself—it shall pass through me as a procession" ("Notes and Fragments," *The Complete Writings*, 9: 30–31).

589. *The Bhagvat-Geeta*, pp. 85–88.
590. Hendrick, *The Bhagvat-Geeta*, p. xiv.
591. *Ibid.*, p. 6.
592. *The Uncollected Poetry and Prose*, 2: 74.
593. *Notes and Fragments*, p. vi.
594. *The Complete Writings*, 10: 14.
595. *Notes and Fragments*, no. 30, p. 163.
596. *The Bhagvat-Geeta*, p. 5.
597. Wilkins also uses the same words: "The [*Geeta*] is a dialogue . . . between *Kreeshna*, an incarnation of the Deity, and his pupil and favourite *Arjoon*" (*The Bhagvat-Geeta*, Preface, p. 23).
598. *The Bhagvat-Geeta*, pp. 7–8.
599. *The Complete Prose*, p. 279.
600. *Notes and Fragments*, p. 64.
601. *The Complete Prose*, p. 279.
602. *The Bhagvat-Geeta*, p. 8. The account is in pp. 8–9.
603. *Walt Whitman's Workshop*, pp. 190–91.
604. *The Bhagvat-Geeta*, p. 10.
605. *Ibid.*, pp. 10–11.
606. *Ibid.*, p. 23.
607. "A Backward Glance O'er Travel'd Roads."
608. *The Bhagvat-Geeta*, p. 23.
609. *Ibid.*, p. 24.
610. *Ibid.*
611. *The First (1855) Edition of Leaves of Grass*, p. xvii.

612. "Starting from Paumanok," sec. 4.
613. Whitman, too, we may remember, offers a supreme journey along his "open road," in "Song of the Open Road."
614. The reference to "Song of Myself" here is in the final version. The image of "night" when "all things" are dissolved in that which is called the *invisible,* is elsewhere mentioned in the *Gita,* (p. 75).
615. *The Bhagvat-Geeta,* p. 35.
616. *Ibid.,* pp. 99 and 55.
617. *Ibid.,* p. 35. Since what follows is almost a page-by-page study of the *Gita,* its extracts are not individually page-marked, except when they are out of turn.
618. Whitman's poem will hereafter be referred to in the final version which makes his meanings clearer.
619. *Notes and Fragments,* p. 47.
620. *The Bhagvat-Geeta,* p. 29.
621. *The Bhagvat-Geeta,* pp. 99–100.
622. Whitman's entry: "Notes and Fragments," *The Complete Writings,* 3: 276.
623. *The Bhagvat-Geeta,* p. 80.
624. *A View,* 1: 435 n.
625. *The Bhagvat-Geeta,* pp. 79–80 and 84.
626. *Ibid.,* p. 104.
627. *Walt Whitman,* p. 46.
628. *The Bhagvat-Geeta,* p. 80.
629. *Ibid.,* pp. 36, 38, and 39.
630. *Ibid.,* pp. 37–38.
631. *The Uncollected Poetry and Prose,* 2: 80.
632. *The Bhagvat-Geeta,* p. 42.
633. *Notes and Fragments,* pp. 28–29.
634. *The Bhagvat-Geeta,* p. 46.
635. *Notes and Fragments,* p. 18.
636. *The Bhagvat-Geeta,* pp. 49–50.
637. *Ibid.,* p. 58.
638. *The Uncollected Poetry and Prose,* 2: 65.
639. *The Bhagvat-Geeta,* p. 61.
640. *Ibid.,* pp. 71–72.
641. *Notes and Fragments,* p. 37.
642. *The Bhagvat-Geeta,* p. 99.
643. *Ibid.,* p. 93.
644. *Ibid.,* p. 107.
645. "Song of Myself," sec. 40.
646. "A Woman Waits for Me."
647. "Spontaneous Me."
648. "I Saw in Louisiana a Live-Oak Growing." *Notes and Fragments* (p. 51) carries a version of the poem earlier than the published one, but, even "the copy given [there] . . . not by any means a first draft," the first thoughts can only be guessed. The reference to "manly love" in the poem, and the "Calamus" section of its location, need not mislead us, as many a more sublime image or con-

cept, taken from more meaningful sources, has been pressed into service in the poems of that section, as, for example, in "The Base of All Metaphysics," "Of the Terrible Doubt of Appearances," and so on.

649. "Here the Frailest Leaves of Me."
650. *A Critical Guide to Leaves of Grass*, p. 85.
651. *Notes and Fragments*, p. 20.
652. *The Bhagvat-Geeta*, p. 133.
653. *Ibid.*, pp. 56 and 109.
654. *Notes and Fragments*, p. 30.
655. *Walt Whitman Handbook*, pp. 267–68.
656. *The Bhagvat-Geeta*, p. 140.
657. *Ibid.*, p. 145. The following quotations from the account itself are from pp. 147–148.
658. Whitman's words: "Crossing Brooklyn Ferry," sec. 9.
659. R. M. Bucke, "Notes on the Text of Leaves of Grass," *The Conservator*, August, 1896.
660. *The Bhagvat-Geeta*, pp. 151–52.
661. *The Bhagavad-Gita*, translated by J. Cockburn Thomson (Hertford: Stephen Austin, 1855), p. 96.
662. *Ibid.*, p. 12.
663. *Ibid.*, pp. xliii–xliv.
664. Whitman, of course, could have made this detail out of the concept of "avatars" he read about—from the 1845 magazine article on "Indian Epic Poetry" to Wilkins's *Gita*—and so it is not to be held as a proof of his having read Thomson's book when he wrote the lines.
665. Astor's copy was the second edition (London: Parbury Allen & Co., 1832).
666. *In Re Walt Whitman*, p. 33.
667. "Starting from Paumanok," sec. 4.
668. Edward Carpenter, *Days with Walt Whitman*, p. 78.
669. *Translations*, pp. 7–8. The italics in the extracts from Roy are his own.
670. *Ibid.*, p. 78. Similar passages are frequently found in other pages.
671. *Notes and Fragments*, p. 24.
672. *Translations*, pp. 9, 14, and 15.
673. *Ibid.*, p. 15.
674. *Ibid.*, pp. 31 and 70.
675. *Ibid.*, pp. 35 and 69.
676. *Ibid.*, p. 36.
677. *Ibid.*, p. 68.
678. "Song of Myself," sec. 33.
679. *Translations*, pp. 27–28 and 36–38.
680. *Ibid.*, p. 30.
681. *Ibid.*, p. 71.
682. "Whoever You are Holding Me Now in Hand."
683. "In Paths Untrodden."
684. "Whoever You Are Holding Me Now in Hand."
685. *Ibid.*

686. J. Cockburn Thomson, *The Bhagavad-Gita*, p. 44, n.
687. "Whoever You Are Holding Me Now in Hand."
688. *Ibid.*
689. "Scented Herbage of My Breast."
690. "City of Orgies."
691. *Translations*, pp. 111 and 129.
692. "I Hear It Was Charged Against Me."
693. "When I Peruse the Conquer'd Fame."
694. *Translations*, p. 73.
695. *Ibid.*, p. 75–76.
696. *Ibid.*, p. 75.
697. *Ibid.*, pp. 104–105.
698. "A Backward Glance," *The Complete Writings*, 3: 45–46.
699. *Notes and Fragments*, p. 109.
700. "A Backward Glance," *The Complete Writings*, 3: 48.
701. Newton Arvin's words. *Walt Whitman*, p. 194.
702. "Prayer of Columbus."
703. R. M. Bucke, "Memories of Walt Whitman."
704. His own words. *In Re Walt Whitman*, p. 350. Also *Walt Whitman's Pose*, pp. 391–392.
705. The title of a book on Walt Whitman by Cameron Rogers (Garden City, N.J.: Doubleday Page & Co., 1930).
706. From the title of his poem, "Scented Herbage of My Breast."
707. "Notes on the Text of Leaves of Grass," February, 1898.
708. Roger Asselineau, *The Evolution of Walt Whitman*, 2: 302.

Part III

1. *Walt Whitman*, p. 304.
2. Whitman's words. "Song of Myself," sec. 17.
3. Victor Hugo's words in a letter to Whitman. *Walt Whitman's Pose*, p. 135.
4. Whitman's words in "A Backward Glance."
5. Emerson's letter to Whitman, *The First (1855) Edition of Leaves of Grass*, p. ix.
6. *Ibid.*
7. T. F. Wolfe, *Literary Shrines* (Philadelphia: J. B. Lippincott Co., 7th ed., 1897), p. 213. The next quotation is from the same.
8. "Song of Myself," sec. 24.
9. *Notes and Fragments*, p. 57.
10. Malcolm Cowley, "Walt Whitman: The Miracle," *The New Republic*, 18 March, 1946.
11. *A Life of Walt Whitman*, p. 51.
12. "Alias Walt Whitman," *Harper's Magazine*, May 1929; later published as a book, *Alias Walt Whitman* (Newark, N. J.: the Carteret Book Club, 1930).
13. "Once I pass'd Through a Populous City." The point has been discussed in our study.
14. Cowley, "Walt Whitman: The Secret," *The New Republic*, 8 April 1946.

15. "Walt Whitman: The Miracle," *The New Republic,* 18 March 1946.
16. "City of Orgies."
17. "Now Precedent Songs, Farewell."
18. "Democratic Vistas."
19. G. W. Allen, *Walt Whitman: Leaves of Grass* (New York: A Signet Classic, The New American Library, 1964), p. vii.
20. *Notes and Fragments,* p. 126.
21. *Walt Whitman Handbook,* p. 8.
22. Kennedy, *The Conservator,* February 1898. But the poem appears to be a translation of a passage in Michelet's book on birds. See *Walt Whitman Handbook,* p. 212, n. 178.
23. *Notes and Fragments,* pp. 69 and 57.
24. "Whitman and Tennyson," *Nation and Atheneum,* 18 December 1926.
25. Esther Shephard, *Walt Whitman's Pose,* p. 236.
26. *Walt Whitman Abroad,* p. 213.
27. J. A. Symmonds, *A Study of Walt Whitman,* p. 7.
28. *The Complete Writings,* 3 : 65.
29. *Notes and Fragments,* pp. 161 and 179.
30. *Notes and Fragments,* p. 55.
31. "Starting from Paumanok," sec. 5.
32. *Notes and Fragments,* p. 64.
33. *Nation and Atheneum.*
34. *Notes and Fragments,* p. 142.
35. "Walt Whitman: The Poet," *The New Republic,* 20 October 1947.
36. *Walt Whitman,* p. 165.
37. Cowley, "Walt Whitman: The Poet."
38. "Song of Myself," sec. 49.
39. Poem of the same title.
40. "To Him that was Crucified."
41. "Yet, Yet, Ye Downcast Hours."
42. "My 71st Year."
43. *The Complete Writings,* 3 : 276.
44. *Notes and Fragments,* p. 40.
45. Richard Chase, *Walt Whitman Reconsidered,* p. 174.
46. *Walt Whitman's Workshop,* p. 150.
47. "Spontaneous Me."
48. Richard Chase, *Walt Whitman Reconsidered,* p. 49.
49. *Walt Whitman Handbook,* pp. 243–44.
50. G. W. Allen, *Leaves of Grass* (Signet Classic), p. viii.
51. Horace Traubel, *With Walt Whitman in Camden,* entries for September 13, 1888, and November 20, 1888; also for October 20, 1888.
52. It is curious that Whitman himself once declared: "So I may go down to history, if I go at all, as a merry-maker wearing the cap and bells rather than as a prophet or what the Germans call a *Philosoph.*" ("Camden Diary of Horace Traubel," *American Mercury,* October 1924.)

SELECT BIBLIOGRAPHY

A. *Bibliographies*

Allen, Gay Wilson — *Twenty-five Years of Walt Whitman Bibliography: 1918–1942,* Boston: The F. W. Faxon Co. (1943).

Wells, Carolyn & Goldsmith, Alfred F. — *A Concise Bibliography of the Works of Walt Whitman,* Boston and New York: Houghton Mifflin & Co., 1922.

Shay, Frank — *The Bibliography of Walt Whitman,* New York: Friedman's (1920).

Triggs, O. L. — "Bibliography of Walt Whitman," *The Complete Writings of Walt Whitman,* New York and London: G. P. Putnam's Sons, Vol. X.

B. *Catalogues of Whitman Material*

Detroit Public Library — *Walt Whitman: A Selection of the Manuscripts, Books and Association Items Gathered by Charles E. Feinberg,* . . . Detroit, 1955.
An Exhibition of Works of Walt Whitman . . . Detroit, 1945.

Duke University Library — *Walt Whitman; A Checklist of an Exhibition of Manuscripts and Books from the Trent Collection . . .* Durham, N. C., 1955.

Frey, Ellen Frances — *Catalogue of Whitman Collection in the Duke University Library,* Durham: Duke University Library (1945).

New York Public Library — *Walt Whitman: The Oscar Lion Collection,* N. Y.: New York Public Library (1953).

The Swartz Collection Sales Catalogue of Whitman Material — New York: American Art Association, Anderson Galleries (1936).

American Library, London — *Walt Whitman Catalogue of an Exhibition of Manuscripts, Letters and Books . . .* London: U.S.I.S. (1954).

Library of Congress — *Walt Whitman: A Catalogue Based upon the Collection of the Library of Congress with Notes,* Washington, D. C.: Govt. Printing Office (1955).

C. *Works by Whitman*

The Complete Writings of Walt Whitman, edited by R. M. Bucke, T. B. Harned and H. L. Traubel, N. Y.: G. P. Putnam's Sons (1902), 10 vols.

Leaves of Grass, Reproduced from the Facsmile First Edition (1855) with an Introduction by C. J. Furness, N. Y.: Columbia University Press (1939).

Leaves of Grass: the First (1855) Edition, edited with an Introduction by Malcolm Cowley, New York: The Viking Press (1959).

The Uncollected Poetry and Prose of Walt Whitman, Collected and Edited by Emory Holloway, Garden City, N. J. and Toronto: Doubleday, Page & Co. 1921).

The Complete Prose Works of Walt Whitman, Boston: Small, Maynard & Co. (1907).

Walt Whitman's Workshop, A Collection of Unpublished Manuscripts, edited with an Introduction and Notes by C. J. Furness, New York: Russel & Russel, Inc. (1928), (1964); and Cambridge: Harvard University Press (1928).

Notes and Fragments, left by Walt Whitman, edited by R. M. Bucke, London, Ontario: A. Talbot and Co. (1899).

Rivulets of Prose, edited by Carolyn Wells and Alfred F. Goldsmith, New York: Greenberg (1928).

Pictures; an Unpublished Poem by Walt Whitman, edited with an Introduction and Notes by Emory Holloway, New York: June House (1927).

Faint Clews and Indirections: Manuscripts of Walt Whitman and His Family, edited by Clarence Gohdes & Rollo G. Silver, Durham, N. C.: Duke University Press (1949).

Walt Whitman of the N. Y. Aurora: A Collection of Recently Discovered Writings, edited by Joseph Jay Rubin and Charles H. Brown, Pennsylvania State College, Bald Eagle Press (1950).

The Gathering of the Forces: Editorials, Newspaper Contributions etc., of Walt Whitman, edited by Cleveland Rodgers and John Black, New York and London, G. P. Putnam's Sons, 1920.

I Sit and Look Out: Editorials from Brooklyn Daily Times by Walt Whitman, selected and edited by Emory Holloway & Vernolian Schwarz, New York: Columbia University Press (1932).

Walt Whitman's Backward Glances, edited, with an Introduction on the Evolution of the Text, by Scully Bradley and John A. Stevenson, Philadelphia: University of Pennsylvania Press (1947).

New York Dissected; A Sheaf of Recently Discovered Newspaper Articles by the Author of "Leaves of Grass," edited by Emory Holloway & Ralph Adimari, New York: Rufus Rockwell Wilson (1936).

Walt Whitman and the Civil War; A Collection of Original Articles and Manuscripts, edited by Charles I. Glicksberg, Philadelphia: University of Pennsylvania Press (1933).

The Complete Poetry and Selected Prose of Walt Whitman, edited by Emory Holloway, New York: Random House (1938).

Walt Whitman's Dairy in Canada, edited by W. S. Kennedy, Boston: Small, Maynard and Co. (1904).

The Half-Breed and Other Stories, edited by Thomas Ollive Mabbott, New York: Columbia University Press (1927).

Walt Whitman's Civil War, edited by Walter Lowenfels, assisted by Nan Braymer, New York: Knopf (1960).

An 1855–56 Notebook: Toward the Second Edition of "Leaves of Grass," edited with an Introduction and Notes by Harold W. Blodgett, with a foreword by Charles E. Feinberg, and additional notes by William White, Carbondale: Southern Illinois University Press (1959).

Walt Whitman's Backward Glances: A Backward Glance O'er Travel'd Roads and Two Contributory Essays Hitherto Uncollected, edited with an Introduction by Scully Bradley and John A. Stevenson, Philadelphia: University of Pennsylvania Press (1947).

Wound-Dresser: Letters Written to His Mother from the Hospitals in Washington during the Civil War, edited by R. M. Bucke, with an Introduction by Oscar Cargil, New York: Bodley Press (1949).

Calamus: A Series of Letters Written during the Years 1868–80, by Walt Whitman to a Young Friend (Peter Doyle), edited with an Introduction by R. M. Bucke, Boston: Laurens Maynard (1897).

Letters Written by Walt Whitman to his Mother from 1866 to 1872, Together with Certain Papers Prepared from Material now First Utilized, edited by Thomas B. Harned, New York and London: G. P. Putnam's Sons (1902).

An American Primer, With Facsimiles of the Original Manuscript, edited by Horace Traubel, Boston: Small, Maynard & Co. (1904).

Walt Whitman & Rolleston: A Correspondence, Bloomington: Indiana University Publication (1951).

D. *Whitman Material Collections*

Berg and Oscar Lion Collections in the Public Library of New York.

John Pierpont Morgan Collection in the John P. Morgan Library of New York.

Harned Collection in the Library of Congress, Washington, D. C.

Walt Whitman Foundation, Camden, N. J.

Rare Book Department of the University of Pennsylvania, Philadelphia, Pa.

Charles E. Feinberg Collection, Detroit, Mich.

E. *Journals and Newspapers Read by Walt Whitman, of the Years 1840–1855*

> *The Westminster Review*
> *Blackwood's Magazine*
> *The Whig Review*
> *Graham's Magazine*
> *The Edinburgh Review*
> *Sartrain's Magazine*
> *Harper's Weekly*
> *The Penny Magazine*
> *The Dial (1840–1844)*
> *The Eclectic*

F. *Books on Walt Whitman*

Allen, Gay Wilson
Walt Whitman Abroad, Syracuse, N. Y.: Syracuse University Press (1955).
Walt Whitman As Man, Poet and Legend, Carbondale: Southern Illinois University Press (1961).
The Solitary Singer: A Critical Biography of Walt Whitman, New York: The Macmillan Co. (1955).
Walt Whitman Handbook, Chicago: Packard and Co. (1946).
American Prosody, New York: American Book Co. (1935).

Arwin, Newton — *Whitman,* New York: The Macmillan Co. (1938).

Asselineau, Roger — *The Evolution of Walt Whitman: The Development of a Personality,* translated by Richard P. Adams and the Author, Cambridge: Harvard University Press (Vol. I, 1960, Vol. II, 1962).

Bailey, John — *Walt Whitman,* London & New York: The Macmillan Co. (1926).

Barrus, Clara — *Whitman and Burroughs: Comrades,* Boston: Houghton, Mifflin and Co. (1931).

Bazalgette, Léon — *Walt Whitman, the Man and his Work,* translated by Ellen Fitzgerald, Garden City: Doubleday (1920).

Binns, Henry Bryan — *A Life of Walt Whitman,* London: Methuen and Co. (1905).

——— — *Walt Whitman and His Poetry,* London: G. G. Harrap & Co. (1915).

Blodgett, Harold — *Walt Whitman in England,* Ithaca, N. Y.: Cornell University Press (1934).

Brooks, Van Wyck — *The Times of Melville and Whitman,* New York: E. P. Dutton (1947).

Bucke, Richard Maurice — *Walt Whitman,* Philadelphia: David McKay (1833).

——— — *Cosmic Consciousness,* New York: E. P. Dutton (1923).

Burroughs, John — *Notes on Walt Whitman as Poet and Person,* New York: American News Co. (1867).

——— — *Whitman; A Study,* Boston: Houghton, Mifflin and Co. (1896).

Canby, Henry Seidel	*Walt Whitman, An American,* Boston: Houghton, Mifflin and Co. (1943).
Cargill, Oscar	*Intellectual America: Ideas on the March,* New York: The Macmillan Co. (1941).
Carpenter, Edward	*Days With Walt Whitman, With Some Notes on His Life and Works,* London: George Allen (1906).
Carpenter, F. I.	*Emerson and Asia,* Cambridge: Harvard University Press (1932).
Carpenter, G. R.	*Walt Whitman,* New York: The Macmillan Co. (1909).
Chari, V. K.	*Walt Whitman in the Light of Vedantic Mysticism,* Lincoln: Nebraska University Press (1964).
Chase, Richard	*Walt Whitman Reconsidered,* New York: William Sloane Associates (1955).
Christy, Arthur	*The Orient in American Transcendentalism,* New York: Columbia University Press (1932).
Conway, Moncure D.	*Emerson at Home and Abroad.* London: Trubner & Co. (1883).
Daiches, David	*Literary Essays,* New York: Philosophical Library (1957).
De Selincourt, Basil	*Walt Whitman: A Critical Study,* London: Martin Secker (1914).
Donaldson, Thomas	*Walt Whitman, the Man,* New York: Francis P. Harper (1896).
Dowden, Edmund	"The Poetry of Democracy: Walt Whitman," *Studies in Literature: 1789–1877,* London: Kegan Paul and Co. (1878).

Faussett, Hugh I'Anson · *Walt Whitman: Poet of De-mocracy,* New Haven: Yale University Press (1942).

Frothingham, O. B. · *Transcendentalism in New England,* New York: G. P. Putnam's Sons (1876).

Goddard, H. C. · *Studies in New England Transcendentalism,* New York: Columbia University Press (1908).

Guthrie, William N. · "Walt Whitman, Camden Sage," in *Modern Poet Prophets,* Cincinnati: The Robert Clarke & Co. (1897).

Hindus, Milton, ed. · *Leaves of Grass One Hundred Years After* (Essays by several critics), with an Introduction by Milton Hindus, Stanford: Stanford University Press (1955).

Holloway, Emory · *Whitman; An Interpretation in Narrative,* New York: Knopf (1926).

——— · *Free and Lonesome Heart: The Secret of Walt Whitman,* New York: Vantage Press (1960).

James, William · *Varieties of Religious Experience,* New York: Modern Library, Longman's, Green & Co. (1925).

Johnson, Maurice · *Walt Whitman, as a Critic of Literature,* Lincoln: Nebraska University Press (1938).

Keller, Elizabeth (Leavitt) · *Walt Whitman in Mickle Street,* New York: M. Kennerley (1921).

Kennedy, William Sloane · *Reminiscences of Walt Whitman,* London: Alexander Gardner (1896).

——— · *The Flight of a Book for the*

Lawrence, D. H.

Long, Haniel

Masters, Edgar Lee

Matthiessen, F. O.

Mercer, Dorothy F.

Miller, James E.

O'Connor, William Douglas

O'Higgins, Harvey J.

Otto, Rudolf

Pearce, Roy Harvey, ed.

World, West Yarmouth, Mass:
Stonecraft Press (1926).
*Studies in Classic American Lit-
erature,* New York: T. Seltzer
(1923).
Selected Literary Criticism,
New York: The Viking Press
(1956).
*Walt Whitman and the Springs
of Courage,* Santa Fe: Writers'
Editions Inc. (1938).
Whitman, New York: Charles
Scribner's Sons (1937).
*American Renaissance: Art and
Expression in the Age of Emer-
son and Whitman,* New York:
Oxford University Press (1941).
*Parallels between Leaves of
Grass and Bhagavadgita* (Ph.D.
dissertation, University of Cali-
fornia, 1933).
*A Critical Guide to "Leaves of
Grass,"* Chicago: University of
Chicago Press (1957).
*The Good Gray Poet: A Vin-
dication,* New York: Bunce and
Huntington (1866).
Alias Walt Whitman, Newark,
New Jersey: The Carteret Book
Club (1930).
*Mysticism East and West: A
Comparative Analysis of the
Nature of Mysticism,* New
York: Macmillan and Co.
(1932).
*Whitman; A Collection of
Critical Essays,* Englewood
Cliffs, N.J.: Prentice-Hall
(1962).

——— *The Continuity of American Poetry,* Princeton, N.J.: Princeton University Press (1961).

Perry, Bliss   *Walt Whitman; His Life and Work,* London: Archibald Constable Co.; New York: Houghton Mifflin and Co. (1906).

Rivers, W. C.   *Walt Whitman's Anomaly,* London: George Allen (1913).

Rogers, Cameron   *The Magnificent Idler: The Story of Walt Whitman,* Garden City: Doubleday Page & Co. (1926).

Santayana, George   *The Poetry of Barbarism,* New York: Scribner's (1927).

Shephard, Esther   *Walt Whitman's Pose,* New York: Harcourt, Brace and Co. (1936).

Stevenson, R. L.   *Familiar Studies of Men and Books,* N.Y.: Scribner's Sons (1896).

Symmonds, John Addington   *Walt Whitman, A Study,* London: George Routledge; New York: E. P. Dutton (1893).

Thomson, James   *Walt Whitman, the Man and the Poet,* London: Bertram Dobell (1910).

Traubel, Horace   *With Walt Whitman in Camden;* Vol. I—Boston: Small, Maynard & Co. (1906). Vol II —N.Y.: D. Appleton & Co. (1908). Vol. III—N.Y.: Mitchell Kennerly & Co. (1914). Vol. IV—Philadelphia: University of Pennsylvania Press (1953).

Trowbridge, John Townsend   *My Own Story; With Recollections of Noted Persons,* Boston: Houghton, Mifflin and Co. (1903).

Warfel, Harry Redcay, ed.   *Studies in Walt Whitman's Leaves of Grass,* Gainesville, Fla.: Scholars' Facsimiles & Reprints (1954).

Willard, Charles B.   *Whitman's American Fame,* Providence: Brown University Press (1950).

Winwar, Frances   *American Giant: Walt Whitman and His Times,* New York: Harper and Bros. (1941).

Wolfe, Theodore F.   *Literary Shrines; the Haunts of Some Famous American Authors,* Philadelphia: J. B. Lippincott Co. (1897), 7th edition.

G. *Collections of Essays on Walt Whitman*

Start with the Sun; Studies in Cosmic Poetry, edited by James E. Miller, Karl Shapiro and Bernice Slote, Lincoln: University of Nebraska (1960).

In Re Walt Whitman, edited by Horace Traubel, R. M. Bucke and Thomas Harned, Philadelphia: David McKay (1893).

Walt Whitman: Man, Poet and Philosopher, (Three essays by David Daiches, G. W. Allen, and Mark Van Doren), Washington, D.C.: Library of Congress (1955).

H. *Articles on Walt Whitman*

Adams, Charles M.   "Whitman's Use of Grass," *American Notes and Queries,* VI (Feb. 1947), 167–68.

Allen, G. W.   "Regarding the Publication of the First 'Leaves of Grass'," *American Literature,* XXVIII, 78–79 (1956).

Baker, Elsa   "What Whitman Learned from the East," *Canada Monthly,* 10 (011), 438–43.

Bergman, Herbert   "Sir Edwin Arnold and Walt

Whitman," *Notes and Queries,* CXCIII, 366 (Aug. 21, 1948).

Boatright, Mody C. "Whitman and Hegel," *Studies in English* (The University of Texas Bulletin) IX, 134–50 (July 8, 1929).

Bowers, Fredson "The Earliest Manuscripts of 'Passage to India' and its Notebooks," *Bulletin of New York Public Library,* LXI (1957) 319–52.

———— "The Manuscript of Whitman's 'Passage to India'," *Modern Philology,* LI, 102–17 (Nov. 1953).

Cairns, W. B. "Swinburne's Opinion of Whitman," *American Literature,* III, 125–35 (May 1931).

Campbell, Killis "The Evolution of Whitman as Artist," *American Literature,* VI, 254–63 (Nov. 1934).

Chari, V. K. "Whitman and Indian Thought," *Western Humanities Review,* XIII, 291–302 (1959).

Coffman, S. K. Jr. "Form and Meaning in Whitman's 'Passage to India'," *PMLA,* LXX, 337–49 (June 1955).

Cooke, Alice Lovelace "A Note on Whitman's Symbolism in 'Song of Myself,'" *Modern Language Notes,* LXV, 228–32 (April 1950).

Conway, Moncure D. "Walt Whitman," *Fortnightly Review,* VI, 538–48 (Oct. 15, 1866).

Cowley, Malcolm "Guru, the Beatnick and the Good Gray Poet," *New Republic,* October 26, 1959.

———— "Walt Whitman—the Miracle," *New Republic,* March 18, 1946.

"Walt Whitman—the Philosopher," *New Republic,* September 29, 1947.

"Walt Whitman—the Secret," *New Republic,* April 8, 1946.

"Whitman—the Poet," *New Republic,* October 20, 1947.

"Whitman: A Little Anthology; Lyrical Passages from 'Leaves of Grass,' selected with Commentary," *New Republic,* July 25, 1955.

"Walt Whitman's Buried Masterpiece," *Saturday Review,* October 31, 1959.

Eby, E. H.   "Did Whitman Write 'the Good Gray Poet?'", *Modern Language Quarterly* 11: 445–49 (December 1950).

Eleanor, Sister Mary   "Hedge's 'Prose Writers of Germany' as a Source of Whitman's Knowledge of German Philosophy," *Modern Language Notes* 61: 381–88 (June 1946).

Erskine, John   "A Note on Whitman's Prosody," *Studies in Philology* 20: 336–44 (July 1923).

Feinberg, Charles E.   "A Whitman Collector Destroys a Whitman Myth," *Papers of the Bibliographical Society of America* 52: 73–92 (1958).

Finkel, William L.   "Walt Whitman's Manuscript Notes on Oratory," *American Literature* 22: 29–52 (March 1950).

Fulghum, W. B. Jr.   "Whitman's Debt to Joseph

Gostwick," *American Literature* XII, 491–96 (Jan. 1941).

Furness, C. J.
"Review of Winwar's *American Giant: Walt Whitman and his Times*," American Literature 13: 423–32 (Jan. 1942).

Fussel, Edwin
" 'Leaves of Grass' and Browning," *American Literature* 31: 77–78 (1959).

Garrison, Charles E.
"Walt Whitman, Christian Science, and Vedanta," *Conservator* 15 (1905).

Goodale, David
"Some of Walt Whitman's Borrowings," American Literature 10: 202–13 (May 1938).

Hendrick, George
"Mrs. Davis' Claim Against the Whitman Estate," *Walt Whitman's Birthplace Bulletin* 4: 6–8 (October 1960).

Holloway, Emory
"Walt Whitman's Love Affairs," *The Dial* 119: 473–83 (November 1920).

Howard, Leon
"For a Critique of Whitman's Transcendentalism," *Modern Language Notes* 47: 79–85 (Feb. 1932).

Hungerford, Edward
"Walt Whitman and His Chart of Bumps," *American Literature* 2: 350–84 (Jan. 1931).

Kinnaird, John
"The Paradox of an American Identity," *Partisan Review* 25: 380–405 (1958).

Lovell, John Jr.
"Appreciating Whitman: 'Passage to India,'" *Modern Language Quarterly* 21: 131–41 (June 1960).

Marks, Alfred H.
"Whitman's Triadic Imagery," *American Literature* 23: 99–126 (March 1951).

Moore, John B. | "The Master of Whitman," *Studies in Philology,* 23: 77–89 (Jan. 1926).

Myers, Henry Alonzo | "Whitman's Conception of the Spiritual Democracy, 1855–56," *American Literature* 6: 239:53 (Nov. 1934).

O'Higgins, Harvey | "Alias Walt Whitman," *Harper's Magazine* 158: 698–707 (May 1929).

Paine, Gregory | "The Literary Relations of Whitman and Carlyle with Especial Reference to their Contrasting Views of Democracy," *Studies in Philology* 36: 550–63 (July 1939).

Parsons, Olive W. | "Whitman the Non-Hegelian," *PMLA* 58: 1073–93 (Dec. 1943).

Platt, I. H. | "Whitman's Superman," *Conservator* 16: 182–83 (February 1906).

Ross, E. C. | "Whitman's Verse," *Modern Language Notes* 45: 363–64 (June 1930).

Sixbey, G. L. | "Chanting the Square Deific—A Study in Whitman's Religion," *American Literature* 9: 171–95 (May 1937).

Smith, Fred M. | "Whitman's Debt to Sartor Resartus," *Modern Language Quarterly* 3: 51–65 (March 1942).

—————— | "Whitman's Poet-Prophet and Carlyle's Hero," *PMLA* 55: 1146–64 (Dec. 1940).

Stovall, Floyd | "Main Drifts in Whitman's Poetry," *American Literature* 4: 3–21 (March 1932).

Wiley, Autrey Nell

"Reiterative Devices in 'Leaves of Grass,'" *American Literature* 1: 161–70 (May 1929).

Woodward, Robert H.

"Journey Motif in Whitman and Tennyson," *Modern Language Notes* 72: 26–27 (Jan. 1957).

INDEX

511

The Roots of Whitman's Grass

T. R. RAJASEKHARAIAH

Ever since 1855, when the first edition of Walt Whitman's *Leaves of Grass* was dramatically thrust upon the world, attempts have been made to explain how the undistinguished journalist was suddenly transformed into a poet of genius. The transformation has been variously explained as the result of a "miracle"; of an "illumination"; of a soul-stirring "sexual experience"; of faith in a phrenological chart of "bumps." The only agreement has been that the transformation was sudden. Only a few people, notably Emerson and Thoreau, sensed that India's literature might have provided the stimulus for the new Titan to create those "incomparable things said incomparably well."

T. R. Rajasekharaiah did not believe in any of these theories, nor did he believe Whitman's downright denial of Oriental knowledge. *The Roots of Whitman's Grass* is a study of sources to which Whitman had access in the public libraries of New York for the seven or eight years before publication of *Leaves of Grass*. Nearly all the philosophies of India were at hand in translation, ready to be adapted, extended, diminished, and versified, and furnishing "grass" roots indeed if the connection with Whitman's poetry could be traced.

The Roots of Whitman's Grass painstakingly traces the connections, and also convincingly demonstrates Whitman's use of the strange mystical writings.